# WOMANKIND

# WOMAN
### beyond the

**ALDINE · ATHERTON**

*Chicago · New York*

# Nancy Reeves

# KIND

## *tereotypes*

*with parallel readings*
*selected and annotated by the author*

## The Author

Nancy Reeves, member of the Bar in California and New York is a distinguished lawyer and lecturer who has been active for many years in the field of women's rights. In addition to her numerous articles on the subject, she prepared a radio series entitled "Woman's Place" in 1966, has made many television appearances, and has taken part in conferences in Copenhagen, Moscow, the Hague, and Lausanne, dealing with women's problems. Ms. Reeves has been a visiting lecturer at several European and American universities, and this book itself was developed out of a course she conducted at UCLA in 1969, one of the first courses on women taught for credit at the university level.

First published 1971 by
Aldine · Atherton, Inc.
529 South Wabash Avenue
Chicago, Illinois 60605

Second Printing 1972

Library of Congress Catalog Card Number 79-140013

ISBN 202-30170-2, cloth; 202-30171-1, paper

Printed in the United States of America

*for*

**SADIE GOLDHABER**

*gallant spirit*

# PREFACE

When I was a small girl, I used to spend the summers with my San Diego grandmother. She had a carved old-world weather house with two doors from which alternate figures emerged as barometric indicators. Since San Diego climate is rather constant, the vacation days would follow one another and I would only see the little man. "Grandmother," I would ask, "where is the little woman?" "The little woman," responded my grandmother, "is in the house where she belongs." "Grandmother," I would persist, "when will the little woman come out of the house?" "The little woman will come out of the house when there's a change in the weather."

This book is being published now because there has been a change in the weather. But the reflection and research on which it is founded go back almost to the San Diego days, to a long-standing curiosity about the riddle of woman's place, a curiosity that has stimulated me to step back from the familiar and study it. Karl Mannheim has written: "Every epoch has its fundamentally new approach and its characteristic point of view, and consequently sees the 'same' object from a new perspective." In this sense, the focus of my private pursuit has now become a public issue. An old riddle has new relevance, as the traditionally invisible woman swings into view.

The question remains, however, why now? What has caused the change in the weather? I do not think that events of this dimension are cyclical, that society oscillates like a pendulum from one perspective to another so that what is hidden at one stage suddenly appears at another. Nor am I persuaded that changes such as this are a simple response to ardent militancy. Rather the militancy itself may be triggered by the tenor of the times, not in a mechanical but in an historical sense.

The dilemmas and directions of women in society are not fortuitous. They are the resultant of multiple factors that determine the drift of the whole cultural complex. The first feminist revolution cannot be considered meaningfully apart from the social realities of its epoch, including the technological upheaval of the first industrial revolution. The current feminist revolution cannot be assessed apart from our living context of revolutions in communication, in cybernetics, in fertility choice, in the rising expectations of subject peoples.

This is not to say that the human actors play no role, only that there is a connection between thought and the kind of world we experience, that psychic awareness and social circumstances have reciprocal effects. Concerned crusaders can accelerate or decelerate the course of events, but they are not the single determinate cause of change. In fact, emancipation from social determinism increases proportionately with insight into the range of underlying variables, not the least of which is the time dimension.

It has been conventional for scholars to study women as a constant psychological phenomenon, severed from the ecology of the human condition, untouched by the temporal process. This work is an effort to discern images of woman in the mirrors of our century and of the century that looms ahead. It is also an effort to mark out a new field where the social roots of woman's place can be scrutinized with academic rigor.

The book itself can be used in a number of ways. It can be read straight through, moving in sequence from the angle of vision of the writer to that of the various authors represented in the anthology of parallel readings. Or it can be approached as a series of segments — of chapter and parallel reading units — connected by explanatory bridges. Again, Part One: *Stereotypes,* along with its related readings, can be considered as an organic whole before Part Two: *Assumptions* (and the related readings) is examined. For the student who would continue the search, source materials that I found most useful are listed at the end of the volume.

I wish at this juncture to register my debt to the spirited women of the past, colleagues across the centuries who have helped me expand the temporal reach. And I salute the spirited women of the present, colleagues across the generation gap, who have helped me extend the experiential reach. I must particularly single out Alena Jech, who first conceived the idea of a course on women at the University of California at Los Angeles (which I subsequently taught) and who, serving officially as teaching assistant and unofficially as tutelary ally, pressed me to prepare the syllabus that was the nucleus for this work.

I wish also to thank Christine Valentine, Associate Editor of Aldine · Atherton, and to express appreciation for her perceptive aid in searching out examples for the photo essay. Finally, I am grateful to my publisher, Alexander J. Morin, for his technical expertise, sensitive guidance, and unfailing support.

# CONTENTS

Contents xi

## The View from the Sexual Ghetto

## Readings in Parallel

# Images of Woman

# INTRODUCTION

> The sufferings of growth, the agony of
> sentimentality that tries to hold life by
> "institution" and establishment and
> extend the fleeting hour until the
> simple inevitable becomes high tragedy
> — are they not all punishment for
> violation of the first simple law of
> Freedom: the law of organic change?
>
> FRANK LLOYD WRIGHT

Surveyed as a whole, every age has its characteristic approach to the great human dilemmas, including the question of woman's place. Today, in an epoch of equalization, it is not surprising to find the second sex ranged with excluded and subject peoples in a revolt sparked by rising expectations and revolutionary possibilities. Unfortunately, as with other emotionally charged issues, most discussion goes forward on the basis of folklore and folk myth. It will therefore be the object of this work to study the concept of woman through an analysis first of *stereotypes of role:* preformed patterns of place; and second, of *assumptions of reasoning:* preformed patterns of thought. These two approaches will serve as alternate lenses for viewing the same phenomenon. In addition, each chapter will be followed by readings constituting still another focusing lens. Since the subject, woman, does not shift, there will be an overlap of parallel ideas seen in different perspective. This is essential to the design, and should help to fracture the universals of what Clyde Kluckhohn has termed "culturally standardized unreason."[1]

3

*Part One* will examine the principal stereotypes that define concepts of woman:

> in relation to herself as human identity
> in relation to man as human mate
> in relation to society as human matrix.

*Part Two* will examine the principal assumptions that underlie conventional dialogue:

> of history as imperative
> of anatomy as imperative
> of psychology as imperative.

*Part Three* will project the arc of the future in an effort to read the messages of time, and to integrate woman's place with the multiple factors that determine the human condition.

For I believe the integration of women cannot be accomplished by each female fomenting her single rebellion. And I believe the consequences following on the failure of that integration are not limited to personal tragedy. They penetrate every layer of the social experience. A woman's place shapes and fashions all places; it cannot be abstracted from the decisive variables that rock the planet. Today, this means it must be relevant to the exponential rate of contemporary change.

From that vantage, the woman question is not for women only; the integration of women is not woman's work — for we are all wrapped in the same bundle of destiny.

If, in my concern with technical and cultural mutations, I question too insistently the certainties of the past, it is because I believe with Sir James Frazer that "like the chameleon the candid enquirer should shift his colors with the shifting colors of the ground he treads."

# PART ONE                    STEREOTYPES


## I. *The Identity of Woman as Woman* ►•─•─•─•─•─•─•─•─◄


### *1.* The Traditional Approach

►•─•─•─•─•─•─•─•─•─•─•─•─•─•─•─•─•─•─•─•─•─•─•─•─◄

> When one attempts such an
> examination he cannot but be
> surprised that such far-reach-
> ing conclusions, based on such
> tenuous evidence, should have
> received so much credence.
>
> HAROLD F. BLUM


Custom makes women invisible in periods of social equilibrium, for we do not
see what habit renders familiar. But when the pattern is threatened, suddenly
the little woman who wasn't there appears, is rediscovered, and counseled. A
host of mentors start coaching from the sidelines. Some say: "Run, Run!" and
others: "As you were. Go back, go back to home plate!" What follows are
illustrations of this counsel down through the ages and up to the minute.

*Xenophon,* the Greek historian:

> War, politics and public speaking are the sphere of man; that of woman is to keep
> house, to stay at home, and to receive and attend her husband.[1]

*Hannah More,* the English bluestocking:

> That providential economy which has clearly determined that women were born to
> share with men the duties of private life, has clearly demonstrated that they were
> not born to divide with them its public administration.[2]

*Parallel readings for this chapter appear in the section entitled "Inner Space."

5

*Mrs. A. J. Graves,* whose book *Woman in America* was published in 1858:

> A good woman . . . submits with cheerful acquiescence to that order in the conjugal relation which God and nature have established.[3]

You have probably noted that these quotations appeal to God, Providence, and Nature as authority for the design. In our time the counsels are parallel, but the source of authority has shifted.

*Dr. Ralph S. Banay,* psychologist:

> Women are restless and dissatisfied because they cannot or will not accept their physical destiny.[4]

*Dr. Arthur Mandy,* psychiatrist, Johns Hopkins University:

> Frigidity, as we see it today, is an outgrowth of woman's running away from her biological destiny, which is to be wife, mother, and homemaker.[5]

*Dr. Richard Centers,* psychologist, UCLA:

> Modern woman's attempt to be a "man by day and woman by night" has led to a confusion that is breeding tension and broken homes and could conceivably influence the national birth rate.

Although he recognizes the fact that this is an era of social transition, Dr. Centers maintains:

> One thing is certain. If mankind is to survive, woman cannot completely escape the feminine role imposed by her biological destiny.[6]

Here the appeal is to the authority of the organism, perhaps another form of Nature, but at least the terms have changed; God, Providence, and Nature have given way to biological destiny.

There are other types of counsel which, instead of appealing to authority, cite the horrors that have resulted because the design has been violated. The angriest man I have discovered is *Philip Wylie.* In *Generation of Vipers* he writes:

> Mom got herself out of the nursery and the kitchen. She then got out of the house. [Here I skip a part. He then goes on] . . . she also got herself the vote, and, although politics never interested her (unless she was exceptionally naive, a hairy foghorn, or a size 40 scorpion) the damage she forthwith did to society was so enormous and so rapid that the best men lost track of things.

Wylie then lists events he believes concomitant with what he calls "Mom's first gracious presence at the ballot box." These include:

> . . . political scurviness, hoodlumism, gangsterism, labor strife, monopolistic

thuggery, moral degeneration, civic corruption, smuggling, bribery, theft, murder, homosexuality, drunkenness, financial depression, chaos, and war.[7]

In the next two instances, a new factor has been added. These critics not only cite the horrors resulting from woman's assumption of a role outside the home, they even point to the horrors attending woman's assumption of a dominant role *within* the home.

First, *Dr. Maurice E. Linden,* Director of Mental Health, Philadelphia. Deploring the increasing importance of women within the family as a form of "non-feminine aggressiveness," he attributes "such widespread and increasing mental health problems as alcoholism, the addictions, character neuroses, tension and the psychotic and neurotic problems of aging" to this change.[8]

Second, *Dr. Joseph C. Rheingold,* in his massive study *The Fear of Being a Woman,* points to maternal destructiveness as the agent responsible for "the confusions and anxieties of contemporary life, the loss of self-identity, the reversal of sexual roles, and the breakdown of marriage and the family."[9]

Another approach is somewhat indirect. It does not say going out of the home is bad; it just says staying in the home is better.

Here is the comment of a journalist, *Hal Borland:*

> The greatest woman in history is — the American Housewife . . . . I don't deny myself that the shop talk of wives is not always as interesting as the reminiscences of actresses or lady wrestlers. But few professional career women live a life one-half as exciting or satisfying as that of the ordinary housewife. Motherhood, the art of raising children, is an endless drama, a ceaseless adventure.[10]

*Dr. Russell Caldwell,* Professor of History, University of Southern California:

> Today's woman seems to ignore the fact that she is a woman. She is determined to become man's equal in the business and professional worlds and is sacrificing her greatest claim to glory in the process — her femininity.[11]

And, on a somewhat more primitive level, *Dr. John A. Schindler,* in his book *Woman's Guide to Better Living:*

> Lady, Yours is the Important Work . . . there is no one more important than you, there is no place more important than your home . . . . There are some people who may be handling gigantic sums of money, or managing huge engineering projects, directing thousands of people, or charting the course of a nation, but none of them are doing a more important and significant work than you are, even though *they* occupy the limelight . . . the homemaker can be proud of her accomplishments and achievements, proud of being a glorified, world-moving, scullery maid.[12]

The same thing is said, but with far more sophistication, by *Helene Deutsch* in her major work, *The Psychology of Woman.* The point, in the subsequent quotations which I have abridged, is not that this is better, but that since you can't do the other, this is better:

> Woman's intellectuality is to a large extent paid for by the loss of valuable feminine qualities; it feeds on the sap of the affective life and results in impoverishment of this life.

And further on:

> For intuition is God's gift to the feminine woman; everything relating to exploration and cognition, all the forms and kinds of human cultural aspiration that require a strictly objective approach, are . . . the domain of the masculine intellect, . . . against which woman can rarely compete.[13]

And finally, a few words from *Dr. Theodore Reik,* Director of the New York Society for Psychoanalytic Psychology. This is from an article entitled "Women Love Men, but Men Love Work":

> Women, who form the chain of all organic beings, are at home in the world and rarely feel the urge to find out all about it.

And then comes the crucial line:

> A man's self-evaluation is strictly dependent on how successful he is in his work.
> A woman's self-evaluation is dependent on the kind of man who chooses her.[14]

To sum up, what is the model for woman that develops from these insinuations and assertions? It is that woman is primarily homemaker, wife, and mother. The private is her exclusive sphere. The public world of work and politics belongs to man. Rivalry with man in these pursuits is unnatural and dangerous. Woman cannot successfully enter the intellectual realm because her genius is affective and any knowledge she might have should be derived intuitively. It is her destiny to be nurturing and passive.

How then does one evaluate this model and its categorical imperatives? I can think of three methods. First, it can be tested intrinsically, by the criteria of logic. That is, standing alone, are the supportive statements founded in precise reasoning? Second, it can be tested historically, to see if it is validated by the patterns of the past. And the third method is to test it cross-culturally, to determine whether it holds true in other contemporary societies.

Let me illustrate each of these methods using the essence of the counsels we have just heard.

I begin with logic because, as George Bernard Shaw has noted, people tend to use their reason to support their prejudices. Many of the logical fallacies have resonant Latin names. They should ring pleasantly to the ear after the strident voices just heard.

There is, for example, the fallacy *secundum quid,* which includes the error of founding a sweeping generalization on the basis of a few specifics. (I shall move along in swift summary because logic is a large subject. But I think even a few samples can serve as a grid to test the rigor of the reasoning.) Most of the statements, if you remember, began with the word "woman." In fact, the writer really had in mind the particular circle of women of his time and his experience. Yet in its full scope the word — and consequently the generalization — encompasses half of humanity throughout history. A little data is a dangerous thing. One has only to open a window on the world to discern more differences among women than there are between men and women of distinct cultures, countries, and classes.

Then there is the fallacy *ignoratio elenchi,* which has three subdivisions, all of which are pertinent here. The first one, *ad hominem,* means "to the man" (I suppose, in our context, we should title it "to the woman") because it applies to the situation where one tries to win an argument by attacking the character of a person. I don't think I have to dwell on this. Attacking the character of the ladies is a favorite sport of Sunday supplements, and one or two of our own experts seem to have succumbed to the same temptation. The second part of the fallacy *ignoratio elenchi* is entitled *ad populum,* or appealing "to the crowd." In our quotations, this appeal was made through the tug of the great abstractions: motherhood, the family, love, the child, femininity. And finally, again under the same heading of *ignoratio elenchi,* we find the fallacy *ad baculum,* which means appealing "to fear." If you recall, several of the critics, deploring the change in woman's role, aroused fear by predicting this new feminine casting would result in frigidity, broken homes, homosexuality, and even war.

Another fallacy that besets us all is called *ad verecundiam,* and means the appeal "to revered authority." The pronouncements I have cited contained appeals to Nature, to Providence, to God, and, most prevalent in our own time, to biological destiny.

Let us move now to the fallacy termed *petitio principii,* or "begging the question." It embraces the concept *circulus in probando,* which means the conclusion is contained in the premise. I think the best way of illustrating this fallacy is to remind you of the quotations where femininity is argued and femininity is assumed. You will recall that one of our critics asserted that when woman wishes to become man's equal, she is sacrificing her greatest claim to glory: her femininity. But it is precisely the indispensable components of femininity that are at issue. This is what we are seeking to learn.

Another fallacy has the lovely name *post hoc, ergo propter hoc:* "after this, therefore because of this." Chanticleer, the cock in Rostand's famous play, observed that after he crowed, the sun came up. Therefore, he reasoned, it was his crowing that caused the sun to rise. This is the kind of logic that lists the many ills of contemporary society (as you remember Philip Wylie did), notes that woman's role has been shifting in recent years, and concludes that it is because her role has shifted that these ills have occurred.

From this brief survey of logical fallacies and their application to pronouncements in favor of the traditional woman, I think it is clear that the arguments offered are not based in precise reasoning. In fact, they can be compared to the summation to the jury of one lawyer who said: "These, gentlemen, are the conclusions on which I base my facts." They also remind me of the *New Yorker* cartoon showing a determined-looking chap in the jury box stating: "I don't listen to the evidence, I like to make up my own mind."

Francis Bacon, who was a great student of logic, offered this rule of thumb which our experts might ponder:

> In general, let every student of nature take this as a rule, that whatever his mind seizes and dwells upon with particular satisfaction is to be held in suspicion.

We are now ready to apply the second method, the historical, to see if the traditional model is validated by precedent. Surveyed as a whole, the historical position of women is germane because most of the experts, attuned to the traditional theme, assume it pervaded the past and is therefore imperative today. The gist of their counsel is, consequently: Go back. But the question remains: Go back — where?

Their guideposts seem to point to the self-sustaining farmhouse prior to the industrial revolution. Whether this home really had all the virtues ascribed to it is irrelevant. It is quite another matter, however, to imply that it was the home designed by God, Providence, Nature, or biological destiny as the universal prototype. To do so is to signify that all other habitations throughout history transgressed those authorities.

For change is a constant, perhaps the only constant in human life. To study immemorial woman is to discover the extraordinary mutability of her role. It is time, I think, to recall that today's woman is the descendant of that primitive woman who had no home to which to devote her exclusive energies, unless we consider a rudimentary hut or a cave a country seat, and who worked side by side with her mate to gather food for survival. True, there was in many groups a division of labor between the sexes, but its character was often fortuitous. In one society, fishing was a woman's task; in another, a man's. Only agriculture was, at the level of hoe technic, consistently woman's work. It may even have been woman's discovery: the domestication of plants following from the collection of plants by our foremothers. And it became, among many peoples, woman's monopoly, the magic of female fertility counting as the compelling factor to make crops grow. From agricultural indispensability came economic power and social significance for women, reified in customs that tend to reverse our conception of appropriate sex roles. Let me illustrate this concretely, using the words of the missionary Lafitau in his description of the League of the Iroquois:

> All authority rests in the women of the country. The fields and all harvests

belong to them. They are the soul of the councils, the arbiters of war and peace, and the guardians of the public fisc. It is to them that the prisoners are delivered. They arrange for the weddings, govern the children, and determine the laws of inheritance according to their blood.[15]

This was confirmed by an ethnologist writing a century later: "woman's influence was absolutely paramount. Chiefs, warriors and councils were all obliged to yield to her demands."[16] Other groups that transpose our archetypes are cited by Margaret Mead:

No culture has failed to seize upon the conspicuous facts of age and sex in some way, whether it be the convention of one Philippine tribe that no man can keep a secret, the Manus' assumption that only men enjoy playing with babies, the Toda prescription of almost all domestic work as too sacred for women, or the Arapesh insistence that women's heads are stronger than men's.[17]

As the sociologist Viola Klein notes:

The reason inducing Margaret Mead to adopt such radical relativism with regard to sex temperaments was the observation that among the three primitive societies which she investigated, one, the Arapesh, displayed homogeneously a temperament which we, according to our conceptions, would call feminine; the other, the Mundugumor, showed uniformly characteristics which we should attribute to men only; whereas the third society, that of the Tchambuli, has institutionalized contrasting sex temperaments for men and women which, however, represent a complete reversal of the sex attitudes of our own culture — and this in spite of the existence of formal patrilineal institutions.[18]

To be sure, these examples refer to rather small groups. But, looking across the centuries, we must consider that today's woman is also the descendant of those Egyptian women who, according to Herodotus, roamed about in the market squares while their men sat at home at the looms.[19] Standing alone, such a report is open to question as a credulous traveler's tale, but its general import is consistent with what we learn from other authorities, both ancient and modern. Thus Diodorus Siculus, another ancient traveler, notes: "the husband, by the terms of the marriage agreement, appertains to the wife, and it is stipulated between them that the man shall obey the woman in all things."[20] Marriage contracts that have come down to us from various periods in Egyptian history confirm the strong economic and social position of women. And, in a negative way, this is also confirmed by Sophocles, who ridiculed the men of Egypt as the "women's slaves of the Nile."[21] Even such a modern scholar as W. Max Müller, who considers the Diodorus text quite incredible, nevertheless states: "No people, ancient or modern, has given women so high a legal status as did the inhabitants of the Nile Valley."[22] We are all inclined to doubt a report when its truth appears to us incomprehensible; but it is provincial in time scale to assume ancient societies must have resembled our own.

Coming a little closer to our own period, we learn that on the American continent our government found it necessary to take cognizance of matrilineal tradition among Indians, requiring signatures of tribal women to make land transactions legally binding. We must also recall that today's woman is a descendant of those women who, before the industrial revolution, were members of guilds, plied trades, harvested crops, managed commercial enterprises, and supervised the home workshops. Their activities have been woven into our very language, the words *spinster* and *brewster* indicating the sex of those who made the cloth and the beer in that period. True, this may have been accomplished as a family industry, but in the words of one scholar: "Mankind lulled by its faith in the 'eternal feminine' . . . having once named a place 'the home' thinks it makes no difference whether it consists of a workshop or a boudoir."[23]

In the same vein, a writer on early colonial women comments:

> It was one thing to be the lady of a southern tobacco plantation or the wife of a New England merchant; it was quite another to be a pioneer raising a family in western Massachusetts or the Allegheny valleys, the self-supporting widow of a Marblehead fisherman, or a servant girl working out her indenture period.[24]

But the "women kidnapped from city streets, or sold out of crowded prisons and brought to this country to serve as indentured servants had something to look forward to."[25] No such vision sustained the women torn from the African continent and sold as slaves. They, too, were our foremothers.

With the advent of the industrial revolution, upper class women remained in the home, but the workshops moved out, and lower class women followed them to the factory. Then, as now, critics yearned for a return to the feudal past, and castigated women for their change in role as though the sex had contrived it. This was, and is, patent error. But, as George Bernard Shaw once wryly remarked: "Still a thing that nobody believes cannot be proved too often."

In my rapid summary, I must attest that today's woman is also the descendant of those mill girls who were the first employees of early industry. Parenthetically, it should be added that the second major labor force was the children — so that among the most vulnerable sectors of the population, not only was the choice foreclosed for needy women to remain in the home, the very children were required to earn their living away from it. The hours ran from 12 1/2 to 15 a day, as for example:

> In Paterson, New Jersey, [where] women and children had to be at work at 4:30 A.M. and [continue to] work as long as they could see, with time off for breakfast and dinner, until a strike in 1835 cut the working day to 12 hours.[26]

Although the critics railed, it was not perversity but necessity that impelled women to embrace such a schedule. And, although conditions have been ameliorated, the work most women do today is still drudgery, which they continue to perform not from perversity but from necessity. The critics who deplore, assert, and point with alarm are therefore confusing the obsolete and the fictitious with the contemporary and the real; they cannot withdraw woman from the marketplace, they can only make her uncomfortable there.

In sketching the mutability of woman's role and the multiple forms of the home in which she has dwelt, and contrasting them with the universal proto-type espoused by the critics, I am reminded of the exquisite painting by Sasseta called "The Gift of the Magi." It depicts the Three Wise Men and their retainers on horses, descending a low hill. In the foreground is the Star of Bethlehem; in the background, however, one discovers the pink Sienese archi-tecture of the fifteenth century, and the company is attired in the Italian costumes that were fashionable in the artist's lifetime. In the same sense, our articulate mentors see the past with the eyes of the present. This is not surpris-ing when we consider that each age moves imperceptibly into the next. For although change is a constant, history registers as a series of stills. It is as if we lived within the framework of the paradox posed by Zeno, the Greek philosopher who denied the principle of motion because, it was argued, as one goes from A to B he is, at any given moment, at rest at an intermediate point.Therefore, he cannot be moving. Similarly, the silent revolutions that proceed through the ages are rarely perceived by those at rest within a given period of the continuum. I am beginning to suspect that only when violent cataclysms topple the eternal verities is the distance between past and present sharply discerned. More often, the dynamics of motion becomes, as with Zeno, a branch of statics, and nowhere is this more likely than in the famous place that is woman's, long assumed to be fixed for all time.

But even if nature is the common law, culture is its codification: "form follows function," as the architects have it. Woman's patterns are cut to fit the cloth of the community in which she finds herself. A newspaper story high-lights this principle. It reports an interview with the general secretary of the National Man's Legion, which had sought to make it unlawful for a female to hold any job a man might hold. Explaining the organization's lack of success, the secretary declared: "This group was formed in 1940. But then the war came along, and women were needed. It knocked our program on its ear, you might say."[27]

We are now in a position to consider the third method of testing the traditional model: cross-cultural analysis of contemporary societies. For I believe the variations in pattern that exist abroad validate my judgment that form follows function. The interplay of role and social scenario in the concrete present cannot be as easily reduced to the imaginative constructs that simplify the past. One has only to call the name of a country to summon a picture that belies precedent. In Sweden, where I spent several years, there was at that period (in the fifties) a marked need for woman's labor. The wrong sex was welcome in all professions, with the exception of the ministry (and even that has since been revised), and in most of the trades. Participation was made feasible through social facilities: nursery schools, after-school care, plant cafeterias, shopping aides in factories, a civil service category of home helpers to cope with sick children and other emergencies, cooperative housing that included tenant restaurants, catering service, laundries, maids, tutors — to the end that the family life of the working woman was not deflected by chores. This is a far cry from the traditional model. Yet, our critics notwithstanding, it has not sounded the death knell of time-honored sexual relationships. Rather, the enlarged base of shared experience, according to one sociologist, seems to have heightened the salience of sex qua sex. In fact, she writes: "visitors are struck by the erotic atmosphere of that society."[28]

By the same token, in Israel, where necessity dictated outsize efforts by early settlers to reclaim the land, the inefficiency of single unit economy and duplicated time and motion were dissipations they could not afford, and new forms were created. Most widely known is the form called the kibbutz, a kind of shared life characterized by mutual economy, self-government, and pooled services. Division of labor is concomitant with division of property among all able-bodied adults. I spent some time in such a community and observed its design for living in practice. Parents have their quarters; children theirs. Men and women both participate in management, and men and women both work. Children join their parents in leisure periods and, since there is no commuting, they know where to look for one another even when otherwise occupied. When I saw the modern, machine-filled kitchen and sampled the cuisine in the glass-walled central dining room, I was reminded of Thomas More's aphorism: "And also it were a Follye to take the payne to dresse a badde diner at home, when they may be welcome to good and fyne fare so neighe hande at the hall."[29] After the meal, parents gravitate to the children's quarters and the goodnight ritual. Later they may go to the cultural center or take coffee with friends. There are no babysitter problems; offspring are guarded by a staff of teachers, nurses and housekeepers. To make a home, to raise a family, are tasks incumbent on both sexes. Both engage in work, politics, and the full range of intellectual life.

It need scarcely be said that another society that deviates from the "divine blueprint" is that of Soviet Russia. In the drastic revision of its economic life, the energies of women were indispensable, and new designs were developed to mitigate the double burden. These take the form of crèches, kindergartens, children's camps, boarding schools, canteens for public catering, plant cafeterias, pioneer palaces, and factory services. Although the theoretical goal of complete integration of women at all levels and in all arenas has still to be achieved, the old strata separating the sexes have been interpenetrated. I visited the Soviet Union in 1960 and again in 1964. Like most industrialized nations, its employment of women is commensurate with epochal change. The distinction lies in the extent of that change: from serf labor to cybernetics in a single generation. Utilization of women is therefore more extensive and more matter-of-fact than in countries that developed more gradually. It is taken for granted that women work; it is not surprising to see them as university heads and lathe operators, as engineers and laborers, as tractor drivers and officials. I was sick in a hospital and found myself surrounded by women: nurses, maids, orderlies, technicians, doctors. I did not see a single man in the four days I was there. In Leningrad, I met honored artists and a deputy mayor. In Tashkent, I was presented to the president of the Uzbek Republic and to the chairman of its Supreme Court. In Tbilisi, I met an agronomist, a vintner, and an authority on leather. These women all had private lives, but they were not traditional women.

Surveyed as a whole, none of the societies I have described fosters traditional women. Yet they are viable societies. Whatever our judgment of these new webs of life, whether we subscribe to their values or salute their ideologies, we must admit they work. Their designs for living are not problem-free, but the time-honored forms also pose dilemmas. The only question that is relevant is whether they function, whether they are viable. If they do, and if they are, then this casts doubt on the assertion that it is woman's destiny to be what the traditional model defines. The refutation is inherent in the range of totally different patterns obtaining in other societies. Had such variant designs been destructive of organic imperatives, they would have generated disastrous consequences. Since, on the contrary, these forms were (and are) functional and viable, it is clear that the sententious formulations rest on fragile frames.

In disputing the universal application of the traditional model by the techniques of logic, by an analysis of the past, and by a look at other countries today, I do not, of course, question the legitimacy of a preference for this model. I only maintain that a preference is not a precept; that a frozen world is an artificial construct; and that a model abstracted from the temporal process offers little guidance to the form that follows function for the American woman today.

## 2. The Challenging View

*All liberation depends upon
the consciousness of servitude.*

HERBERT MARCUSE

A new woman is an old phenomenon. She appears front stage center in periods of social turbulence, and each age imagines that it alone has produced her, it alone has launched her in her challenging role. Yet, if we look back, Lysistrata's winged words are still relevant and Nora's slammed door still echoes. Forms change, but the underlying dialogue between those who favor full integration and those who point to the famous place that is woman's continues. When society is at rest, the debate subsides. When society is in flux, it becomes the issue of the day. A nineteenth-century verse entitled "The Times That Try Men's Souls" describes the mood of our times as well as that of the writer's:

> Confusion has seized us, and all things go wrong,
>   The women have leaped from "their spheres,"
> And instead of fixed stars, shoot as comets along,
>   And are setting the world by the ears![1]

Just as the idea of the new woman has appeared before, so the issues raised in the contemporary dialogue are not so very different from those considered in the past. What then are the components of the challenging view? First, the claim to full participation in all fields of work, including politics and govern-

*Parallel readings for this chapter appear in the section entitled "Not for Ourselves Alone."

16

ment; second, the right to equal training and to equal pay; third, the pressure for institutional change that would ratonalize the double burden of personal and public responsibilities. These components are, in turn, based upon two ideas:

a)    sexual roles are socially created (that is, neither providence nor anatomy blueprints them for all time, but rather they are socially developed and therefore subject to social amendment);

b)    far from being deleterious, it is meliorative both for the woman and for her family if she has a wider function.

What follows will be a series of contrapuntal ideas representing the recurring themes of past and present, based on the same underlying assumptions, but keyed to the needs and the style of each generation. I think they reveal the continuity of the challenging view and something of its historical range.

On the importance of work, the rallying call was voiced by Olive Schreiner more than a half century ago in her classic, *Woman and Labor:*

> In that clamor which has arisen in the modern world, where now this, and then that, is demanded for and by large bodies of modern women, he who listens carefully may detect as a keynote, beneath all the clamor, a demand which may be embodied in such a cry as this: Give us labor and the training which fits for labor! We demand this, not for ourselves alone, but for the race.[2]

On the right to participate in politics and government, Aristophanes poses this scene with Lysistrata:

> "Husband," I say with a tender solicitude, "Why have you passed such a foolish decree?"
>
> Viciously, moodily, glaring askance at me, "Stick to your spinning, my mistress," says he, "Else you will speedily find it the worse for you! War is the care and the business of men!"
>
> ... "What! You unfortunate, shall we not then, then when we see you perplexed and incompetent, shall we not tender advice to the state!"[3]

And, in Roman times, Hortensia exclaimed:

> "Why should we pay taxes when we have no part in the honors, the commands, the statecraft for which ye contend against one another so disastrously?"[4]

Closer to our own time, we have the lively report of Lucy Stone, as a young girl, writing to her brother:

> It was decided in our Literary Society the other day that ladies ought to mingle in politics, go to Congress, etc., etc. What do you think of that?[5]

Contemporary advocates of the challenging view also begin with the pivotal issues of work and of political participation. In the face of announcements that

more women are in the labor force than ever before, and that openings for
women are being made at all government levels, the new campaigns might
seem unnecessary. But the change is not as substantial as the statistics and the
headlines imply. To begin with, the term *labor force* encompasses unemployed
as well as employed workers, a significant increment for women especially,
whose jobless rate is consistently higher than that for men. Further, reports
of millions of American wives working outside the home convey a roseate
picture that fails to specify that of all employed women, only one-third hold
full-time jobs; one-third are full-time workers only part of the year, and one-
third are part-time, part of the year. And finally, women still have only token
footing in the prestige occupations and are established only in the sexual ghetto
of "women's fields"—at the low end of the skill ladder and at the bottom of
the pay scale. As one astute observer remarks:

> The startling phenomenon is not the much-advertised, relatively insignificant
> increase in the numbers of American women who now work outside the home,
> but the fact that two out of three adult American women do *not* work outside
> the home, and that increasing millions of young women are *not* skilled or
> educated for work in any profession.[6]

Hidden obscurely in the ballyhoo is the sobering truth that 85 per cent of
the top professional and technical jobs in the United States today are still held
by men. This results, as the Report of the President's Commission on the
Status of Women points out, in a low proportion of women in public office,
since "few women possess the practical experience obtained at middle and
upper levels of administrative and executive responsibility"[7] and consequently
lack the public visibility that would be the basis for such posts. So, fifty years
after the passage of the Nineteenth Amendment, there are thirteen women in
the 92nd Congress, with the pattern more or less the same at other levels of
government. Clearly, the presence of a few commoners in the castle does not
make a revolution.

Let us now consider the second component of the challenging view—the
right to equal training and equal pay—and begin once again with the vigorous
expressions of the past. On the crucial role of equal training, here is Charles
Brockden Brown, an American writer who, in 1793, published *Alcuin, A
Dialogue on the Rights of Women:*

> The lady speaks: "You might as well expect a Laplander to write Greek spon-
> taneously, and without instruction, as that anyone should be wise or skillful
> without suitable opportunities. I humbly presume one has a better chance of
> becoming an astronomer by gazing at the stars through a telescope than in
> eternally plying the needle or snapping the scissors. To settle a bill of fare, to lard
> a pig, to compose a pudding, to carve a goose, are tasks that do not, in any
> remarkable degree, tend to instill the love of, or facilitate the acquisition of

literature and science. Women are generally superficial and ignorant because they are generally cooks and sempstresses."[8]

The parallel situation today is summed up by Helen Rosenau:

The processes of form require power of concentration, an aptitude which is diametrically opposed to the education of the average housewife. . . . Indeed, housekeeping is perhaps a real education in the diffusion of thought . . .[9]

On the issue of equal pay, Sarah Grimké, famous as an abolitionist, found that the prevailing concept of women's inferiority

bears with tremendous effect on the laboring classes, and indeed on almost all who are obliged to earn a sustenance, whether it be by mental or physical exertion—I allude to the disproportionate value set on the time and labor of men and women. As for example, in tailoring, a man has twice or three times as much for making a waistcoat or pantaloons as a woman, although the work done by each may be equally good. In those employments which are peculiar to women, their time is estimated at half the value of that of men. A woman who goes out to wash, works as hard in proportion as a wood sawyer, or a coal heaver, but she is not generally able to make more than half as much by a day's work.[10]

Current conditions are indicated by the President's Commission on the Status of Women:

The difference in occupation distributions of men and women is largely responsible for the fact that in 1961, the earnings of women working full time averaged only about 60% of those of men working full time. But in various occupations where both sexes were employed, the levels of women's earnings were likewise demonstrably lower than those of men.[11]

So, from Sarah Grimké's day to ours the figure for women's earnings has moved from 50 to 60 per cent of the wages of men.

Even the advance in education, now available to women more or less without discrimination, is counterfeit equality, for open doors without opportunities might as well be closed. It seems marvelous that current writers, agonizing over women's attenuated motivation, do not seem to connect low sights with limbo scholarship. The ultimate evidence is offered by little Sally in *Peanuts:* "I never said I wanted to be somebody important. All I want to do when I grow up is to get married and be a good wife and mother—why should I have to go to kindergarten for that?"

Pressure for institutional change, the third component of the challenging view, has also been exerted in earlier periods from Sir Thomas More's *Utopia,* where the drudgery of the private household is abolished, and child care, cooking, and nursing are all community tasks, to the feminists as illustrated by Winifred Holtby, who in 1934 wrote in her *Women:*

For the sake of human happiness, justice, intelligence and welfare, I should like
to see all family homes and amateur housekeepers abolished for the space of one
generation, because at present the price we pay for these luxuries is too high.[12]

Vaulting to the present, we find a similar theme in Alice Rossi's article, "An
Immodest Proposal: Equality Between the Sexes."[13] Although hers really is a
very modest proposal compared with the projections of old militants, it does
spell out an institutional design to expedite that equality. This includes a
course in practical mothering for stand-ins, a network of child care centers,
and a reconsideration of our suburban pattern of living in view of the isolation
problems it poses.

The argument recalls the fantastic truth turned up by the President's Commission that across the country licensed day care is available to only some
185,000 children—despite the fact that in nearly half a million families with
children under six, the mother is the sole support. A recent survey, moreover,
reported 400,000 children under twelve whose mothers work full time and for
whose supervision no arrangements whatsoever had been made. In the face of
this evidence, the Commission concludes that the failure to provide such
services reflects, primarily, a lack of community awareness of the realities of
modern life.

As I indicated earlier, the three components of the challenging view—the
right to participate in all occupations, the demand for equal pay and equal
training, the pressure for institutional change—rest upon two philosophical
ideas. The first, that sexual roles are socially created and consequently subject
to social change, was in the past grounded in logic. Consider the simple
statement of Judith Murray which appeared in 1790:

Should it still be vociferated, "Your domestic employments are sufficient"—I
would calmly ask, is it reasonable, that a candidate for immortality, for the joys
of heaven, an intelligent being, who is to spend an eternity in contemplating the
works of Deity, should at present be so degraded, as to be allowed no other ideas,
than those which are suggested by the mechanism of a pudding or the sewing
of the seams of a garment?[14]

In terms of the modern temper, sex as the constant basis for role differentiation is questioned on more scientific ground. Cross-cultural and cross-histori-
cal studies join issue with ethnocentrism. And, as I remarked at the beginning
of this discussion, patterns of primitive cultures can no longer be accepted as
eternal verities while viable industrial societies, which controvert them, are
overlooked. Old universals of biological determinism are impugned by the
growing sophistication respecting the enormous diversity of human life and its
social ecology.

We are now in a position to examine the second underlying idea of the
challenging view: that the widest function of the woman is beneficial to the

family. Contending for this principle, Socrates renders the argument in his own dialectical style. Addressing a friend, he inquired:

"Is there any one whom you oftener trust with important matters than your wife?"

"No one."

"Is there anyone with whom you converse less?"

"Few, if any."

"You married her when quite a young girl, or at any rate when she could have seen and heard little."

"Quite so."

"Well then, it would seem much more wonderful if she *did* know how to speak and act than if she failed therein. There is nothing like looking into it."[15]

And Stendhal, referring to the development gap between marriage partners and to its unfortunate consequences, writes:

[The husband may] find a good heart that will share his sorrows, but he is always obliged to turn his thoughts into small change if he wishes to be understood, and it would be ridiculous to expect reasonable counsel from an intellect that has need of such a method in order to seize the facts.[16]

On the relationship of wide function to motherhood, there is this affirmation from an English feminist, describing the sequela of that struggle:

We shared a joy of life that we had never known. Most of my fellow fighters were Wives and Mothers. And strange things happened to their domestic life. Husbands came home at night with a new eagerness. As for the children, their attitude changed rapidly from one of affectionate toleration for poor darling mother to one of wide-eyed wonder. Released from the smother of mother love —for she was too busy to be more than casually concerned with them—they discovered that they liked her.[17]

Of course, this observation was made before the concept of parental availability was propounded; but its counterpoint in today's setting is offered belatedly by a few maverick sociologists. Speaking of the traditional mother functioning exclusively in the home, one writes:

In myriad ways the mother binds the child to her, dampening his initiative, resenting his growing independence in adolescence, creating a subtle dependence which makes it difficult for the child to achieve full adult stature.[18]

And, like an echo of the comment of the English feminist, one finds the surprising counsel: "A healthy dose of inattention is needed by children."

This new judgment is reinforced by studies of working mothers that tend to impugn negative assumptions about their issue. Some studies even go so far as to conclude that the best way to encourage independence and responsibility in the child is for the mother to be a living model of these qualities herself.

In reviewing these contrapuntal voices, do I seek to prove that there is nothing new under the sun? Not at all. Yet it is just this that current writers, even those offering the challenging view, imply when they assume a constant universe. Most significantly, like their predecessors they focus on marketplace activity as the touchstone of liberation. The proposals they advance today were progressive when feminism was young. But have they looked at the market picture lately? Unfortunately, yesterday's slogans are not always relevant in today's world. We are currently experiencing the effects of technological revolution, and one of the components of that cataclysm is automation.

> In 20 years, other things being equal, most of the routine blue-collar and white-collar tasks that can be done by cybernation will be.[19]

Since most women's jobs are on the lower rungs of the employment ladder, the likelihood is pretty clear that their number will shrink rather than expand in these circumstances. This probability, then, would appear to underscore arguments advanced to persuade women to learn higher skills — based on the theory that there will always be room at the top. It is a troubling thought, however, that even here we may not be dealing with long-term perspectives. Already many sectors of middle management and of upper echelon specialties are being eliminated. What is the willing woman to be trained for? How can we be sure that those who head for the top now will not be redundant by the time they are qualified? Dr. Robert M. Hutchins has predicted:

> The relentless advance of automation means one thing is sure: a smaller and smaller proportion of the population is going to be able to find work.[20]

Given the consequent scramble for places, and given the traditional cultural values that have frozen women into subordinate positions, why should we imagine there will be a thaw at the pinnacle? The fact is that the route of jobs even of significant jobs, as a way for women to be integrated is being swiftly by-passed by scientific events. In disregarding the ascendant industrial revolution and its impact on cultural design, writers about women today are as far outside the real dilemmas of our time as their subjects are outside the mainstream.

When scholars consider the condition of man, they ponder objective structure; when they consider the condition of woman, they are preoccupied only with subjective milieus. Man's condition is assumed to be third person plural; woman's condition is presumed to be first person singular. Yet, as I have tried to indicate, it is a fragmentation of reality, now as never before, to focus on the role of women without making a profound analysis of the tendencies and the trends in the social matrix.

Erik H. Erikson has observed that women are tempted to go back to their place whenever they feel out of place. To offset such regressive reaction, we must beware of fostering false illusions. Early nineteenth-century prescriptions may be no more than wishful thinking in terms of our strange new world. There is a curious remoteness about today's students of women who, at a time when the whole relation of people to work is being reconceived and re-evaluated, are still beguiled by the question of whether women should work outside the home.

Homo sapiens first gained his living through hunting and gathering. Then he planted and reaped. Later he labored at jobs. Now we are entering a stage when we may all live as only some do today: from income. In such a context, nothing less than a full analysis of contemporary life, and the challenge to invent social machinery that will be relevant to it, is the real road to integration for men, and also for women, in the United States today.

## II. *The Relation of Woman and Man as Mates*━━

### 3. The Masculine Mystique

>━●━○━●━●━●━●━○━●━○━●━○━○━●━○━●━○━●━●━●━●━○━●━○━●━●━●━●━○━●━●━━(

It appears that ordinary men take wives because possession is not possible without marriage, and that ordinary women accept husbands because marriage is not possible without possession; with totally differing aims the method is the same on both sides.

THOMAS HARDY

There are two Americas, the male and the female, separated by a psychological gulf scarcely bridged by the culture's ingenious devices for keeping them coupled. In both Americas, people are pressured to become satellites of the family planet, but each sex moves in a separate orbit, scarcely meeting as they traverse their daily round.

A current version of the female orbit, one much debated in recent years, has been termed "the feminine mystique." In our context, it is a variant of the traditional model, for it is founded on biological determinism, defining woman in relation to nest and brood, but adding a new environment, the split-level suburb. In protest against the segregation implied by this stereotype, we have heard much questioning, much re-examination of old rationales. There is, however, a tendency in such neofeminism — at least at the popular level — to view women as victims; to view men as autonomous beings, even as victi-

*Parallel readings for this chapter appear in the section entitled "The Good Provider."

mizers, giving rise in new form to that ancient lawsuit: the battle of the sexes.

I think this is error, that in fact the equation is not so simple, and that correlative with the feminine mystique there is a hidden masculine mystique. Reflecting the modern temper, just as women are defined in terms of reproductive function in the mystique that focuses on them, so men are defined in terms of pecuniary function in a parallel mystique. Both these mystiques, and the two social hemispheres that derive from them, are in turn predicated upon the assumption of an irrevocable dichotomy in the basic natures of women and of men, an assumption largely untested because of the ethnocentrism with which we all view what touches us immediately.

By way of illustration, consider the study of more than 600 women in Chicago designed to learn in what order of importance they viewed their roles in life. Most considered themselves mothers first of all. The sample group were then asked to do the same for their husbands.

> Did these women — suburban wives in their thirties, with a family income of between $6,000 and $10,000, urban wives with a median age of forty-nine and a family income from $5,000 to more than $16,000 — see their mates primarily as husbands? As fathers? Or as breadwinners? The answer, startling though it is, isn't difficult to guess. Nearly 65 percent of the wives in both groups stated unequivocally that the most important role of the man of the family is, in their eyes, his bread-winning one. Father came in second; husband a poor third.[1]

Since whatever is, is likely to be accepted as eternal verity, such social patterns projected on the sexes appear inevitable, and the consequent distance between the sexes is perceived as an integral part of the human condition. "His" and "hers" seem to be fixed for all time: men must work and women must weep; her job is to be fruitful and multiply, his job is to be good provider — successful hunter in the financial jungle.

The contemporary model for the American male, seen in this perspective, appears through spectacles especially constructed by our times and our circumstances. It is a model tethered to the present and congruent neither with all pasts nor all futures. Moreover, in the instrumental view that fixes man as good provider, born to bear all external stresses, it goes without saying that woman can fulfill herself solely through the achievements of her mate. "Why do women have to fight their natures all the time?" asks a married civil engineer. "Why can't they just relax and let us take care of them, like the good Lord intended?"[2]

Here I am reminded of some lines from Ogden Nash:

> How simple was the relationship between the sexes in the days of Francesca di
> Rimini.
> Men were menacing, women were womeny . . .

which conclude:

I attribute much of our modern tension
To a misguided striving for intersexual comprehension.[3]

But there are other causes for "our modern tension" — heightened competition and the quest for security, which together take an incredible toll of the American male. For he must bring home not only the bacon to his entitled wife and expectant offspring, but also a whole cornucopia of glittering commodities. And he is required to carry this burden alone.

> When Dr. Mirra Komarovsky asked the husbands in her blue-collar study what subjects they would be most reluctant to discuss with their wives, their answers included the following: anything having to do with the job; financial worries . . . hopes, dreams, and dissatisfactions (anything having to do with the man's inner core).[4]

Lee Rainwater and associates, in their study of the workingman's wife, report that many women do not even know where their husbands work or exactly what they do to earn their paychecks.

The perils of this design for living are unforgettably captured by Osborn in a cartoon showing man and woman walking a tightrope above an abyss, holding hands and balancing three children on their shoulders. But even this departs from the pervasive stereotype, which would dictate that the man stand alone on the tightrope, carrying the little woman, too.

In return for all this stress and effort, the male prototype tends to expect rewards that, in the main, fail to materialize. First, he finds that his work, which he has been taught should constitute the alter ego of self, is by and large meaningless. In Richard Yates' *Revolutionary Road,* the antihero Frank defines his condition as "one of hundreds of tiny pink men in white shirts, forever shifting papers and frowning into telephones."[5] This is what work is for millions of men in America today. Clearly a life spent in such paltry activity, if it has at the same time been identified as the core of vital sex performance, is bound to lead to a sadly diminished sense of masculinity. As C. Wright Mills has written, "a bureaucracy is no testing field for heroes."

Second, his relationship with wife and children tends, in most families, to be essentially functional and, consequently, alienated. The bonds that should be ties between organic beings are reduced to partial contacts for particular ends.

In 1887, Ferdinand Tönnies published his major work, *Gemeinschaft und Gesellschaft*, which distinguished between two essentially different bases of human association: one, a unit derived from status, such as the family; the other, a unit derived from contract, such as a business venture. In the first, *Gemeinschaft,* members of the group are bound together as whole persons; in the second, *Gesellschaft,* individuals enter the relationship with only a fraction of their being, that part which is connected with the end in view.

Commenting on this model, Fritz Pappenheim notes:

In the *Gemeinschaft* unity prevails, in spite of occasional separation; in the *Gesellschaft* separation prevails, in spite of occasional unity.

So deep is the separation between man and man in *Gesellschaft* that "everybody is by himself and isolated, and there exists a condition of tension against all others." Thus, *Gesellschaft* becomes a social world in which latent hostility and potential war are inherent in the relationship of one to another.

In terms of historical development,

Tönnies holds that society is moving away from an age where *Gemeinschaft* was predominant towards an age where *Gesellschaft* prevails.[6]

Certainly this is no surprise at the level of work, since home industry and the family farm as bases for making a living are disappearing life styles. But it is surprising to find increasingly functional attitudes of family members toward one another. There is, however, mounting evidence that individuals enter the most intimate relationships with only a fraction of their beings, for ulterior ends, and with attitudes of "latent hostility and potential war" — in short, with all the indicia of contract or *Gesellschaft*.

And yet, why should we be surprised? William Dilthey has observed that all the manifestations of energy that shape an era are akin to one another. Certainly we, in the United States today, are not unaware that alienation is one of the "manifestations of energy" that shape our era; and that most people are so absorbed in the relentless pursuit of their interest that this foreshortened view determines their encounter with reality. Why should we then be surprised to find the same pattern present in encounters between the sexes?

I have referred to a study showing that women see their husbands primarily as breadwinners and themselves primarily as mothers. We have no data on how men see their wives and themselves, but I would speculate that the findings would be modified to this extent: before they become mothers, wives to men would be sex objects; men, to themselves, would continue breadwinners. In this context, the atmosphere of *Gesellschaft* would imply an exchange of exclusive sexual availability for every-ready economic support. The difficulty in this kind of bargain, however, in addition to its focus on function in place of person, is that there is a point of satiation in sex, but none in acquisitiveness.[7]

In effect, a great many American women seem to be saying, "You want to prove your manhood — produce." Thus, an astute motivation researcher, Dr. Ernest Dichter, advises companies to use wives to get more production out of their employees: "It is the wife of the salesman who can often be used to stimulate him and urge him to make more money."[8] Myron Brenton offers this vignette of the effect of such pressures on family life: "Some wives know just how to use the masculine stereotypes to twist the knife. One mother of six, chiding her husband for not showing more get-up-and-go, shoved his paycheck under his nose and said: 'This looks like a receipt for a woman's paycheck instead of a man's.' "[9]

Pressured in public and pulverized in private, is it any wonder that most American males respond to neofeminism with incredulity: "What do the women want? They already have everything."

To the masculine eye, it is the man who pays and pays while even the most demanding wives don't have to enter the competitive arena of the marketplace. Such men do not understand that women's frustration derives from foreshortened opportunities, from being stereotyped and restricted; that even the pleasures of comfort and security can be vitiated by a sense of uselessness.

It is a curious sidelight on this complex of patterns that it is the very emancipated woman, scorning parasitism and ready to share the economic burden, who is the most resented. Beleaguered males are certainly ambivalent about little women:

> "Here's the gal," they think. "What does she have to prove? All she has to do is keep the damn house clean, and that's only for me or for the people we invite into our home. Whereas the man goes out into the cold cruel world; he has to be good on his job; he has to be competitive; he has to bring home the bacon; he has to be a good lover; he has to be potent; he has to live up to his kids' expectations of him."[10]

But having identified his masculinity with money-making, the same beleaguered male feels altogether threatened by the new breed of females:

> Many a male feels genuinely alarmed by a woman who can match wits with him, beat him in a debate, more quickly solve a problem in calculus, or write a better piece of advertising copy. He uneasily tells himself she is "cold" and "unfeminine" . . . . He feels a threat to his traditional male superiority.[11]

We must remember, however, that "Man is a unique animal species in that he is also an historical development." [12] To take pointer readings in the present does not always help us to reconstruct the past or to project the future. "The Flintstones" tells us little about our stone age ancestors; current dichotomies do not define the limits of the twenty-first century.

On the other hand, even in tracing the evolution of patterns that mark the history of human division of labor, it is necessary to offer a cautionary word: experts disagree. There are those who believe that variations are superficial modifications of form but that basic roles for men and for women have not changed and must not change; that such forms are integral to the divine or the biological blueprint.

Thus, a contributor to a symposium on the family swings easily from the paleolithic to the present in documenting man's discontent:

> The primitive man roamed far and wide and freely as a hunter; the woman cowered in the protection of the cave. The home is usually the world to the woman; often it is a cage to the freedom-loving male. The English club and the

old-time (no women allowed) saloon represent attempts in the modern world to achieve this freedom. The nagging female's "Where have you been all this time?" is part of the agony of lost freedom.[13]

Here the enemy is change, that change which thwarts the underlying drives of the male archetype.

Other scholars, as they survey the pace of change and the continuous transformations that mark its trajectory, conclude that the "evolution of social structures is linked up with...the questions of social ecology."[14] In their view, it is this evolution that affects human actors, not only in relation to the patterns of their lives, but also in relation to images of self, formed and reformed at the intersection between tradition and process. From this vantage point, it is in terms of historical development that man must be defined, and therefore no single formula will fit him.

> Neither his anatomy nor his psyche fix his destiny. He creates his own destiny as he responds to his experienced situation, and both his situation and his experiences of it are complicated products of the historical epoch which he enacts. That is why he does not create his destiny as an individual but as a member of society. Only within the limits of his place in an historical epoch can man as an individual shape himself.[15]

In this sense, just as people feed data into machines, so society feeds data into people. What comes out as opinion, attitude, model, image, is the fascinating resultant of personal and cultural heritage, of personal and cultural programming.

The gap between male and female in such perspective is not a universal constant, but rather the distance between public and private that developed with the first industrial revolution. Whereas home and workshop were once one, and the design for earning a living was interwoven with the design for living, this is no longer true.

Today the hemisphere of the public has been assigned to the male and the hemisphere of the private to the female. Each sex has become a symbol for its territory. The conflict between them can then be seen as a reflection of the longing of each to be part of the other's sphere, to link the public with the private in our schizoid world, to embrace the whole of life.

In his charming volume, *Letters to a Young Poet,* Rilke foreshadows the dream:

> And perhaps the sexes are more related than we think, and the great renewal of the world will perhaps consist in this, that man and maid, freed of all false feeling and aversion, will seek each other not as opposites, but as brother and sister, as neighbors, and will come together *as human beings,* in order simply, seriously and patiently to bear in common the difficult generation that is their burden.[16]

## 4. Marriage à la Mode

>═●═○═●═○═●═○═●═○═●═○═●═○═●═○═●═○═●═○═●═○═●═○═●═○═●═○═●═○═●═○═●═○═●═○═●═(

Physics has begun to uncover
a new conundrum in the
worlds of matter and anti-
matter, occupying the same
space and time but locked off
from each other by their ob-
verse natures, forever twin yet
forever sundered.

I. F. STONE

Revolutionaries of the past sought to mold the new woman along two basic lines: wide range and full function. The focus of the first was personal growth beyond the private; that of the second, a place in the social sun. Contending for this view, they were confident that only when a new design for living was created would romantic love flourish and men and women be free to find one another in joyous equality.

The efforts of the feminists have been fruitful. Barriers to range and function have come tumbling down. Then why the recurrent discontent? And where is the projected erotic millenium?

One difficulty is that women today have been persuaded to walk the new roads with bound feet, to encumber their rights with their privileges. Consequently, the gap in development that our foremothers struggled so resolutely to close is still with us. Only its form has changed. Women today roam the

*Parallel readings for this chapter appear in the section entitled "So Dearly Joined."

campuses but they are, in the main, caricatures of the dream; intellectual pursuit has been largely eclipsed by the mating game. Gifted coeds with a world to win have narrowed their sights and delimited their goals to "object: matrimony." Some do it with backward looks; the majority rush forward to the still, small life. For, superseding personal inclination, social models press our young women to hitch their wagon to a spouse, not a star, and few have the courage to be deviant.

And so, despite the modern temper, that development gap between husband and wife which was, in the feminist view, the major impediment in the path of true love, remains a striking feature of marriage in our time. Education for him is an investment in the future. For her, it has become the pearl in the apron pocket.

Nor is this pattern limited to privileged groups. It pervades every social level. As Margaret Mead has astutely observed, the styles of behavior set by the fortunate "inform the daydreams and minister to the discontents of the groups who do not share in them."[1] All individuals, all classes, are offered the model of the little woman, and intrinsic to that model is the development gap.

With this stunting of growth, it is not remarkable that contemporary American women also suffer from the dependency syndrome, a malady the old militants were certain would disappear once woman had free access to the marketplace. It could scarcely have occurred to those early feminists, in their effort to win the franchise of occupational choice, that their granddaughters would still elect to be domestic relations; that a time would come when the majority of new women would view this option not as a ticket to autonomy but as a raincheck for emergency.

It is conceivable that the development gap and the dependency syndrome will be modified by current soul-searching. But I think it is fair to say that the pacesetters, the middle class models who are provided with opportunity and not pressed by necessity, conduct their lives in the old context. They can still be described as myopic hitchhikers: myopic because they have limited their sights, hitchhikers because they travel on their husbands' shoulders (and use their sex to climb on board).

Perhaps we have here the reason that scholars, when they consider the condition of man, weigh his relation to the universe; but when they consider the condition of woman, continue to weigh only her relation to man. For the universe of many women is still suspended from a thin gold ring. And, for many men, this is still the total conception of women. Thus, the condition of woman becomes confused with the circumstance that, for her, marriage is a way of earning a living; that she can get her keep by getting a husband; that her sex function can be a marketable skill.

This combination — this confounding of the economic with the emotional — introduces profound variables to the conjugal equation. It was for this reason that early militants, searching for solutions, agitated for a new form of alliance, with love and money finally unravelled from one another, where each partner would be financially free, where they would come together solely from reciprocated tenderness.

Olive Schreiner wrote passionately of this goal:

> For the first time in the history of the modern world, prostitution, using that term in its broadest sense to cover all sexual relationships based, not on the spontaneous affection of the woman for the man, but on the necessitous acceptance by woman of material good in exchange for the exercise of her sexual functions, would be extinct; and the relation between men and women become a co-partnership between them.
>
> So far from the economic freedom and social independence of the woman exterminating sexual love between man and woman, it would for the first time fully enfranchise it.[2]

Olive Schreiner was writing at a time when the right to function productively, particularly in the professions, was a burning issue. Today, there is less gross discrimination which would make imperative the interweaving of affection with economic survival, but the pattern prevails. With all the tide of recent change, the largest sector of our feminine population still gain their living through marriage. It is unquestionably the most popular profession.

I do not here argue the objective necessity of this arrangement, other things being equal. The right to a spectrum of other occupations may be an empty one if jobs are not available. Nor do I question the economic contribution of housewives, given contemporary designs for living. With single-unit structure and servantless households, it is clear that numbers of women perform necessary tasks. I merely observe that for the majority of American women, sex and security are still centered in the same relationship. The very folkways bear testimony, as in the revealing remark: "She used to be a laboratory assistant, but now she's married."

The underlying assumption here points to yet another motive for the choice of marriage as a means of livelihood. When a woman earns her own way, her social level is rarely very high; she is tied, even in the professions, to the less honorific tasks of the occupational compass: those with least prestige and lowest pay. So painful is it still for a woman to make her way upward under her own power that only the hardiest persist. The majority soon discover that an ambitious woman can go higher faster through judicious mating than by any other ladder. It is a more permanent course, too, because if she has been effective, after the climb to the altar, she's set for life. In sociological jargon, "Marriage remains the only major path of social mobility for women in our society."[3]

In recent years, this choice has been further reinforced by our marvelous fixation on boudoirs and babies. The biological cycle, whether interpreted by skillful Freudians or by the folksy slicks, covers dependency with a sacred aura. With so many pressures and so many persuasions, it is scarcely surprising to find the whole range of womanhood — the moronic, the mediocre, the meteoric — all attached to the same female model deep in the heart of the home. This despite the fact that "American girls spend more time as apprentice mothers with their dolls than they will as adult women with their own babies, and there is half a lifetime still ahead by the time the youngest child enters high school."[4]

Now, in the course of utilizing marriage for vertical mobility a very interesting thing occurs. The man, out in the arena, is challenged constantly in his work — even if it is only to keep a firm hold on his job — and is thus required to measure himself against external criteria. The woman, since she is using *his* motion to propel *her* onward, is immune both to challenge and to criteria. Wives and mothers are good wives and good mothers by definition, not by performance. Only misanthropes point the finger at American womanhood; only hucksters talk about tattletale gray. Following on this lack of standard, this affirmation by "being" — presently, imperceptibly, even partners who commence marriage as intellectual equals begin to experience the development gap.

But, by and large, couples are not equally educated. The accepted pattern is for husbands to have more schooling, wives to have less; and as the years of togetherness accumulate, the differential widens. No one has seriously refuted the sardonic remark that Washington is full of fascinating men and the women they married when they were very young. Yet these embarrassing spouses of the illustrious may once have been as charged with potential as the very young men. The critical variable is that, living the horizontal life, the women's mental muscles have atrophied. This means that among the leisure classes, wives have become human ornaments; among the lower classes they have become the one-woman band. Identity is, at each level, imprisoned in futile forms; role proficiency involves little intellectual rigor.

Here is the picture of the development gap at the power elite level:

> The President has broken the total Congressional membership of 535 into about a dozen groups of roughly equal size, and he is having these groups one by one down to the White House along with their wives for the strangest meetings the old mansion has ever seen.
>
> Mrs. Johnson takes the wives off to see a movie, to look at the White House decor or something of the sort. The President leads the men into the Oval Room and there lays out for both parties what he is doing and intending to do all across the board in public affairs.[5]

Another illustration, this time of the life styles of middle class professionals, also delineates the distance between spouses. It is taken from the convention issue of the State Bar of California *Reports* and lists, side by side with such programs for the attorneys as "Discovery in Administrative Proceedings," "The Uniform Rules of Evidence," and "The Revision of the Penal Code," the following item: "The Lawyers' Wives will staff the hospitality desk, the coffee bar and the art exhibit." It was also announced that they would have a "Fashion Luncheon."[6]

If this is how it goes in privileged circles, I suppose we should not be surprised to find the development gap also present in the blue collar class. A booklength study of the stay-at-home workingman's wife notes that her range of experience rarely extends beyond the personal; that she is bounded by the doorstep and the block; that men to her, her husband included, are personified instruments of the public world which she does not know and does not comprehend; and that her "sense of inferiority to the male is marked." So remote are these women's lives, so vulnerable, so passive, that some "have difficulty saying exactly what their husbands do at work or where his company is located."[7]

The effect of the distance between husband and wife is, then, among all groups and at all levels, invariably negative. Wherever they stand, they have difficulty communicating across the development gap. In each instance there is also a diminution of the spouses: of the wife because she exists in limbo, of the husband because he becomes inured to tiny talk. The end result is that each lives in two communities: the community of partners and the community of peers. This is evident at social functions where the differently charged sexes are drawn to the anode and the cathode of the living room. At the male pole, arena concerns: work, politics, sports, stock market; at the female pole, distaff concerns: children, clothes, health, home.

Even among young people, who now tend to marry while still in school, the old patterns begin imperceptibly to supplant the new. Although they may start together, he winds up with a Ph.D., she with a "Ph.T.," the consolatory degree for "putting hubby through." True, there is here a departure from the past. In this early stage, the wife, instead of earning her living through marriage, makes the marriage possible by earning both livings. An election has been made that the husband's career has priority; the bride becomes breadwinner so that he can stay with the books. No doubt the young woman's sacrifice (if it was that) was appreciated, but the division of labor begins to divide interests too. Routine work keeps her in a narrow channel, while he goes on to increasingly more complex levels of thought. In most cases, her career is eclipsed. The wife who puts her husband through, winds up through. By the time he acquires the significant degree and she is awarded the sop to her pride, the relationship of peers has been fractured. At this point, he takes up the earning responsibility as a professional, while her profession becomes marriage. Then, like their elders, these fresh young couples are left to make their way in two communities: the community of partners and the community of peers. Whirling in separate but not at all equal orbits, they may no longer be within hailing distance of one another.

Development gap and dependency syndrome, then, despite the furor of the feminists, despite the motion of change, show that woman in America today is not yet the equal sex. She continues to be the ornamental sex, the domestic sex, and the auxiliary sex. There are those who challenge this conclusion, arguing: "It takes both of us to keep his job." This is borne out by a *Fortune* study that reports the executive view: "When a man comes to work for us . . . we think of the company as employing the family."[8] But even if it is true that the wife is a rider in the employment contract, that scarcely spurs her development. Nor does it help her in attaining autonomy to function as hostess, emergency typist, housekeeper, chauffeur, soothing syrup, pillow listener, goad. Admittedly, the corporation perspective is not unique. It is entirely consonant with other directives that assume it is woman's destiny to achieve her fulfillment through others. The new wrinkle is that, instead of being the tactful little lady behind the scenes, the company wife has been promoted to stage manager, as one firm after another discovers the profits that accrue from domestic prodding.

But even without company intervention, the desire to be supported in the style to which her neighbors are accustomed makes many a woman a constant manipulator. From the sanctuary of complete infallibility — she can't fail since she doesn't have to try — she issues directives. I found samples of this pattern in the novel *In Vivo,* by Mildred Savage, which tells the story of company scientists searching for an antibiotic. The author takes the characters from laboratory to bedroom, from the ambience of work colleagues to that of bosom companion, and we see each, now from the angle of partnership, now from the angle of peer. In fascinating counterpoint to the problems of research and the politics of rivalry in the professional world, there is a scene like this:

> "I think I'll quit."
> She looked up quickly at that. "Don't be ridiculous."
> "I'm thinking of it."
> "You're not going to quit," she said. "You're going to stay right where you are. Where else are you going to get this much money?"

Another discouraged scientist, tired of the in-fighting and troubled by an ulcer, says to his wife:

> "And if you want the truth, I'd like to get as far away from it as possible."
> "Now let me tell you something," she said. "As long as Enright is working on this, you're going to work on it and you're not getting far away. You've only been chemical director for six years, so don't get any ideas that you've had it. Do you know Max Strong would love to have your job? Why should he be satisfied to be assistant director if he can get director? I know that type — he'd like to be president. Well, if he ever gets to be director, it'll be when you get to be vice president. And not before. So don't think you're going to back away from this and let him take over by default — just because it gives you a stomach-ache."[9]

Why the men are so compliant is not very clear to me, except that I think there may have been a power reversal deriving, in some measure, from a false sense of egalitarianism and an unquestioning acceptance of stereotyped role. Also, he has been exposed to the competition so his defenses are down, while she, isolated and supported in her self-righteousness by the prevailing mores, can remain omniscient.

There are those who challenge my classification of modern woman as the underdeveloped and dependent sex on the theory that marriage is a partnership; he gains the living, she keeps the house; he produces money, she produces heirs; his the business beat, hers the biological one — bed, board, and babies. There are several answers. First, if the woman is a partner, she is a limited one. A recent California court decision illustrates this. It held that a wife's travel expenses are tax deductible if she accompanies her husband on a business trip, despite the fact that she does not perform any duties of a business nature. The appeals court held:

> The critical inquiries are whether the dominant purpose of the trip was to serve her husband's business purpose in making the trip and whether she actually spent a substantial amount of her time in assisting her husband in fulfilling that purpose . . . . It is true that, on these trips, most of Mrs. Disney's activities in helping her husband fulfill some of his business purposes in making the trip were of a kind which she would normally engage in while they were both at home. But the added factor here is that the husband has, because of company policy, been put to the additional expense of paying his wife's travel expenses so that she could assist him in this way on the road.[10]

It was pointed out elsewhere in the court's opinion that the wife spent much of her day in her hotel room or shopping, attending to such matters as the care of her husband's laundry, taking telephone calls, and performing other activities of a "wifely" character.

One has only to reverse the design, to have the husband go along on a wife's business trip to see what the partnership idea of the wife implies: handmaiden duties. Clearly, since a husband does not perform such services, it is not likely that his travels as consort would be similarly tax deductible. In point of fact, many professional women complain they are at a competitive disadvantage precisely because they have no wives.

Still another point is clarified here; namely, that those citing the distaff side as proof of the wife's partnership status are confusing marriage with domestic service. Women specialized to sex, reproduction, and housework may do useful things, but their role is dependent and auxiliary and rarely lends itself to functional development. (A recent study of the mentally retarded reports that feeble-minded girls make exceptionally good housekeepers and nurse-maids. It should be added that they are also adequate sex partners and have the organic potential to reproduce themselves.) In fact, housekeeping and child care have been defined as the supreme education in diffusion of thought—a life design diametrically opposed to that vital ingredient of development: concentration. Further, the circumstance that family labor in servantless houses has an economic value, given the current institutional setting, should not obscure the fact that these services do not make a wife economically independent. This is a crucial distinction in a cash nexus society and one that effectively disposes of the peer concept implied by the word *partnership.*

Even the women who are beginning to question the soft sell contained in feminine mystique ideology have not, by and large, escaped the implications of the development gap and the dependency syndrome. Most make their forays into the fuller life from the protective custody of their husband's solid incomes. Although they are no doubt sincere in their discovery that happiness is a state of stretch not of slack, their dream, as they weep into their Metrecal, seems to be self-realization, first person singular. This is a tiny revolution, a far cry from the creative insurgency of the old feminists who were concerned with self-realization for the human race. Moreover, they tend to turn the guns of their frustration on the very husbands who finance their uprising, and so the new becomes but another version of an old controversy, the battle of the sexes.

Solutions for diminished woman and harassed man yoked in a kinship system that has lost its meaning can only be derived contextually. For we are an accommodating species; our brains program their neural network to resemble the social one. I think we must seek guidance in de Tocqueville's reflection:

> I am tempted to believe that what we call necessary institutions are often no more than institutions to which we have become accustomed . . . that in matters of social constitution, the field of possibilities is much more extensive than men living in their various societies are ready to imagine.[11]

Manifest content, then, is not to be trusted; we must view the familiar with extreme skepticism. For the tensions of our personal lives reflect instabilities in the social matrix that have shaken all the old verities. Old mutualities between the sexes have disappeared; new ones relevant to new conditions have not thus far been designed. Yet, where there is no mutuality, "sex ends by being only another expression of hostility."[12] Only with new paradigms can the changing identities of men and women be institutionally harmonized; only when women are liberated from their bondage to underdevelopment and dependency, and when men are liberated from their obligation to support them in that suspension, can marriage be meaningful today.

In the stirring language of Olive Schreiner:

> It is for love's sake yet more than for any other that we look for that new time when love is no more bought and sold, when it is not a means of making bread . . . . Then love will come . . . a strange sudden sweetness . . . not sought for, but found.[13]

Marriage will then cease to be a profession, a design for making a living, and become instead a peer relationship where the sexes as comrades can try to rivet together the shattered fragments of the world.[14]

## 5. Law the Laggard

—•—o—•—o—•—o—•—o—•—o—•—o—•—o—•—o—•—o—•—o—•—o—•—o—•—o—•—o—•—o—•—

The truth is, we are in the
midst of such terrible errors
on the subject of woman and
her veritable rights that it is
frightful to think of.

LEO TOLSTOI

In the old days, those incapable of entering into a contract were infants,
children, idiots, the insane, and married women. Family life has changed since
then, but family law still lags behind reality. The reason for this is that the law
is largely a museum of mummies in which the forms of the past are preserved,
wrapped in amended layers of the present. Thus we find, in the traditional
cases, that husband and wife are termed *baron* and *femme,* harking back to
feudal times, and in the corpus of common law, analyzed by Blackstone in his
famous *Commentaries,* that husband and wife are considered one person. He
writes: "The very being or legal existence of the woman is suspended during
the marriage, or at least is incorporated and consolidated into that of the
husband; under whose wing, protection, and cover she performs everything;

*Parallel readings for this chapter appear in the section entitled "Domestic Relations."

and is therefore called in our law a *femme couverte.* Upon this principle of a union of person in husband and wife, depend all the legal rights, duties, and disabilities that either of them acquire by marriage."[1]

The feminists were up in arms about some of these "legal rights, duties, and disabilities" acquired by marriage, for to them it seemed clear that the law merging man and wife into one person meant that the man became that person. When Lucy Stone and Henry Blackwell were married, to take one instance, they joined hands at their wedding and read aloud a statement which declared: "This act on our part implies no sanction of, nor promise of voluntary obedience to such of the present laws of marriage as refuse to recognize the wife as an independent, rational being, while they confer upon the husband an injurious and unnatural superiority."[2] This was a form of conscientious objection.

While historically it is true that between 1839 and 1950 most states passed legislation recognizing the right of married women to hold property — the first of the layers of amendments wrapped around the corpus of feudal law — and while additional layers have been added over the years, the original body of doctrine still defines the form and determines the philosophy of marital contract and marital condition. We should not, therefore, be surprised to find that some of the "rights, duties, and disabilities" stemming from Blackstone's time, and founded on the legal fiction of the unity of husband and wife, still exist. As the President's Commission on the Status of Women noted in 1963, "In every State, one kind of disability or another limits the legal rights of married women."[3]

The most important derivative of feudal law, in my opinion, is that which still vests in the husband primary legal responsibility for family support.) Blackstone defined this principle in these words: "The husband is bound to provide his wife with necessaries by law, as much as himself; and if she contracts debts for them, he is obliged to pay them."[4] In the book I consulted on this point, a previous reader had noted in the margin: "Still true today." In analyzing the extent to which it is "still true today," a distinction must be made between the 42 states where earnings and property acquired during marriage are owned separately by the spouses, and the 8 states, all in the West or the Southwest, where earnings and most property acquired during marriage are owned in common. Today, in the separate-property states, a wife has no legal right to any part of her husband's earnings or property, aside from basic support. If she does not have her own resources, she is completely dependent on her husband's largesse. Today in the community-property states, whatever is acquired during marriage becomes part of a mutual fund, but the husband manages and controls that fund.

The fiction has faded, but the fact remains that the husband still determines the state of the marital union. And although the wife often has a secondary obligation for family support, particularly if the husband is in need, these are again amended layers wound around an old concept. They result from the new philosophy that I have called "the challenging view," which postulates that a woman is an individual with an independent identity. But they leave intact "the traditional approach," based upon the fictional unity that designates the man as primary provider to family and responsible party to society.

Thus, while Married Women's Property Acts were passed and other legislation was conceived in an attempt to implement new realities, the body of organic law has not been recreated; rather it has continued, with some small modifications, to confirm the patterns of the past.

This means the law has become a mosaic of both philosophies. And it is significant that the recent Report of the President's Commission reflects both philosophies. For, whereas it presses for partnership status of the spouses, at the same time it recommends the retention of principles that go back to the *femme couverte*. Thus, one paragraph states: "In view of the child-bearing and home-making functions of the wife . . . the husband should continue to have primary responsibility for support of his wife and minor children."[5] Any self-respecting feminist of the past would have been really aroused by this relegation of the wife with the minor children, as an equivalent albatross on the husband's shoulders.

So we have the curious legal situation that children over 21 are assigned greater financial burdens and greater financial autonomy than a wife. No matter what her age, she is classed with the juveniles. Second, this proposal makes no distinction between childbearing wives and other wives, between wives responsible for the rearing of minor children and wives whose children are grown. Finally, the proposal does not differentiate between the Judy O'Gradys who do, in fact, manage a household in the most direct sense, doing the scrubbing and the washing, the cooking and the tending, and the Colonel's ladies whose homemaking consists of symbolic courtesies. According to this definition, "a wife's a wife for a' that."

The contrasting philosophy is expressed in this quotation from the Commission Report: "However, in line with the partnership view of marriage . . . the wife should be given some legal responsibility for sharing in her own support and that of her children to the extent she has sufficient means to do so."[6] Of course, this does not require a woman to find "sufficient means to do so." It is only suggested that if she happens to have funds she should be required to share them. The parasitic woman remains the legal prototype.

The same ambivalence is present in the proceedings of a recent legal conference on the status of married women. Here the recommendation was offered that each spouse have a legally defined right in the earnings of the other and in the property acquired through those earnings. This was related to the new partnership concept of coverture where each mate makes a different but equal contribution. From the discussion, it was clear that the division of labor envisioned was nonetheless the traditional one: husband hunting the dollar, wife tending the domicile. An example was given of a woman saying, "You're making $10,000 so I ought to be able to buy this and this and this." And her man responding, "No." The speaker said the wife can argue and protest, "But it's our money." However, outside of the eight community-property states, in a legal sense, it's not; it's his money. And even in the community-property states, he can still say "no" because at the legal level he is vested with authority to manage the community. So the proposal that each spouse have a right in the earnings of the other means, essentially, that the wife shall be entitled to some of her husband's take, or as the British put it, to be part owner of the man's pay packet. Although the conference carefully considered partnership sharing of income, the question of partnership contribution of income was largely overlooked. The underlying assumption was still very much as it was in feudal times — that the husband is destined to be the primary provider.[7] I have observed that when pushed to the pinch node, this is justified on biological grounds; namely, that childbearers must themselves be borne. On the other hand, the logic is generalized to continue prior to and long after childbearing and even if no children are in the picture.

Obsolete forms of social existence are a powerful distorting factor. Even when the need for change is recognized, the formulations tendered are unconscious testimony to the dependence of the present on the past. As one speaker phrased it: "Normally, it is the husband's money and the wife asks for it. But the wife makes a different but equal contribution in that she works and serves, thus giving him the freedom to go out and earn the family income."[8] A British advocate of this concept supported it in these words: "The cockbird can feather the nest only because he is not required to spend most of his time sitting on it."[9] Although I think a case can be made for the argument that the brood hen performs activities of economic value in relation to her nest, the distinction is that in relation to society she is still dependent upon the economic activities of her mate. If the husband dies, or if the husband leaves her, her housework and child care will not pay the rent, nor the grocer, nor the department store; they will not cover the installments due on the car, TV, and dinette set. If she has no earning capacity, she must attach herself to another man. A legal right to the husband's earnings does not free a wife from the humiliation of economic dependency.

Once again, solutions grafted upon patterns of the past do not resolve dilemmas of the present. And we have not progressed as far as we might think from the time Jane Austen depicts, when Charlotte Lucas, reflecting on her engagement to Mr. Collins, muses: "Mr. Collins, to be sure, was neither sensible nor agreeable; his society was irksome, and his attachment to her must be imaginary. But still he would be her husband. Without thinking highly either of men or of matrimony, marriage had always been her object; it was the only honorable provision for well-educated young women of small fortune, and however uncertain of giving happiness, must be the pleasantest preservation from want."[10] That is what, I believe, is still true today: marriage as the pleasantest preservation from want.

Examining the subject cross-culturally, let us take some pointer readings in how the marital contract has been reappraised in other countries. The law of the Soviet Union leaves husband and wife free to choose a profession or occupation, and includes this interesting clause: "Which is to be house-maker is decided by mutual consent of the parties."[11] Sweden has a parallel provision to the effect that each spouse must contribute to the maintenance of the marriage by income or by homemaking. And the Polish section on this point reads: "Both spouses are obliged according to their strength, gaining possibilities, and estate, to contribute to the satisfaction of the needs of the family formed by their union. Fulfillment of this duty can also wholly or partly consist in personal efforts to bring up children and work in the common household."[12]

From my point of view, the last is the most enlightened of the codes I have seen. I think it is instructive that its content was developed through dialogue between laymen and lawyers after a campaign was launched inviting popular reaction to draft proposals under consideration by the legislature. The result was a flood of communications. These were scrutinized and discussed before the final code was adopted.

Just as the legal form of marriage harks back to an earlier period, so the legal principles and the legal philosophy respecting dissolution of marriage are similarly based. To quote Blackstone again, "for the canon law, which the common law follows in this case, deems so highly and with such mysterious reverence of the nuptial tie that it will not allow it to be unloosed for any cause whatsoever that arises after the union is made, and this is said to be built on the divine revealed law."[13] Contemporary conditions have caused us to amend that concept to the degree that all states now recognize divorce on at least one ground. Nevertheless, the underlying form of the law, rooted in ecclesiastical dogma, regards the rupture of the union, of the fictional oneness, as sin, and permits such rupture only upon the basis of guilt, the most significant guilt being adultery. I'd like to quote a paragraph from the very first case I studied on adultery to indicate the atmosphere in which such guilt is usually established.

The evidence is that the defendant went to the Grand Central Station with his handbag, met a woman not his wife, . . . took her with her hand-baggage, to a hotel in a cab, registered her with himself as his wife, had a room assigned to them, . . . and immediately went with her into the lift, . . . taking their baggage with them. A witness waited in the hotel until midnight to see if he came down, but did not see him. There is no description of the woman, nor of their demeanor toward each other . . . Though opportunity was shown, inclination, it is said, was not. But seeking such bedroom privacy was evidence of inclination stronger than any ordinary act of affection between them at the station or in the cab. What did they register in a hotel as a man and wife and retire to a bedroom for? We have it of old [and here the judge quoted from Burton's *Anatomy of Melancholy*], "it is presumed he saith not a *pater noster*" there.[14]

Fault or guilt continues to be emphasized both in the granting of decrees and in awards of alimony. True, proposed legislation in various states and newly minted legislation in California suggest an emerging countertrend. It is, however, undeniable that for the most part all of the insights of psychology, all of the data of casework, which together reveal so much about the root causes of marital discord, seem to have left virtually unshaken the traditional legal attitudes on "guilty" conduct of a spouse.

In view of the earlier discussion of the husband as primary provider, I think it is striking that in addition to the usual grounds from which guilt is drawn, some states also recognize nonsupport as a ground for granting a wife a decree of divorce. Moreover, when dissolution is ordered, forty-eight states provide for permanent alimony to the wife to be awarded at the court's discretion. Here, in effect, the law guarantees social insurance for the "unemployed wife."

The same tension between traditional and contemporary trends is reflected in what is essentially the poor man's divorce: desertion. For the man who opts out is now sought under the Uniform Reciprocal Enforcement of Support Act. I think it is a profound commentary on our values that the states, which cannot get together on the machinery of dissolution, so that domestic relations codes are still the greatest stronghold of states' rights doctrine, have been able to find common ground in pursuing the little man who isn't there.

As in the area of marital entanglement, cross-cultural examination of marital breach also provides new perspectives. Not surprisingly, the most radical approaches appear in the codes of the most radical states. Soviet law, for instance, does not follow the tradition of a list of causes from which guilt may be drawn. One of their jurists writes: "Life is highly complex and varied, and judicial practice shows that causes which are valid in one case may be invalid in others."[15] So the law in Russia provides one criterion: the criterion of necessity. The Family Code of Poland approaches the issue in a similar fashion. It states: "In case of a complete and durable breakdown of married life each of the spouses can demand that the court dissolve their marriage by divorce."[16] Current California proposals for divorce reform are in the same philosophical framework, in which the key issue is, like the phrase in the *Ladies' Home Journal*, "Can this marriage be saved?"

I believe even these few indicators of approaches at variance with our own should modify any facile assumptions that familiar customs and familiar laws reflect eternal verities. Clearly, there are many possible plots for plays featuring the same old characters: papa, mama, and the children.

It is a commonplace that the law moves ponderously behind social and economic change; but family law, it seems, lags behind all other fields. Even while we are preparing for the future at other levels of life, there seems to be an underlying conviction that, particularly in the private sphere, it will unfold in an orderly manner from the practices of the present. Robert Sinheimer, in a recent issue of the *Bulletin of the Atomic Scientists*, urges the importance of anticipation in a world of flux, and points to the injustice and the suffering that might be mitigated had we but a modicum of reliable foresight, and the resolution to use it. In our time, he writes, we are moving out of a world we never made, but were biologically adapted to, to a world of our own creation. We are becoming free not only from the "external tyrannies and caprices of toil, famine and disease, but from internal constraints of our animal inheritance, our physical frailties, our emotional anachronisms, our intellectual limitations.[17] Isn't the last the perfect definition of the foundations of family law and the fictions of woman's position there?

Lawyers have become aware of the new findings of specialists through the use of the computer, but they employ this marvelous instrument to search out old precedents, precedents that have largely become irrelevant. Sociologists are debating the personal consequences of woman's re-entry into the work force at a time when the industrial equation is moving toward the complete elimination of humans as automatons, and when, according to Buckminster Fuller, the very word "worker" will soon have no current meaning. Psychiatrists are urging women to fulfill themselves "naturally" in their predestined role of motherhood, even as it becomes more clear that the very right to give birth to life, as today the right to take life, will have to be controlled to preserve some semblance of population balance.

Mummified legal systems preserving yesterday's antique verities distort our lives even when they are liberally wrapped in layers of social relevance. The revolutionary force of new ecological patternings requires a sweep-out of all inherited systems that aren't necessarily so, including those applied to the hot little kingdom of family folklore.

The splitting of the atom has also split the legal fiction of man and wife as one person. Population density and "the pill" have undermined the biological determinism upon which woman's legal role has been founded. Potential plenty for all, and the redundancy of man as automaton, have jettisoned the first person singular support concept that underlies domestic relations.

It is time to overturn the patterns of arbitrary customs, codes, and mores; to look upon our unprecedented situation with pristine eyes; and to make new and bold social blueprints based not upon legal fictions but upon transcendant realities.

# 6. A House Is Not a Homestead

The home background out of which our new young woman has come is still coloured by the ideas of the past, and its obligations cling about her feet.

RAY STRACHEY

Families in the United States think in one world and live in another. They cannot relate to the real: it is hidden. Nor can they implement the fantasy: reality intrudes. Yet this failure to fuse social myth with social fact is not diagnosed as cultural astigmatism. Rather, because of our emphasis on individual autonomy, the mote is sought in the subjective eye, precipitating a search for causes and meanings directed inward and backward, toward the personal and the past. Sociology gives way to psychology; institutions are eclipsed by the ego. This is how it is at the thinking level. But at the living level, actuality has a momentum of its own: the real transcends the myth. We have then the curious paradox that, as each household strives toward the impossible ideal, the empirical direction of change is true to life. The difficulty is that the new, the valid, the contemporary patterns are distorted in the mirrors of myth, so that each family sees itself guiltily as deviant.

What, then, is that myth and why is it so compelling? It is a projection of the American family as a free-standing, self-contained unit with significant productive functions, patriarchal in character, and rural and rooted

*Parallel readings for this chapter appear in the section entitled "Woman's Place."

45

in design. There once was such an American family. It existed during the household economy of the colonial period, and in the early stages of western migration. At that time, most people who were white and free owned land and pooled their efforts, as kinship units, to produce what they needed, to protect themselves from enemies and the elements, to pass along what knowledge they had, to amuse themselves when the day was done, and to pray together. So hardy was this group, so appealing to romantic imagination and national pride, that the image of its life style survived long after its foundations in land ownership were undermined.

Indeed its image survives to this day. Our version is the consumer family, which, though conceived on Madison Avenue, is bred from stout colonial stock. It is pictured as ruggedly independent and eternally young, living the full life in a split-level ranch house removed by manorial lawns from the rest of suburbia and, in fact, from the rest of the world. The father, master in his own house, leaves it cheerfully each morning to try his mettle in the marketplace. His wife, fresh and deft, applies herself to technicolor tasks while the tow-headed children tumble. Effortlessly, the good provider puts down deep roots of security at his evergreen desk in the city; serenely, the timeless nurturer sustains her own, ensuring their climb straight up the beanstalk of vertical mobility.

The real family looks at these pictures with despair. Both the pioneer pattern and its consumer mutant appear to it not as illusory conceits, but as conclusive standards. This causes strain at many levels and in almost all circles, for the proffered models are not only present, they are pervasive. All classes see the same films, television shows, musical comedies. All read the same newspapers and magazines. All are assaulted by the same advertisements. As Margaret Mead observes: "Subtly, insistently, continuously, the standard American culture is presented to rich and to poor, to newcomer and even to aborigine."[1]

What are the imperatives of this design for living, and why are they unreal for the contemporary family? Most important is the imperative of self-sufficiency. Our stalwart ancestors are reputed to have produced all they consumed and to have withstood adversity in splendid isolation. Actually, this pattern, in its pure form, existed only for a very brief period; as rapidly as was possible, the self-sufficiency of the isolated family of the frontier disappeared.[2] Indeed, the advantages of group life, where members could work together at tasks beyond the power of a single family, have occurred to people throughout recorded history. Of course, nostalgia has no use for history, but the fact remains, according to the great anthropologist, Bronislaw Malinowski, that:

> In spite of repeated theoretical assertions as to the existence of the "closed household economy"... the fuller our knowledge of the relevant facts, the better we see on the one hand the dependence of the family upon the rest of the community and on the other hand the duty of each individual to contribute not only to his own household but to those of others as well.[3]

If the family was not self-sufficient after the westward trek, how can we hold up this imperative as a model today, in the century of the organization man? At the beginning of the 1800's, four-fifths of the working population of the United States were self-employed. As early as 1870, this was true of only one-third, and by 1940, of only one-fifth. In 1950, it was one-sixth; in 1960, one-eighth; and in 1965, one-ninth, as America increasingly becomes a nation of employees, with labor markets, not control of property, determining how people live. This means not only that today's family has become a dependent entity, but that it no longer produces anything (except perhaps meals) in the home. Production takes place in the factories of field and industry. The family now specializes in consumption — and a consuming unit cannot be self-sufficient.

Nor can it be self-contained. A dependent consuming unit hangs by a thread in the marketplace. At the economic level there is no cushion in time of crisis: no kitchen garden for victuals, no homestead for rude shelter. Desertion, divorce, abandonment, and breakdown proliferate as individuals attempt to summon private resourcefulness in situations where the single unit is helpless. Even at the emotional level, the contemporary family is exposed to the elements. The large traditional circle spanned the generations and provided a compass of function and a cluster of personalities with scope for individual affinities. Contrast this with the nuclear family marooned in a metropolis and turning inward on itself. If today's togetherness is an attempt to recapture the home as a refuge, it is self-defeating. The entire complex of a segmented society invades the living room. And though the longing for personal creativity and control has popularized home-centered living, we fail to recreate the essence of that pattern. First, we fail because humans require social range for mental health, and the narrow circle available in the average parent-children unit diminishes that range — so that the very concentration on a few intense relationships becomes the cause of their distortion. And, second, we fail because the privacy of the home has become, by and large, a conforming, mass private. Each unit develops like every other, stamped out by the same insistent social machinery. It is a private that "chooses" the car-of-the-year as its treasure, the book-of-the-month as its culture, the song-of-the-week as "our song."

This introduces another facet of the dogma: rugged individualism. The mythic traditional family was endowed with magical independence, creative energy, and a homely ingenuity that made it equal to any challenge. Each member of this hardy group is assumed to have been a "character," conquering circumstance. Even if we do not accept the materialist conception that the generic type of an epoch is molded by its productive mechanism — by what is produced and by how it is produced — we must concede that today's mass production of products and of life styles does not develop unique personalities. Power over occupational activity has been stripped from the person. The market determines where he works; the boss decides when he works; the machine dictates how he works. The result is a life style that eclipses the individual for the significant segment of his days, with standardization of technique flowing into standardization of thought. The ego becomes a cog in the labor-saving organization.

The rootedness of the American family is also belied by prevailing conditions. Fully one-fifth of the population are annual migrants, parts of our urban centers experiencing complete residential turnover every year. Much of this wandering is in search of jobs or better jobs, but even when they improve their lot, such families are vulnerable islands in the impersonal ocean of a great city.

Here is exposed yet another deviation from the myth: namely, that the American family is no longer rooted in the soil. "The rugged familism which extended the frontier and gave the tenor of individualism to America has disappeared except as it is still found in isolated rural and mountain areas."[4] In 1890, sixty-four per cent of families lived on farms. Now the figure is about eight per cent. The whole country has become a bunch of city slickers. Our natural habitat is the tenement, not the homestead; our direction of expansion is vertical, not horizontal.

Nor can the urban family solitary in the asphalt jungle perform the functions of the backwoods family alone in the forest. The trusty musket has been supplanted bv the cop on the corner; the slate in the kitchen has given way to the school chalkboard; the prayers by the hearth have moved to the cathedral. The urban family around the television set cannot recapture the atmosphere of the rural family around the oil lamp. Entertainment appliances now provide ready-mix products for the passive consumer; even recreation in the home is no longer homemade.

Some authorities applaud this withdrawal of earlier functions, assuming the family can now specialize in more important areas: in developing human potential, in creating an atmosphere of love and order. The fallacy here is that although the family has forfeited its economic self-sufficiency, it continues to be an economic unit. It is difficult to create an atmosphere of love and order when there is hunger in the house or, less drastically, when there is anxiety about unemployment, illness or death . . . and bills mount. For the family is not only an economic unit, it is a *dependent* economic unit. The whole subjective complex is suspended from the social rafters. And when that structure fails in economic security or in social justice, human potential goes by the board.

Yet the myths of personal autonomy persist. Problems, if they appear at all in the smooth-flowing pattern of the illusion, are identified as purely emotional. Romantic love is made to carry the whole weight of living. The dream is the constant — only the individual is variable. And when he fails as consumer, or when the labor market makes him obsolescent, he alone is at fault. As Margaret Mead notes:

> The one-room shack, the coldwater flat, the thousand deviations from the American home, are glossed over as accidents, as having nothing to do with the picture

of the self. So American soldiers in Europe in World War II looked with perfect honesty at British slums and said, "No American lives like that." The British who had seen pictures of the Dust Bowl, of the Back of the Yards area in Chicago, or the back-streets of Southern cities, quite naturally thought the Americans were lying. But they were not lying, they were simply speaking, as they had always learned to speak, about the ideal, which to them was the truth about Americans. People in America of course live in all sorts of fashions, because they are foreigners, or unlucky, or depraved, or without ambition; people live like that, but *Americans* live in white detached houses with green shutters. Rigidly, blindly, the dream takes precedence.[5]

It is this dream that made the recent documentation of poverty in America a discovery. And it is this dream that imposes the pressure of failure upon the individual man and the individual woman who find they cannot implement it. The "self-reliant" man knows he is not self-reliant. The "modern" woman knows she cannot meet the measure of *Vogue, Photoplay*, and *Ladies' Home Journal*.

For side by side with the myth that there is for the American woman but one honorable occupation — housewife — appears the interesting reality that most women in the United States today have the experience of working outside the home at some period of their lives. This development is one of the most revolutionary changes of our time. It is reflected in the status downgrading of "occupation: housewife" despite its stereotyped glorification. But with the downgrading has come doubt about alternative occupations. How is it better to pound a typewriter than to push a vacuum cleaner? How is it better to manage a group of kindergartners than to supervise one's own sprouts? Where is the emancipation? Certainly, it is not from drudgery. But there is a sense in which a woman's release, even to routine employment, constitutes a gain; namely, in that she is no longer dependent on marriage as the only way of earning her living. Indeed the game must be worth the candle, for, with her assumption of new functions, the American woman has not been relieved of old ones. She is all this and housewife, too. If she kisses the family goodbye each morning, she must convert to housewife each evening. No eight-hour day here — the new is just tacked on to the traditional.

This presents yet another aspect of the myth: that the nuclear family can provide security for the child. To quote one authority: "It is perhaps not an exaggeration to say that this is the first time in the history of mankind that the whole responsibility of establishing a family has been put on two persons."[6] In contrast to other countries where it is accepted that in an industrial community one pair of parents cannot attend to all the things that control their children's destiny, in the United States do-it-yourself at the family level has become an article of faith. We fail to see that home-centered lives in child-centered homes are precarious islands in the impersonal sea of a technological society — and that all our life-lines stem from that society.

When parents are poor, children may have to work. According to a Department of Labor Report: although "child labor has all but disappeared in industry . . . small children are permitted to toil in the fields, often at hazardous jobs. As many as one-tenth of the migrants are children under 14, and more than one-fifth of all migrant workers are 14-17 years old."[7] When parents are underprivileged, children may be culturally deprived. A report of school superintendents in the fourteen largest cities in the nation noted that while in 1950 only one out of ten school children in their cities could be classified as "culturally deprived," by 1960 it was one out of three; and the ratio is still rising. The superintendents feared that, by 1970, one-half of the students in America's largest urban areas would come from deprived families.[8] Even among privileged families, as I have already indicated, the emphasis on the hot little kingdom of privacy brings deprivation to the child. The substitution of particularity for range, in the narrow confines of the nuclear family, means that the very absorption with relationships tends to promote their imbalance.

If, then, it is a fallacy to believe that two parents can ensure the welfare of their children, how much more vulnerable is the single parent family where one adult stands alone against the elements. Yet as our society becomes more fragmented, partial families become more prevalent.

For the American family that lives behind the billboards and on the wrong side of the television screens deviates markedly from the consumer picture. It may have a woman at its head; ten per cent of U.S. families do. It may lack children; twenty-seven per cent of families are composed solely of husband and wife. It may contain the children of three "sets" of parents: your children, my children, and our children. It may be a doubled-up group or it may be a partial group. It may live in a farmhouse, a city flat, or a trailer camp. Its members may be Black, they may be Buddhist, they may be old. And, in the middle of the affluent society, we have newly discovered that the American family may be poor.

So effective is the dogma of individual responsibility and the fantasy of self-sufficiency that each family attempts to devise personal solutions for the gravest social problems. A recent Census Bureau survey turned up the fact that more than 400,000 children under twelve years old have to fend for themselves while their mothers work.[9] Since other studies demonstrate that mothers of young children usually stay home if their husband's income is adequate, and since widowed and divorced mothers are likely to be the sole wage earners in partial families, it is clear that most working mothers of young children leave the home for reasons of social necessity. Yet no comprehensive child care program has been in existence in the U.S. since World War II. Each mother is left to make or fail to make "individual arrangements." The vaunted century of the child still produces "latchkey children," while the experts carefully conclude:

The increasing participation of mothers in paid employment has not been accompanied by a general demand for an expansion of public child care facilities, and there is little sentiment in favor of moving in this direction *merely* in order to make it easier for mothers to go to work. [Emphasis added.][10]

Here we encounter a species of exceptionalism which argues that the patterns of community responsibility developed in other industrial societies are not suited to the American scene. With a national income that is the highest in the world, the portion allocated for such child care services is the lowest. In addition to their extensive child care programs, most technologically advanced countries "except the United States make payments to all families with children regardless of income levels in recognition of the fact that the standard of living of the family declines as the number of its members increases."[11] Further, the United States is alone among 51 industrial countries of the world in having no federal law providing maternity protection for women workers. Nor, according to *Womanpower,* "does there appear to be any significant body of opinion which looks to legislation as a means of establishing maternity leave programs which provide both income and job security."[12]

The justification for this approach is also offered in other fields, such as health insurance, public housing, guaranteed income, protection of the aged: it is that Americans object to regimentation, that their "long tutelage to the soil" has made them a resourceful and ingenious people who can do their own managing, thank you. But the fact that this ingenuity has not translated the affluent potential into the adequate actual continues to be a haunting paradox. It can only be resolved when the myths are dissipated and the organic connection between the family and the social matrix stands revealed; when we begin to think and live in the same world; when we are ready to embrace the present, and face the truth that a house is not a homestead.

# III. *The Relation of Woman and World as Milieu* ▬•▬•▬•▬•▬•▬•▬•▬•▬•▬•▬•▬•▬•▬•▬•▬•▬•▬•▬•▬•▬•▬

## 7. In the Marketplace
▬•▬•▬•▬•▬•▬•▬•▬•▬•▬•▬•▬•▬•▬•▬•▬•▬•▬•▬•▬•▬•▬

> For the Colonel's Lady
> an' Judy O'Grady
> Are sisters under their
> skins!
>
> RUDYARD KIPLING

More than a century ago, Olive Schreiner, in her classic, *Woman and Labor,* cried:

> We demand that in that strange new world that is arising alike upon the man and the woman, where nothing is as it was, and all things are assuming new shapes and relations, that in this new world we also shall have our share of honored and socially useful toil.[1]

Her plea epitomizes the goals of privileged women who had been excluded from the economic process with the advent of the industrial revolution. It does not, in any sense, represent the aspirations of the great majority of women for whom honors were beyond the horizon, and who had never known any way of life but "socially useful toil."

The Colonel's Lady and Judy O'Grady may be sisters under the skin, but the pattern of their days was then, and still is, vastly different. Technological

*Parallel readings for this chapter appear in the section entitled "Fair Trade."

change for the wives of the gentry, once busy with family industry and management of the manor, meant enforced leisure and the defilement of dependency. Technological change for the wives of the lowly meant following the machine to the factory and a new vulnerability in the marketplace. The Colonel's Lady was out of work; Judy O'Grady was only out of the home. The very word *toil* came to have an entirely different meaning for the two groups. To advantaged women, it was the symbol of social integration, of usefulness and autonomy. To ordinary women, it was what it had always been, a necessary burden. Thus while the Colonel's Lady fought for status, Judy O'Grady struggled for remission from drudgery. While the rebels of the middle class demanded full participation in the world of work, the rebels of the working class sought protection from the sweat shop bosses.

This dichotomy has been present throughout the history of feminism. As one of the trade union figures of an earlier period reported ruefully:

> For many of the secure middle class ladies the suffrage movement was a mere feminist fad. I tried to get them to see that not the vote alone was important, but its proper use in building a better society.[2]

With the exception of a few perceptive leaders like Susan B. Anthony, the distance was immense between those at the bottom of the economic ladder and those trying to climb onto it. The former sought differential treatment as a safeguard against those special forms of exploitation to which women were liable; the latter were fed up with their protected lives and saw all differential treatment as a setback.

It is important to remember, however, that only a dynamic fraction of each of these groups raised banners and campaigned. The great majority of women, then as now, accepted the patterns handed down to them. The sequestered but secure woman of the classes lived, in the description of Elizabeth Barrett Browning,

> . . . A harmless life, she called it a virtuous life,
> A quiet life which was not life at all
> (But that, she had not lived enough to know.)[3]

And the employed but exploited woman of the masses lived, in the words of Leonora Barry, an early trade unionist,

> [with the] hope and expectancy that in the near future marriage [would] lift [her] out of the industrial life to the quiet and comfort of a home.[4]

So, for the socially inert of both groups, the ideal was identical; however some lived it, while for others it was a wistful dream. But for the socially involved of both groups — labor leaders and middle class suffragists — the goals were vastly different. Even in our own time, the programs of business and professional women who press for literal parity via an Equal Rights Amendment, and of laboring women who are committed to practical parity via protective legislation, are based in conflicting philosophies.

Our ancestors called it *toil* and we call it *work,* but from the foregoing, it seems evident that neither women toilers then nor women workers now can be meaningfully considered as a single category. No more than a single statistic — of millions of women in the labor force — can usefully reflect the disparate occupational patterns of the sisters under the skin. The two categories, have been climbing different mountains, and the milestones of their ascent must be mapped separately. It is because this has not been done that woman's equivocal status, despite apparent breakthroughs, continues to be so puzzling.

Why is it that, with so many trained women in employment, men still fill 17 out of 20 leading professional and technical jobs?* Why, since it has been repeatedly demonstrated that women are efficient workers in a wide spectrum of skills, do their wages still average 60 per cent of those earned by men? Why is it that women not only have a higher rate of unemployment than men, but that the gap has been widening in recent years? Why is the percentage of women seeking higher degrees declining? Why is there an accelerating trend for men to fill administrative positions even in the so-called women's fields?

I do not intend to examine all these questions in this context, but I'd like to indicate a frame of reference from which they might be approached. I call the mountain that middle class women have been climbing "the mountain of structural inclusion," and the most important element in that structural inclusion has been work: work as the measure of usefulness, and work as the key to independence. Therefore, it is not surprising, when announcements are made of increasing numbers of women in the labor force, of the expansion of women's employment in nearly all occupational groups, that some observers interpret these signs as "integration at last." Closer inspection, however, reveals that the apparent motion is peripheral to established patterns; it has not disturbed them.

The overwhelming proportion of privileged women are as economically redundant today as when they were historically uprooted. Yawning hours, busy futility, and oppressive freedom still sap their potential. Marriage still serves as their most popular profession. It requires the least training and

---

*"Despite the increased diversification in women's professional employment, women continue to hold a disproportionately small share of positions in the leading professions. Although women have traditionally made up a large part of the teacher corps, in 1964 only 22 percent of the faculty and other professional staff in institutions of higher education were women. . . . Although women are heavily represented in the health fields, in 1964 only 6 percent of physicians were women. Similarly women had only token representation among scientists (8 percent), lawyers (3 percent), and engineers (1 percent). Moreover, a recent survey by the *Harvard Business Review* states that 'the barriers (to the employment of women in management positions) are so great that there is scarcely anything to study.' . . . *More than one-fifth of employed women with 4 years of college were working as service workers (including private-household), operatives, sales-workers, or clerical workers in March 1965. A startling 7 percent of employed women who had completed 5 years or more of college were working in the same unskilled or semi-skilled occupations"* (emphasis added). *Fact Sheet on Women in Professional and Technical Positions,* U. S. Department of Labor, Women's Bureau, November, 1966 (WB 67-164).

provides the most security. It ensures vicarious status and, after the preliminary skirmish in the mating arena, it imposes no conditions. As I have said
earlier, a wife and mother is a good wife and mother by definition, not by deed,
and every normal female is presumed to be a qualified applicant.

These are the rewards. But there are also penalties, the most painful being
(especially as the children enter school and grow away) the underlying sense
of uselessness which Thomas Huxley has declared is the severest shock the
species can sustain. For, in a cash nexus society, to be outside the economic
structure is also to be outside the mainstream of purposeful activity — to be
irrelevant — and no amount of bowing to the lovely ladies can conceal this
fact. Current soul-searching has been triggered by a naive rediscovery of these
penalties, and with the rediscovery has come a bemused reconsideration of why
most women in the United States have abandoned the struggles and compro-
mised the victories of their forebears. According to the 1969 *Handbook on
Women Workers,* "In 1968, 41 million women were not in the labor force, and
35 million of these devoted their full time to housekeeping."[5]

Why have women accepted this style of living? Most answers refer to the
layered realm of the unconscious. While I have no doubt that there are psychological differences between women and men, I see them as effects as well as
causes. One does not have to probe very far to discover that formal freedom
does not equal integration, that open doors without opportunities might as well
be sealed. These, too, can be causes. And these, too, can be the reason that
earnest exhortations cannot compete with the traditional stereotype. Cultural
imperatives reinforce the still, small life, and women twist their psyches to fit
it. This may not be plucky, but it is practical. What today's little woman learns
in the employment agency quickly sends her back to the safety of the hearth.
For as George Eliot remarks in *Felix Holt,*

> there is no private life which has not been determined by a wider public life, from
> the time when the primeval milkmaid had to wander with the wanderings of her
> clan, because the cow she milked was one of a herd which had made the pastures
> bare.[6]

And what today's little woman discovers about do-it-yourself at the family
level, even if she is successful in the marketplace, also quickly sends her back
to the safety of the hearth. For single unit households without social ameliora-
tions mean an additive life of amateur improvising. Tasks are not rationalized;
there is no division of labor. Child care, meal making, and all the other
mechanics of life continue to devolve on the individual, who must make or fail
to make "arrangements." The professionalism that is so highly valued in other
areas of American life is eschewed in this one. Mother knows best how to rear,
to cook, to nourish, to motivate.

So women whose realities are shaped by the cybernetic era must still explain
themselves, conduct their days, in terms of a model devised two thousand years

ago. Maternity leaves, maternity sabbaticals, after-school care, first-rate pre-kindergartens, well-prepared food from community kitchens, housecleaning teams, emergency aides — all tried in various combinations in other countries — remain outside the realm of rational possibility here. The ingenious people of extraordinary technological imagination fail completely in sociological imagination. This was not so during the war, when women were needed. All kinds of innovations were offered and accepted with minimal fuss.

Today, conditions are different; women are a contingent element in the labor market. Motherhood remains the only career that is a female monopoly. However resourceful, intelligent, ambitious, or restive a woman may be, she is not likely to bypass the role toward which she is directed by the wider society.*

In focusing on the influence of the outside on the inside, am I not risking the error of simple determinism? I do not think so. My thesis is not that the economic button controls humans as if they were automata, but that the state of the economy affects the limits of personal range. Then the persuaders take over and make those limits attractive. The rewards are certified, the penalties suppressed. Nor is the pattern limited to the design for making a living. Every cultural process has its corresponding caveat. Taken together, they constitute a social mandate that sets the broad design of people's lives. The single strand is drawn through the warp and the woof of the whole tapestry. The values of the culture then strengthen that design; they legitimate it; it becomes the style in thought and action and the majority embrace it. In fact, in our open society, they choose it. But it is not a free choice — in the sense of subjective impulse acting upon a spectrum of alternatives. For, by and large, the individual can only yea say or nay say; accept the mode or turn aside from it, remembering that if she rejects what is sanctioned, she must be prepared to suffer the bedevilments of deviation. In this, the ultimate sense, biography is always bounded by history — which has imperatives that cannot be unilaterally exorcised.

Stark as it sounds, the underlying reality affecting the limits of women's role in America today is that they are technological supernumeraries. True, men are also becoming irrelevant to the industrial process, but as a category, they are the primary work force. Women have been, save in time of crisis, the secondary one. Today, with a labor crisis in reverse, with the ratio of people to equipment diminishing, a large sector of the secondary work force must be siphoned off to the suburbs. That's how the structural script reads. And that is why two out of three adults of the wrong gender can, with cultural blessing, take no part (except consumption) in economic activity, and why there are

*"After some time such competitively disadvantaged actors may lose their hopes of ever marketing their skills. . . .If this should happen, the objective relinquishment of the role is subjectively completed." Hans Gerth and C. Wright Mills, *Character and Social Structure* (New York: Harcourt, Brace and World, 1964), p. 393.

virtually no social measures to expedite such economic activity. As a consequence, a century after the beginnings of feminist struggle, middle class American women still patrol the biological beat — bed, board, and babies — and women's status in our country is still suspended from a little gold ring.*

Seeking to explain this paradox so long after suffrage and other victories, contemporary writers are caught up, for the most part, in the legitimations: the social agencies that reinforce the design. They are startled to find in magazines, on television, among the popularizers of Freud, as well as among the planners of curricula and the conferrers of grants, that truth is used like an accordion — pulled out or squeezed tight, as needed. Outraged, they indict the manipulators. Yet these, though visible, are merely secondary levers providing social sanction for what has become socially exigent. Change is justified and change is concealed by pretending that things are what they were before, are what (it is insisted) they have traditionally been. Manipulating the manipulators, however, is the prime mover — change itself, change and its causes, change and its consequences.

In sum, female labor today is, as it has been for decades, a marginal sector of the labor market: standby machinery to be increased and decreased as needed. The current increase cannot be interpreted as progression, for the provisional status of female labor has not been altered. Although, because of population growth and technological refinement, the degree of expansion looms large it does not justify straight-line projection, for contraindicators are also significant. Today, the United States is in transition between the first and the second industrial revolutions, and phenomena associated with both patterns are both present. This is puzzling unless one recognizes the fact of process and the nature of the revolution that is passing and of the one that is impending.

The first industrial revolution multiplied the muscles of men. But in its context, man is still needed: he sets the tool, starts the motor, supervises performance, corrects error, keeps parts in order. Although the machine extends human energy, the human being attached to the machine must still feed his energy into it. This combination of puissant man and primary machine has traditionally been classified as blue collar work, and traditionally considered a masculine preserve. As machines become more sophisticated, however, less and less physical power is required of the human attendants. In effect, blue collar work is transformed into white collar work.

Women are then recruited. We find the Colonel's Lady retreating to the home while Judy O'Grady enters the market; the data show that in March 1967 although over a third (37 per cent) of married women were employed,

---

* "... and in consequence, the modern man finds himself in the impossible position of being required to maintain a person over whose conduct and movements he has no control whatever." Meyrick Booth, *Woman and Society* (New York: Longmans, Green and Co., 1929), fn. p. 83.

only 14 per cent of this group had husbands with incomes of $10,000 or more. This means to me that whereas in the past, a woman supplemented her husband's earnings by taking in washing, or sewing, or lodgers, today she works in a laundry, a factory, or a hotel. Styles have changed, but the design for living remains the same; namely, that a certain proportion of the female population has always been required to earn its keep, married or not, and that in our time, too, it continues to do so.

Has the proportion changed? Again I quote from the *Handbook:* "The percentage of women workers among all women of working age advanced from 20 percent in 1900, to 29 percent in 1940, and to 42 percent in 1968."[7] Perhaps some of this increase reflects the campaigns of the feminists, but there is the nagging doubt that it may reflect a change in situs rather than in status, that the woman who once found means to supplement her husband's income at home must now find employment outside the home to the same end. The relative number, in these circumstances, may not be greater — the women may just be more visible and more countable.

Even assuming that the figures are exactly what they seem, and that more women have been drawn into the labor force, not only for financial reasons but "to reap the psychic rewards that come from achievement and recognition and service to society,[8] (to quote the Women's Bureau), have they in fact reaped those rewards? Have they obtained their "share of honored toil" as demanded by Olive Schreiner?

There's no need to go to statistical handbooks for the answer; one has only to look at the morning paper. A picture of the President and his Cabinet. A picture of the Congress. A picture of the hierarchy of the Council of Churches. A picture of an AFL-CIO convention. A picture of the officers of the American Medical Association, of the Joint Chiefs of Staff, of corporation moguls, of financial giants, of governors, of scientists, of judges. The exclusion from honored toil is still virtually complete. The gauge of woman's achievement can still be found mainly on the society page under marriage announcements and in the vital statistics column under births.

I call the mountain that working class women have been climbing "the mountain of safeguards against exploitation." Work for this group being a fact of life, it was the circumstances attending that work that they sought to ameliorate through equal opportunity, equal training, equal pay, job security, maternity leave, maternity benefits, child care facilities, and freedom of association. Have they succeeded? The big news about equal opportunity is the passage of the Civil Rights Act of 1964, which includes a ban on sex discrimination in private employment.

On the negative side, however, it must be noted that the mere fact that such legislation is hailed as a victory so long after the feminist struggle can only be evidence that women are still a contingent and vulnerable group in the marketplace, that they are still used as a classical labor reserve, supplementing men when there is a shortage, and replacing men when processes make it possible and wage differentials make it profitable.

To women, as to other marginal groups, have been transferred the hostilities engendered by boom-and-bust production, with its cargo of job competition and threatening unemployment. This is probably the origin of the recurrent myth that women work for pin money, a concept that varies from slur to attack in direct relation to the condition of the economy. (The purist will be entertained by the current meaning of the term compared with its derivation. Once pins were scarce in England and were sold on the first two days of January. Women saved all year to accumulate the sum necessary to buy a few pins. This became their "pin money.")

It is unfortunate that, even among sophisticated union leaders, the pin money myth is often an article of faith, used to justify an inertia in respect to women that is detrimental to the labor movement as a whole. Frieda S. Miller, former director of the Women's Bureau, has enunciated a principle, ignored by labor leaders at their peril:

> It is an axiom of wage theory that when large numbers of workers can be hired at lower rates of pay than those prevailing at any given time, the competition of such persons for jobs results either in the displacement of the higher paid workers or in the acceptance of lower rates by those workers. Over a period of time this pressure tends to depress all wage levels and, unless this normal course is averted by direct action, it results eventually in lower levels of earning for all, with a resulting reduction in purchasing power and in standards of living. Because of their new . . . training and skills, women are, as never before, in a position to be used by unscrupulous employers as wage cutters.[9]

Yet, despite the grave danger that wage differentials pose, a relatively small proportion of the female labor force has been drawn into trade unions. The original bias, "blue collar and for men only," which made it necessary for women to obtain through law what men obtained through organization, underlies current practice. With all the talk of organizing the unorganized, and despite the fact that the majority of the unorganized are women, most labor groups continue to do business as usual. I once checked the index of a national AFL-CIO convention report and found no references at all under the words "maternity" or "child care." If women do become members, they are expected to fit unionism's creaky Procrustean bed. It seems clear to me that the labor movement has missed the significance of woman's employment position. The traditional woman, who no longer exists, carries more weight at its council tables than the contemporary breathing members.

The consequence of labor's inertia becomes clear when one discovers that the proportion of working wives is highest in families where the husband is unemployed; and that, in some depressed areas, female labor has become the mainstay of the family. Such a trend goes counter to received patterns of

American society and reminds one uneasily of the "she towns"* of the nine-teenth century. Then, too, men were unemployed and industry put out the "women wanted" sign. An 1893 newspaper item reads:

> A singularity that is met with in the factory towns of Maine, is a class of men who may be rightly called housekeepers. Anyone visiting some of these workers' homes shortly after the noon hour, will find the men, wearing an apron, washing dishes. At other hours of the day they may be seen making the beds, dressing the children, scrubbing or cooking.[10]

In his book *The Better Half*, Andrew Sinclair draws a parallel picture of conditions in the thirties:

> In fact, since women were cheaper to hire in the depression,they got the lioness's share of what jobs there were available. The female labor force grew faster in the thirties than it had done in the previous two decades, while men in their millions were forced to stay at home with the children and fret at their woman's role. The depression did much to bring equality in work and homemaking to the sexes, by putting women in the factory and men in the house.[11]

Will the Civil Rights Act of 1964 prevent such a development today? I do not think so, for it is aimed at banning discrimination *against* women, not correcting conditions of discrimination *for* them. Low rates in the "feminine fields" continue largely untouched. And, if the men want to enter such fields, they will find Frieda Miller's principle in effect; namely, that the rate of pay has already been fixed: a low "woman's rate" suited to a "woman's job."

Another reason why employers may be discovering women's virtues is that female workers fade into the domestic landscape when they are no longer needed, so that, as the National Manpower Council has candidly noted, "the ill effects of laying off personnel during periods of recession are substantially modified."[12] In addition, since one-third of working women are engaged only part-time, they are available at overtime hours on a straight pay basis, save employers paid lunch hours and coffee breaks, may not work enough to accumulate leave or other benefits, and are probably more difficult to unionize due to their variable schedules. At this point, one begins to wonder whether the current ballyhoo is really directed at womanpower expansion or whether manpower substitution is in the wings.

Even if we stipulate that today's promoters of the lady on the job are sincere, isn't an increased labor force a curious objective at a time when automation makes minds and muscles redundant? True, politicians are not among our most sophisticated analysts: their designs, their vocabularies, even their reveries, stem from a long distant past. But it is quite another matter for sociologists, labor leaders, and liberals to rejoice because there is "progress" in women's

---

*This was a term applied to industrial centers where women were the primary labor force and men remained in the home.

employment today. Certainly brave words and some deeds make it appear that goals sought through years of struggle have finally been reached. The difficulty is that yesterday's slogans do not necessarily spell advance in today's world. They may be illusive. They may be exploited for regressive ends. They may be irrelevant. We cannot afford to be too ingenuous when faced with a won war.

What is it that the many come to praise in the woman at work? They praise her docility. They praise her naivete. They praise her availability. They praise her disappearance into the kitchen when they no longer need her.

They may mean that women are attractive employees because they make only 60 per cent of the income of men; they may mean women have winning ways because they work part-time and won't build up much seniority or fringe benefits; they may mean, "Let's employ the women because when they're laid off they won't rate much insurance." They may even mean, "Let's keep women employed when the men are laid off, and then we won't have to carry the families on relief." It's time to wonder whether they have come to bury woman and not at all to praise her.

This, then, is the position of women in the final stages of the first industrial revolution and the basis on which current optimistic forecasts are predicated. But, in addition to all the analytical mistakes and sophistries committed within that framework, the incredible error lies in the fact that the glowing projections completely overlook the second industrial revolution which is already upon us. That, the cybernetic revolution, not only extends the human being, it releases him; the new robots have an artificial nervous system that disemploys the mortal one; for the first time in history the silver cord between man and machine has been severed. Already, in basic production, the evidence is strong that these robots outnumber human workers. Nor does it require much imagination to surmise that women, who are now being sought to tend sophisticated machines, may soon be superseded by more sophisticated machines that need no tending. Women may be cheap labor, but robots are cheaper. It is, however, argued that clerical and service work will continue to be expanding fields. In fact, the white collar computer is already in full operation. As one authority notes:

> Airlines, banks, brokerage houses, . . . virtually all sectors of the American economy, are discovering the simple fact that computers cut labor costs.[13]

If this is the trumpet of prophecy, can services be far behind? In the words of another thoughtful analyst:

> The service trades seem a weak reed to lean on. Self-service and automatic vending machines are invading every department of retailing.[14]

Although labor unions, waking from their long institutional sleep, are beginning to take notice of women workers, they can no longer stem the tide of regressive change by simple recruitment. But they, and other groups concerned with the welfare of people at work, do have a new and urgent responsibility to match a developing and creative technology with a developing and creative society. To do this, the design must be drawn with imagination against a background of reality. This cannot be done by hailing woman's progress when it is patent that the advantaged woman is still largely excluded from the economic process; nor can it be done by brandishing omnibus statistics and overlooking the disadvantaged woman's drift toward "she towns."

George Bernard Shaw has written: "There are two tragedies in life. One is not to get your heart's desire. The other is to get it." In that context, it is clear that in America today, both the Colonel's Lady and Judy O'Grady have yet to experience the second tragedy.

## 8. The Pearl in the Apron Pocket

> Within the last century, it has been gravely asserted that, "chemistry enough to keep the pot boiling, and geography enough to know the location of the different rooms in her house, is learning sufficient for a woman."
>
> SARAH MOORE GRIMKÉ

Loving for a living is the life style of two-thirds of American women. They have taken to heart George Bernard Shaw's sardonic counsel, voiced by Mrs. Warren, that the only way for a woman to provide for herself decently is for her to be good to some man who can afford to be good to her. And while it is true that more coeds roam the campuses than ever before, intellectual pursuits are altogether secondary to other engagements. As I have earlier noted, social mores pressure a young woman to hitch her wagon to a spouse, not a star; whatever subjects she garners, her object is matrimony, not matriculation. Clearly, for the first sex, education is a cultural imperative; for the second, it has become the pearl in the apron pocket.

The logic is, moreover, probative. Partnership announcements, as gauges of achievement for men, are to be found in a newspaper's financial section; for women, they still appear on the society page, under weddings. Manifestly more vertical mobility is accomplished through judicious matchmaking than by any

*Parallel readings for this chapter appear in the section entitled "The Doorways of Life."

other effort: The President's wife participates in the inaugural ceremony without standing for election. The wives of astronauts ride in triumphal procession without leaving .terra firma. An ambitious woman soon discovers that the emoluments for turning his head are immeasurably greater than those for using hers.

The philosophy underlying woman's education proceeds therefore on the assumption "in case." That is, in case she doesn't marry, she should have an escape hatch. Since, however, a larger and larger (and younger and younger) percentage of our women today enter the most popular profession, marriage, the escape hatch has become a pigeonhole.

This was vividly illustrated for me in some byplay I observed at a conference of American and Czech women, which opened with introductions around the table, by name and by profession. The Czech leader, presenting her delegation, announced: "This is Mrs. Alpha, who is a member of the parliament with a degree from the University of Prague; and this is Mrs. Beta, who is an officer of a trade union and whose background is in economics; and this is Mrs. Gamma, who is a school teacher; and this is Mrs. Delta, who is the director of a shoe factory." Then the leader of the United States delegation introduced her people, beginning, "This is Mrs. A, who has four children and whose husband is a lawyer; and this is Mrs. B, who has two college-age sons and whose husband is a successful businessman; and this is Mrs. C, who is active in the PTA and whose husband is a professor of chemistry; and this is Mrs. D, who is a widow with twin daughters and whose late husband was a prominent physician." One of the Czech women then turned to her neighbor and said: "We have been told what your husband does, but what do you do?" "Well," came the reply, "my husband works very hard to earn money so that I can attend conferences like this on the status of women." Here, then, is the contemporary version of George Eliot's wry remark in *Mill on the Floss:* "We don't ask what a woman does, we ask whom she belongs to."

Even venturesome spirits, restive in the Freudian enclave but not ready for radical life styles, make their forays into the fuller life under the umbrella of marital status and marital support. They renounce no privilege. They merely want all this and latitude, too. It is a revolution without risk, for freedom is predicated upon the masculine mystique which posits man as primary provider. It is also a revolution without range, for unlike the creative insurgents of the past, these rebels seek self-realization: first person singular. Their foremothers, the "glorious phalanx" who led the suffrage movement, were concerned with the third person plural: self-realization for the human race. In the context of the abolition movement, there was a tie very early between the "peculiar institution" and the "peculiar sex." Today, each individual struggles to achieve her own tiny revolt. Even when women emerge to march, they march as mothers.

Therefore, and in spite of the ferment, these swinging monads, suspended from the domestic rafters, still traverse a narrow arc along the compass of human capacity. Specialized to sex and to service, they suppress individual qualities in favor of clusters of approved characteristics. They have become products of what they do and what they do not do. Sometimes I find myself speculating on how it would be if I could compel a wholesale uncoupling, a severance of all bonds, and declare a moratorium on marriage. In this fantasy, I see myself separating the sexes into two piles. Then I shuffle and remate. Since the full range of human diversity has become the monopoly of men, the women would have to consort with new phenotypes; the men, for the most part, only with variations on a theme.

For we are programmed by our preoccupations. The preoccupations of men, under pressure in the marketplace, demand multidimensional skills. The preoccupations of women in "their place" — whatever their outreach, whatever their efforts at self-realization and continuing education — are fixed by the limits of their primary orbit as family satellites. Their range is circumscribed by that compelling planet with its idealized selfishness and rudimentary scope. All else is auxiliary, random, and episodic. Of the essence, for the Colonel's Lady and for Judy O'Grady, for Jacqueline Onassis and for Jane Doe, is a roster of buying and bedecking, of preening and procuring, of reproducing and rearing, of feeding and furnishing, of gracing and guarding. The style of performance certainly varies with the station in life: there is a significant distance between doing-it-yourself and delegating to a staff, between sales at Penney's and *haute couture* in Paris. But the range is the same, the roles are set, and the fact remains that no one has ever been listed in *Who's Who* for being a superlative wife and mother. And there's the rub.

And there is also the fallacy of the feminine curriculum, the tacit compact not to pass beyond a certain limit. It is a troubling thought that utility, rather than the search for truth that illuminates all human experience, is still perceived as the object of learning. "Would it be impossible," inquires former President Lynn White of Mills College, "to present a beginning course in food as exciting, and as difficult to work up after college, as a course in post-Kantian philosophy would be? Why not study the history and preparation of a Basque paella, of a well-marinated shishkebab, lamb kidneys sautéed in sherry, an authoritative curry; the use of herbs; even such simple sophistications as serving cold artichokes with fresh milk?"[1]   It would not be impossible, but exotic culinary courses are not transmuted into works of intellectual distinction simply because they are mastered in an academic course. The feminine curriculum is a sophist's response to domesticity and its discontents: "Ladies, this is your destiny; if it does not engage your full capacities, complicate it."

The drama of a single life span is so brief, and the exponential rate of change so great, that to engross women in such irrelevancies is to tether the race. For the hallowed blueprint that stereotypes one whole woman to each household finds its sanction, ironically enough, in the idea that mothers must guide their children in growth. How can they provide guidance in relation to a world they never knew? Long ago, the caustic pen of Charlotte Perkins Gilman marked that the prescriptive mother restricted in range, gives disproportionate value to the few things she knows about, magnifying the personal and minimizing the general, so that "her ceaseless reiteration of one short song, however sweet, has given it a conspicuous monotony."[2] This was documentation of another period, when the necessity for a woman's ignorance was an article of faith (learning addled her feeble brain) and when, as this fiery feminist records, there was an absurd effort to place one sex a million years of evolution behind the other, to confine civilization to half the race.

And yet, is today's now-and-then, off-and-on design for second sex living a paradigm of development? Isolated at the height of their powers on suburban islands of subjectivity, how many women train their sights on the larger impersonal sea? True, some have begun to question their private lives, but they have perquisites. The child, reared and motivated on these islands long before he goes to school, has none. The exquisite extensions of human knowledge, the cataclysmic changes in human ecology, all lie beyond the horizon; "Changes in public life," observes Karl Mannheim, "penetrate only very slowly into the inner life of the family. The child, once it has been moulded by the family, can only very gradually transform these primary patterns of action and of attitudes."[3]

It is for this reason that those who have retreated to the byways — educated women, intelligent women — and have lost sight of the highroads, soon become disqualified to guide their children there. And it is for this reason that mothers who have abetted their own arrested development, who have, in the phrase of George Eliot, reduced the great story of this world to the little tale of their own existence, can no longer counsel their young from wide experience or deep wisdom. For wisdom and experience, it has been said, are bought with the price of all that a man or a woman hath. And so there follows for those children the Great Unlearning.

Curiously enough, I did once meet a master of the Basque paella, and it is her son who always comes to mind when I ponder the Great Unlearning. She was vibrant but banal, all of life being for her prefigured in obvious rows, and she kept what her peripatetic doctor husband called "a good kitchen." The talk, when I first met her, turned on food, but by the time she had plunged in with eager expertise, it had vaulted to an abstruse point of protein chemistry and RNA, so that her remark missed quite badly. There ensued one of those painful silences when everyone tries to summon a graceful evasion. Her tall young son recovered first. Leaning over affectionately, he patted her on the head with tender amusement. "Never mind," he murmured, "mommies can cook." Patronizing, to be sure, but also testimony of a reversal of roles: Child had become reassuring parent. But at what cost? Hidden obscurely beneath the surface equanimity, there must have been a fundamental response to culture shock, a drastic revision of the reality level.

"We should surely have learned by now," comments Robert Theobald, "that there is nothing more difficult to unlearn than facts. It is rather like a city: Once you have put the first road through the middle of a city, if the road has been placed in the wrong location it is very difficult to plan the city rationally. In much the same way, once you have begun to teach a child a set of patterns, he will retain them, or at least they will be extraordinarily difficult to unlearn."[4]

I venture to say that the extreme gyrations of the youth of our time have been generated (at least in part) by the very urgency and magnitude of this Great Unlearning. Its radical intensity is scarcely puzzling when one considers, on the one hand, that these are the children molded by the flight to the suburbs, with its illusion of sanctuary, and by the doctrine of permissiveness, with its illusion of personal autonomy. On the other hand, these are also the children whose birth was registered by computer and who all bear the brand of strontium-90 in their bones.

It is fashionable to flay women, to sting them with the whip of their warped biographies. Furthermore, through skillful use of the twin fallacies of false selection and positive instance, they have been made the scapegoats for all the dislocations that beset our era. To the student of human culture, such reasoning in any other field would be dismissed as ludicrous; in relation to women, it passes for expertise. In the presence of dogma so compelling, it seems important to disassociate myself from the trend and to affirm that I have watched American women for many years, have addressed them, commiserated with them, counseled them. I think they are probably the most earnest and conscientious creatures in history!

Insufficient skepticism is, however, their profound error, and this follows, perhaps, from a partial education. Sensitive to the fact that they have been arrested in mid-air, they may be overeager and overready to accept spurious indicia of authority. Moreover, even authentic experts, because of the tradition that the condition of man is his relation to the universe, and the condition of woman is her relation to the nest, tend to disregard the effect of the outside on the inside. Women have thus been reinforced in their illusion of autonomy (with its train of guilt) by the very avalanche of advice that ignores the variables in the human equation. In their fascination with curbstone Freud, they by-pass the evidence that our instinctual inheritance has been wonderfully eclipsed by a cultural structure that creates its own imperatives, its own ecology.

For it is this second nature, intersecting and modifying first nature, that the mentors of women overlook. There was, for example, the issue of *Daedalus* called "Woman in America," where careers were discussed with scarcely any reference to automation, save in relation to household appliances; where the reproductive cycle as we now know it was projected into a distant future, despite exploding populations; where an obsessive analysis of personal patterns moved forward, divorced from the destiny of the planet. There is a strange remoteness about today's students of women who are still beguiled by yesterday's questions: a) whether educated women should ride tandem as careerists and consorts; b) whether part-time function is a Solomon solution for homebound women; c) whether women at work detract from the earnings, or the egos, of men at work — all this at a time when the whole relation of human beings to life and to labor is being reconceived and re-evaluated. On my office wall, I have framed a remark of Pablo Casals: "We are all leaves on the same tree." In discussing the growth of women, how can we forget the condition of the tree?

Nor is it possible to "disregard the message of time." The sequestered and supported wife as feminine prototype is already being supplanted. There is a lag in life styles, as there is in fashion, between what the suburban matron finds on the ready-to-wear rack and the latest Paris decree. By the time biological determinism disturbs the coffee klatch, it has already been superseded by a new model. Education, which was once insurance "in case," is now being offered as prologue and epilogue to the domestic pageant. The new woman is invited to be a split personality; to make the best of both possible worlds; to be all this and woman, too. She is pressed to divide herself vertically: to spend part of her time on the distaff side and part where the action is (in classroom or office); and she is pressed to divide herself horizontally, along a discontinuous curve that begins with woman's place, takes a detour for indoctrination, and winds up in the marketplace.

In my opinion, both these approaches are invalid. They are adjustments to a rear-view reflection of society, to where we have been, not to where we are going. And the adjustments are prescribed not in the tribal institutions that have in fact become obsolete, but in the human beings trapped in those institutions. People are invited to contort themselves so that social forms can remain constant.

Still one must applaud this trend of phases and of stages, for as soon as women move out of "their place" to another place, even if it is only part-time, even if it is only for a fraction of their lives, the old certainties will be shaken. Anybody who is adjusted to any culture, according to Marshall McLuhan, is brainwashed. But even in this context, feminine culture, with its tribal duties and hedonistic imperatives, with the seduction of creature comforts and the terrible temptations of vicarious living, is a special case. The most significant function of indoctrination is to determine the reality level; brainwashing for women shrinks their reality level to the subjective, the first person singular. But cross-cultural experience, even spasmodically, even partially, presents another perspective.

Women might then discover, with de Tocqueville, that necessary institutions are often no more than those to which we have become accustomed. They might see that the field of possibilities is far more extensive than people living in their cellular societies are ready to imagine. Getting out of "their place" and looking back at it from a distance, it might occur to women to ask: "What has being a wife got to do with domestic service? And what has being a mother got to do with chores? And if my life can be split, why can it not be split off from those parts of it? And if we Americans are so effective and ingenious in the rationalization and division of labor, why can't we devise institutions to take care of these robot aspects of woman's existence?"

It might also occur to them to ask, as they note the pressure on their children just to absorb the data overload, and the pressure on their husbands just to keep abreast of their fields: "How can we be expected to function effectively in the modern world by picking up information in bits and pieces during segments of our lives? What kind of professional competence can we achieve going in and out the window in our twenties? And what kind of professional competence can we achieve carting our stranded bodies and miscellaneous minds back to the classroom in our forties?"

And the women whose direction is creative may discover that ideas are like milk — left on the doorstep too long, they turn sour. And the women whose direction is expansive may perceive that, even if they stretch like a jack-in-the-box springing up taller with each experience beyond the doorstep, the proposed design directs that when they come home they must fold themselves into accordian creases to fit back into the previous space. The box, though plush-lined, becomes to an ever greater extent cramped quarters, the more range they have achieved.

"We should treat our minds as innocent and ingenuous children whose guardians we are," wrote Thoreau, "be careful what objects and what subjects we thrust on their attention . . . . Every thought that passes through the mind helps to wear it and tear it, and to deepen the ruts, which, as in the streets of Pompeii, evince how much it has been used. How many things there are concerning which we might well deliberate whether we had better know them."[5]

The last, I think, is the key sentence for women: "How many things there are concerning which we might well deliberate whether we had better know them."

Here is the substantial counterpoise to the argument for a feminine curriculum, the complete rebuttal to the Basque paella. For while the media assume they are flattering the little woman when they term her "Jill-of-all-trades," there are some people who remember how that folk saying ends: "and master of none." In a world of increasing expertise, a little knowledge about a lot of odds and ends is a dangerous thing.

Here, too, is the counterpoise to assumptions about woman's innate capacities. To be effective one must concentrate, and that is not easy when one is bitten by mosquitoes. The proffered patterns, both old and new, are a free-for-all of distractions and of discontinuities. It need scarcely be interposed that some women, in spite of these distractions and discontinuities, do reach their full potential. But for most women, "culturally imposed forms and individual experiences may," in the sensitive words of Loren Eiseley, "keep permanently closed the doorways of life."[6] At this moment I am hopeful, as I see more and more women shifting frames, that they will be inspired to surpass received culture, to test primordial imperatives against contemporary realities, to wonder why in a revolutionary era domestic patterns must be traditional. It may then become obvious that seesawing between dust motes and atoms demands an extraordinary acrobat; and that, to return to our original metaphor, pearls must be polished, or they lose their luster.

# PART TWO         ASSUMPTIONS

## Prelude

Men rarely learn what they
think they already know.

BARBARA WARD

"Nature," notes a reflective geologist, "lives in motion."[1] But man, it seems, seeks certainties. Losing his foothold in shifting sands of dynamism and diversity, he tethers himself to custom as cultural mooring, and then reacts to that custom as second nature. Official myth becomes determinal imperative; subjective construct becomes objective paradigm, a symbol of safety in the face of disconcerting change. For "men respond as powerfully to fictions as they do to realities, and . . . in many cases they help to create the very fictions to which they respond."[2] In this way we mediate between what Walter Lippmann has described as "the world outside and the pictures in our heads."

The social fictions in our context are the cluster of assumptions that protect us from stumbling against concrete conditions which traduce the familiar, which might threaten the foundations of our universe. Such inference is, moreover, deep-rooted in those areas of human experience that are highly charged with emotion, that intersect personal values and private lives. The position of women is such an area.

Studying the spectrum of pronouncements on this subject, one discovers, for all the difference in viewpoint between academician and man-in-the-street, a surprising uniformity in underlying postulates. For scholars and laymen share the illusions of their epoch. Both are predisposed to employ such simplifications and polarities as will reduce the "great blooming confusion of reality"[3] to manageable proportions. Surveyed as a whole, the layman's failure to cast off cultural moorings gives rise to folklore and unaffected prejudice; the scholar's failure promotes presuppositions treated as constants and a priori notions transmuted to data for rigorous analysis. Both do mischief, for they both abridge reality. But the scholar's naivete has the greater consequence since he, as expert, tends to project distorted images as unassailable fact.

This is not to say that scholars and reporters are consciously deceitful. It is rather because we are all prisoners of our place and time. Just as, in physical science, it has been discovered that the position of the observer affects the data observed, so in social science the norms of a society exert an influence on the perception of facts — resulting in codifications of preconceived reality. "A member of a given society . . . actually grasps reality only as it is presented to him in this code."[4] In such contradiction between concrete reality and categorical concept, individuals are delimited and social solutions denied. People — in our case, women — are frozen into familiar forms, and thought processes are arrested short of the full range of relevant possibility. In this process, one discovers, barely perceptible beneath the surface of most affirmation, both lay and learned, the same basic assumptions:

1. *The past is imperative.*
Here the whole sweep of the history of women is viewed as static and institutionally coordinate, with invariable patterns that delineate the fixed contours of female nature.

2. *The organism is imperative.*
Here the anatomy of the second sex is viewed as a paramount physiological design that determines the absolute range of woman's social function — that is, her destiny.

3. *A cultural universe divided by sex is imperative.*
Here psychological traits are viewed as sex-linked certainties, forever separating masculine and feminine role, talent, and temperament. The body fixes the limits of the soul. The social distance between the sexes is conceived as an integral part of the human condition.

Many years ago, Francis Bacon wrote, "The subtlety of nature is greater many times over than the subtlety of argument." In the same vein a scientist of our own time, Albert Einstein, when asked how he pursued his discoveries, once responded, "I challenge a basic assumption." To test the basic assumptions in our context, it will be necessary to lift what Bertolt Brecht calls the things of everyday life out of the realm of the self-evident: to view that which is "natural" as though it were extraordinary.[5] This means that we must scrutinize the social landscape reserved for women as though we were cosmic tourists, unburdened by the baggage of preconception, who can focus on the familiar with pristine eyes.

## 9. Remembrance of Things Past: The First Assumption

> Pardon him, Theodotus: he is
> a barbarian and thinks that
> the customs of his tribe and
> island are the laws of nature.
>
> GEORGE BERNARD SHAW

The history of women is written in invisible ink. In conventional chronicles, the past emerges as a pageant of single sex societies, with fully half the human race out of sight. Man was *homo faber,* adapting himself and modifying his environment across the centuries. Woman was *femina genitalis,* eternally gravid, preprogrammed, and static. Dynamic man and immutable woman are tacitly assumed as normative absolutes. Such assumption is, moreover, woven into all conjecture about the human condition — the condition of man, as I have earlier suggested, being his relation to the universe, that of woman being only her relation to the nest. The consequence is that man is projected as "mankind." Variation, the nature of process, of dialogue between species and environment, punctuated by a changing ecology, received and devised, are temporal events apart from immemorial woman. The history of the race charts the course of man.

"But the fact that one ignores something," writes Karl Mannheim, "by no means puts an end to its existence."[1] Excavating the layers of the past, we continually turn up scattered data that impugn our preconceptions, social shards that might form meaningful mosaics when cemented together. It is from

*Parallel readings for this chapter appear in the section entitled "Women in the Establishment."

74

these that we must seek to reconstruct the concealed and the forgotten so that society may once again emerge as a bisexual organism.

We must, therefore, view with some skepticism the wanton simplifications of most students of human culture when the subject is women. Taking change-lessness and continuance for granted, they tend to see women in each epoch as extraneous to public endeavor. Selective awareness is transposed, with only a shift in costume and convenience, to an undifferentiated past. Suburban matron is projected backward as paradigm. Divorced from the economy, dependent in the domicile, the symbols of her status become historical impera-tives, the benchmarks of feminine gender for all todays and yesterdays. And, to be sure, if we accept this as truth, what account is there to offer about perpetual confinement in a timeless sexual ghetto?

Yet, at a deeper level, "the first duty of the inquirer is to respect the complexity of the facts" (Stuart Hampshire). If we would avoid *ethnocentrism,* a vision bounded by familiar social scaffolding, and *chronocentrism,* a projec-tion of contemporary patterns on all possible pasts, we must examine the evidence upon which current beliefs rest. *Historia,* in Greek, means an inquiry. Our inquiry is into the designs offered as the given. Our goal is to evolve a standard, not only for making comparisons with other periods, but also for responding to the question classically posed by Sigmund Freud: "What does woman want, dear God? What does she want?"

In terms of the modern temper, we see reality, with Whitehead, as a system of functional relationships. Whatever its beginnings, our social structure rests on five basic pillars: the military, the religious, the political, the economic, and the kinship orders — institutional forms that serve the ends of violence, deities, power, production, and procreation. Underlying enormous diversity, these are the main categories that define our reality. "By delineating these institutional orders, which form the skeletal structure of the total society, we may conven-iently analyze and compare different social structures. Any social *structure,* according to our conception, is made up of a certain combination or pattern of such institutional orders."[2]

Using this approach, a swift glance reveals that women in America today are visible only in the kinship order, the patterned regulation of "legitimate sexual intercourse, procreation, and the early rearing of children."[3] Surveyed as a whole, the feminine gender remains essentially outside the other orders, particularly at the levels of decision. Let me demonstrate this in rapid sum-mary.

## PATTERNS IN THE INSTITUTIONAL ORDERS OF THE PRESENT

Starting with the *military,* for good or ill, it is clear that women are in total eclipse, being neither commanders nor conscripts. As uniformed handmaid-ens, they may occupy inconsiderable posts in a few auxiliary corps, or serve as token generals for public relations, but the matter of might belongs to man, along with the fantastic arsenal of power concentrated there. Armies, navies, and air forces, as well as the officers who deploy them on the maps of the world, are a sex apart. Women are praised as the peaceful sex, and invited to become Gold Star Mothers, to offer up their sons in sacrifice upon the altars of the tribal gods. And that's the end of it. They remain far outside the arenas of decision.

We can say, if we like, that the design is different in the *religious* order — certainly the foot soldiers of the flock are likely to be female — but the pontiffs, patriarchs, and padres are, as the titles suggest, invariably male. The worship of Mary has not elevated matriarchs to primacy. And since, in the interlocking directorates of power, eminence, not numbers, carries weight, there is no question that women remain outside the sources of religious authority.

A century after the suffrage struggle began, fifty years since passage of the Nineteenth Amendment, we must also concede that the male monopoly of the *political* order has not been transformed. Women volunteers who venture into the *res publica* remain traditional hewers of wood and drawers of water: doorbell ringers, raffle vendors, telephone recruiters, and stamp lickers. The new tokenism may prescribe that the ladies appear on the platform, but they still don't hammer out the planks. Nor have they yet made their way behind what Carrie Chapman Catt called the locked doors where real decisions are made. No women manipulate political machines; no women hold pre-eminent public offices. Even among the 52 women in Congress from 1911 to 1953, 25 were replacements for defunct marriage partners, accidental walk-ons from the wings. This has led one writer to counsel that for the potentially aspiring female, the ideal husband is a Congressman with a poor life expectancy. The door of opportunity for women in politics, as in other fields, opens from the bedroom. Women may apply for a mate's berth on the floundering ship of state, but captain's jobs continue to be "for men only."

Patently, the *economic* order is also the preserve of men. There are no female industrial tycoons, Wall Street barons, or banking moguls. There is only an army of aides. We must, therefore, in analyzing this order, be careful to distinguish between inclusion relative to production and inclusion relative to power. Women do not appear at the decisive levels. But more than one-third of American women do function in the labor force, thereby violating the mythic cliché that they are destined for dependency. However, the remaining nearly two-thirds are completely outside the economic order; as conspicuous consumers or as diligent drudges, their contact with goods and services is entirely vicarious. Even at the apex of the triangle, among the women who have everything, the breezy assertion that they are taking over the economy is as casually based as most statements about the distaff side. Balancing the fact that about half of the property in our country is in women's names is the countervailing evidence that, in most cases, it is held in name only. To sum up, women who seek their fortunes through work do not acquire wealth, and women who do acquire wealth have their fortunes made and managed for them. And neither more women in the labor force nor more women in the upper tax brackets has meant more women at the pinnacles of power.

We come finally to the *kinship* order, undeniably woman's place. And we face the recurrent question: why is she so restive there? I venture to suggest it is because of the widespread discovery that this order has virtually no relation to the functioning system. For the life stream of industrial societies, despite our custom to deny it, is money not blood, and production, not reproduction, has transcendent value. Kinship institutions, therefore, in the present period have but marginal utility and peripheral importance. Their triumphs have been relegated to the vital statistics columns and to the woman's page. This may be one reason why a sentimental patina from the past is utilized to film over dilemmas posed by inconvenient fact. It involves, perhaps, our heritage of magic; as in some remote time, the shaman created the event by naming it, conjuring sociologists today find matriarchies in the American heartland. Unfortunately for these theories of petticoat power, autocrats of the breakfast table do not dominate society. In our cash nexus culture, the private is altogether parenthetical to the public. By law and by custom, the structural irrelevance and the subordinate rank of the kinship order are consistently ratified. (If wives have learned to maneuver behind the bedroom door, that is a prescriptive right of mistresses and paramours. So did Mme. Pompadour, but no one called her monarch or matriarch for all that.)

In the present design, as has been demonstrated, significant institutions do not merely mark off a hemisphere defined by the traditional division of labor, they comprehend the full range of social geography. Reserved for women, until the test tube takes over, there remains only the biological peninsula. And from this ground plan comes the absolute, the transposition of vision, that makes the kinship order, as we know it today, the area of predestined segregation for the second sex. From it is derived the assumption that women are fated from time immemorial to be outsiders in every other order. Magnifying the insular in space and the immediate in time, regularities in the social landscape are perceived as constants, obvious and inevitable; sanctioned roles are abstracted from the temporal design that has produced them. The present is presumed to define the past, and the past to circumscribe the future.

To challenge the roots of this assumption, to question whether it really has always been so, involves an effort to dissect strands of truth from layers of distortion and suppression. For, as I have already observed, women have, by and large, been considered an epiphenomenon by those who kept the records, and even more, by those who later interpreted them. We are obliged to proceed, therefore, by pointer readings that cast doubt upon the parochial and the superhistorical, as we may find them in each of the orders previously considered.*

---

*Gerth and Mills, to whose work I am indebted for the idea of institutional orders, offer this cautionary word: "Just what institutional orders exist in a more or less autonomous way is a matter to be investigated in any given society. In some societies the institutions of the kinship order may perform functions which, in more segmented societies, are performed by specifically

POINTER READINGS IN INSTITUTIONAL ORDERS OF THE PAST

Beginning with the *military* order once again, there are hints in the history of peoples of the ancient world that women were not always pacific nor sequestered. Recent archeological "excavations which have brought to light statuary groups of female hunters or warriors, evidently votaries of the goddess like the Korai on the Athenian acropolis,"[4] lend color to legends of the Amazons, which fascinated the Greeks. Diodorus of Sicily, who was at work on his *Chronica Majora,* a history of the world, as early as 56 B.C., tells us:

> The Amazons were a people ruled by women, and their way of life was very different from ours. The women were trained for war, being obliged to serve under arms for a prescribed period, during which they remained virgins. After being discharged from military service they resorted to men for the sake of having children, but retained in their own hands the control of all public affairs, while the men led a domesticated life just like the married women in our society.[5]

Further to the East, we have the narrative of Matthew Paris describing the wives of the Mongols of Jinghis Khan, whose fierceness caused him to remark, "[they] fight like men."[6] And in Europe, there are numerous traces of women as soldiers. One authority has gone so far as to surmise that the Valkyries of Nordic and Teutonic myth were regarded as feminine ideals at a time when it was considered woman's role to share all dangers with her husband or her brothers. This is corroborated by the tale of the Red Maiden, a storied Norwegian woman, who, it is said, led an army in Ireland in the tenth century. It has also been reported that military service for Celtic women was not, in fact, abolished in Ireland until the year 590. Then there are the exploits of the British Queen Boadicea, who led her people against the Roman legions and who is quoted as boasting that the women were quite as good warriors as the men.[7]

But even if none of this ever happened, or if it did not happen precisely as reported, the fact that it was once conceivable is a datum of history.

Coming closer to our own time, Arab history is full of the warlike deeds of women; they not only participated in conflict, but are reported to have often turned the tide of battle, saving the lives of their men. And, in various parts of the world, monarchs, including the kings of Dahomey and of Siam, as well as the Nizam of Hyderabad, kept an Amazonian guard.[8] Most recently, we have the documentation of the *New York Herald Tribune* (Paris edition) of December 2, 1964, describing the Amazon army of 5,000 which formed an elite body in the military force of Dr. Hastings Banda, the founder and first premier of the African state of Malawi. This female corps was said to have been

political institutions. Any classification of institutional orders in terms of function should be seen as an abstraction which sensitizes us to the possibilities and enables us to construct and to understand the concrete segments and specific functions of any given social structure." *Character and Social Structure* (New York: Harcourt, Brace and World, 1964), pp. 27–28.

instrumental in achieving Malawi's independence and, at the time of the report, guarded the crucial boundary with Tanganyika.

On the American continent, it has been chronicled that Columbus and his companions were attacked by female archers,[9] and, according to an eyewitness report, the Klamath Indians, fighting government troops in 1854, included women:

> One day the savages came suddenly upon them . . . filling the air with a perfect shower of arrows. But not a male barbarian was in sight. Before them, in serried line of battle, their women were moving to the charge, while the warriors slunk behind them, discharging their arrows between the women.[10]*

Other examples, drawn from every region, could be cited, testimony to the fact that at various periods in history, in legend and in record, women have participated in the military order.

Surveyed as a whole, the *religious* order is even more studded with historical instances that belie our preconceptions. The ancient world was full of priestesses. The oldest shrines of Greece at Delphi and Dodona were served by prophetic women, and the Roman vestals presided over the most sacred ceremonies in that civilization. "As in Greece, so in Babylonia and Assyria," writes an Oxford authority, "women were inspired prophetesses of the god."[11] In Egypt, the queen was high priestess of Ra, and in Carthage, women mediated between the Great Goddess and her people.[12]

Turning from lands of antiquity to simpler societies of more recent epochs, we find in the western hemisphere that medicine women were not unusual among North American Indians. This was also true among the Eskimo, where women functioned as shamans or *angakut.* [13] Dr. D. G. Brinton, reporting on the practices of a Central American people at the time of the European conquest, writes "in the sacraments of Nagualism, woman was the primate and hierophant."[14] Among the tribes of the Amazon, old women are said to be the interpreters of the gods.

Sir C. J. Lyall, writing during the period of British rule in India, noted that the Khasi priestesses of Assam performed all the rites and sacrifices, and that male officiants were permitted to serve only as deputies.[15] The numerous "mother fetishes" in Africa, served exclusively by women, testify to the religious significance of women on that continent.

Even the early stages of Christianity confirm this tradition of significant women in the religious order. Making the transition from the worship of Isis, (the Mother-Earth Goddess, who appears under a score of names), where they were accustomed to religious prominence, women were at first permitted to serve as deaconesses. Later the clergy abolished this practice, but they had then to contend with heresies, such as Montanism, in which women continued to

---

*The ethnocentric vision of this reporter is revealed in his use of terms: the male fighters were "warriors," the female fighters were "women," and the Indians, to be sure, were "savages" and "barbarians."

be admitted to high rank. The persistent cult of Mary was probably also an issue, since it contravenes the teaching about women of nearly every one of the early Church Fathers.[16]

Evidence of women as rulers of tribes in simpler societies and as heads of state in more complex ones are numerous in the *political* order. The oldest existing fragment of Hebrew literature refers to the Jewish tribes as led by a woman (Judges 4-5). Among the Arabs, too, many of the judges and chiefs were women, and ruling queens, from the Queen of Sheba to Zenobia, occupied a prominent place in their history.

Of the ancient world, Claudian reports, "The female sex rules among the Sabians and a large proportion of the barbarians is under the armed domination of queens."[17] Plutarch says that the Spartan women were "the only women in Greece who ruled over their men."[18] In Homeric poetry, there are sovereign queens in no fewer than five realms, and Virgil describes Italic tribes, led by Queen Camilla, who reigned over the Volsci. When the Carthaginian general, Hannibal, marched through Gaul, an agreement drawn up between him and the inhabitants states that any difference of opinion regarding the damage done by his troops was to be decided by the supreme council of Gallic women.[19] In Tibet, there was a highly organized entity called by Chinese analysts *Nu-Kuo* or "the Kingdom of Women."[20]

Such glimmerings from the distant past are supplemented by more recent descriptions of tribal societies where women were politically significant. I have already referred to the Iroquois (see chapter 1); an extensive treatment of the role of women in African societies appears in the parallel reading for this chapter by Annie M. D. Lebeuf.

Finally, it should not be overlooked that there have been queens of great power within historical memory: Elizabeth I whose reign marked one of the most celebrated periods of British rule, Christina of Sweden whose court became a magnet for the intellectuals of her time, Catherine the Great of Russia, one of the most remarkable sovereigns of the modern period, and Empress Tz'u Hsi of China, who was in the forefront of resistance to foreign encroachment, encouraging the daring Boxer Rebellion. If power in the female person had violated immemorial tradition, it could not have been countenanced even among royal female persons, particularly since such power also implied the divine right of queens.

We now reach the *economic* order and the need to determine whether women have always been dependent there — and powerless — to the degree they are today. We have no pointer readings about half-glimpsed events in the early mists of history, but rudimentary reflection lifts the veil. Until homo sapiens could wrest surplus from a modified environment, there were no expendable individuals. The united efforts of the whole community were required to feed the chain of energy in the search and the struggle for continuing existence. Specialized function in sex and kindred service was unimaginable. Women must have ranged and run, hunted flora and fauna, contrived shelter and sought safety, in addition to bearing and caring for young, for these activities were the essentials of survival.

Even in later, more segmented societies, social surplus was a narrow quantity; the circle of privilege was small, and toil continued to be an imperative for most women. It seems marvelous, as one reaches across the centuries, to discover to what extent our "facts" are fantasies. It is not even essential to search out subtle points in exotic places; a surprising amount of evidence is in plain sight, unseen only because of our preconceptions. Thus, contravening the idea that women stay home and men support them, we have only to read again the verses from *The Odyssey* which every schoolboy must study.

Consider the lament of the woman slave, as overheard by Odysseus on his beggar's couch:

> Here were standing the mills of the prince of the people.
> These were worked by the women, a dozen in number, that toiled there
> Making the meal of the wheat and the barley, the marrow of mortals.
> All of the rest were sleeping, for ground was the whole of their wheat-grain.
> She was the weakest, and now was alone and incessantly toiling.

Then, calling on Zeus, she exclaims:

> Also for me, poor wretch, accomplish the prayer that I utter:
> O for the last and the latest of all their delightful carousings
> Here in the halls of Odysseus to-day to be held by the suitors!
> Yea, for the men have loosened my knees with this pitiless labour,
> Grinding the grain — so now let them finish their feastings for ever![21]

From another age, we have the voice of another slave, Sojourner Truth, responding, at a suffrage conference, to a clergyman's argument based on the weakness and helplessness of women:

> Look at my arm! I have ploughed and planted and gathered into barns, and no man could head me — and ain't I a woman? I could work as much and eat as much as a man when I could get it — and bear the lash as well! And ain't I a woman? I have borne thirteen children, and seen most of 'em sold into slavery, and when I cried out with my woman's grief, none but Jesus heard me — and ain't I a woman?[22]

It should not be necessary to represent that, although special groups could be exempt from primary production as technology transformed environment, the great majority of social populations, irrespective of age and sex, were forced to labor. Women then certainly participated in production, but did they share economic power? There is evidence that they were not always excluded from decisive roles.

In Vedic India, according to the *Rig-Veda*, women frequently owned great wealth, and were sought for the sake of their possessions.[23] Briffault reports that women in ancient Arabia "were commonly the owners of wealth; they possessed large flocks and herds, and their husbands so commonly acted as the herdsmen of their wives' flocks that the phrase 'I will no longer drive thy flocks to pasture' was àn habitual formula of divorce."[24] Petrie has stated that, in Egypt, "As late as the XIXth Dynasty there was still surviving the idea that a man was only a boarder in a woman's house." All landed and house property was in the hands of the women. The same phenomenon is noted by Aristotle in respect to the women of Sparta.[25]

Representative of a later period among peoples whose wealth also lay in the land, there is a 1907 study of the Khasis of Assam where "in the most primitive part of the hills, the Synteng country, [the woman] is the only owner of real property, and through her alone is inheritance transmitted."[26] Among the Navaho, where wealth may be in the form of herds, women are frequently the owners of sheep.[27] Kroeber, reporting on the customs of the Zũni, writes, "The house belongs to the women born of the family."[28] Here the husband comes to dwell, both residence and marriage tie depending on his good behavior.

And where economic well-being depended on trade, there are indications of women in North America trading in furs,[29] of those in Africa trading in vegetable produce, baskets, mats, pottery and salt.[30] Bancroft writes that in Nicaragua "a man might not enter the market, or even see the proceedings, at the risk of a beating."[31] And in Central Asia, tradition long reinforced the observation of Marco Polo that "the women do the buying and selling."[32]

These pointer readings are not intended to be more than suggestive of data that contradict facile assumptions. As Elise Boulding comments:

> The social invisibility of women makes it difficult to document the roles of women in any society, in whatever stage of industrialization, and therefore difficult to document common assumptions. Recent efforts of the UN Commission on the Status of Women to gather data from member countries on the status of women has dramatically underlined the fact that most data-gatherers and record-keepers are men. It is no reflection on their competence, only on their culture boundness, that men selectively (and unconsciously) filter out information concerning women. It took a woman economist, Polly Hill, to discover that the food wholesalers in Ghana, reported in the census as men, were in fact almost exclusively women. . . . Our problem, then, is to document the undocumented![33]

Although in later periods, particularly in the middle ages, parish records reveal the multiple activities of "the distaff side" in the management of estates, in home industry, in trade, and in finance, women never again attained the economic power held in antiquity. Even so, as late as the seventeenth century, "the idea was seldom encountered that a man supports his wife: husband and wife were then mutually dependent and together supported their children."[34]

Then came the revolution that replaced more hands than ever before in human history, and it affected women at all levels. Wives of the lowly became contingent and vulnerable; wives of the privileged lost all economic function. It was at this point that women fell out of the history books.

With successive technical mutation, increasing sectors of women have found themselves either marginal or expendable: the former moving in and out of the home in response to the push and tug of market conditions, the latter becoming full-time females. Yet the point is that, since history rarely documents the lives of ordinary people, it is the patterns of privilege that we have inherited as prototypes. Once established, moreover, they are claimed to be perennial, and irrelevance and dependency become the imperative model for all.

There is no need to cite instances of the participation of women in the *kinship* order. Our task is rather to examine whether it had the same significance in the past as it has in the present. Looking across the centuries to tribal societies, where clan or phratry organized the total life, and where human replenishment through the capacity to be fruitful and multiply was a crucial variable, it is clear that prominence in the kinship order could mean organic relation to power. For cultural forms have their roots in ecology. Though there are doubtless requisite functions for all social systems, the institutions that fulfill these functions are not always comparable entities. The outside position of the woman in the kinship order today tells us nothing about earlier organization, when she had no home to guard (unless we think also in terms of a lean-to or a cave) and where the next generation was toted unceremoniously to where the action was.

Very simply, then, how people are used depends on what needs to be done. There was a time when women were more likely to build the homes than be sequestered in them; there was a time when domestic economy was all the economy there was. The huts of the Australian, the black camel-hair tents of the Bedouin, the yurta of the nomads of Central Asia, the earth lodges of the Omaha, and the pueblos of the Hopi were all the exclusive work of women. Further, the primitive human home was also "the primitive State, the primitive factory, the centre of all those activities which social evolution has transferred to the council house, the office, the workship, and the field."[35] Every form of production, hide and leather work, basketry, pottery, spinning, weaving, dyeing, was carried on in its environs. And this continued into the home industries and guild crafts of later ages when the habitation was a hive of activity. Even "in the rude castle or grand establishment of the feudal lord, the mistress of the household was usually no languid lady or mere attendant ministering to the wants of an imperious male"[36] — she had onerous duties. Woman was part of the establishment; the whole range of the wider society was reflected in the domestic arena; the second sex helped develop the social surplus that has since rendered *it* surplus.

For the full-time housewife and mother is a recent phenomenon, a by-product of technological unemployment; and symbiosis long preceded parasitism as the economic relation between the sexes. Therefore in response to Freud's question, "What do the women want?" the answer is they want to function as insiders. And when it is asked why they seek to crash a man's world, the answer is they are not trying to enter a man's world, they only wish to re-enter *the* world: there is no other.

The life behind the record is, as has been seen, elusive and difficult to grasp, but it casts doubt upon the stereotype, upon the historical assumption of woman's eternal exclusion. The only adequate history of women is woven into the history of humanity and its dynamic adventure upon a spinning globe. If this be heresy, let it be recalled that "Heretics are the only . . . remedy against entropy of human thought."[37]

## 10. The Living Fossil: The Second Assumption

> What was decided among the prehistoric protozoa cannot be annulled by an act of Parliament.
>
> THEODORE REIK

The philosopher Alfred North Whitehead has counseled: when questioning the ideas of an epoch, do not focus on those positions that are explicitly defended. Rather, he says, "There will be some fundamental assumptions which adherents of all the variant systems . . . unconsciously presuppose. Such assumptions appear so obvious that people do not know what they are assuming because no other way of putting things has ever occurred to them."[1] The consistency of assumptions, of unambiguous norms, about women in history leads one to suspect that they are rooted in just such an "obvious" way of putting things — the belief that things must have always been that way deriving from an even deeper conviction that woman has always been that way, that is, in durance to her organism.

If we would test this assumption, we must examine it at two levels: to what extent is it biologically imperative, and to what extent is it socially relevant? In such process, we must consider the concept of the weaker sex in relation to the two most consistently cited factors: differential in force, and differential in generative function. Together, they are seen as universal constants, debarring women by definition from independent social range and from integrated social role. Sustenance is suspended from sex: participation is confined to the sexual ghetto. Male then is deemed norm, female abnorm. Male is the pro-

*Parallel readings for this chapter appear in the section entitled "A Case of Identity."

ducer, female the reproducer. Male is the social actor, female the biological instrument.

STATURE AND STRENGTH

Beginning with strength and the stowaway ideas of height, weight, stamina — and the absolutes they imply — it is to the physical anthropologists we must turn for verification. For, as Walter Goldschmidt has written, "If we are endeavoring to explain human history rather than merely recount it, to explain social behavior rather than merely record it, we must put forth such efforts as we can to make our explanations verifiable. . . . That is the only way to [test] a causative statement other than by an appeal to common sense (i.e., folk attitudes)."[2] One such authority cautions: "Men are, on the average, taller than women, but stature is so variable, in our species, that this is not a reliable criterion of sex, while differences in weight are even less distinctive."[3] Since, moreover, ours is a plastic species, the variability is not only genetic; it is affected by environment, custom, race, diet, and the state of technology.

In addition to individual differences, where one finds the "range of stature in both sexes is so great . . . that many women are taller than many men,"[4] even average differences are not absolute but vary from population to population. The mean differences in the height of men and women, for example, range from two inches for the Klamath Indian to almost eight inches for the Shilluk of Sudan, so that it is virtually impossible to sex-type by height unless population parameters are known.[5] It has also been reported of certain groups that the women are equal in size and strength, or even larger and stronger than the men. These observations are found in the journals of early travelers, missionaries, and ethnologists, describing phenotypes and patterns that prevailed before extensive European acculturation. One, writing in 1872, described female Bushmen as being on the average four centimeters taller than the men.[6] Another, depicting the Dahomey in 1890, noted "the women are generally tall, muscular and broad, and the men smooth, full-breasted, round-limbed and effeminate-looking."[7] Stephen Powers, in his work on Indian tribes of California, wrote in 1877 that the women of the Shastika were "larger and stronger-featured" than the men.[8] Tibetan women have also been reported to be taller and stronger than Tibetan men, by some observers, and of equal stature, by others. "As Tibetans dress and wear their hair alike, it is sometimes difficult to tell whether any one person is a man or a woman."[9] This difficulty in distinguishing the sexes is also related respecting the Bantu of the Lower Congo, in 1888, and the Patagonians, in 1869.[10] Writing on human variation a century later, two contemporary anthropologists state: "It does seem true that the Malay populations of Southeast Asia. . .or the Indians of the Amazon Basin do display less [physical] differentiation between the sexes" than do European peoples.[11]

Most individuals, moreover, never fulfill their genetic potential. The wide margin between possibility and realization has been offered as explanation for the marked deviation in size revealed by such studies of differentials as the famous one comparing Swiss migrants to California and their native-born children. It is a concept that can be applied to women. Diet, to take one instance, has been shown to have a significant effect on the phenotype.

> In many parts of the world, women eat apart from the men, girls get the soup while boys get the meat. . . . Boy babies may be suckled longer (to make them strong) or weaned earlier (to make them independent). Such child-rearing practices may be expected to have a marked effect upon stature and weight.[12]

Muscular activity is another determinant.

> Secondary sex characteristics are not completely under genetic control, and can be affected by cultural and environmental factors. For example, cultural heightening of genetic secondary characteristics occurs frequently with regard to physical strength. . . . This difference [of strength between the sexes] is often increased, however, by the tendency for males in most societies to perform those activities requiring rapid and extreme exertion.[13]

The reverse also seems to be true. Numerous writers report on the strength and endurance of tribal women. Edward S. Curtis, describing the Apsorake Indians of North America, notes:

> The rigors of this life made the women as strong as the men; and women who could carry a quarter of a buffalo apparently without great exertion, ride all day and all night with a raiding war-party, or travel afoot two hundred and fifty miles across an unmarked wilderness of mountains, plains, and swollen streams in four days and nights, were not the women to bring forth puny offspring.[14]

Sir Richard F. Burton comments in *First Footsteps in East Africa:* "In muscular strength and endurance the women of the Somals are far superior to their lords."[15] And Champlain, writing in 1615, states that the Huron and Algonquian women were expected to attend their husbands from place to place in the fields, filling the office of pack-mule in carrying the baggage and in doing a thousand other things. Yet it would seem that this hard life did not thwart their development, for he adds that among these tribes there were a number of powerful women of extraordinary height.[16] In Formosa among the Chinwan, W. Joest, a German ethnologist, reported in 1882 that the women carried burdens that the men were unable to handle.[17] On the other hand, in Bali, "where males do little heavy lifting. . . both males and females have slender somatypes."[18]

Such variability is demonstrated not only in obscure and distant societies but also here and now.

> Anthropologists tell us that, as civilized man depends more and more on machines to do his heavy physical labor, and as women become more and more

athletic, there is a tendency for the two sexes to become more and more alike in skeletal musculature.[19]

And finally there is the matter of social selection. Where small round women are the models of femininity, small round women will be those most likely to be invited to reproduce themselves.

> Male sexual selection [in recent history] has been confined to physical charac-
> teristics, and while it has given to woman all the beauty and grace that she
> possessed, it tended rather to dwarf her stature, sap her strength.[20]

For all the tremendous differences, there does, however, seem to be a statistical limit, both in size and strength.

> In general, . . . the man's height is about a sixteenth greater than the woman's,
> or somewhat over three-quarters of an inch more to every foot of her size.[21]

Style of life and the cultural patterning of sex-typed roles do not, on the other hand, strictly follow these somatic norms. Despite known mean differentials in height, weight, skeletal mass, and muscular development, stimulated in males by the androgens, women have not been held immune from heavy labor. In all societies, including our own, they have been required to do taxing manual work. Reporting on a journey in Africa in 1955, Dr. Grantly Dick Read, the authority on natural childbirth, writes: "It is the women who do the work, and when I say 'work' I refer to *manual labor* as well as motherhood and bringing up the children."[22] In our own culture, Jane Swisshelm, commenting on conditions in the America of 1853, remarked ironically:

> It is well known that thousands, nay millions of women in this country are
> condemned to the most menial drudgery such as men would scorn to engage in,
> and that for one-fourth the wages; that thousands of them toil at avocations
> which public opinion pretends to assign to men. They plough, harrow, reap, dig,
> make hay, rake, bind grain, thrash, chip wood, milk, churn . . . and who says
> anything against it? But let one presume to use her mental powers . . . take up
> any profession . . . which is deemed honorable and requires talent, and . . . What
> a fainting fit Mr. Propriety has taken! Just to think that [she] should for-
> sake . . . woman's sphere — to mix with the wicked strife of this wicked
> world![23]

Although the specific drudgery may be different, countless women of our own time are required to toil at equally onerous tasks. For the function of norms is often to obscure reality. The manifest content, that woman's "obvious" physical limitations inhibit her grasp upon the world, confirms only the rationalized appearances of things. What follows is a classic example of how such manifest content is communicated:

> No matter how expert, how long-trained, a top flight woman golfer simply
> can't drive a golf ball as great a distance as a top flight male golfer; she simply

doesn't have the strength to do so. Naturally, this strength difference has manifold implications for the tasks and activities to which the woman will turn — despite certain of the primitive societies where what we think of as the male and female roles are reversed."[24]

The train of reasoning here demonstrates that when we examine reality through the periscope of the present, we may not only be culture-bound but also concept-bound. Whitehead says: "Thought is abstract; and the intolerant use of abstractions is the major vice of the intellect. This vice is not wholly corrected by the recurrence to concrete experience. [In our illustration, the woman golfer.] For after all, you need only attend to those aspects of your concrete experience which lie within some limited scheme."[25] (Such as eliminating from consideration those societies with strong women who have never heard of golf.) Here, the fact that top-flight women golfers, in the environment for which the doctor who made this remark speaks, "simply don't have the strength" tells us nothing about the potential of women in golf across time and across cultures. The ethnocentrism of the easy dismissal of "certain primitive societies" tells the story. For we do not look at the world with pristine eyes. What we see is "edited by a definite set of customs and institutions and ways of thinking."[26] In such editing about women, it is clear, biologically determined universals have been broadly assumed. Transcending time and abridging tradition, the weaker sex is perceived as a living fossil, a fixed bundle of rudimentary absolutes.

The implications of human inheritance mean, however, even for woman, that there is a very narrow scope for biologically transmitted behavior. The very convictions that the doctor enunciates testify to this truth, for he reflects the cultural process that transmitted to him the crystallized tradition. "Naturally," he remarks, "this strength difference has manifold implications for the tasks and activities to which the woman will turn. . . ." These words appeared in 1963 when the major social issue in the country was automation; when we as a people were faced with the reality that such human labor as followed closely the metabolic processes of biological life was becoming redundant; when arranging abstract symbols could command a salary of $1,000 an hour, but heaving a shovel might earn a wage of no more than $1,000 a year. Despite our custom to deny it, the "tasks and activities to which woman will turn" come as a response not to private physiology, but to the "manifold implications" of cultural design. Strength differences may be significant where strength is the definitive energy source, but in the United States today, we have the atom. And those "tasks and activities" where women are not welcome are, as Jane Swisshelm so sharply noted, tasks and activities where strength is not the issue.

The assumed absolute respecting woman's strength and stature is, then, a variable affected by social imperatives and individual difference. All women are not little women, and even those who are are not disqualified for the rigors of public existence as a result of their physical frailty. If woman's grasp upon the world, to use Simone de Beauvoir's felicitous phrase, is less extended than man's, the reasons lie elsewhere. Muscle power is not today, if it ever was, the crucial passport to the country of the power elite.

### REPRODUCTION AND REARING

But, as I have already suggested, biological determinism has two components, and one usually finds them coupled. Distinctions of strength and reproduction are, as will be seen, extrapolated to signify specialized function of a cultural order. The following are two judicial expressions of the unquestioned norm. The first is based on Louis Brandeis' famous brief in *Muller vs. Oregon,* decided in 1908.

> Woman has always been dependent upon man. He established his control at the outset by superior physical strength, and this control in various forms, with diminishing intensity has continued to the present. . . . Even though all restrictions on political, personal, and contractual rights were taken away, and she stood as far as statutes are concerned, upon an absolutely equal plane with him, it would still be true that she is [so] constituted that she will rest upon and look to him for protection; that her *physical structure and a proper discharge of her maternal functions* . . . justify legislation to protect her from the greed as well as the passion of man.[27] [Emphasis added.]

The second is from an earlier case, *Bradwell vs. Illinois* (1873):

> *The natural and proper timidity and delicacy* which belongs to the female sex evidently unfits it for many of the occupations of civil life. The constitution of the family organization, which is founded in the divine ordinance, as well as the nature of things, indicates the domestic sphere as that which properly belongs to the domain and functions of womanhood. The harmony, not to say identity of interest and views which belong, or should belong, to the family institution is repugnant to the idea of a woman adopting a distinct and independent career from that of her husband . . . . The permanent destiny and mission of woman are to fulfill *the noble and benign offices of wife and mother.*[28] [Emphasis added.]

Woman, then, was not only weak, she was subject to childbirth, the old word "confinement" suggesting the ambience surrounding the female who reproduced herself. It was assumed that most women were with child most of the time, and this may, indeed, have been the case, as the clusters of infant headstones in the old cemeteries mutely testify. For women brought forth a series of young before any survived and, all too often, they themselves failed to survive the ordeal of producing excessive progeny. (Alexis de Tocqueville, visiting a frontier outpost in the 1830's, gives a touching picture of a delicate woman, worn out from multiple births, watching her brood with mingled melancholy and joy.[29]) Marriage meant children, by choice as well as by foreordination; such matings as did not produce them were, at various points in history, automatically dissolved. It was even customary in some parts of the world for the marriage ceremony to be deferred until the woman was pregnant, the young man slipping through the window during the courtship period. It is interesting to note that in early Japanese society the very word for marriage signified "to slip by night into the house."[30]

Certainly, in the conditions of continual bearing and rearing, the hazards of childbirth were very real. Moreover, they were compounded by superstition and dogma: "Even the use of anesthesia during childbirth was regarded by the Anglican Church, for a time, as a violation of basic femininity, for did not the Bible say she should bring forth her children in sorrow?"[31]

Today, by contrast, most prospective mothers move in their accustomed rounds in the months before the baby is born. Sometimes, not always, the tempo is slower. The process of delivery is likely to take place under medical supervision, and current obstetric practice inclines toward early ambulation (by the second or third day), discharge from the hospital on the fifth day, and some three weeks of curtailed activity at home. (The increasing interest in concepts of natural childbirth tends to streamline even these timetables.) Then there are three or four months of nursing and an even longer period of nurturing. But neither can be classified as disabilities, nor are they tasks that, even traditionally, only the biological mother can perform. Children have been fed by wet nurse and by bottle; they have been cared for by fathers, grandparents, governesses, and child-care specialists, not to speak of sisters and cousins and aunts. In any case, and whatever the arrangement, before long they grow up.

Recently, on television, a feminist was being interviewed. "And while you are out here agitating for women's rights," demanded the master of ceremonies, "who is at home minding your children?" "I'd have done a bad job if they needed minding," she replied, "for they are 18 and 21 years old." Even in societies where women die young, as Margaret Mead has pointed out, they can devote not more than half their lives to childbearing. In societies where women are long-lived, they devote only a third of their lives to that function. In the United States today, the average woman completes her family of 2.45 children by the time she is 30, and is somewhere in her middle thirties when they are all in school.

So there is a large and youthful body of graduated mothers who are nevertheless socially defined by their "natural calling." But there are also women without children: who have not had any, who cannot have any, who will not have any, and who should not have any, yet who are similarly defined. Moreover, the revolutions of fertility choice and population pressure imply entirely new patterns of human increase. Still the assumption remains constant. A woman is a womb, ever susceptible to the disease of pregnancy, ever engaged in upbringing, ever doomed by nature to a dependent existence. Whatever her age or condition, the biological blueprint tethers her to the species and binds her to the bedroom. This is rationalized as a law of nature, the balanced doctrine of separate but equal. Unfortunately for this theory, even a certified ghetto can still constitute limbo. The difficulty with dichotomies is that they are only persuasive when true.

The question then remains: why is the childbearing aspect of femininity so persistently emphasized as the significant one? Dr. Mead reports: "In many societies girls before puberty and women after menopause are treated very much as men. A society that has not defined women as primarily designed to bear children has far less difficulty in letting down taboos or social barriers."[32]

The answer may be subsumed in the concept of role — where there is no productive role assigned, only the reproductive one is instrumental. As an articulate and candid woman remarked in course of a recent symposium: "I need to have children to place myself." Certainly many women in America, as I mentioned earlier, are occupied in the marketplace, but that does not seem to modify the madonna-and-child model. By contrast, in food-gathering and food-growing cultures, where social patterns confirm woman as producer, there are likely to be additional dimensions to femininity, and childbearing and rearing may not be viewed as functional disabilities.

> In food-gathering cultures, such as those of the Bushman of South Africa and the Australian aborigines, the fact that a woman is pregnant or that an hour ago she gave birth to a child is generally responsible for no deviation whatever from her customary manner of living, except for the additional task of nursing.[33]

There is time out for parturition, a traditionalized period of recovery, and then continued activity in the business of life, with infant slung from hip or shoulder, hung in the trees, or laid on a mat. Older children help with the work and with the siblings, conducting free-form al fresco child-care centers. In such groups, being feminine means being strong, enduring, courageous, competent, and responsible.[34]

In reproduction and rearing, as in strength and stature, the somatic state is affected by the social order; dynamic adjustment alters the biologically given. Boscana, in his fascinating account of the San Juan Capistrano Indians of southern California, documents this principle:

> What is wonderful and for which we should bless God, as regards these women, was the facility and happiness which they had in the bringing forth of children; it can be stated that they scarcely felt at all the pains of childbirth, which did not last half an hour, and many times the woman was alone, and she herself after having given birth cleaned the baby, and after passing the afterbirth washed herself of all the mess of the childbirth . . . and shortly afterwards they would set themselves to working at whatever was necessary to be done about the house. . . .In their present state of being Christians, the Creole women of the Mission no longer have this facility, which they had in their gentile condition;

I attribute it to the exercise which they used to have when they were gentiles, since many of them now have more idleness, for finding herself pregnant, she no longer works at anything unless it be something short and easy.[35]

Even in our own time and place, I have heard of a woman in Nebraska who left her hoeing to produce a son, then returned to the field to continue her row. But, as the doctor who told me this story remarked, her condition was probably quite different from that of a woman who had done nothing all her life to feed her family but open the refrigerator door.

It is hazardous to infer a constant genotype from the mutable phenotype. "We have heard a great deal lately," wrote the scientist Julian Huxley, "about the physical disabilities of women. Some of these alleged impediments, no doubt, are really inherent in their organization, but nine-tenths of them are artificial — the product of their mode of life."[36]

To sum up, caution forbids sweeping aside all differences in biogenetic endowment, but such evidence as has been accumulated relates a number of observable differences to nongenetic factors. The possibility cannot therefore be ignored that bodily constitutions, including cardinal points of sexual dimorphism, are variable, within limits not yet determined, in relation to surrounding phenomena.

It would be simplistic to postulate woman's relation to production as the crucial variable affecting constitutional potential. But I suggest it is important, and it reveals the intimate causal relation between cultural concepts and somatic capacities. Among preliterate societies, practices of polygyny, lactation up to three years, and infanticide were other variables that differentiated human from nonhuman primate females.* Even contraception was not unknown. Dr. Grantly Dick Read reports secret contraceptive knowledge among various tribes he visited in Africa, and a paper read at the Conference of the Americas in Peru, in August 1970, refers to contraceptive herbs known to certain peoples in the southern part of the hemisphere. The extent to which the relation between culture and biology and its philosophical meaning has been, in part, reversed, is illustrated by another remark, this time in a jocular vein, by the professor of obstetrics previously quoted:

> When you come right down to it, perhaps women just live too long! Maybe when they get through having babies they have outlived their usefulness — especially now that they outlive men by so many years. That is a rather shocking

---

* This is in marked contrast to the nonhuman female primate. "Her primary focus, a role which occupies more than 70 per cent of her life, is motherhood. . . . A female raises one infant after another for her entire adult life. . . . What is 'normal' for the nonhuman primate female and for the human female are substantially different ways of life. . . . If we think of what is normal for a nonhuman primate female, it is caring for young, pregnancy, and lactation. No adult female monkey or ape has ever been observed which was too old to go through estrus cycles and reproduce. Very old females have been observed — but all were still bearing young. There appears to be no menopause for the nonhuman primate." Phyllis C. Jay, "The Female Primate," in Farber and Wilson (eds.), *The Potential of Woman,* pp. 3, 11.

way of pointing up a question which many gynecologists are asking today, namely, "Is a woman's postmenopausal status a normal, physiologic condition, or is it actually a pathologic, disease state?" Take note of what obtains in the rest of the animal kingdom. Rarely is there found among the higher animals in nature a female surviving much beyond the age of reproductive life.[37]

If, as most scholars assume, what is now has always been, there is no need to puzzle about how women were transformed from cultural participants into agents of propagation. The moment the idea is conceived, however, that it may not always have been so, at that moment there also arise the questions, when did the transformation occur, and what were the forces that triggered it. For speculation along these lines, one must turn to those who recognized the riddle, the mavericks. This unorthodox band, some of whom had great gifts, were handicapped by the crude state of anthropological knowledge in their time, and by an intellectual fashion that tended toward symmetrical systems and unilinear sequences. Although their conclusions must be approached with caution, they are nevertheless a source of suggestive conceptual clues.

Thorstein Veblen, for example, was persuaded that women were the first possessions, the first form of property. Prior to this development, he believed, the most archaic communities were poor, nonpredatory, and without concepts of individual ownership. From the possession of women came other forms of appropriation and ownership-marriage, as a form of coercion.

Johann Jacob Bachofen, studying the myths of classical peoples, scandalized his contemporaries when he argued the existence of sexual promiscuity, prior to crystallized forms of the family, in the archaic past. This, he reasoned, made paternity uncertain so that descent must have been reckoned in the female line. He further advanced the hypothesis that the transition to monogamy, with a woman belonging to one man exclusively, came after struggle between opposed social forms, with patriarchy emerging triumphant. This struggle was symbolized as contention between two sets of deities, dramatized in the *Oresteia* of Aeschylus.

Lewis Henry Morgan, beginning his study of kinship with the Iroquois, developed as his most controversial proposition the idea that unilateral descent through the mother was a universal phenomenon that, in all societies, had preceded descent through the father. This idea cut across the grain of entrenched belief, particularly when Marx's collaborator, Frederick Engels, picked up the theme and argued that if property and power once flowed from females, there must have been a time when women were not socially irrelevant. Morgan further upset his colleagues by postulating various forms of group marriage as precursors of monogamy, and suggesting that the transformation from the system of mother-right to father-right occurred when property increased beyond subsistence requirements, and when doubt about paternity raised the question of legitimate heirs.

The particular heresies of the mavericks mentioned here, and of a number of others who raised a storm, were that they laid down absolute sequences in designs of human living, and that they related those sequences to other social inventions — specifically, in the cases of Veblen, Morgan, and Engels, to property relations. This put in question the eternal form of the family. Across the planet, the traditional assumption had been that the family had experienced no mutation since the time of Adam and Eve, or their counterparts. The mavericks, in contrast, saw the history of the family as a progressive narrowing of the circle of conjugal relations. Although much of their reasoning is today considered more as curiosity than as scholarship, the research of these men has not been impugned as much as the conclusions drawn from it. For our purposes, it is not necessary to enter the fray. It is sufficient to cite them as pioneers of the concept that the family — and the position of women relative to it — has taken many forms in history, and that existing peoples testify to the marvelous variety in human designs for living.

Moreover, the idea that the progressive definition of individual paternity was a late development, connected with ideas of personal possession, matches other evidence that the position of women was not always congruent with today's assumptions. Not the least interesting is the light such a formulation throws on the obsession with female seclusion and female chastity. For if a woman is faithless, in this context, she might bring another man's children into her husband's house to become heirs to his property. To ensure that his possessions followed his blood, the woman thus became the most perdurable part of these possessions as each man sought to ensure a womb of his own, a safe repository for his seed. It seems persuasive to reason that it was at this point in social evolution that sex became a possessive privilege and woman a biological instrument.

Rousseau testifies to such philosophy quite explicitly: "The husband ought to be able to superintend his wife's conduct, because it is of importance for him to be assured that the children, whom he is obliged to acknowledge and maintain, belong to no one but himself."[38] This is also borne out for an earlier period by Roman law. "If thou dost take they wife in adultery," says Cato, "thou mayest kill her without trial and with impunity; but, if thou dost commit adultery thyself, she shall not and dare not so much as lay a finger on thee."[39] Similarly, under the Code Napoléon, undisputed paternity did not impose monogamy on men, the right of conjugal infidelity being secured to them so long as they did not bring their concubines into the house.

By a fascinating transposition of ideas, such as one sometimes encounters in cultural history, the focus on *certain* paternity reversed the physiological facts. Aeschylus has Apollo assert:

> The mother is not procreatrix to her child;
> She only the awakened life doth keep and bear.
> The father is the procreator; she but keeps
> The forfeit for her friend, unless a god destroy it

> I will submit a proof that cannot be denied.
> For one can have a father, yet no mother have.
> Minerva, daughter of the great Olympian Zeus,
> Within the darkness of a mother's womb ne'er rested,
> And yet no goddess e'er gave birth to fairer offspring.

James Campbell remarks that Adam told Eve she was taken from his rib, "whereas we know, as Eve knew and her serpent knew, that woman is not born of man, but man of woman."[41]

From such conceptions, it was a short step to the idea of woman as temptress. Although she was postulated to be supererogatory in nature, man nevertheless needed her to produce his young. He knew he must secure her chastity, yet he also knew that, when he himself was unchaste, it was with a woman. Clearly, women were seductive and impure. So, among the early Christians, Gregory Thaumaturgus testifies: "Moreover, among all women I sought for chastity proper to them, and I found it in none. And verily, a person may find one man chaste among a thousand, but a woman never."[42] The ultimate attitude and curious anger are conveyed by Tertullian. This is how he addressed women:

> Do you not know that each one of you is an Eve? The sentence of God on this sex of yours lives in this age: the guilt must of necessity live too. You are the devil's gateway; you are the unsealer of that forbidden tree; you are the first deserter of the divine law; you are she who persuaded him whom the devil was not valiant enough to attack. You destroyed so easily God's image, man. On account of your desert, that is death, even the Son of God had to die.[43]

It is a troubling thought that when this pathological view of human reproduction was scuttled by Freud, even he reverted to the premises of an older phallic religion and continued to view "the sex" as a biological agency, but a deficient one, in that she lacked the vital organ of her species. "Every philosophy," says Whitehead, "is tinged with the colouring of some secret imaginative background, which never emerges explicitly into its trains of reasoning."[44] This may explain why the victories of the early feminists did not affect the basic condition of women. The demonstration of facts — that they could function outside the home, that they were intelligent beings, that they had human capacities — did not alter ideas. Custom regarding woman's place, laws regarding woman's mating and its consequences, remain rooted in the philosophy that continues to view woman as a body who belongs to somebody. The young rebels of today sum it up in the phrase "barefoot and pregnant." To this must be added the locus of her proper milieu: the home, a setting not of sentimental refuge but of sequestration to ensure chastity.

If, therefore, we return to Dr. Freud and his echoing query: *Was will das Weib?"* the answer is she wants autonomy. She wants to be perceived not as a human female but as a female human. Seen in this perspective, the agitations of the current Eves, who have eaten the apple of feminism, for sexual freedom, sexual dignity, and for experiments beyond monogamy, are logical reactions to stereotyped body image. And the agitation for the right to abortion and the right to bear children outside wedlock, for celibacy, and for new forms of child care is a logical reaction to institutionalized patterns of body ownership.

Jacob Bronowski, poet and scholar, has observed that "at the basis of human thought lies the judgment of what is like and what is unlike." Across the years, woman has been unlike: a bearer of beings, not a being herself. To continue Bronowski's idea, "When science shifts that judgment, it makes as profound a shift in these values. The Greeks built a wonderful civilization, yet it did not outrage their sense of values to hold men in slavery. They did not feel the slave and citizen to be alike men. By the end of the eighteenth century, it was felt in the western world that all white men are alike; but William Wilburforce spent a lifetime in persuading his generation that black slaves and white are alike in human dignity. Science helped to create that sensibility, by widening the view of what is like and what unlike."[45] In terms of the modern temper, we can say that we live in an epoch of equalization that is steadily expanding the areas of likeness between peoples, shifting values founded in xenophobia. Perhaps we are on the verge of the crucial discovery that woman and man are alike human, that all children are our children, and that we share a common destiny in the cosmic age.

## 11. Portrait of a Lady: The Third Assumption

>—•—◦—•—◦—•—◦—•—◦—•—◦—•—◦—•—◦—•—◦—•—◦—•—◦—•—◦—•—◦—•—◦—•—◦—•—◦—•—◦—•—◦—•—◦—•—◦—•—<

> . . . as if femininity were an
> incurable disease with which
> they had been born. . . .
>
> R. H. TAWNEY

Woman has been taught that love and life contend. As living fossil, she has been restricted to one virtue, one passion, one occupation. The third assumption is also based on the imperative of the organism — this time as the crystallizing agent of cultural capacities. It is founded in the idea that body determines soul, that the feminine psyche is a pattern fundamentally woven into the human fabric, that woman's personality, like woman's place, is biologically imprinted, with sex a branch of bio-typology from which consistent symmetries can be predicted. Once again we encounter a concept of foreordination, of absolute correspondence between the genetic and the cultural. Physique becomes an immutable factor in psychology, fixing the range and contour of feminine nature, imposing a permanent limit to station in life.

One finds, however, on searching out the particular traits termed feminine, "a bland affirmation of clashing contradictions."[1] No account is taken of serious discrepancies. The conclusions of diligent scholars are not congruent, and descriptions of intellect, emotion, character, personality are all offered in semantic dossiers untethered to analytical principles or concrete referents. Here, to take one instance, is the classical Aristotelian definition:

*Parallel readings for this chapter appear in the section entitled "The Nature of Nurture."

Woman is more compassionate than Man, more ready to weep, but at the same time more jealous, more querulous, more inclined to abuse. In addition she is an easy prey to despair and less sanguine than Man, more shameless and less jealous of honor, more untruthful, more easily disappointed and has a longer memory. She is likewise more cautious, more timid, more difficult to urge to action, and she requires a smaller quantity of food.[2]

And here is an excerpt from Martin Luther's *Table Talk*:

Men have broad and large chests, and small narrow hips, and more understanding than the women, who have but small and narrow breasts, and broad hips, to the end they should remain at home, sit still, keep house, and bear and bring up children. . . . A woman is, or at least should be, a friendly, courteous, and a merry companion in life, whence they are named, by the Holy Ghost, house-honours, the honour and ornament of the house, and inclined to tenderness, for thereunto are they chiefly created, to bear children, and be the pleasure, joy and solace of their husbands.[3]

And more recently, Havelock Ellis:

Women dislike the essentially intellectual process of analysis; they have the instinctive feeling that analysis may possibly destroy the emotional complexes by which they are largely moved and which appeal to them. Women dislike rigid rules, and principles, and abstract propositions. They feel that they can do the right thing by impulse, without needing to know the rule, and they are restive under the rigid order which a man is inclined to obey upon principle.[4]

In this case, as in others where rhetoric stands alone, language succeeds (as I. A. Richards shows) in hiding from us almost all the things we talk about. Somatic design is presumed to determine personality configuration — but what configuration?

As in physics, where the position of the observer affects the data observed, it is not altogether irrelevant that most capsule renderings of the qualities of women come from men. And man observes, as Virginia Woolf vividly notes, "through the black or rosy spectacles which sex puts upon his nose."[5] Moreover there is a line of development in the definitions. The initial idea was that woman is a deformed human. Aristotle considered the female a mutilated male suffering from "a kind of natural defectiveness," and stated that "there is only one thing they have not in them, the principle of soul."[6] This view coincides with that of Freud, who also saw woman as a damaged reflection of man, all her traits representing response to her basic defect in lacking the essential organ. This leaves "ineradicable traces on her development and character formation" and is responsible, in Freud's judgment, for tendencies toward envy, jealousy, lack of a sense of justice, narcissism, and vanity. That "vanity is partly a further effect of penis-envy, for they are driven to rate their physical charms more highly as a belated compensation for their original sexual inferiority."[7]

The second phase in the development of definitions of woman is marked by the discovery that, in Tennyson's words, "Woman is not an undeveloped man, but diverse," that she is in every respect the opposite of man. A nineteenth-century French philosopher reflected this perspective when he wrote:

> There are thus two human souls, that is a masculine soul and a feminine soul. Thus, woman not only has a soul, whatever impertinent misogynists may have thought, but she has a soul essentially different from ours, a soul which is the inverse of ours, inverse and complementary. *Different* in mind and heart, *different* in imagination and character, intimately and essentially different woman brings us a new spiritual world and not only a more or less watered down re-edition of the spiritual world of man.[8]

Here is a modern statement, that of Erich Fromm, in the same vein:

> There is a masculinity and femininity in character as well as in sexual function. The masculine character can be defined as having the qualities of penetration, guidance, activity, discipline and adventurousness; the feminine character by the qualities of productive receptiveness, protection, realism, endurance, motherliness.[9]

Although the language is the language simply of difference, the meaning, in most cases, is derogation, for the qualities assigned to women are not the ones the culture values; the dualism maintains a separate that is not equal. Even a maverick like Robert Briffault, who challenged many of the historical assumptions of woman's place, is drawn to such polarities:

> Women are innately conservative and, if it is true that a man learns nothing after forty, it may be said that a woman learns nothing after twenty-five. Her intelligence differs in kind from masculine intelligence.[10]

Nietzsche, in the course of arguing the importance of dualism as a conceptual tool, also reveals where he stands in the controversy:

> To be mistaken in the fundamental problem of Man and Woman is to deny the abysmal conflict and the necessity of an eternally hostile tension: perhaps even to dream of the same rights, the same occupations, the same demands, the same duties; this is a typical sign of shallow-patedness.[11]

The definitions are, for all their tremendous differences, rooted in the "obvious," and the authors, for the most part, offer no verification; for who needs to defend the inevitability of the familiar? Derogation ranges from the folk formula of Sporting Life (in *Porgy and Bess*) that "a woman is a sometime thing" to the formidable opinion of Dr. Samuel Johnson delivering himself on the subject of women preachers:

> Sir, a woman's preaching is like a dog's walking on his hind legs. It is not done well, but you are surprised to find it done at all.[12]

Consistency with cultural conceptions of the "divine blueprint" and its implementation in a particular time and place ranges from the observation by Oscar Browning, the Cambridge don, that "irrespective of the marks he might give, the best woman was intellectually inferior to the worst man,"[13] to the views of the Arapesh, who insist that women's heads are stronger than men's.[14] What is, is presumed to be normative.*

With the advance of scientific rigor, however, elemental archetypes are no longer accepted on faith; efforts are exerted in various disciplines to seek out the relationship between sex and gender. "So far," however, "those who believe in such organic correlations of constitution with psychic traits have not isolated its mechanisms."[15] The research has taken paths ranging from primatology to physiological experiments, from studies of sexual anomalies to psychological testing for personality traits and patterns of learning.

The most important finding in this wealth of material seems to be the intricacy of the process of growing and of being, and the inadequacy of single factors and static causal weights to account for the dynamism and complexity of human life. Certainly, since homo sapiens is an animal, it would be strange to find that biological differences make no difference. The problem is, however, that homo sapiens is also a human animal, the most significant aspect of that humanity being that he is culture-bearing. "Culture is not only our creation but our creator."[16] Among intervening variables, culture is one of the major factors affecting mental phenotype. Humans are subject to nature's laws and to man-made mores as well, for our *nature* is cultural. As the physical anthropologist Frederick S. Hulse writes:

> The physical aspects and the cultural aspects of being human are so intimately related to one another that attempts to separate them are not only fatuous but dangerously misleading. We have come to realize that there is no real conflict between nature and nurture, but that genetic systems and their environments react upon each other in most subtle ways. In just the same sense, human biology and human culture are in a state of dynamic interdependence upon one another. Attempts to explain either one without taking the other into account are doomed to failure.[17]

In the interest of analysis, however, there have been a number of attempts to connect biological givens with the divergent social designs prescribed for men and women. In primatology, for example, it has been observed among such animals as the rhesus monkey that females tend to be submissive and passive in social interaction while males seem to be predisposed to aggression. From such evidence it has been suggested that a similar dimorphism may exist

---

*The mechanism here might be termed the distorting mirror effect. Lord Chalfont has described it as "a cumulative process of misperception in which the distorted images are self-confirming." Lord Chalfont, "Prospects of Peace," *Bulletin of the Atomic Scientists,* vol. XXII, no. 5 (May 1966), p. 4.

in humans, dictating a parallel behavior pattern. Authorities who are skeptical of such equivalence point to the fact that in certain anthropoid apes, notably the chimpanzee and the gibbon, the reverse can occur. Also, Maslow and his associates, writing on the dominance-subordination syndrome in infrahuman primates, report that either male or female can become the dominant or the subordinate individual in contrived laboratory situations. Since their status is independent of gender, doubt is cast on the sex-linked nature of the behavior.

Other scholars question the significance of patterns of instinctive behavior in comprehending the origins of cultural conduct. No living primate can be directly traced to man's ancestors. And homo sapiens, even in the most rudimentary societies, does not function through automatic expression of primate nature. "There is a quantum difference, at points a complete opposition," writes Marshall Sahlins, "between even the most rudimentary human society and the most advanced subhuman primate one. The discontinuity implies that the emergence of human society required some suppression, rather than a direct expression of man's primate nature."* Thus aggression related to food supply, and strife related to sexual congress, were impulses that had to be brought under control in the interest of the economic adaptation of the group.

Man alone is not a formidable animal; it is only as he learned to join with his fellows in mutual projects that he could struggle to survive. Harmony then became a precondition to continuing existence. "As Frank Beach of Yale University has pointed out, a progressive emancipation of sexuality from hormonal control runs through the primate order. This trend culminates in mankind, among whom sex is controlled more by the intellect — the cerebral cortex — than by glands. Thus it becomes possible to regulate sex by moral rules; to subordinate it to higher, collective ends."[18] If cortical mediation affects primate impulse in an area as urgent as sex, the simple projection of primate patterns as an explanation for the complexities of cultural conduct promotes a conclusion based in tenuous evidence. To many scholars it is an inadequate model, reducing the range and variety of human life to the single factor of biological determinism.

Another research approach is concerned with the effect of hormones on human behavior. The hypothesis is that since males and females differ in their sex hormones, and since sex hormones enter the brain, there may be a correla-

---

*"This is not to slander the poor apes, to suggest that their social behavior is necessarily innate and unlearned. Yet it is clearly the product of their nature, of animal needs and reactions, physiological processes and psychological responses. Their social life therefore varies directly with the organic constitution of the individual and the horde. In an unchanging environment the social characteristics of a given subhuman primate species are unchanging, unless or until the species is organically transformed. The same cannot be said about human social arrangements. We are all one species, but our social orders grow and diversify, even within a constant environment. . . . This liberation of human society from direct biological control was its greatest evolutionary strength." Marshall D. Sahlins, "The Origin of Society," *Scientific American* (September 1960), vol. 203, p. 77.

tion between hormone function and personality traits. Results so far have, in the opinion of critics of this approach, only demonstrated differences in physiological state. The problem still to be solved is "whether these differences are at all relevant to behavior. For a particular physiological state can itself lead to a multiplicity of felt emotional states and outward behavior, depending on the social situation."[19] It is also not without significance that "present methods of measurement do not reveal any differences between young boys and girls in the concentration of male or female hormones present in their bodies, even though their social behavior might suggest the presence of such a difference. This might be taken to mean that the differences in social behavior could not be a product of differential hormonal factors in the two sexes."*[20]

Such a conclusion is reinforced by the fascinating research of Dr. John L. Hampson, Dr. Joan Hampson, and Dr. John Money at the Endocrine Clinic of the Johns Hopkins Hospital, who studied sex anomalies: people whose original sex assignment was incorrect or ambiguous because of the appearance of their external genitalia. These individuals were reared as members of the sex to which they did not physiologically belong; nevertheless, their gender role and orientation were found to be congruent with the assigned, not the organic, psychosexual function. The team was persuaded, as Dr. John Hampson reports, that there is no convincing evidence that sex hormones "act as a single causal agent in the establishment of an individual's gender role and psychosexual orientation,"[21] but rather that gender role appears to be learned.

> In place of a theory of innate constitutional psychologic bisexuality we can substitute a concept of psychosexual neutrality in humans at birth. Such neutrality permits the development and perpetuation of many patterns of psychosexual orientation and functioning in accordance with the life experiences each individual may encounter and transact.[22]

Moreover, when later efforts are made to reassign gender consistent with chromosomal sex or predominant physical attributes, unless such reassignment occurs at a very early age (between 18 months and 3 years), marked psychological problems result. Such attempts are usually unsuccessful.

A third avenue of investigation is that of differential psychological testing of capacities and aptitudes. Henry Higgins (in *My Fair Lady*) was not the only one who wondered why can't a woman be more like a man: there has been a long history of puzzlement about questions of intelligence and sex-linked

---

*David A. Hamburg, one of the leading experimenters in this area, administered male hormones to pregnant subhuman primates and observed increased incidence of rough-and-tumble play, and other behavior associated with males, in the female offspring. He concluded that in primates sex-specific hormones govern social as well as sexual behavior. Where no measurable hormone is found, he suggests the ingenious theory that sex differences in social behavior may be related to endocrine influence even though no difference in hormone concentration appears at the time the behavior is observed. David A. Hamburg and Donald T. Lunde, "Sex Hormones in the Development of Sex Differences," in Maccoby (ed.), *The Development of Sex Differences,* pp. 9–21.

traits. It comes then as nothing new, perhaps, that research to date has turned up no consistent evidence of sex differences in intelligence. Dr. Higgins speaks with primary certitude when he states:

> Women are irrational,
> That's all there is to that.
> Their heads are full of cotton, hay, and rags.

But the scholars, in their own kind of language, come to an opposite conclusion:

> When large unselected groups are used, when age is taken into account, when possibilities of bias in test content are allowed for, startling differences between the sexes either in average tendency or in variations fail to emerge.[23]

On the other hand, by high school age, differentials do appear in spatial ability, in some aspects of analytic ability, in verbal ability, and in mathematical reasoning. The question arises, then: are these variables of sex or of gender?*

In attempting to answer this question, linkages have been sought between intellectual performance and personality characteristics. Thus, where girls are found to be more field-dependent and less analytical, it has been suggested that this performance level is related to the cultural imperatives for girls to be more dependent and conforming.

> Why should there be any relationship between the cluster of personality dispositions that we may call the dependency cluster and individuals' characteristic modes of dealing with a stimulus array? Two possible reasons suggest themselves. First, an individual who is dependent and conforming is oriented toward stimuli emanating from other people; perhaps he finds it difficult to ignore these stimuli in favor of internal thought processes. . . . Dependent children have been shown to be more distractible . . . . Tasks calling for sequential thought may be hindered by a heavy reliance on external, interpersonal cues.[24]

Dependency, then, and conformity, the qualities that are appropriate to woman's place, interfere with first-rate intellectual functioning. The scholars are confirming what the feminists have been asserting. There is also data that connect level of aspiration with achievement, and numerous studies that reveal a curve away from accomplishment, despite high IQ, in girls as they approach puberty. Such "achievement drop-off among girls as they reach maturity is linked to the adult female sex role."[25]

> They seem to feel that proficiency in problem solving is not "feminine," especially when competing with men. It has been found that the problem-solving ability of women can be improved by restricting the group being studied entirely to women, by using female experimenters, and by reducing the masculine content

*Researchers use this terminology to distinguish between the biologically given and the culturally learned.

of the problems. The failure of women to compete successfully with men in problem situations seems to be due primarily to conflicting motives rather than to lack of ability.[26]

The correlations are then with gender expectations. To return to Professor Higgins:

> Can't a woman learn to use her head?
> Why do they do everything their *mothers* do?
> Why don't they grow up like their *fathers* instead?

And once again to the scholarly counterpoint:

> Sex-role training is seen as beginning at birth, with the use of blue blankets for boy infants and pink ones for girls; the roles are "drilled in" intensively and continuously throughout childhood. . . . In their explanation of sex-typing, social learning theorists invoke well-known, experimentally verified principles of learning. The factors that are central are differential and selective rewards and punishments, generalization, mediation, modeling and vicarious learning.[27]

We find, then, that personality has an evolution. It is affected by what C. Wright Mills has termed "the imperial reach of social worlds into the intimacies of our very self."[28] Women in the feminine subculture reflect the disabilities of those signed off from their civilization. It follows that no generalization about differential behavior is permissible so long as there is a differential environment. We are programmed by our preoccupations.

At the root of psychological reasoning in the field of sex-typing is the concept of polarities, that dualism which Nietzsche believed to be a *sine qua non* for profundity. There is a fascination with masculine-feminine measurement and a correlation of scores with various capacities. Unfortunately,

> The generally low intercorrelations among the measures may make it difficult to interpret the results of studies of sex-typing. The findings of one study may not support (or may even contradict) those of another, not because the conclusions based on one set of data are faulty, but rather, because the studies used vastly different, uncorrelated operational measures of sex-typing.[29]

This means essentially that the scholars used concepts of polarity taken from the popular culture. In one test, young children are offered toys (dolls, cribs, dishes, knives, boats, racing cars) and are assessed as masculine or feminine in relation to those they choose. "Older children, adolescents, or adults are asked to indicate their agreement or disagreement with statements indicative of masculine and feminine attitudes or interests (e.g., I enjoy participating in active sports)."[30] The matrix of the society then becomes the given, and, of course, society has already traditionalized the presumed difference along role lines. All that the researchers are doing is measuring the success of that traditionalization, using the definitions reflected in mores and folklore. Their rigor in technique cannot compensate for their field-dependency in concept. They apply value-free methods and objective measurement to uncalibrated stereotypes. Thus we find such conclusions as "the brighter boys were considerably more feminine and slightly less masculine than their less intelligent peers." And "children who were more skillful at spatial tasks than verbal or numerical tasks tended to be low in masculinity if they were boys, high in masculinity if they were girls." The key to the results is revealed in this summary statement from Eleanor Maccoby:

> The studies cited so far indicate that analytic thinking, creativity, and high general intelligence are associated with cross-sex typing, in that the men and boys who score high are more feminine, and the women and girls more masculine, than their low-scoring same-sex counterparts.[31]

The sociologist Robert K. Merton has observed that deviance results from the conflict between cultural paths and cultural possibilities. The cross-sex types then are deviants, violating "normative" standards, transcending the soap opera plots and daring to depart from the straitjackets of a sex that thinks and a sex that feels. Perhaps the tests should be asking what makes an optimum human being and testing for that optimum human being. If there were any distinctions between the sexes, one could then examine biographical differences in a search for causes. Then and only then, if no explanation were found, could one begin to construct a masculinity – femininity axis.

Robert Lowell has commented that we are all dealers in used furniture. In accepting the stigmata of sex as the critical element of difference between people, we are harking back to the naive observations of our primitive ancestors, who also believed that the stars were something to tell fortunes by. In an open-ended search, new classifications of human personality might be found. It may be that the physical differences between individuals are not the decisive ones. And it may indeed be that polarized reasoning cannot encompass the dialectical nature of process.*

This is reinforced by another type of study, crosscultural research like that of Margaret Mead, where it appears that personality is a plastic quality and related to the expectations and designs found in the social matrix. Having experienced, like other anthropologists, the transposition of vantage that comes from living in another culture, she is cautious in postulating the "innateness" of difference. Describing the three New Guinea tribes referred to earlier, who have internalized quite different patterns of approved personalities for the two sexes, she concludes:

---

*"To think in polarities . . . is merely a habit without regard for the real structure of things, and excusable only as a preliminary step in the explanation of the world. If one observes carefully enough, true opposites are not found. . . . Warm is not the opposite of cold. Dark is not the opposite of light, love is not the opposite of hatred. . . . There is no polarity between activity and passivity, between aggression and submission, between rest and motion. . . . I have never found two opposite strivings as the basis of so-called ambivalence . . . masculinity is not the opposite of femininity." Paul Schilder, *Goals and Desires of Man*, quoted in Helen Merrell Lynd, *On Shame and the Search for Identity* (New York: Science Editions, Inc., 1966), pp. 137-138.

Human nature is almost unbelievably malleable, responding accurately and contrastingly to contrasting cultural conditions. . . . Standardized personality differences between the sexes are of this order, cultural creations to which each generation, male or female is trained to conform.[32]

The task is to fracture the universals, to deal with what Clyde Kluckhohn has called "culturally standardized unreason." Only when this has been effected will we be able to put woman up against a wall and measure her.[33]

# PART THREE
# PROJECTIONS AND CONCLUSIONS

## 12. The Arc of the Future

>-•-o-•-o-•-o-•-o-•-o-•-o-•-o-•-o-•-o-•-o-•-o-•-o-•-o-•-o-•-o-•-o-•-o-•-o-•-o-•-o-<

> The visible world is no longer
> a reality, and the unseen world
> is no longer a dream.
>
> W. B. YEATS

We see with the eyes of our culture. William James tells the story of a tribe of skilled canoe makers reacting to the visit of a steamship to their shores. They were fascinated by the lifeboats, but oblivious of the liner. Epictetus makes the same point in reverse: not things, he says, confuse men, but opinions of things. And the opinion of things, the very awareness of things, is traditionalized by social norm and social caveat.

Blacks and women, the young and the poor, have been among us for a long time. Their invisibility "then" and the spasm of recognition[1] that accompanies their emergence "now" are matters of social focus. Conversely some few appear in every culture who transcend the proffered perspective. We call them simpletons or seers. Such visionaries look at the world through lenses that modify perception of the mainstream culture, for not only are they persons of their time and their place, but they have the vantage of individual gifts or of a subculture — artist, philosopher, scientist, outsider. Looking so along the arc of the future, they register a different dream from those who gaze with the eyes of the predefined and the given.

We find in consequence that there were those in other ages who questioned the position of woman as service industry. And we find the axis of their discourse and the issues they raised were not so very different from those that agitate dissidents today. The women then and the women now chronicle the same indignities, the same inequities, across the chasm of centuries. Could they cross the bridge of time, meet and talk, they would, unlike other historical analogues, immediately understand one another. For the patterned disparities continue to be modal: marginal work life, political exclusion, social subordination, and auxiliary status, in terms of the specific; along with biological determinism (with its corollary of separate but equal), in terms of the general ideology. Now, as then, the essential title to the human estate is clouded by the disability of gender. And now, as then, overarching other issues, remains the question of autonomy.

Why then, if they had the same insights and mounted parallel struggles, did the first feminists fail? And what does this portend for the prospects of the new? The women in 1848 were certainly militant. At their founding convention they resolved:

> That woman has too long rested satisfied in the circumscribed limits which corrupt customs and a perverted application of the Scriptures have marked out for her, and that it is time she should move in the enlarged sphere which her great Creator has assigned her.[2]

Just as one group of women in 1966 declared:

> NOW is dedicated to the proposition that women, first and foremost, are human beings, who, like all other people in our society, must have the chance to develop their fullest potential.[3]

The crucial point was identified with one voice, then and now, that men are male *humans*, women human *females*. In the old vocabulary, they spoke of

> a mortifying consciousness of inferiority which embitters all enjoyment[4]

and a terrible awareness of

> natures turned awry for want of space to burgeon their powers.[5]

And in the new:

> Modes of acceptance and rejection in social behavior may not create genius, but they can thwart the effective expression of genius.[6]

> The brightest and best girls get the message: don't try for the really challenging work.[7]

> There are more whooping cranes in all North America than lady legislators.[8]

Clearly the attainment of specific rights has not added up to autonomy. Biologically bounded and precategorized, women are still cut off by cultural proscription from social integration. Feminist struggle, therefore, continues not because women seek to be like men, but rather because the power of self-determination has been labeled: for men only.

History, Merleau-Ponty has observed, is ambiguous. We are not certain, looking backward, that we can assess the variables that determined the rate and direction of the current of change that flowed into our present. Nor can we say how it might have been if the pressures had been different.* But we can compare the objective conditions, both public and private, within which the two campaigns of feminism set their course.

At the level of production, we can compare the first industrial revolution with the second, one adding a new energy source to lighten toil, the other introducing unlimited energy that can make toil as a human necessity obsolete. In terms of that segment of the population called women, the first transformation, with its substitution of machines for muscle power, meant some hands were expendable. As already noted, upper class women ceased to have an economic function, while lower class women became a marginal labor force for the care and feeding of marginal machines. It was, however, the utilization of some women, albeit at the periphery of performance and power, that was seen as the entering wedge, and feminists sought to extend that inclusion. For honored toil was the social test of human worth. Concrete function defined identity, and the nature of such identity opened or kept permanently closed the doors to autonomous being. Insiders were relevant. Outsiders were cut off from social nourishment and the generative force of self. In seeking to escape irrelevance, women were therefore obliged to struggle for marketplace inclusion. "You have monopolized," cried Olive Schreiner, "all the honorable employments." Economic integration became the symbol not only of status, but of autonomy.

Vision, on the other hand, is not the only variable. One has to take account of the social matrix. The first feminist movement arose in response to the extrusion of a given number of persons from the production of goods and services, following the discovery of new sources of energy. Yet despite profound change the economy was still an economy of scarcity: there was a finite limit to growth — in terms of available energy and resources, a saturation point — in the use of human beings.

For reasons still not altogether understood, women were the most significant group that became expendable at the inception of that industrial leap. And their number grew. As technology developed, more and more lower class women

---

* It has been suggested that concentration on the suffrage issue, to the neglect of other possible strategies, was the crucial error of the first feminists, and that it arose from failure to understand the complex nature of their struggle. I'm afraid this is oversimplification. The vote was the clearest issue, chosen as slogan and symbol, to galvanize interest. It was also seen as condition precedent to participation in decision-making, and thence to participation in all social orders. But the ultimate goal was autonomy, and the feminist leaders were sophisticated enough to know that autonomy was not a simple sequel to suffrage.

were siphoned off; and, as the social surplus increased, more and more upper class women became outsiders. Structural transformation, together with a mix of cultural determinants, thus rendered a whole sex extraneous to the essential machinery of society.* Moreover, given the technological conditions then obtaining, along with the existing structural design, it is important to emphasize that women could have been integrated only if another group had been turned out.† It was an either/or system; a certain proportion of the population was bound to be extraneous. Feminist agitation did not, perhaps could not, alter the formula. For although it is possible, as has been suggested in recent writing, that the first feminists failed in strategy, we cannot know whether they were not, for their time, dreaming the impossible dream.††

We do know that the neofeminists are accelerating the course of history. The world is not changing; it has changed. Although much of the new is as ambiguous as Merleau-Ponty's picture of the past, objective conditions have been transformed at crucial nodes. Magnificent potential is, however, perverted, not by poverty of vision, but by failure of cognition. An after-image lag insulates conditions, unprecedented and prodigious, from comprehension. We continue to think and to act in terms of a superseded universe. Classical debate continues. The old lawsuit — the battle of the sexes — goes forward apart from stupendous new variables in the social equation. Engaged and unaware, the women seek to enter and the men to defend an establishment that has become obsolete. The ultimate paradox is to find searching women straining to discover a new relationship to society, a new identity, in an old functionalism.

The cybernetic revolution, the second industrial revolution, has changed all the rules and transformed all the reference points. "Only an extraordinarily elaborate exercise in social camouflage," writes John Kenneth Galbraith, "has kept us from seeing what is happening."[9] The principle of feedback implies that the human element — the element of operation and control — left over after the first industrial revolution can now be dispensed with. Machines can be built to control their own operations, and the limiting factor of human capacity, which hampered earlier forms of mechanization, can be transcended. Even in areas of judgment, the ability of the computer to deal simultaneously with a multitude of variables and to handle an enormous quantity of information means it can explore possible courses of action in fractions of minutes. Further, we are no longer confined to fossil fuels; energy output, particularly in terms of the atom, is virtually unlimited. Even resources are no longer restricted to the familiar raw materials found in nature.

*This was not literally true, as has been pointed out in earlier chapters, but it was true in definition and in stereotype, and most significantly, in patterns of power.
†This may explain the extent of the fury directed against them.
††Their goals could perhaps have been achieved, without such extrusion, through the complete restructuring of society. But this would have meant an alliance with other movements and a revolutionary ideology; in short, an entirely different scenario.

This sets the stage, for the first time in human history, for an economy of abundance: a capacity to produce enough for all without depriving any. The consequence is a mutation of life on earth "potentially as basic as that experienced through the slow process of evolution from animal to human."[10] New definitions of identity, new goals synchronous with the new conditions are now the imperative.

Yet, perhaps in consequence of their position as outsiders, particularly their position as outsiders in the scientific professions, the challenging campaign of the new feminists proceeds in an old context. They continue to struggle for work, in order to achieve identity, at a time when human displacement can be predicted in relation to any task that can be programmed, when new conditions presage a phasing out of most work. "Cybernetics and automation will revolutionize working habits, with leisure becoming the practice and active work the exception — and a privilege reserved for the most talented."[11] To struggle effectively, one must understand the arena. As Norbert Wiener says: we live in a world "in which there is condign punishment, not only for him who sins in conscious arrogance, but for him whose sole crime is ignorance of the gods and the world around him."[12]

The present is pregnant with the future in a sense unprecedented in human history. Every aspect of human life will be determined by decisions taken, or not taken, at this critical juncture. For contemporary society is yoked to the economy of the first industrial revolution and the technology of the second. One reins us in while the other gallops. We think in terms of scarcity in a context of unlimited abundance, as institutions limp behind possibilities. The key issue of our time, then, the pivotal challenge, is to direct technical transformation toward human ends. There is no need for us to be sorcerer's apprentices. But this implies a break with the folklore of current abstraction and a creative plan congruent with the facts of current reality.

Women must be part of this appraisal, this recasting, this metamorphosis. In focusing on their status as an isolated problem in a superseded framework, they will not only be unable to achieve their ends, they will find themselves outside the new dynamism. When new identities are dealt out, they may even find themselves relegated once again to the sexual ghetto — to a postindustrial apartheid. For in an entirely neoteric sense, feminine autonomy is now a viable option, but it is implicit in the power to move forward into a quite different state of human life, given the new evolutionary potential; it is not simply a function of feminine militancy. Once again, patterns of integration can neither be considered nor realized apart from process.

Let me project the problems and the possibilities first in terms of today, then in terms of the middle distance, and finally in terms of the more distant future. In each case I shall attempt to make a connection between social design and the feminine subculture.

Beginning with the here and now, it is necessary to bear in mind that 80 per cent of the female labor force in the current economic market are semiskilled. The jobs they do are the simplest to structure (clerical and routine service) and clearly the most likely to be phased out by computer technology.[13] As soon as women are no longer cheaper to employ than machines, when their wages and perquisites exceed what it would cost to have George do it, employers will surely install George. At the same time, since computers represent a considerable investment, employers are inclined to keep people as long as they profitably can. This may explain some of the curious allies the new feminists have been finding in their struggle for the passage of the Equal Rights Amendment. That proposal would do away with state-by-state protective legislation, adopted at various periods because of woman's vulnerable position in the work force. In California, present wage orders for women in agriculture, to take one instance, provide for a minimum of $1.65 an hour. Should such orders become a dead letter as a result of the proposed Constitutional amendment, a female agricultural worker employed on a farm doing interstate business would fall under the federal minimum wage of $1.30 an hour; one who was employed on a farm doing only intrastate business would be at the mercy of the individual employer.* Such differentials, if they appeared, could go far to keep semiskilled women competitive with the cost of automated labor. This is not to suggest conspiratorial action by management, but just to point out the name of the game, which is profits. In an intricate economy, every action has multiple consequences.

Similarly, new structural realities affect skilled and professional women workers. In the past, as has been indicated, there was a need for numbers of humans to deal with machines. This was the essence of the assembly line, the instrumental bond between proletariat and power tool. Today, human robots are becoming increasingly obsolete. The new proletarian has a Ph.D., for the essence of the cybernetic process is programming, and programming requires know-how. The new labor force is composed of those competent to perform such less structured tasks as are still consigned to the human organism.

From an employer's point of view, it is always advantageous to increase the available pool of that sector of labor in which he is interested, for then he does not have to compete with other employers for personnel. If, in the present stage of production of goods and services, educated people are in demand, women with this kind of background may be welcome. But an increased labor pool also means more people than jobs, converting what might have been a seller's into a buyer's market. This not only widens management's range of choice, but, since competition is a powerful salary depressant, it also tends to cut costs. Moreover, neither the Civil Rights Act of 1964 nor the Equal Rights Amendment, if adopted, would serve as safeguard against the sort of wage shaving

---

*Union contracts, of course, set wages by agreement, but only a small proportion of the female labor force in the United States (one out of seven) is organized.

implied here: the semiskilled worker may be in a "woman's field," the professional worker may be hired at the going (depressed) rate.

From this standpoint, the campaigns of contemporary feminists can become a command performance, if the women are not sophisticated enough to know when they are advancing their own cause, and when they are being co-opted. For it is not sufficient to struggle, however earnestly, in the body of the whale; one must study the anatomy of leviathan.

We come now to the middle distance, the period in the future for which contradictions between the momentum of cybernation and the inertia of cultural design imply chaos. Can such a condition be averted? If people are not to be extruded, and employment is to continue to be the source of function, identity, and income, it will be necessary to press for redirection of focus, for expansion of the economy by programming economic endeavor around critical social needs: helath, education, transport, housing, conservation, ecology. "Most of these activities and institutions are now short-changed. With abundance to support the expanding portion of the population engaged in them, . . . for some time to come, we can be sure, the real work that remains to be done in the world will stave off the specter of universal leisure."[14] In pressing for solutions to their own situation, women must also press for solutions to major social ills. This is necessary not only because women as part of the citizenry are suffering from the consequences of the general social decay, but also because only if such expansion of the economy occurs will there be any hope of their social integration in the old sense, as a work force.*

Finally we come to the long-range projection when, futurists speculate, most humans will no longer be required to toil. In such a civilization, identity would have to be redefined; for if most people are outside production, their identity could no longer have a functional reference point. By the same token, the traditional bond between income and toil would be severed. Human survival could not be suspended from functions that had been phased out. In an economy of plenty, people would have the right to live, not through making a living, but by virtue of being alive. Identity would then have to be derived from individual qualities in the human scale rather than in the operational one.

A new concept not only of man, but of woman, of humans, would come into being. Human extrusion from tasks unworthy of human energy would be seen as a positive mutation — the loss of rote labor, of obligatory toil — as blessing and release. Human identity would then be related to labors of love: to the more subtle tasks of private purpose and social priorities befitting that brave new world. Unemployment in such a context would spell, not catastrophe, but liberation from the bonds of necessity, the prerequisite for the "good life" in

*Such effort is also important as a safeguard against the use of women as a substitute labor reserve. In some parts of the country, it appears that women are becoming primary breadwinners as men are laid off. This usually means a cut in family income. Such patterns of change caricature liberation goals.

the Greek sense. This was the term employed by Aristotle to denote the life of the citizen which "was not merely better, more carefree or nobler than ordinary life, but of altogether different quality. It was 'good' to the extent that by having mastered the necessities of sheer life, by being freed from labor and work, and by overcoming the innate urge of all living creatures for their own survival, it was no longer bound to the biological life process."[15] The Greeks could achieve this state, this ability to embark on the "good life" — perfecting living rather than making a living — because they had slaves. For us, the second industrial revolution means available slaves without guilt.

But none of this can occur without anticipation, without setting a course. And here again it is important for women to know the options and to participate in the decisions. In terms of that challenge, women's relegation to the "humanities" as their academic place puts them at a distinct disadvantage: it is as though they were still attentive only to pictographs in an age of the picture tube. For it has been said, "Our older theories contribute no more to predictive power than astrology." The generalizations they foster are tied essentially to "myth and totem, and consolidated by tradition. . . . The contention that persons ignorant of technology can function in a democracy to any effect when the society is a technological one is dubious. Understanding is not only a prerequisite of control, it *is* control."[16] To be scientifically and economically literate becomes imperative for those seeking to challenge official definitions of reality at times of great structural shifts.

The first feminists, like the second, in seeking a new identity through public function, were also explicitly resisting the prevailing identity imposed by private function; then as now dissenting women had an outsider's perspective on the given. Ellen Key argued for sex freedom and the right to motherhood without matrimony, Charlotte Perkins Gilman lifted the curtain of illusions about the home, exposing the social stunting of the dependent woman specialized to sex and private service, and of the smothered child "permanently injured in character by this lack of one of humanity's most precious rights — privacy." With characteristic acerbity, she summed up the situation: "The home is the cradle of all the virtues, but we are in a stage of social development where we need virtues beyond cradle size."[17] Utopian colonies were founded where marriage was abolished, monogamy was questioned, and children were regarded as the human harvest of the community. But, as with the public goals, the conditions of their time were not consistent with their vision.

By contrast, technology has revolutionized for us every aspect of the given, including the sphere of the private. Fertility choice has changed the equation between woman and her body. Increased survival at both ends of the life span has altered the equilibrium between woman and society. True, vision can transcend structure; Leonardo could conceive of flying machines. But technology is a limiting factor; he could not build them. Implementation of ideas rests upon a scientific base of possibilities. Thus the first feminists could fight their hearts out in favor of voluntary motherhood, but their cause was limited by the involuntary nature of pregnancy. They could insist on sex relationships as peers, but they found themselves to be peers with consequences. They could challenge the definition of woman as breeder but would be treated as heretics so long as babies were needed to balance the death rate — and no other forms of generation had yet been discovered.

The politicians of the period crucified Margaret Sanger in her struggle for birth control. It is not enlightenment that causes their counterparts today to endorse planned parenthood or to launch trial balloons suggesting premiums for small families and penalties for large ones. They are responding to objective conditions. Legalized abortion, too, will come — sooner, perhaps than if women were not actively insisting on it, but it will come — because conditions make it imperative. Even politicians learn, in time, which way the wind blows.

Similarly, the biological revolution that has made it possible to have sex without propagation is beginning to pave the way for propagation without sex. Artificial insemination is already a fact. Other discoveries are on the horizon.

> Hitherto . . . it has been usual for a child to be born of two parents of differing sex, both of whom were alive at the time of his/her conception. Such tedious limitations are rapidly disappearing, with unforeseeable consequences for marriage and the family as we know it. Thanks to techniques for storing the male seed, it is already the case that a child may be conceived long after the death of the father. And a woman might bear a child to her grandfather one day. Indeed, research now in hand may make it possible for a woman to bear a child without male intervention, or even for a child to be born without the comfort of a maternal womb. The parents, if any, may be able to specify the sex of the child in advance, and even change it.[18]

The rage of women comes from the latent contradictions of a new freedom in an old framework. In an epoch of equalization, women are unprepared for the reality level of the power elite in the public sphere, which still perceives them as unpersons. Seeking parity on the basis of performance, they are dismayed to find employers and politicians relating not to particular women, but to the pictures in their heads.[19] In an era of liberation, women are unprepared for the reality level of their partners in the private sphere, who still perceive them as epiphenomena. Seeking free relationships with enlightened men, women are astonished to find that being female still carries penalties, despite the pill; that although patterns have been redefined, women have not. Change, then, in both hemispheres, is accepted as convenience, but there is a reluctance to recognize change in either social or personal life as having a radical character, as implying a comprehensive transformation of the reality level. This resistance continues despite cybernetic and biological events that are redesigning homo sapiens into a new species.

As might be expected, it is easier to change the public than the private reality level. When the nation needed Rosie the Riveter, working women became the new paradigm, utilization of child care centers a patriotic duty. After the war, nobody ever heard of such a thing. But personal patterns are another matter:

once they are internalized, emotions come into play. The young man, whose fancy has been programmed, may not be able to perceive or relate to women beyond the pictures in his head. This limits the range of personalities with whom he can be intimate and often results in the projection of his dream upon a woman he does not recognize and in marriage to a myth. That love which "can become an intensification of seeing, a looking into hidden possibilities" [20] never begins. There is no commitment to a real person; the coming together is symbolic and instrumental. This is perhaps the deepest pain women experience — that they are invisible not only in their public lives, but in their most intimate private ones.

But when the woman is a shadow, the identity of the man is also arrested. Harry Stack Sullivan, who was interested in the impact of cultural forces on personality, believed that apart from personal relations there is no self, that "an individual can be understood only in terms of the social relations that produced him."[21] Other scholars who have explored the concept of identity submit that the "ability to enter into relations of intimacy and mutuality opens the way to experiences in which the self expands beyond its own limitations in depth of feeling, understanding, and insight."[22] They also suggest that without such expansion, there can be no love.

> It takes a certain audacity on the part of the philosopher-psychologist to talk about Love. . . . Love is so much pushed into the background that many people do not believe in the . . . existence of Love, or consider it to be only a comforting illusion of poetry. . . . There is a deeply grained embarrassment or shame even in admitting a sincere yearning for Love. In our present-day culture there is no great difficulty in talking about sexuality, particularly if it is considered as a successful performance. . . . But Love is deeply taboo.
>
> In the transcendence of Love there is no anxiety nor struggle for self-assertion, for in the we-ness the Self is received as a gift of grace.[23]

As I have hinted previously, that "we-ness" is at the mercy of the existential situation, a situation not entirely self-made; it is affected by "the imperial reach of social worlds into the intimacies of our very self."[24] That imbalance, already noted, which pervades the public sphere — of a new technology and an old structure, of unprecedented potential and inherited philosophy — also pervades the private. The conventional young are mated by computer and married into a feudal institution. The radical young dispense with formalities and are betrayed by the fifth column in their heads.

Nor is it sufficient to point to lags. Rather than explain something as a persistence from the past, we ought to ask, counsels C. Wright Mills, why it has persisted. Feminists today address themselves to the social cost of keeping women down. But as I have already suggested, there is also the social context that offers a different account rendered. The domestic orbit in an irrational society, if nothing else is changed, may be a structural imperative even if it can be proved to be an imbecile life style. By the same token, the lag at the personal level, the patterns that tie couples into irrelevant knots, may also have the structural function of keeping the battle lines in the bedroom.* Proceeding by trial and error in private designs for living is a circuitous route to fundamental change, for the critical determinants of destiny occur in the social arena.

> Men are much more than political animals, but there are times when they must be this above all, or else they lose all their other beings. If this is such a time, then reveling in other features of the self may be irresponsibility.[25]

Feminists know much of this. But in mounting their campaigns for change they tend to be more frontal than analytical. Yet it is a truism that historically all effective social changes, revolutionary reconstructions of reality, were guided and strengthened by the mappings and projections, by the unique imaginations and systematic studies of reflective giants: from Plato to Paine, Mazzini to Marx, Garrison to Gandhi. Women must be added to that roster. Agitation at the level of the immediate is only one phase of political motion; it is part of the pressure, but it is no substitute for plan. Emily Green Balch, one of America's Nobel Peace Prize winners, has written

> How far capable of a long plan are we, of dealing with ends that are not obvious, that are intricate and complex and not to be won by booms and cataclysms of effort?[26]

Random passion is no substitute for intellectual rigor. Even the heady experience of coalition must be analyzed. The feminist movement, like all broad efforts, is composed of disparate elements. It is important to know to what extent they can be fused and to what extent they can only come together on special issues.

There are at least three categories, the conservative, the liberal, and the radical, who differ not so much in terms of tactic as in terms of conceptualization and criteria of change. Karl Mannheim has written that for the conservative, utopia is today. To transpose this idea, conservative feminists see little wrong with current institutions beyond the fact that they are excluded from them. The slogan raised is therefore: "Me too!"

Liberals, however, locate their utopia in the future. They conceive of many changes, but their strategy is abstract. They tend to rely on the logic of what should be as the essence of their effort, on language as the ultimate reality. They feel they have completed their task when they have shown what is rational and right. Their campaign cry tends to be: "It isn't fair!"

The utopia of the radical is also in the future, the distinction between radical and liberal being what the term implies, that the former go to the root of social phenomena. They deal not only with what should be but with what is, and why it is. This is, to be sure, also the classical sociological vantage point. Their

---

*This is evident in current dialogue in the black community where men and women confront one another, seeking private definitions of self, unaware that their dilemmas derive from wider issues, that they are the resultant of multiple social elements.

blueprint for tomorrow is drawn in terms of the persistent modalities of today. They deal with real institutions in a real setting and with an evaluation of tendencies toward change. Their slogan is: "Look here!"

In the current movement, these lines are blurred as all questioning women seek to discover one another. One finds, moreover, virtually no radicals in the sense in which I am using the term here. The most militant women cry with the liberals, albeit more forcibly, "It isn't fair!" True, their blueprint for tomorrow is different from that of the liberals, for they insist they want no part of the establishment; but like the liberals, they take few pointer readings in reality.

The imperative that the new women have still to meet is anticipation of the arc of the future and an integration of their goals with its course. Among the futurists this is called scenario writing. Usually women have no part in the process either as writers or as role-players. Just as students of paleolithic man construct patterns of primitive women that are low-browed versions of their own wives camping out, futurists project into the twenty-first century little women with conveniences. Or, among the group that Caroline Bird has termed "The New Masculinists," the projection is in terms of "updating women's traditional role"[27] to include politics, the new stereotype being that women are tender-minded and can bring their special grace* into the public arena to save us all from destruction. This treats modern stratified society as though it were a simple folk culture, run by the influence of psychological states. It is time, perhaps, for women to write scenarios, taking account of variables that men, because of their programmed vision, overlook. In the presence of so compelling a need, I shall venture to begin.

*In the immediate future,* feminists will discover the shape of the phenomenal, factual world and its implications for their goals. This will come about in part because they will develop patterns of consultation with women experts in their own movement, who can project the arc of the future. For, in the language of Karl Mannheim, we cannot calculate a priori what a thing should be like and what it will be like: "We can influence only the general trend of the process of becoming."[28] Only in terms of that general trend can projections, not only of probable, but even of desirable futures be made. And only in terms of such projections will it become clear that the drive to enter the system without modifying it cannot be accomplished. The slogan will then become: divide the available work and cut the working day.† This would make it possible for men and women to share both public and private spheres of living.

---

*Virginia Woolf, reacting to this kind of reasoning, wrote: "But a desire to worship woman as a higher moral influence tends, in real life, to restrict her freedom almost as much as a conviction of her inferiority." Herbert Marder, *Feminism and Art, A Study of Virginia Woolf* (Chicago: University of Chicago Press, 1968), p. 14.

†Such a change would be even more imperative should the conflict in Southeast Asia end, and men presently tied down to military tasks return to the civilian labor force.

Abortion as a legal expedient would be realized, but a new slogan, "Birth control for men," as a more efficient method of fertility choice, would be raised. Shorter hours of toil would mean, in intact families, a division of parental responsibility. But child care centers would still be sought, not as parking places for the offspring of working parents, but as environments for optimum rearing in an interdependent society.

*In the middle distance,* the system would be further modified by a recognition that technology, although its misuse has disfigured human existence, can also, with wisdom, be used to reconstruct it. As intractable social problems became the target, new sources of employment, mainly 'in the public sector, would be developed. Women, along with members of other underprivileged enclaves, would be recruited, with work apportioned in ratio to available persons and hours prorated accordingly. A moratorium on marriage would be sought to separate the strands of love from those of security in the mating bond. New definitions of coupling and uncoupling would be developed, free from concepts of property and possession, for as Justice Holmes wrote, there can be no freedom of contract where there is no equality of status. Nursery schools would become part of the school system just as kindergartens are today. There would be the beginning of an effort to establish standards of parenthood, with the growing realization that good producers do not necessarily function as good rearers. Birth control could occur at the level of insemination either by virtue of individual choice, or as Paul Ehrlich has suggested, through the use of temporary sterilants in reservoirs.

Social blueprints would have an entirely new significance as the magnificent potential for human life came to be more generally perceived. The imaginative qualities of individuals, including those of women, would be newly valued as treasuries of social vision, as survival came to depend on adaptation to unprecedented reality.

*In the long range,* "irreversible movement into a contingent future"[29] would provide the choice, as Buckminster Fuller has phrased it, between Oblivion and Utopia. The oblivion he refers to would result from the misuse of technical skill and its consequence in nuclear death; his utopia would result from the creative use of technology which has made abundance realizable, along with the scuttling of ideas and configurations rooted in an ecology of scarcity. This also implies the end of war, an institution born in scarcity and stemming from the need to compete for finite materials. In time, natural resources will no longer constitute a limiting factor, as synthetics which are almost "no nature and all technology"[30] take their place and as virtually inexhaustible energy sources replace fossil fuels. Struggle in such a context would have no purpose, for the incentive to seek spoils will have disappeared. Toil as human enterprise could be dispensed with, as the need vanishes for human hands and human nervous systems as instruments of survival. The whole shape of existence would be transformed. "Life as an end," is, as Marcuse has observed, "qualitatively different from life as a means."[31] And since "variety and possibility are inherent in the human sensorium,"[32] new personalities would emerge, new identities develop. These would arise untethered to the somatypology of our culture in a definitional field transcending sex or age, color or race.

For competition is the ultimate determinant of the quality of life as we know it, both at the public and at the private level, and possession is the ultimate goal. All our values are enclosed in that reality. "Attitudes evolved in an age of scarcity have led to glorification of accumulation of personal and national wealth . . . until (they have become) the highest imperative of social ethics, . . . the paramount social aim." People vying with people is the very stuff of history, of art, of literature. "The streets and squares of all capitals are dedicated to such national heroes and adorned by their statues; folksongs glorify their deeds; the greatest poems and novels have them as protagonists."[33]

Such a spirit of oppugnancy also pervades the private. Men compete for women, women compete for men, men and women, in the most intimate relations, compete with one another. Even children become symbols of competitive achievement. So profound is this adaptation to marketplace psychology that conflict between opposing forces is interpreted as the essential trigger in human impulse. Freud's entire system of intersexual function is founded in mechanisms of attack and defense, of aggression and submission, of antithetical goals. Relations between man and woman become the battle of the sexes; relations between parents and children are staged in the arena of the Oedipal complex.

Since ideas arise and grow in the enveloping element, such compression of human nature may no longer be the norm when the world of reality is no longer a threat to individual desires, when competition of each against all is no longer an operative necessity. People will then become mutually enhancing, joining with one another for mutual ends. Affection, not possession, will be the social fulcrum, as economic man and biological woman are superseded, as people achieve identity free from function. All will then live, as only some do today, from income. Even honored work will not be the basis of worth or wage. The ability to pay and the capacity to own will no longer be the indicia of power.

Since concepts of flesh and blood derive from impulses of ownership, the family as we know it will also probably fade away. As the great geneticist H. J. Muller has pointed out, "a family life of deep fulfillment can just as well develop where it is realized that the genetic connection lies only in our common humanity."[34] The debate about monogamy will decline as individuals explore their natures to learn where they belong in the continuum between fidelity and license. I suspect there will be experimentation in youth, exclusive relationships after the discovery of identity — for there is a rare pleasure in multidimensional understanding and in mutual memory — and uncelibate singleness in later years because of uneven decline.* For, as a consequence of the "revolutionary change in man's relationship to nature, we can proceed to the necessary revisions in our relationships with one another." These will not occur only in private life since "one of the aspirations that now becomes feasible . . . is self-government."[35] With toil obsolete, all can become citizens in the Greek sense, addressing themselves passionately to the unrealized dreams of the democratic process.

Starting out with women, I have reached utopia. And yet it is this vision that is the critical determinant of their sociological destiny. Inherited dimentions of reality have become illusions. Fantastic utopias have become realistic projections. The changing scale and scope of our lives means that "the world alters as we walk on it."[36] The search for new directions must not be hobbled by old doctrines: we dare not cripple our imaginations by factors of fixity. A mighty cultural revolution waits in the wings.

*Unless the biological revolution solves the problems of disease and degeneration.

# NOTES

## Introduction

1. *Mirror for Man* (Greenwich, Conn.: Fawcett Publications, Inc., [Premier Books], 1963), p. 26.

## Chapter 1   The Traditional Approach

1. Xenophon, *Oeconomicus,* quoted in John Langdon-Davies, *A Short History of Women* (New York: The Literary Guild, 1927), p. 159.

2. Hannah More, quoted in Irene Clephane, *Towards Sexual Freedom* (London: Lane, 1935) and cited by Viola Klein, *The Feminine Character* (New York: International Universities Press, 1949), p. 24.

3. Mrs. A. J. Graves, *Woman in America* (New York: Harper and Bros., 1858), quoted in S. D. Schmulhausen and V. F. Calverton (eds.), *Woman's Coming of Age* (New York: Horace Liveright, 1931), p. xv.

4. Ralph S. Banay, *Life,* June 22, 1947, p. 112.

5. Arthur Mandy, quoted by Alton L. Blakeslee, "Over-Aggressive Wives Can Spoil Marriage, Psychiatrist Declares," *Los Angeles Times,* March 23, 1958.

6. Richard Centers, quoted in "Women's Careers Held Leading to Confusion," *Los Angeles Times,* May 2, 1955.

7. Philip Wyle, *Generation of Vipers* (New York: Farrar and Rinehart, 1942), p. 188.

8. Maurice E. Linden, quoted by Patricia McCormack, "Matriarchy Ruins Family Life, Nations," *Los Angeles Times,* November 10, 1960.

9. Joseph C. Rheingold, *The Fear of Being a Woman,* quoted by Robert R. Kirsch, *Los Angeles Times,* August 2, 1964.

10. Hal Borland, quoted by Eve Merriam, "Are Housewives Necessary," *The Nation,* January 31, 1959.

11. Russell Caldwell, *Los Angeles Times,* November 11, 1959.

12. John A. Schindler, *Woman's Guide to Better Living 52 Weeks a Year* (Englewood Cliffs, N. J.: Prentice-Hall, 1957), p. 155.

13. Helen Deutsch, *The Psychology of Woman,* 2 vols. (New York: Grune and Stratton, 1944), vol. I, p. 290 et seq.

14. Theodore Reik, as quoted in *This Week* magazine, February 5, 1961.

15. Joseph François Lafitau, *Moeurs des sauvages amériquains comparés aux moeurs des premiers temps,* 2 vols. (Paris: 1724), vol. I, p. 70, quoted in Helen Diner, *Mothers and Amazons,* ed. and trans. by John Phillip Lundin (New York: The Julian Press, 1965), p. 181.

16. Lucien Carr, "The Social and Political Position of Women among the Huron-Iroquois Tribes," *Sixteenth Annual Report of the Peabody Museum of Archaelogy and Ethnology* (Cambridge, Mass.: 1883), p. 211, as cited by Robert Briffault, *The Mothers,* 3 vols. (New York: Macmillan, 1927), vol. I, p. 317.

17. Margaret Mead, quoted in Klein, *Feminine Character,* p. 130.

18. Klein, *Feminine Character,* p. 130.

19. Herodotus, *Historiae,* ii, 35, The Loeb Classical Library, trans. A. D. Godley, 4 vols. (New York: Putnam, 1931), vol. I, p. 317.

20. Diodorus Siculus, *Bibliotheca historica,* I, 27, The Loeb Classical Library, trans. C. H. Oldfather, 10 vols. (New York: Putnam, 1933), vol. I, p. 87.

21. George Moritz Ebers, *Aegyptische Studien,* quoted by Mathias and Mathilde

124

Vaerting, *The Dominant Sex,* trans. by Eden and Cedar Paul (New York: George H. Doran, 1923), p. 252.

22. W. Max Müller, *Die liebespoesie der alten Aegypter* (Leipzig: 1899), p. 6, quoted by Robert Briffault, *The Mothers,* vol. I, p. 386.

23. Alice Clark, *Working Life of Women in the Seventeenth Century* (London: Routledge, 1919), p. 8.

24. Eleanor Flexner, *Century of Struggle* (Cambridge, Mass.: Belknap Press of Harvard University Press, 1959), p. 6.

25. *Ibid.,* p. 18.

26. *Ibid.,* p. 54.

27. Eugene B. Baron, quoted by Patricia McCormack, "Male Legion's Goal: Women in Home," *Los Angeles Times,* July 20, 1961.

28. Alice Rossi, "Equality Between the Sexes," in "The Woman in America," *Daedalus, Journal of the American Academy of Arts and Sciences* (Spring 1964), p. 648 fn.

29. Sir Thomas More, *Utopia* (London: Dent, 1910), p. 63.

## Chapter 2   The Challenging View

1. Maria Weston Chapman, "The Times That Try Men's Souls," quoted in Eleanor Flexner, *Century of Struggle* (Cambridge, Mass.: Belknap Press of Harvard University Press, 1959), p. 48.

2. Olive Schreiner, *Woman and Labor* (New York: Stokes, 1911), p. 27.

3. Aristophanes, *Lysistrata,* quoted by G. Lowes Dickinson, "The Greek View of Women," in *The Woman Question,* ed. by T. R. Smith (New York: Boni and Liveright, 1918), pp. 7–8.

4. Hortensia, quoted by Alice Ames Winter, *The Heritage of Women* (New York: Minto, 1927), p. 53.

5. Lucy Stone, quoted in Flexner, *Century of Struggle,* p. 42.

6. Betty Friedan, *The Feminine Mystique* (New York: Norton, 1963), note 3, ch. 6, p. 388.

7. *Report of the President's Commission on the Status of Women, American Women,* 1963 (Washington, D.C.: U.S. Government Printing Office, 1963), (0-693-825), p. 51.

8. Charles Brockden Brown, *Alcuin: A Dialogue on the Rights of Women,* quoted in Bernard Smith (ed.), *The Democratic Spirit* (New York: Knopf, 1941), p. 172. (The original work appeared in 1793.)

9. Helen Rosenan as quoted in Klein, *Feminine Character,* p. 181.

10. Sarah Grimké, as quoted in Flexner, *Century of Struggle,* p. 53.

11. *Report of the President's Commission on the Status of Women,* p. 28.

12. Winifred Holtby, *Women* (London: Lane, 1934), p. 146.

13. Alice Rossi, "Equality Between the Sexes," *Daedalus, Journal of the American Academy of Arts and Sciences* (Spring 1964), pp. 607–652.

14. Judith Murray, (pseud., Constantia) "The Equality of the Sexes," *Massachusetts Magazine,* 1790, quoted in Flexner, *Century of Struggle,* p. 16.

15. Socrates, quoted in Winter, *Heritage of Women,* p. 39.

16. Stendahl (Henry Beyle), "On the Education of Women," in Smith (ed.), *The Woman Question,* p. 92.

17. Ida Alexa Ross Wylie, "The Little Woman," *Harper's,* vol. 191 (November 1945); pp. 407–408.

18. Alice Rossi, "Equality Between the Sexes," p. 622.

19. Donald N. Michael, *Cybernation: The Silent Conquest,* A Report to the Center of the Study of Democratic Institutions (Santa Barbara, Calif., 1962), p. 44.

20. Robert M. Hutchins, "What Kind of World," *Los Angeles Times,* April 19, 1963.

## Chapter 3    The Masculine Mystique

1. Myron Brenton, *The American Male* (New York: Coward-McCann, 1966), p. 194.

2. *Ibid.,* p. 53.

3. Ogden Nash, "It's About Time," *Marriage Lines* (Boston: Little Brown, 1964), p. 84.

4. Brenton, *The American Male,* p. 60.

5. Richard Yates, *Revolutionary Road* (Boston: Little, Brown, 1961), p. 120.

6. Fritz Pappenheim, *The Alienation of Modern Man* (New York: Monthly Review Press, 1959), p. 67.

7. Aldous Huxley, *Point Counter Point* (New York: Harper and Bros., 1928); see Philip Quarles' Notebook, p. 295.

8. Ernest Dichter, quoted in "The Playboy Panel: The Womanization of America," *Playboy,* vol. 9 (June 1962), p. 48.

9. Brenton, *The American Male,* p. 97.

10. *Ibid.,* quoting Paul Vaharnian, p. 39.

11. Morton M. Hunt, *The Natural History of Love* (New York: Knopf, 1959), p. 382.

12. Hans Gerth and C. Wright Mills, *Character and Social Structure* (New York: Harcourt, Brace, 1964), p. 480.

13. Russel V. Lee, "The Agony of Conforming: The Male Parent," in Seymour Farber, Piero Mustacchi, and Roger H. L. Wilson (eds.), *Man and Civilization: The Family's Search for Survival* (New York: McGraw-Hill, 1965), p. 134.

14. P. Chombart de Lauwe, Introduction to "Images of Women in Society," *International Social Science Journal,* UNESCO, vol. XIV, no. 1 (1962), p. 7.

15. Gerth and Mills, *Character and Social Structure,* p. 480.

16. Rainer Maria Rilke, *Letters to a Young Poet,* trans. by M. D. Herter (New York: Norton, 1934), p. 38.

## Chapter 4    Marriage à la Mode

1. Margaret Mead, *Male and Female* (New York: Morrow, 1949), p. 281.

2. Olive Schreiner, *Woman and Labor* (New York: Stokes, 1911), p. 258.

3. Alice Rossi, "Equality Between the Sexes," in "The Woman in America," *Daedalus, Journal of the American Academy of Arts and Sciences* (Spring 1964), p. 611.

4. *Ibid.,* p. 614.

5. William S. White, "President, Congress Sing Close Harmony," *Los Angeles Times,* March 9, 1965.

6. *Reports:* The State Bar of California, Convention Issue (August-September, 1964).

7. Lee Rainwater et al., *Workingman's Wife* (New York: Oceana, 1959), pp. 70, 71, 86.

8. William H. Whyte, Jr., "Corporation and the Wife," *Fortune,* vol. 44 (November 1951), p. 111, quoting William Given, chairman of American Brake Shoe Company.

9. Mildred Savage, *In Vivo* (New York: Simon and Schuster, 1964), pp. 312, 158, 159.

10. Gene Blake, "Executive May Deduct Wife's Travel Expenses," *Los Angeles Times,* July 21, 1969.

11. Alexis de Tocqueville, *Democracy in America* (New York: Harper and Row, 1965). First published in 1835–1839.

12. May Sarton, *The Small Room* (New York: Norton, 1961), p. 63.

13. Olive Schreiner, *The Story of an African Farm,* first published in 1833, as quoted by Klein, *Feminine Character,* p. 20.

14. This phrase is from Virginia Woolf.

## Chapter 5    Law the Laggard

1. William Blackstone, *Commentaries on the Law of England* (1765–69), vol. I., pp. 442–444.

2. Eleanor Flexner, *Century of Struggle* (Cambridge, Mass.: Belknap Press of Harvard University Press, 1959), p. 64.

3. *Report of the President's Commission on the Status of Women, American Women,* 1963 (Washington, D.C.: U.S. Government Printing Office, 1963), (0-693-825), p. 47.

4. I Black. Com. 442-444.

5. *Report of the President's Commission on the Status of Women,* p. 48

6. *Ibid.*

7. *Report of a Conference on the Legal Status of Married Women* presented by the National Association of Women Lawyers, Northeastern Region, (October 1965).

8. Marie W. Kargman, as reported in *The Patriot Ledger* (Mass.), Oct. 8, 1965, p. 10.

9. Sir Jocelyn Simon, address, National Council of Civil Liberties, as reported in *Women* (London), May 1965, p. 21.

10. Jane Austen, *Pride and Prejudice* (New York: Dodd, Mead, 1945), p. 87. First published in 1813.

11. *Code of Laws,* RSFSR, governing "Marriage, the Family and Guardianship," Art. 9, as quoted by Grigory Sverdlov, *Marriage and Family in the USSR* (Moscow: Foreign Languages Publishing House, 1956), p. 48.

12. *Family and Custody Code,* Title I, Part 2, Art. 27, adopted February 25, 1964, *Journal of Law of the Polish People's Republic,* No. 9, Warsaw, March 5, 1964.

13. I Black. Com. 440–441.

14. Kerr v. Kerr, Appellate Division of the Supreme Court of New York, 1909. 134 App. Div. 141.

15. Grigory Sverdlov, *Marriage and the Family,* p. 37.

16. *Family and Custody Code,* Title I, Part 4, Art. 56, Para. 1.

17. Robert Sinheimer, "The End of the Beginning," *Bulletin of the Atomic Scientists,* vol. 23 (February 1967), p. 12.

## Chapter 6    A House Is Not a Homestead

1. Margaret Mead, *Male and Female* (New York: Morrow, 1949), p. 246.

2. Hazel Kyrk, *The Family in the American Economy* (Chicago: University of Chicago Press, 1953), pp. 6–7.

3. "Marriage," *Encyclopedia Brittanica,* 14th edition, vol. XIV, p. 943.

4. Reuben Hill, "The Changing American Family," *The Social Welfare Forum,* 1957, Official Proceedings of the National Conference on Social Welfare (New York: Columbia University Press for the National Conference on Social Welfare, 1957), p. 69.

5. Margaret Mead, *Male and Female,* pp. 257–258.

6. Paul Popenoe, *Family Life,* American Institute of Family Relations, April 1959.

7. *Hired Farm Workers in the United States,* BES Series, Washington, D.C., U.S. Dept. of Labor, Employment Security Bureau (June 1961).

8. "Big Trouble in Our City Schools," *Look,* September 26, 1961.

9. *Census Bureau Survey,* May 1958, as reported in *Child Care Arrangements of Full-Time Mothers,* Children's Bureau Publication 378, Washington, D.C., U.S. Government Printing Office, 1959.

10. *Womanpower,* National Manpower Council (New York: Columbia University Press, 1957), p. 350.

11. Eveline M. Burns, *Social Security and Public Policy* (New York: McGraw-Hill, 1956), p. 4.

12. *Womanpower,* p. 350.

## *Chapter 7    In the Marketplace*

1. Olive Schreiner, *Woman and Labor* (New York: Stokes, 1911), p. 65.

2. Eleanor Flexner, *Century of Struggle* (Cambridge, Mass.: Belknap Press of Harvard University Press, 1959), p. 201.

3. Elizabeth Barrett Browning, "Aurora Leigh," book one, line 289, in *The Complete Poetical Works of Mrs. Browning* (Boston: Houghton Mifflin, 1900), p. 258.

4. Leonora M. Barry, quoted in Flexner, *Century of Struggle,* p. 200.

5. *1969 Handbook on Women Workers,* Women's Bureau of the U.S. Department of Labor (Washington, D.C., U.S. Government Printing Office, 1969), p. 12. (Bull. 294).

6. George Eliot, *Felix Holt, The Radical* (London: Panther, 1965), p. 56.

7. *Handbook on Women Workers,* p. 7.

8. *1965 Handbook on Women Workers,* Women's Bureau of the U.S. Department of Labor (Washington, D.C., U.S. Government Printing Office, 1965), p. 5. (Bull. 290).

9. Frieda Miller, "Who Works, Where, and Why," in *Report on 1948 Women's Bureau Conference,* U.S. Department of Labor (Washington, D.C.: U.S. Government Printing Office), p. 17. (Bull. 224).

10. August Bebel, *Women and Socialism* (New York: Socialist Literature Co., 1910), fn. p. 128.

11. Andrew Sinclair, *The Better Half* (New York: Harper & Row, 1965), p. 347.

12. *Work in the Lives of Married Women,* National Manpower Council (New York: Columbia University Press, 1958), p. 70.

13. Dr. R. H. Davis, of Systems Development Corp., as quoted in an article by Irving S. Bengelsdorf, "Man Faces Computers with Rising Distrust," *Los Angeles Times,* May 24, 1965.

14. Robert M. Hutchins, "Are We Educating Our Children for the Wrong Future?" *The Saturday Review,* vol. 48 (September 11, 1965), p. 67.

## *Chapter 8    The Pearl in the Apron Pocket*

1. Lynn White, quoted in Mirra Komarovsky, *Women in the Modern World* (Boston: Little, Brown, 1953), pp. 7–8.

2. Charlotte Perkins Gilman, *Woman and Economics* (Boston: Small, Maynard, 1898), p. 53.

3. Karl Mannheim, *Systematic Sociology* (New York: Grove Press, 1957), p. 30.

4. Robert Theobald, "Education for a New Time," in *Journal,* United Church of Christ—Council for Higher Education (March 1967), p. 4.

5. Henry David Thoreau, quoted in Loren Eiseley, *The Mind as Nature* (New York: Harper & Row, 1962), pp. 41–2.

6. Eiseley, *Mind as Nature,* p. 51.

## *Prelude to Part Two*

1. James Hutton, quoted in Loren Eiseley, *The Firmament of Time* (New York: Atheneum, 1966), p. 25.

2. Walter Lippmann, *Public Opinion* (New York: Macmillan, 1922), p. 27.

3. *Ibid.,* p. 45.

4. Dorothy Lee, *Freedom and Culture* (Englewood Cliffs, N.J.: Prentice-Hall, 1959), p. 105.

5. Bertolt Brecht, *Schriftzen zum Theater* (Berlin and Frankfurt: Suhrkamp, 1957), pp. 76, 63.

## *Chapter 9    Remembrance of Things Past*

1. Karl Mannheim, *Ideology and Utopia* (New York: Harcourt, Brace, 1936), p. 4.

2. Hans Gerth and C. Wright Mills, *Character and Social Structure* (New York: Harcourt, Brace, 1964), p. 26.

3. *Ibid.*

4. George Thomson, *Studies in Ancient Greek Society: The Prehistoric Aegean* (New York: International Publishers, 1949), p. 182.

5. *Ibid.* fn. 163, citing Diodorus Siculus, 3. 52.

6. Matthew Paris, *Chronica Magna (Chronicles and Memorials of Great Britain and Ireland)*, edited by S. Henry Richards Luard, 7 vols. (London, 1872–83) vol. IV, p. 77, cited by Robert Briffault, *The Mothers*, 3 vols. (New York: Macmillan, 1927), vol. I., p. 455.

7. Briffault, *The Mothers*, vol. I, pp. 457–458, cites these sources. For the Valkyries: K. Von von Müllenhoff, *Deutsche Altertumskunde*, 5 vols. (Berlin, 1883–1900), vol. IV, p. 205. For the Red Maiden: Knut Gjerset, *History of the Norwegian Peoples*, 2 vols. (New York, 1915), vol. I, p. 76. For the Celts: Douglas Hyde, *A Literary History of Ireland* (London, 1899), p. 234; and J. A. MacCulloch, *The Religion of the Ancient Celts* (Edinburgh, 1911), p. 72. For Boadicea: Xiphilinus, Epitome of Dio Cassius, *Histor. Roman.*, lxii. 6. Ed. Reimari (Hamburgi, 1752).

8. Briffault, *The Mothers*, vol. I, pp. 454–455, cites for the Arabs: R. Geyer, "Die arabische Frauen in der Schlacht," *Mitteilungen der anthropologische Gesellschaft* (Wien, 1909), 39, pp. 149 et seq.; and for the other locales: John Duncan, *Travels in Western Africa in 1845 & 1846*, 2 vols. (London, 1847), vol. I, p. 240; H. Schaafhausen, *Anthropologischen Studien* (Bonn, 1885), p. 661; and H. Mouhot, *"Voyage dans les royaumes de Siam, Cambodge, de Laos,"* Le Tour du Monde (Paris, 1863), p. 238.

9. Pietro Martire in G. B. Ramusio, *Navigationi et Viaggi* (Venetia, 1559), vol. III, fol. 28, cited by Briffault, *The Mothers*, vol. I, p. 453.

10. Stephen Powers, *Tribes of California, U. S. Geographical and Geological Survey of the Rocky Mountain Region. Contributions to North American Ethnology* (Washington, 1877), vol. III, p. 248, cited by Briffault, *The Mothers*, vol. I, p. 452.

11. A. H. Sayce, *The Religion of Ancient Egypt and Babylonia* (Edinburgh, 1902), pp. 455, 466, cited by Briffault, *The Mothers*, vol. II, p. 515.

12. Briffault, *The Mothers*, vol. II, p. 515.

13. Briffault, *The Mothers*, vol. II, pp. 518–519, cites J. Hunter, *Memoirs of a Captivity among the Indians*, p. 273; and H. J. Rink, *Tales and Traditions of the Eskimos, with Sketch of their habits, religion, language and other peculiarities.* Transl. (Edinburgh, London: 1875), pp. 42, 53, 58.

14. D. G. Brinton, *Nagualism. A study in Native American Folklore and History* (Philadelphia, 1894), p. 33, cited by Briffault, vol. II, p. 522.

15. Sir C. J. Lyall, in P. R. T. Gurdon, *The Khasis* (London, 1907), p. xxiv, cited by Briffault, vol. II, p. 520.

16. Joseph McCabe, "How Christianity Has Treated Women," in S. D. Schmalhausen and V. F. Calverton (eds.), *Woman's Coming of Age* (New York: Horace Liveright, 1931), p. 51.

17. Claudian, in *Eutropius*, 1.820: "Sabaeis imperat his sexus, reginarumque sub armis barbariae magna pars jacet." The Loeb Classical Library, trans. Maurice Platinauer, 2 vols. (New York: Putnam, 1922), vol. I, p. 163.

18. Plutarch, *Lycurgus*, xiv, *and Agis*, vi, cited by Briffault, *The Mothers*, vol. II, p. 400.

19. Helen Diner, *Mothers and Amazons*, ed. and trans. by John Philip Lundin (New York: Julian Press, 1965), 253.

20. George Thomson, *Ancient Greek Society*, p. 156.

21. Homer's *Odyssey*, translated by H. B. Cotterill (London: George G. Harrap, 1911), pp. 275–276, Book XX, lines 106–119.

22. Sojourner Truth, quoted in Eleanor Flexner, *Century of Struggle* (Cambridge, Mass: Belknap Press of Harvard University Press, 1959), p. 91.

23. *The Rig-Veda*, auth. trans. by Adolf Kaegi, with additions to the notes by R. Arrowsmith (Boston: Ginn, 1886), 352, p. 75, citing 10, 27, 12: "To how many a

maiden does the wooer, who desires to become her husband, show affection for the
sake of her admirable treasures . . ."

24. G. W. Freytag, *Arabum Proverbia,* 2 vols. (Bonn, 1838–43), vol. I, p. 498;
W. Robertson Smith, *Kinship and Marriage in Early Arabia,* edited by S. A. Cook
(London, 1903), p. 116, cited by Briffault, *The Mothers,* vol. I, p. 375.

25. W. M. Flinders Petrie, *Social Life in Ancient Egypt* (London, Constable, 1924),
pp. 73-74; Aristotle, *Politic,* viii, 6. 2. 3. The Loeb Classical Library, trans. H. Rack-
ham (New York: Putnam, 1932), p. 139.

26. C. J. Lyall in P. R. T. Gurdon, *The Khasis* (London, 1914), pp. xix-xx, cited by
Thomson, *Studies in Ancient Greek Society,* p. 152.

27. Katherine Luomala, *Navaho Life of Yesterday and Today* (Berkeley, Calif.:
U.S. Department of Interior, National Park Service, 1938), p. 62.

28. A. L. Kroeber, "Zuni Kin and Clan," *Anthropological Papers of the American
Museum of Natural History* (New York, 1927), xviii, part ii, p. 47.

29. J. G. E. Hechewelder, *Memoirs of the Historical Society in Pennsylvania*
(Philadelphia, 1876), vol. XII, p. 158.

30. John H. Weeks, "Anthropological Notes on the Bangola of the Upper Congo
River," *Journal of the Royal Anthropological Institute* (London, 1909–1910), XXXIX,
xl, p. 118. "If a woman sold anything from her garden the money was hers, and her
husband had no claim upon it; he might borrow it, but he would have to pay it back
like a loan from an outsider."

31. H. H. Bancroft, *The Native Races of the Pacific States,* 5 vols. (New York,
1875–76), vol. III, p. 145, cited by Briffault, *The Mothers,* vol. I, p. 485.

32. *The Book of Ser Marco Polo,* edited by Col. Henry Yule, 2 vols. (London:
John Murray, 1903), vol. I, p. 252.

33. Elise Boulding, "Dissertation Summary: The Effects of Industrialization on the
Participation of Women in Society," Ann Arbor: The University of Michigan, Ph.D.
dissertation, 1969, p. 9, citing Polly Hill, "A Plea for Indigenous Economics: The
West African Example," *Economic Development and Cultural Change,* vol. 15, no. 1
(October 1966), p. 17.

34. Alice Clark, *Working Life of Women in the Seventeenth Century* (London:
Routledge, 1919), p. 12.

35. Robert Briffault, "The Evolution of Woman," in Schmalhausen and Calverton
(eds.), *Woman's Coming of Age,* p. 17.

36. Mary R. Beard, *Woman as a Force in History* (New York: Macmillan, 1946),
pp. 219–20.

37. Evgeni Zamyatim, "On Literature, Revolution, and Entropy," in Patricia Blake
and Max Haywards (eds.), *Dissonant Voices in Soviet Literature* (New York:
Pantheon, 1962), p. 14.

## Chapter 10   The Living Fossil

1. Alfred North Whitehead, *Science and the Modern World* (New York: Macmillan, 1949), p. 71.

2. Walter Goldschmidt in a letter to the *New York Review of Books,* January
26, 1967.

3. Frederick S. Hulse, *The Human Species: An Introduction to Physical Anthropology* (New York: Random House, 1965), p. 174.

4. *Ibid.,* p. 331.

5. Roy G. D'Andrade, "Sex Differences and Cultural Institutions," in Eleanor E.
Maccoby (ed.), *The Development of Sex Differences* (Stanford: Stanford University
Press, 1966), p. 175.

6. Gustav Fritsch, *Die Eingeborenen Süd-Afrika's* (Breslau: 1872), cited by Robert Briffault, *The Mothers,* 3 vols. (New York: Macmillan, 1927), vol. I, p. 443.

7. Alfred Burdon Ellis, *The Ewe-speaking Peoples of the Slave Coast of West Africa* (London, 1890), partly adopting the words of Burton, cited by Briffault, *The Mothers,* vol. I, p. 443.

8. Stephen Powers, *Tribes of California, United States Geographical and Geological Survey of the Rocky Mountain Region. Contributions to North American Ethnology,* vol. iii (Washington, 1877), cited by Briffault, *The Mothers,* p. 444.

9. Carleton S. Coon, *The Origin of Races* (New York: Knopf, 1962), p. 26.

10. R. C. Phillips, "The Lower Congo, a Sociological Study," *Journal of the Anthropological Institute,* vol. xvii (London, 1888); and J. Hutchinson, "The Tehuelche Indians of Patagonia," *Transactions of the Ethnological Society,* vol. vii (London, 1869), both cited by Briffault, *The Mothers,* vol. I, pp. 446–447.

11. James F. Downs and Hermann K. Bleibtreu, *Human Variation: An Introduction to Physical Anthropology* (Beverly Hills, Calif.: Glencoe Press of the Macmillan Co., 1969), p. 205.

12. Stanley M. Garu, "Cultural Factors Affecting the Study of Human Biology," in Yehudi A. Cohen (ed.), *Man in Adaptation, The Biosocial Background* (Chicago: Aldine • Atherton, 1968), pp. 52–53.

13. D'Andrade, "Sex Differences and Cultural Institutions," in Maccoby (ed.), *Development of Sex Differences,* p. 175.

14. Edward S. Curtis, *The North American Indian,* 20 vols. (Cambridge, Mass.: University Press, 1909), vol. IV, p. 3.

15. Sir Richard F. Burton, *First Footsteps in East Africa* (London, 1856), cited in Briffault, *The Mothers,* vol. I, p. 443.

16. Quoted in Frederick Webb Hodge (ed.), *Handbook of American Indians, North of Mexico* (Washington, D. C.: Smithsonian Institution, Bureau of Ethnology, 1912), part 2, p. 969.

17. W. Joest, "Beiträge zur Kenntniss der Eingebornen der Inseln Formosa und Ceram," *Verhandlungen der Berliner Gesellschaft für Anthropologie* (Berlin, 1882), cited by Briffault, *The Mothers,* vol. I, p. 445.

18. D'Andrade, "Sex Differences and Cultural Institutions," in Maccoby (ed.), *Development of Sex Differences,* p. 175.

19. Clara Thompson, "Femininity," in Albert Ellis and Albert Abarbanel (eds.), *The Encyclopedia of Sexual Behavior* (New York: Hawthorne, 1961), p. 422.

20. Lester F. Ward, *Pure Sociology,* 2nd ed. (New York: Macmillan, 1916), p. 372.

21. Amram Scheinfeld, *Women and Men* (London: Chatto and Windus, 1947), p. 125.

22. Grantly Dick Read, *No Time For Fear* (New York: Harper, 1955), p. 143.

23. Jane Swisshelm, *Letters to Country Girls* (New York, 1853), cited by Eleanor Flexner, *Century of Struggle* (Cambridge, Mass.: Belknap Press of Harvard University Press, 1959), pp. 113–114.

24. Edmund W. Overstreet, "The Biological Makeup of Woman," in Seymour M. Farber and Roger H. J. Wilson (eds.), *The Potential of Woman* (New York: McGraw-Hill, 1963), pp. 19–20.

25. Alfred North Whitehead, *Science in the Modern World* (New York: Macmillan, 1949), pp. 26–27.

26. Ruth Benedict, *Patterns of Culture* (New York: Penguin Books, 1946), p. 2. (First published 1934.)

27. Muller v. Oregon, 208 U.S. 412, 52 LAW. ED. 551, 28 SUP. CT. REP. 324 (1908).

28. Bradwell v. Illinois, 83 U.S. 130, 21 LAW. ED. 442 (1873).

29. Alexis de Tocqueville, *Democracy in America* (New York: Harper & Row, 1965), cited in Flexner, *Century of Struggle,* pp. 6–7.

30. E. Sidney Hartland, *Matrilineal Kinship and the Question of its Priority,* Memoirs of the American Anthropologic Association (Lancaster, Pa.: The New Era Printing Company, Jan.-March, 1917), vol. IV, no. 1, p. 13.

31. Morton M. Hunt, "The Male Revolt," in Farber and Wilson (eds.), *Potential of Woman,* p. 264.

32. Margaret Mead, *Male and Female* (New York: Dell, 1968), p. 229.

33. Ashley Montagu, *The Natural Superiority of Women*, rev. ed. (New York: Macmillan, 1968), p. 17.

34. Thompson, "Femininity," in Ellis and Abarbanel (eds.), *The Encyclopedia of Sexual Behavior*, p. 423.

35. John P. Harrington, *A New Original Version of Boscana's Historical Account of the San Juan Capistrano Indians of Southern California* (Washington, D.C.: The Smithsonian Institution, 1934), p. 30.

36. Julian Huxley in a letter to the *London Times*, quoted by Ward, *Pure Sociology*, p. 371.

37. Overstreet, "The Biological Makeup of Woman," in Farber and Wilson (eds.), *Potential of Woman*, p. 22.

38. Jean Jacques Rousseau, *Discourse on Political Economy*, quoted by Elizabeth Mann Borgese, *Ascent of Woman* (New York: George Braziller, 1963), p. 142.

39. George Thomson, *Studies in Ancient Greek Society* (New York: International Publishers, 1949), p. 93. Citing Aulus Gellius, 10. 23.

40. Aeschylus, *The Eumenides* in the *Oresteia*, as quoted by August Bebel, *Woman and Socialism* (New York: Socialist Literature Co., 1910), trans. Meta L. Stern, p. 36. The same passage, lines 558–666, appears in a translation by Richard Lattimore (Chicago: University of Chicago Press, 1953), p. 158, lines 558–666.

41. James Campbell, Introduction to Helen Diner, *Mothers and Amazons,* ed. and trans. by John Philip Lundin (New York: The Julian Press, 1965), p. x.

42. James Donaldson, *Woman: Her Position and Influence in Ancient Greece and Rome, and among the Early Christians* (London: Longmans, Green, 1907), p. 183, citing *Metaphrasis in Ecclesiasten*, c. 7, 28.

43. *Ibid.,* p. 182, citing Tertullian, "De Cultu Feminarum," 1, I.

44. Whitehead, *Science and the Modern World,* p. 11.

45. Jacob Bronowski, *The Common Sense of Science* (Cambridge, Mass.: Harvard University Press, 1951), p. 134.

## Chapter 11    Portrait of a Lady

1. The phrase is Paul Goodman's, used in another connection.

2. Aristotle, *De animalis historia,* quoted by Klein, *Feminine Character,* p. 168.

3. Martin Luther, *Table Talk,* first published in 1566, ed. and trans. by William Hazlitt (London, 1884), pp. 299–300.

4. Havelock Ellis, *Man and Woman,* pp. 407–408, quoted by Klein, *Feminine Character,* p. 47.

5. Virginia Woolf, *A Room of One's Own* (New York: Harcourt, Brace, 1929), p. 143.

6. Aristotle, *De generatione animalium,* quoted by Klein, *Feminine Character,* p. 169; and *Selections,* W. D. Ross (ed.) (New York: Scribner's, 1927, 1938), pp. 194, 195.

7. Sigmund Freud, *The Psychology of Woman,* p. 160, quoted by Klein, *Feminine Character,* p. 73.

8. Jean Izoulet, *La Cité Moderne, métaphysique de la sociologie,* quoted from Cath. van Tussenbroek, "Over de Aequivalentie van Man en Vrouw" (Amsterdam, 1898), quoted by Klein, *Feminine Character,* p. 169.

9. Erich Fromm, *The Art of Loving* (New York: Harper, 1956), p. 39.

10. Robert Briffault, *The Mothers,* abridged ed. (New York: Grosset & Dunlap, Universal Library, 1963), p. 431.

11. Frederick Nietzsche, quoted by Klein, *Feminine Character,* p. 169.

12. Samuel Johnson, quoted by Virginia Woolf, *A Room of One's Own,* p. 94.

13. Oscar Browning, quoted by Virginia Woolf, *ibid.,* pp. 92 – 93.

14. Margaret Mead, *Sex and Temperament in Three Primitive Societies* (London: Routledge, 1935), pp. xix-xx.

15. Hans Gerth and C. Wright Mills, *Character and Social Structure* (New York:

Harcourt, Brace, 1964), p. 40.

16. Fredericks S. Hulse, *The Human Species* (New York: Random House, 1965), p. 466.

17. *Ibid.,* p. 461.

18. Marshall D. Sahlins, "The Origin of Society," *The Scientific American,* vol. 203, (September 1960), p. 80.

19. Naomi Weisstein, "Kinde, Kuche, Kirche as Scientific Law," *Women,* vol. 1, no. 1, p. 19, citing Schacter and Singer (1962).

20. Eleanor E. Maccoby, "Sex Differences in Intellectual Functioning," in E. Maccoby (ed.), *The Development of Sex Differences,* (Stanford: Stanford University Press, 1966), pp. 49 – 50.

21. John L. Hampson, "Determinants of Psycho-sexual Orientation," in Frank A. Beach (ed.), *Sex and Behavior* (New York: Wiley, 1965), p. 115.

22. *Ibid.,* p. 125.

23. Kuznets and McNemar (1940, p. 217), quoted by Edwin C. Lewis, *Developing Woman's Potential* (Ames: Iowa State University Press, 1968), p. 43.

24. E. Maccoby, "Sex Differences in Intellectual Functioning," in *Development of Sex Differences,* p. 45.

25. *Ibid.,* p. 31.

26. Lewis, *Developing Woman's Potential,* p. 56.

27. Paul H. Mussen, "Early Sex-Role Development," in David A. Goslin (ed.), *Handbook of Socialization Theory and Research* (Chicago: Rand McNally, 1969), p. 713

28. C. Wright Mills, *Images of Man* (New York: George Braziller, 1960), p. 17.

29. Mussen "Early Sex-Role Development," p. 710.

30. *Ibid.,* p. 709.

31. E. Maccoby, "Sex Differences in Intellectual Functioning," pp. 34–35 (including earlier quotes).

32. Margaret Mead, *Sex and Temperament,* pp. 190–191.

33. This is an adaptation of a phrase from Virginia Woolf.

## *Chapter 12   The Arc of the Future*

1. The phrase is Robert Heilbroner's used in another connection.

2. *Declaration of Sentiments,* adopted at first woman's rights convention, Seneca Falls, New York, quoted by Aileen S. Kraditor, *Up from the Pedestal* (Chicago: Quadrangle Books, 1968), p. 187.

3. *Statement of Purpose,* adopted at organizing convention of the National Organization of Women, quoted by Caroline Bird, with Sara Wells Briller, *Born Female* (New York: McKay, 1968), p. 220.

4. Constantia on the "Equality of the Sexes" (1790), quoted by Kraditor, *Up From the Pedestal,* p. 33.

5. Anna Garlin Spencer, *Woman's Share in Social Culture,* (1912), quoted by Kraditor, *ibid.,* p. 107.

6. C. Mildred Thompson, "Women's Status — Yesterday, Today, Tomorrow," in *Report on 1948 Woman's Bureau Conference Report,* U.S. Department of Labor (Washington, D. C.: U.S. Government Printing Office), p. 51. (Bull. 224).

7. Bird, *Born Female,* p. 164.

8. Charlotte Reid, 1967, quoted by Bird, *ibid.,* p. 44.

9. John Kenneth Galbraith, "Labor, Leisure, and the New Class," in John G. Burke (ed.), *The New Technology and Human Values* (Belmont, Calif: Wadsworth, 1966), p. 183.

10. Zbigniew Brzezinski, *America in the Technetronic Age* (New York: Columbia University School of International Affairs, 1967), p. 5.

11. *Ibid.,* p. 6.

12. Norbert Wiener, *The Human Use of Human Beings* (Garden City, N. Y.: Doubleday, 1950, 1954), p. 184.

13. Donald N. Michael, "Some Speculations on the Social Impact of Technology," in Robert Perrucci and Marc Pilisuk (eds.), *The Triple Revolution* (Boston: Little, Brown, 1968), p. 200.

14. Gerald Piel, "Consumers of Abundance," Center for the Study of Democratic Institutions, (June 1961), p. 10.

15. Hanna Arendt, *The Human Condition* (Chicago: University of Chicago Press, 1958), pp. 36, 37.

16. John Wilkinson, "Second Edition/The Quantitative Society," *The Center Magazine*, Center for the Study of Democratic Institutions, vol. II, no. 4 (July 1969), p. 71.

17. Charlotte Perkins Gilman, *The Home: Its Work and Influence* (New York: McClure Phillips, 1903), quoted by William O'Neill in *Everyone Was Brave* (Chicago: Quadrangle Books, 1969), pp. 42, 43.

18. Gordon Rattray Taylor, *The Biological Time Bomb* (London: Thames & Hudson, 1968), p. 11.

19. This is Walter Lippman's phrase quoted earlier.

20. Helen Merrell Lynd, *On Shame and the Search for Identity* (New York: Science Editions, 1958), p. 239.

21. *Ibid.*, p. 156.

22. *Ibid.*, p. 159, citing Erik Erikson, *Childhood and Society*, pp. 129–131; and "Growth and Crises of the Health Personality," in Kluckholn and Murray (eds.), *Personality in Nature, Society, and Culture* (New York: Knopf, 1956), pp. 221–222.

23. Edith Weigert, "Existentialism and Its Relation to Psychotherapy," *Psychiatry*, vol. 7 (November 1949), pp. 404–405, quoted in Lynd, *On Shame and the Search for Identity*, p. 160.

24. C. Wright Mills, *Images of Man* (New York: George Braziller, 1960), p. 17. I have already used this concept of Mills in the chapter "Portrait of a Lady."

25. C. Wright Mills, "Pragmatism, Politics and Religion," in Irving Louis Horowitz (ed.), *Power, Politics and People* (New York: Oxford University Press, 1963), p. 165.

26. Emily Green Balch from a pamphlet in the archives of the *Women's International League for Peace and Freedom*.

27. Bird, *Born Female*, p. 160.

28. Karl Mannheim, *Ideology and Utopia*, trans. Louis Wirth and Edward Shils (New York: Harcourt, Brace, 1936), p. 126.

29. Norbert Wiener, *Human Use of Human Beings*, p. 51.

30. Eugene Rabinowitch, "Responsibility of Scientists in Our Age." editorial in *Bulletin of the Atomic Scientists*, vol. XXV, no. 9 (November 1969), p. 26.

31. Herbert Marcuse, *One Dimensional Man* (Boston: The Beacon Press, 1964), p. 17.

32. Norbert Wiener, *Human Use of Human Beings*, p. 52.

33. Both quotations in this paragraph are from Eugene Rabinowitch, "Twenty-five Years Later," *Bulletin of the Atomic Scientists*, vol. XXVI, no. 6 (June 1970), pp. 6, 34.

34. H. J. Muller, "Human Evolution by Voluntary Choice of Germ Plasm," *Science*, vol. 134, no. 3480 (September 8, 1961), p. 647.

35. Both quotations are from Gerard Piel, "The Advent of Abundance," *Bulletin of the Atomic Scientists*, vol. XIX, no. 6 (June 1963), p. 6.

36. Robert Oppenheimer, as quoted in *SDC Magazine*, Systems Development Corporation, Santa Monica, Calif. (August 1969), p. 7.

# The View from the Sexual Ghetto

## List of Photographs

138

139

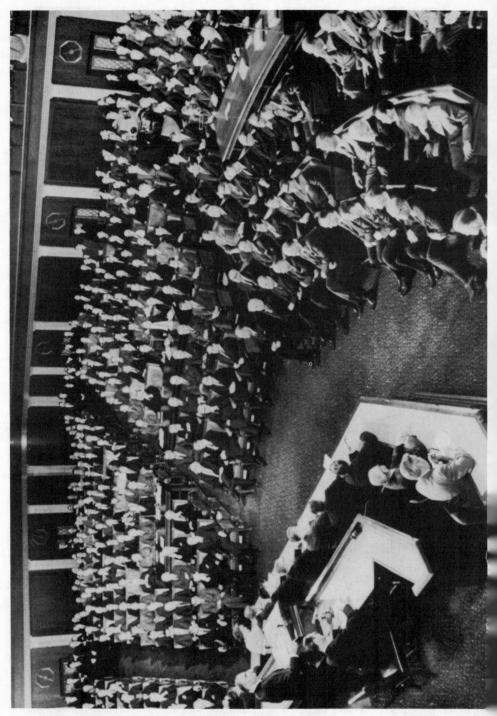

143

147

150

151

# Readings in Parallel

# 1. Inner Space━०━●━●━०━●━●━०━●━●━०━●━●━०━●━●━०━●━●━०━●━●━०━●━●━०━●━●━●━

> What if some space be assigned to the useful and elegant arts of female industry?
>
> CHARLES BUTLER

The traditional model postulates that woman is primarily homemaker, wife, and mother; that her qualities are nurturing and passive; that she is destined to inhabit the private as her exclusive sphere. In the readings that follow, this model is illustrated as it appears in the language and circumstances of various social periods.

*First* Ischomachus offers the classical conception of a wife as queen bee, docile, domesticated, discreet, but busy, for in her "covered place" she is charged with the indoor tasks and cares of producing children, clothing, and comestibles. Even though such a woman has servants, she cannot be idle: her place is indoors, but that inner space is a hive of activity. (God is cited as authority for this design.)

*The second selection* depicts the ideal of the American lady in the nineteenth century. She is presumed to have been formed in a smaller mold than man to suit her for domestic life. Unlike Ischomachus, Charles Butler does not picture this woman's place as a hive, but as a refuge of rest and refreshment. The talents and disposition of the lady are to be auxiliary to others: modeling the minds of children, fascinating through elegance and grace, and contributing to the comfort of her family, as daughter, sister, mother, wife, in the inner

*Parallel readings for Chapter 1, "The Traditional Approach."

155

space of the home. (Providence and the Scriptures are cited as authorities for the design.)

*The third reading* is from an informal criticism of the ideas of John Stuart Mill on the emancipation of women. It was written by Sigmund Freud, who used the opportunity to sketch his own ideal of women, as different beings destined for calm, uncompetitive activities related to house management and child care — which, he says, demand the whole of the feminine identity. Although he specifies the domestic duties that must occupy women in such interior existence, Dr. Freud's chief emphasis is on those tender attributes that invest her with the capacity to be a loved object. (Nature is cited as authority for the design.)

*The last reading* describes an interpretation of children's play by Erik Erikson, who concludes that the sexes use space differently: boys erecting exterior scenes (with high structures, motion, and conflict) and girls devoted to interior scenes (with low walls, static content, and peace). This is construed as paralleling the morphology of sexual difference; as reflecting a social pattern of tranquil feminine love for family and child versus high masculine aspiration; and as a matter of anatomic construction, which dictates profound difference between the sexes in their experience of the ground plan of their bodies. Dr. Erikson takes the idea of inner space far beyond the concept of milieu (the home) and projects it to include sex dichotomies in history, technology, and exploration of interplanetary space. Traditional woman, in his formulation, is literally out of this world. (The organism is authority for the design.)

## How Ischomachus Trained His Wife

>●━●━●━●━●━●━●━●━●━●━●━●━●━●━●━●━●━●━●━●━●━●━●━●━●━●━●━●━●━●━●━●━<

*Xenophon*

"Ah, Ischomachus," said I, "that is just what I want to hear from you. Did you yourself train your wife to be of the right sort, or did she know her household duties when you received her from her parents?"

"Why, what knowledge could she have had, Socrates, when I took her for my wife? She was not yet fifteen years old when she came to me, and up to that time she had lived in leading strings, seeing, hearing and saying as little

From Xenophon, *Oeconomicus,* trans. by E. C. Marchant, in the Loeb Classical Library (Harvard University Press), VII 4-48, pp. 415-429.

as possible. If when she came she knew no more than how, when given wool, to turn out a cloak, and had seen only how the spinning is given out to the maids, is not that as much as could be expected? For in control of her appetite, Socrates, she had been excellently trained; and this sort of training is, in my opinion, the most important to man and woman alike."

"But in other respects did you train your wife yourself, Ischomachus, so that she should be competent to perform her duties?"

"Oh no, Socrates; not until I had first offered sacrifice and prayed that I might really teach, and she learn what was best for us both."

"Did not your wife join with you in these same sacrifices and prayers?"

"Oh yes, earnestly promising before heaven to behave as she ought to do; and it was easy to see that she would not neglect the lessons I taught her."

"Pray tell me, Ischomachus, what was the first lesson you taught her, since I would sooner hear this from your lips than an account of the noblest athletic event or horse-race?"

"Well, Socrates, as soon as I found her docile and sufficiently domesticated to carry on conversation, I questioned her to this effect:

" 'Tell me, dear, have you realised for what reason I took you and your parents gave you to me? For it is obvious to you, I am sure, that we should have had no difficulty in finding someone else to share our beds. But I for myself and your parents for you considered who was the best partner of home and children that we could get. My choice fell on you, and your parents, it appears, chose me as the best they could find. Now if God grants us children, we will then think out how we shall best train them. For one of the blessings in which we shall share is the acquisition of the very best of allies and the very best of support in old age; but at present we share in this our home. For I am paying into the common stock all that I have, and you have put in all that you brought with you. And we are not to reckon up which of us has actually contributed the greater amount, but we should know of a surety that the one who proves the better partner makes the more valuable contribution.'

"My wife's answer was as follows, Socrates: 'How can I possibly help you? What power have I? Nay, all depends on you. My duty, as my mother told me, is to be discreet.'

" 'Yes, of course, dear,' I said, 'my father said the same to me. But discretion both in a man and a woman, means acting in such a manner that their possessions shall be in the best condition possible, and that as much as possible shall be added to them by fair and honourable means.'

" 'And what do you see that I can possibly do to help in the improvement of our property?' asked my wife.

" 'Why,' said I, 'of course you must try to do as well as possible what the gods made you capable of doing and the law sanctions.'

" 'And pray, what is that?' said she.

" 'Things of no small moment, I fancy,' replied I, 'unless, indeed, the tasks over which the queen bee in the hive presides are of small moment. For it seems to me, dear, that the gods with great discernment have coupled together male and female, as they are called, chiefly in order that they may form a perfect partnership in mutual service. For, in the first place, that the various species of living creatures may not fail, they are joined in wedlock for the production of children. Secondly, offspring to support them in old age is provided by this union, to human beings, at any rate. Thirdly, human beings live not in the open air, like beasts, but obviously need shelter. Nevertheless, those who mean to win store to fill the covered place, have need of someone to work at the open-air occupations; since ploughing, sowing, planting and grazing are all such open-air employments; and these supply the needful food. Then again, as soon as this is stored in the covered place, then there is need of someone to keep it and to work at the things that must be done under cover. Cover is needed for the nursing of the infants; cover is needed for the making of the corn into bread, and likewise for the manufacture of clothes from the wool. And since both the indoor and the outdoor tasks demand labour and attention, God from the first adapted the woman's nature, I think, to the indoor and man's to the outdoor tasks and cares.

" 'For he made the man's body and mind more capable of enduring cold and heat, and journeys and campaigns; and therefore imposed on him the outdoor tasks. To the woman, since he has made her body less capable of such endurance, I take it that God has assigned the indoor tasks. And knowing that he had created in the woman and had imposed on her the nourishment of the infants, he meted out to her a larger portion of affection for new-born babes than to the man. And since he imposed on the woman the protection of the stores also, knowing that for protection a fearful disposition is no disadvantage, God meted out a larger share of fear to the woman than to the man; and knowing that he who deals with the outdoor tasks will have to be their defender against any wrong-doer, he meted out to him again a larger share of courage. But because both must give and take, he granted to both impartially memory and attention; and so you could not distinguish whether the male or the female sex has the larger share of these. And God also gave to both impartially the power to practise due self-control, and gave authority to whichever is the better — whether it be the man or the woman — to win a larger portion of the good that comes from it. And just because both have not the same aptitudes, they have the more need of each other, and each member of the pair is the more useful to the other, the one being competent where the other is deficient.

" 'Now since we know, dear, what duties have been assigned to each of us by God, we must endeavour, each of us, to do the duties allotted to us as well as possible. The law, moreover, approves of them, for it joins together man and woman. And as God has made them partners in their children, so the law appoints them partners in the home. And besides, the law declares those tasks to be honourable for each of them wherein God has made the one to excel the other. Thus, to the woman it is more honourable to stay indoors than to abide in the fields, but to the man it is unseemly rather to stay indoors than to attend to the work outside. If a man acts contrary to the nature God has given him, possibly his defiance is detected by the gods and he is punished for neglecting his own work, or meddling with his wife's. I think that the queen bee is busy about just such other tasks appointed by God.'

" 'And pray,' said she, 'how do the queen bee's tasks resemble those that I have to do?'

" 'How? she stays in the hive,' I answered, 'and does not suffer the bees to be idle; but those whose duty it is to work outside she sends forth to their work; and whatever each of them brings in, she knows and receives it, and keeps it till it is wanted. And when the time is come to use it, she portions out the just share to each. She likewise presides over the weaving of the combs in the hive, that they may be well and quickly woven, and cares for the brood of little ones, that it be duly reared up. And when the young bees have been duly reared and are fit for work, she sends them forth to found a colony, with a leader to guide the young adventurers.'

" 'Then shall I too have to do these things?' said my wife.

" 'Indeed you will,' said I, 'your duty will be to remain indoors and send out those servants whose work is outside, and superintend those who are to work indoors, and to receive the incomings, and distribute so much of them as must be spent, and watch over so much as is to be kept in store, and take care that the sum laid by for a year be not spent in a month. And when wool is brought to you, you must see that cloaks are made for those that want them. You must see too that the dry corn is in good condition for making food. One of the duties that fall to you, however, will perhaps seem rather thankless: you will have to see that any servant who is ill is cared for.'

" 'Oh no,' cried my wife, 'it will be delightful, assuming that those who are well cared for are going to feel grateful and be more loyal than before.'

" 'Why, my dear,' cried I, delighted with her answer, 'what makes the bees so devoted to their leader in the hive, that when she forsakes it, they all follow her, and not one thinks of staying behind? Is it not the result of some such thoughtful acts on her part?'

" 'It would surprise me,' answered my wife, 'if the leader's activities did not concern you more than me. For my care of the goods indoors and my management would look rather ridiculous, I fancy, if you did not see that something is gathered in from outside.'

" 'And my ingathering would look ridiculous,' I countered, 'if there were not someone to keep what is gathered in. Don't you see how they who "draw water in a leaky jar," as the saying goes, are pitied, because they seem to labour in vain?'

" 'Of course,' she said, 'for they are indeed in a miserable plight if they do that.'

" 'But I assure you, dear, there are other duties peculiar to you that are pleasant to perform. It is delightful to teach spinning to a maid who had no knowledge of it when you received her, and to double her worth to you: to take in hand a girl who is ignorant of housekeeping and service, and after teaching her and making her trustworthy and serviceable to find her worth any amount: to have the power of rewarding the discreet and useful members of your household, and of punishing anyone who turns out to be a rogue. But the pleasantest experience of all is to prove yourself better than I am, to make me your servant; and, so far from having cause to fear that as you grow older you may be less honoured in the household, to feel confident that with advancing years, the better partner you prove to me and the better housewife to our children, the greater will be the honour paid to you in our home. For it is not through outward comeliness that the sum of things good and beautiful is increased in the world, but by the daily practice of the virtues.'

"Such was the tenor of my earliest talks with her, Socrates, so far as I can recall them."


## The Female Character

*Charles Butler*

IMPORTANCE OF THE FEMALE CHARACTER

Human happiness is on the whole much less affected by great but unfrequent events, whether of prosperity or of adversity, of benefit or of injury, than by small but perpetually recurring incidents of good or evil. Of the latter description are the effects which the influence of the female character produces. It is not like the periodical inundation of a river, which overspreads once in a year a desert with transient plenty. It is like the dew of heaven which descends at all seasons, returns after short intervals, and permanently nourishes every herb of the field.

In three particulars, each of which is of extreme and never-ceasing concern to the welfare of mankind, the effect of the female character is most important.

First; In contributing daily and hourly to the comfort of husbands, of parents, of brothers and sisters, and of other relations, connexions, and friends,

From *The American Lady* (Philadelphia: Hogan & Thompson, 1839, 1842), pp. 14–16, 17, 19-22.

in the intercourse of domestic life, under every vicissitude of sickness and health, of joy and affliction.

Secondly; In forming and improving the general manners, disposition, and conduct of the other sex, by society and example.

Thirdly; In modelling the human mind, during the early stages of its growth, and fixing, while it is yet ductile, its growing principles of action. Children of each sex are, in general, under maternal tuition during their childhood, and girls until they become women.

Are these objects insufficient to excite virtuous exertion? Let it then be remembered, that there is another object of supreme importance set before each individual; and one which she cannot accomplish without faithfully attending, according to her situation and ability, to those already enumerated; namely, the attainment of everlasting salvation, purchased through the blood of Jesus Christ, for those who walk in the spirit and precepts of his Gospel.

ON THE PECULIAR FEATURES BY WHICH THE CHARACTER OF THE FEMALE MIND IS NATURALLY DISCRIMINATED FROM THAT OF THE OTHER SEX

On the same principle a writer, who ventures to hope, that in suggesting observations on the duties incumbent on the female sex, he may be found to have drawn his conclusions from the source of nature and of truth, should endeavour, in the first place, to ascertain the characteristical impressions which the Creator has stamped on the female mind; the leading features, if such there be, by which he has discriminated the talents and dispositions of women from those of men. For it is from these original indications of the intention of Providence, taken in conjunction with the additional and still clearer proofs of the Divine Will which the Scriptures shall be found to have disclosed, that the course and extent of female duties, and the true value of the female character, are to be collected.

The Power who called the human race into being has, with infinite wisdom, regarded, in the structure of the corporeal frame, the tasks which the different sexes were respectively destined to fulfil. To man, on whom the culture of the soil, the erection of dwellings, and, in general, those operations of industry, and those measures of defence, which include difficult and dangerous exertion, were ultimately to devolve, he has imparted the strength of limb, and the robustness of constitution, requisite for the persevering endurance of toil. The female form, not commonly doomed, in countries where the progress of civilization is far advanced, to labours more severe than the offices of domestic life, he has cast in a smaller mould, and bound together by a looser texture. But, to protect weakness from the oppression of domineering superiority, those whom he has not qualified to contend he has enabled to fascinate; and has amply compensated the defect of muscular vigour by symmetry and expression, by elegance and grace. To me it appears, that he has adopted, and that he has adopted with the most conspicuous wisdom, a corresponding plan of discrimination between the mental powers and dispositions of the two sexes.

The science of legislation, jurisprudence, of political economy; the conduct of government in all its executive functions; the abstruse researches of erudition; the inexhaustible depths of philosophy; the acquirements subordinate to navigation; the knowledge indispensable in the wide field of commercial enterprise; the arts of defence, and of attack, by land and by sea, which the violence or the fraud of unprincipled assailants render needful; these and other studies, pursuits, and occupations, assigned chiefly or entirely to men, demand the efforts of a mind endued with the powers of close and comprehensive reasoning, and of intense and continued application, in a degree in which they are not requisite for the discharge of the customary offices of female duty. It would therefore seem natural to expect, and experience, I think, confirms the justice of the expectation, that the Giver of all good, after bestowing those powers on men with a liberality proportioned to the existing necessity, would impart them to the female mind with a more sparing hand. It was equally natural to expect, that in the dispensation of other qualities and talents, useful and important to both sexes, but particularly suited to the sphere in which women were intended to move, he would confer the larger portion of his bounty on those who needed it the most. It is accordingly manifest, that, in sprightliness and vivacity, in quickness of perception, in fertility of invention, in powers adapted to unbend the brow of the learned, to refresh the overlaboured faculties of the wise, and to diffuse throughout the family circle the enlivening and endearing smile of cheerfulness, the superiority of the female mind is unrivalled.

Does man, vain of his pre-eminence in the track of profound investigation, boast that the result of the inquiry is in his favor? Let him check the premature triumph, and listen to the statement of another article in the account, which, in the judgment of prejudice itself, will be found to restore the balance. As yet the native worth of the female character has been imperfectly developed. To estimate it fairly, the view must be extended from the compass and shades of intellect, to the dispositions and feelings of the heart. Were we called upon to produce examples of the most amiable tendencies and affections implanted in human nature, of modesty, of delicacy, of sympathizing sensibility, of prompt and active benevolence, of warmth and tenderness of attachment; whither should we at once turn our eyes? To the sister, to the daughter, to the wife. These endowments form the glory of the female sex. They shine amidst the darkness of uncultivated barbarism; they give to civilized society its brightest and most attractive lustre.

## A Critique of Mill on Women

*Sigmund Freud*

(A revealing account of Freud's views on women is contained in the following critique. Referring to a translation of the work of John Stuart Mill, which he made in 1880, Freud wrote:)

I railed at the time at his lifeless style and at not being able to find a sentence or phrase that one could commit to memory. But since then I have read a philosophical work of his which was witty, lively and felicitously epigrammatic. He was perhaps the man of the century who best managed to free himself from the domination of customary prejudices. On the other hand — and that always goes together with it — he lacked in many matters the sense of the absurd; for example, in that of female emancipation and in the woman's question altogether. I recollect that in the essay I translated a prominent argument was that a married woman could earn as much as her husband. We surely agree that the management of a house, the care and bringing up of children, demand the whole of a human being and almost excludes any earning, even if a simplified household relieve her of dusting, cleaning, cooking, etc. He had simply forgotten all that, like everything else concerning the relationship between the sexes. That is altogether a point with Mill where one simply cannot find him human. His autobiography is so prudish or so ethereal that one could never gather from it that human beings consist of men and women and that this distinction is the most significant one that exists. In his whole presentation it never emerges that women are different beings — we will not say lesser, rather the opposite — from men. He finds the suppression of women an analogy to that of Negroes. Any girl, even without a suffrage or legal competence, whose hand a man kisses and for whose love he is prepared to dare all, could have set him right. It is really a stillborn thought to send women into the struggle for existence exactly as men. If, for instance, I imagined my gentle sweet girl as a competitor it would only end in my telling her, as I did seventeen months ago, that I am fond of her and that I implore her to withdraw from the strife into the calm uncompetitive activity of my home. It is possible that changes in upbringing may suppress all a woman's tender attributes, needful of protection and yet so victorious, and that she can then earn a livelihood like men. It is also possible that in such an event one would not be justified in mourning the passing away of the most delightful thing the world can offer us — our ideal of womanhood. I believe that all reforming action in

From Ernest Jones, *The Life and Work of Sigmund Freud,* edited and abridged by Lionel and Steven Marcus (New York: Basic Books, 1961), pp. 117, 118

law and education would break down in front of the fact that, long before the age at which a man can earn a position in society, Nature has determined woman's destiny through beauty, charm, and sweetness. Law and custom have much to give women that has been withheld from them, but the position of women will surely be what it is: in youth an adored darling and in mature years a loved wife.

## Reflections on Womanhood

)━●━0━●━0━●━0━●━0━●━0━●━0━●━0━●━0━●━0━●━0━●━0━●━0━●━0━●━0━●━(

### *Erik H. Erikson*

Let me present here an observation which makes my point wordlessly. Since it has already been presented on a number of other occasions, I should admit that I am the kind of clinical worker in whose mind a few observations linger for a long time. Such observations are marked by a combination of being surprised by the unexpected and yet somehow confirmed by something long awaited. For this same reason, I am apt to present such observations to various audiences, hoping each time that understanding may be deepened.

It was in the observation of preadolescent children that I was enabled to observe sex-differences in a nonclinical setting. The children were Californian boys and girls, aged ten, eleven, and twelve years, who twice a year came to be measured, interviewed, and tested in the "Guidance Study" of the University of California. It speaks for the feminine genius of the director of the study, Jean Walker Macfarlane, that for over more than two decades the children (and their parents) not only came with regularity, but confided their thoughts with little reservation and, in fact, with much "zest" — to use Jean Macfarlane's favorite word. That means, they were confident of being appreciated as growing individuals and eager to reveal and to demonstrate what (so they had been convincingly told) was useful to know and might be helpful to others. Since this psychoanalyst, before joining the California study, had made it his business to interpret play-behavior — a nonverbal approach which had helped him to understand better what his small patients were not able to communicate in words — it was decided that he would test his clinical hypotheses by securing a number of play-constructions from each child. Over a span of two years, I saw 150 boys and 150 girls three times and presented them, one at a time, with the task of constructing a "scene" with toys on a table. The toys were

From "Inner and Outer Space: Reflections on Womanhood," *Daedalus,* Journal of the American Academy of Arts and Sciences (Spring 1964), pp. 588-593.

rather ordinary: a family; some uniformed figures (policeman, aviator, Indian, monk, etc.); wild and domestic animals; furniture; automobiles. But I also provided a variety of blocks. The children were asked to imagine that the table was a moving picture studio; the toys, actors and props; and they themselves, moving picture directors. They were to arrange on the table "an exciting scene from an imaginary moving picture," and then tell the plot. This was recorded, the scene photographed, and the child complimented. It may be necessary to add that no "interpretation" was given.

The observer then compared the individual constructions with about ten years of data in the files to see whether it provided some key to the major determinants of the child's inner development. On the whole this proved helpful, but that is not the point to be made here. The experiment also made possible a comparison of all play constructions with each other.

A few of the children went about the task with the somewhat contemptuous attitude of one doing something which was not exactly worth the effort of a young person already in his teens, but almost all of these bright and willing youngsters in somber jeans and gay dresses were drawn to the challenge by that eagerness to serve and to please which characterized the whole population of the study. And once they were "involved," certain properties of the task took over and guided them.

It soon became evident that among those properties the spatial one was dominant. Only half of the scenes were "exciting," and only a handful had anything to do with moving pictures. In fact, the stories told at the end were for the most part brief and in no way comparable to the thematic richness evidenced in verbal tests. But the care and (one is tempted to say) esthetic responsibility with which the children selected blocks and toys and then arranged them according to an apparently deeply held sense of spatial propriety was astounding. At the end, it seemed to be a sudden feeling of "now it's right" which made them come to a sense of completion and, as if awakening from a wordless experience, turn to me and say, "I am ready now," — meaning: to tell you what this is all about.

I, myself, was most interested in defining the tools and developing the art of observing not only imaginative themes but also spatial configurations in relation to stages of the life cycle, and, of course, in checking psychoanalytic assumptions concerning the sources and forms of neurotic tension in prepuberty. Sex-differences thus were not the initial focus of my interest in spatial behavior. I concentrated my attention on how these constructions-in-progress moved forward to the edge of the table or back to the wall behind it; how they rose to shaky heights or remained close to the table surface; how they were spread over the available space or constricted to a portion of the space. That all of this "says" something about the constructor is the open secret of all "projective techniques." This, too, cannot be discussed here. But soon I realized that in evaluating a child's play-construction, I had to take into consideration the fact that girls and boys used space differently, and that certain configurations occurred strikingly often in the constructions of one sex and rarely in those of the other.

The differences themselves were so simple that at first they seemed a matter of course. History in the meantime has offered a slogan for it: the girls emphasized inner and the boys outer space.

This difference I was soon able to state in such simple configurational terms that other observers, when shown photographs of the constructions without knowing the sex of the constructor (nor, indeed, having any idea of my thoughts concerning the possible meaning of the differences), could sort the photographs according to the configurations most dominant in them, and this significantly in the statistical sense. These independent ratings showed that considerably more than two thirds of what I subsequently called male configurations occurred in scenes constructed by boys, and more than two thirds of the "female" configurations in the constructions of girls. I will here omit the finer points which still characterized the atypical scenes as clearly built by a boy or by a girl. This, then, is typical: the girl's scene is an *interior* scene, represented either as a configuration of furniture without any surrounding walls, or by a *simple enclosure* built with blocks. In the girl's scene, people and animals are mostly *within* such an interior or enclosure, and they are primarily people or animals in a *static* (sitting, standing) position. Girls' enclosures consist of *low walls*, i.e. only one block high, except for an occasional elaborate *doorway*. These interiors of houses with or without walls were, for the most part, expressly *peaceful*. Often, a little girl was playing the piano. In a number of cases, however, the *interior was intruded* by animals or dangerous men. Yet the idea of an intruding creature did not necessarily lead to the defensive erection of walls or the closing of doors. Rather the majority of these intrusions have an element of humor and of pleasurable excitement.

Boys' scenes are either houses with *elaborate walls* or *façades with protrusions* such as cones or cylinders representing ornaments or cannons. There are *high towers;* and there are *exterior scenes,* In boys' constructions more people and animals are *outside* enclosures or buildings, and there are more *automotive objects* and *animals moving* along streets and intersections. There are elaborate automotive *accidents,* but also traffic channeled or arrested by the *policeman.* While high structures are prevalent in the configurations of the boys, there is also much play with the danger of collapse or *downfall; ruins* were exclusively boys' constructions.

The male and female spaces, then, were dominated, respectively, by height and downfall and by strong motion and its channelization or arrest; and by static interiors which were open or simply enclosed, and peaceful or intruded upon. It may come as a surprise to some, and seem a matter of course to others, that here sexual differences in the organization of a play space seem to parallel the morphology of genital differentiation itself: in the male, an *external* organ, *erectible* and *intrusive* in character, serving the channelization of *mobile* sperm cells; *internal* organs in the female, with vestibular *access,* leading to *statically expectant* ova. The question is, what *is* really surprising about this, and what only too obvious, and in either case, what does it tell us about the two sexes?

Since I first presented these data a decade and a half ago to workers in different fields, some standard interpretations have not yielded an iota. There are, of course, derisive reactions which take it for granted that a psychoanalyst would want to read the bad old symbols into this kind of data. And indeed, Freud did note more than half a century ago that "a house is the only regularly occurring symbol of the (whole) human body in dreams." But there is quite a methodological step (not to be specified here) from the occurrence of a symbol in dreams and a configuration created in actual space. Nevertheless, the purely psychoanalytic or somatic explanation has been advanced that the scenes reflect the preadolescent's preoccupation with his own sexual organs.

The purely "social" interpretation, on the other hand, denies the necessity to see anything symbolic or, indeed, somatic in these configurations. It takes it for granted that boys love the outdoors and girls the indoors, or at any rate that they see their respective roles assigned to the indoors of houses and to the great outdoors of adventure, to tranquil feminine love for family and children and to high masculine aspiration.

One cannot help agreeing with both interpretations — up to a point. Of course, whatever social role is associated with one's physique will be expressed thematically in any playful or artistic representation. And, of course, under conditions of special tension or preoccupation with one part of the body, that body part may be recognizable in play-configurations. The spokesmen for the anatomical and for the social interpretations are thus both right if they insist that neither possibility may be ignored. But this does not make either exclusively right.

A pure interpretation in terms of social role leaves many questions unanswered. If the boys thought primarily of their present or anticipated roles, why, for example, is the policeman their favorite toy, traffic stopped dead a frequent scene? If vigorous activity outdoors is a determinant of the boys' scenes, why did they not arrange *any* sports fields on the play table? (One tomboyish girl did.) Why did the girls' love for home life not result in an increase in high walls and closed doors as guarantors of intimacy and security? And could the role of playing the piano in the bosom of their families really be considered representative of what these girls (some of them passionate horseback riders and all future automobilists) wanted to do most or, indeed, thought they should pretend they wanted to do most? Thus the boys' *caution outdoors* and the girls' *goodness indoors* in response to the explicit instruction to construct an *exciting movie scene* suggested dynamic dimensions and acute conflicts not explained by a theory of mere compliance with cultural and conscious roles.

I would suggest an altogether more inclusive interpretation, according to which a profound difference exists between the sexes in the experience of the groundplan of the human body. The spatial phenomenon observed here would then express two principles of arranging space which correspond to the male and female principles in body construction. These may receive special emphasis in prepuberty, and maybe in some other stages of life as well, but they are relevant throughout life to the elaboration of sex-roles in cultural space-times. Such an interpretation cannot be "proven," of course, by the one observation offered here. The question is whether it is in line with observations of spatial behavior in other media and at other ages; whether it can be made a plausible part of a developmental theory; and whether, indeed, it gives to other sex-differences closely related to male and female structure and function a more convincing order. On the other hand, it would not be contradicted by the fact that other media of observation employed to test male and female performance might reveal few or no sexual differences in areas of the mind which have the function of securing verbal or cognitive agreement on matters dominated by the mathematical nature of the universe and the verbal agreement of cultural traditions. Such agreement, in fact, may have as its very function the *correction* of what differentiates the experience of the sexes, even as it also corrects the idiosyncrasies separating other classes of men.

The play-constructing children in Berkeley, California, will lead us into a number of spatial considerations, especially concerning feminine development and outlook. Here I will say little about men; their accomplishments in the conquest of geographic space and of scientific fields and in the dissemination of ideas speak loudly for themselves and confirm traditional values of masculinity. Yet the play-constructing boys in Berkeley may give us pause: on the world scene, do we not see a supremely gifted yet somewhat boyish mankind playing with history and technology, and this following a male pattern as embarrassingly simple (if technologically complex) as the play-constructions of the preadolescent? Do we not see the themes of the toy microcosm dominating an expanding human space: height, penetration, and speed; collision, explosion — and cosmic super-police? In the meantime, women have found their identities in the care suggested in their bodies and in the needs of their issue, and seem to have taken it for granted that the outer world space belongs to the men.

## 2. Not for Ourselves Alone

> Men will not be liberated until women are free.
>
> ROBIN MORGAN

Countering the traditional approach we find the challenging view — based in the twin ideas that sexual roles are socially created and that wide function for women benefits the race. More than a century ago, Sarah Grimké for example, declared in her cogent style: *"That intellect is not sexed;* that strength of mind is not sexed; and that our views about the duties of men. . .and the duties of women, the spheres of man and the spheres of woman, are merely arbitrary opinions, differing in different ages and countries, and dependent solely on the will and judgment of erring mortals." From this foundation, the demands of the challengers crystallized about the issues of full participation in the work of the world, of inclusive education, and of structural change to accommodate public as well as private life.

In the pressures of the moment, however, there were in each period more activists than theorists; ritual slogans and constructive passion exceeded penetrating insights. Olive Schreiner belongs to the small group of reflective thinkers devoted to an analysis of the structure and instruments for leverage in the social organism that the feminists sought to transform. The full scope of her profound scholarship is forever lost to us, for the book that she worked on for ten years was destroyed when she was prevented from returning to her home in the Transvaal during the Boer War. The excerpt that follows is taken from

*Parallel readings for Chapter 2, "The Challenging View."

*Woman and Labor*, written as a recollection of the earlier work during her internment in a small hamlet, while the war raged around her. Even this fragment reveals the extraordinary prescience of the author, speaking for our time as clearly as for her own as she relates the impact of technological events on the position of women. For, as Olive Schreiner notes in her Introduction: "Wherever there is a general attempt on the part of the women of any society to readjust their position in it, a close analysis will always show that the changed or changing conditions of that society have made woman's acquiescence no longer necessary or desirable." The issue then becomes not whether change will occur, but rather which direction it should take.

Caroline Bird's article sets forth the directions in which the new feminists have set their sights. As she points out, none of these goals would have startled Mary Wollstonecraft or Elizabeth Cady Stanton (who wrote their agitational documents in 1792 and 1848 respectively). The distinction between earlier campaigns and the current ones lies rather in the character of those "changing conditions of. . .society" which Olive Schreiner anticipated, and which today constitute the very crucible of reality.

## Woman and Labor

*Olive Schreiner*

Is it to be, that, in the future, machinery and the captive motor-forces of nature are largely to take the place of human hand and foot in the labor of clothing and feeding the nations; are these branches of industry to be no longer domestic labors? — then, we demand that in the factory, the warehouse, and the field, wherever machinery has usurped our ancient labor-ground, we also should have our place, as guiders, controllers, and possessors. Is child-bearing to become the labor of but a portion of our sex? — then we demand for those among us who are allowed to take no share in it, compensatory and equally honorable and important fields of social toil. Is the training of human creatures to become a yet more and more onerous and laborious occupation, their education and culture to become increasingly a high art, complex and scientific? — if so, then, we demand that high and complex culture and training

From *Woman and Labor*, 3rd ed. (New York: Frederick A. Stokes Co., 1911), chapters II and III (abridged).

which shall fit us for instructing the race which we bring into the world. Is the demand for child-bearing to become so diminished that, even in the lives of those among us who are child-bearers, it shall fill no more than half a dozen years out of the three-score-and-ten of human life? — then we demand that an additional outlet be ours which shall fill up with dignity and value the tale of the years not so employed. Is intellectual labor to take ever and increasingly the place of crude muscular exertion in the labor of life? — then we demand for ourselves that culture and the freedom of action which alone can yield us the knowledge of life and the intellectual vigor and strength which will enable us to undertake the same share of mental which we have borne in the past in physical labors of life. Are the rulers of the race to be no more its kings and queens, but the mass of the peoples? — then we, one-half of the nations, demand our full queens' share in the duties and labors of government and legislation. *Slowly but determinately, as the old fields of labor close up and are submerged behind us, we demand entrance into the new.*

We make this demand, not for our own sake alone, but for the succor of the race. . . .

In the confusion and darkness of the present, it may well seem to some that woman, in her desire to seek for new paths of labor and employment, is guided only by an irresponsible impulse; or that she seeks selfishly only her own good, at the cost of that of the race, which she has so long and faithfully borne onward. But, when a clearer future shall have arisen and the obscuring mists of the present have been dissipated, may it not then be clearly manifest that not for herself alone, but for her entire race, has woman sought her new paths?

For let it be noted exactly what our position is, who to-day, as women, are demanding new fields of labor and a reconstruction of our relationship with life.

It is often said that the labor problem before the modern woman and that before the unemployed or partially or almost uselessly employed male, are absolutely identical; and that therefore, when the male labor problem of our age solves itself, that of the woman will of necessity have met its solution also.

This statement, with a certain specious semblance of truth, is yet, we believe, radically and fundamentally false. It is true that both the male and the female problems of our age have taken their rise largely in the same rapid material changes which during the last centuries, and more especially the last ninety years, have altered the face of the human world. Both men and women have been robbed by those changes of their ancient remunerative fields of social work: here the resemblance stops. The male, from whom the changes of modern civilization have taken his ancient field of labor, has but one choice before him: he must find new fields of labor, or he must perish. Society will not ultimately support him in an absolutely quiescent and almost useless condition. If he does not vigorously exert himself in some direction or other (the direction may even be predatory) he must ultimately be annihilated.

Individual drones, both among the wealthiest and the poorest classes (millionaires' sons, dukes, or tramps), may in isolated cases be preserved, and allowed to reproduce themselves without any exertion or activity of mind or body, but a vast body of males who, having lost their old forms of social employment, should refuse in any way to exert themselves or seek for new, would at no great length of time become extinct. . . .

The labor of the man may not always be useful in the highest sense to his society, or it may even be distinctly harmful and antisocial, as in the case of the robber-barons of the Middle Ages, who lived by capturing and despoiling all who passed by their castles; or as in the case of the share speculators, stockjobbers, ring-and-corner capitalists, and monopolists of the present day, who feed upon the productive labors of society without contributing anything to its welfare. But even males so occupied are compelled to expend a vast amount of energy and even a low intelligence in their callings; and, however injurious to their societies, they run no personal risk of handing down effete and enervated constitutions to their race. Whether beneficially or unbeneficially, the human male must, generally speaking, employ his intellect, or his muscle, or die.

The position of the unemployed modern female is one wholly different. The choice before her, as her ancient fields of domestic labor slip from her, is not generally or often at the present day the choice between finding new fields of labor, or death; but one far more serious in its ultimate reaction on humanity as a whole — it is the choice between finding new forms of labor or sinking slowly into a condition of more or less complete and passive *sex-parasitism!*

Nevertheless, in the history of the past the dangers of the sex-parasitism have never threatened more than a small section of the females of the human race, those exclusively of some dominant race or class; the mass of women beneath them being still compelled to assume many forms of strenuous activity. It is at the present day, and under the peculiar conditions of our modern civilization, that for the first time sex-parasitism has become a danger, more or less remote, to the mass of civilized women, perhaps ultimately to all. . . .

The parasitism of the human female becomes a possibility only when a point in civilization is reached. . .when, owing to the extensive employment of the labor of slaves, or of subject races or classes, the dominant race or class has become so liberally supplied with the material goods of life that mere physical toil on the part of its own female members has become unnecessary.

It is when this point has been reached, and never before, that the symptoms of female parasitism have in the past almost invariably tended to manifest themselves, and have become a social danger. The males of the dominant class have almost always contrived to absorb to themselves the new intellectual occupations, which the absence of necessity for the old forms of physical toil made possible in their societies; and the females of the dominant class or race, for whose muscular labors there was now also no longer any need, not succeeding in grasping or attaining to these new forms of labor, have sunk into a state in which, performing no species of active social duty, they have existed through the passive performance of sexual functions alone, with how much or how little of discontent will now never be known, since no literary record has been made by the woman of the past, of her desires or sorrows. . . . Finely clad, tenderly housed, life became for her merely the gratification of her own physical and sexual appetites, and the appetites of the male, through the stimulation of which she could maintain herself. And, whether as kept wife, kept mistress, or prostitute, she contributed nothing to the active and sustaining labors of her society. . . .

The conception which again and again appears to have haunted successive societies, that it was a possibility for the human male to advance in physical power and intellectual vigor, while his companion female became stationary and inactive, taking no share in the labors of society beyond the passive fulfillment of sexual functions, has always been negated. . . . The human female, by producing the intellectual and moral atmosphere in which the early infant years of life are passed, impresses herself. . .indelibly on her descendants. Only an able and laboring womanhood can permanently produce an able and laboring manhood; only an effete and inactive male can ultimately be produced by an effete and inactive womanhood. . . . It is this fact which causes even prostitution (in many respects the most repulsive form of female parasitism which afflicts humanity) to be, probably, not more adverse to the advance and even to the conservation of a healthy and powerful society than the parasitism of its childbearing woman. For the prostitute, heavily as she weights society for her support, returning disease and mental and emotional disintegration for what she consumes, does not yet so immediately affect the next generation as the kept wife, or kept mistress, who impresses her effete image indelibly on the generations succeeding. . . .

We have seen that, in the past, no such thing as the parasitism of the entire body or large majority of the females inhabiting any territory was possible. Beneath that body of women of the dominant class or race, who did not labor either mentally or physically, there has always been of necessity a far more vast body of females who not only performed the crude physical toil essential to the existence of society before the introduction of mechanical methods of production, but who were compelled to labor the more intensely because there was a parasite class above them to be maintained by their physical toil. The more the female parasite flourished of old, in one class or race, the more certainly all women of other classes or races were compelled to labor only too excessively; and ultimately these females and their descendants were apt to supplant the more enervated class or race. In the absence of machinery and of a vast employment of the motor forces of nature, parasitism could only threaten a comparatively small section of any community, and a minute section of the human race as a whole. . . .

At the present day, so enormous has been the advance made in the substitution of mechanical force for crude, physical, human exertion (mechanical force being employed today even in the shaping of feeding-bottles and the creation of artificial foods as substitutes for mother's milk!) that it is now possible not only for a small and wealthy section of women in each civilized community to be maintained without performing any of the ancient, crude, physical labors of their sex, and without depending on the slavery of, or any vast increase in the labor of, other classes of females; but this condition has already been reached, or is tending to be reached, by that large mass of women in civilized societies who form the intermediate class between poor and rich. During the next fifty years, so rapid will undoubtedly be the spread of the material conditions of civilization, both in the societies at present civilized and in the societies at present unpermeated by our material civilization, that the ancient forms of female, domestic, physical labor of even the women of the poorest classes will be little required, their place being taken, not by other females, but by always increasingly perfected labor-saving machinery.

Thus, female parasitism, which in the past threatened only a minute section of earth's women, under existing conditions threatens vast masses, and may, under future conditions, threaten the entire body.

If woman is content to leave to the male all labor in the new and all-important fields which are rapidly opening before the human race; if, as the old forms of domestic labor slip from her for ever and inevitably, she does not grasp the new, it is inevitable, that, ultimately, not merely a class, but the whole bodies of females in civilized societies, must sink into a state of more or less absolute dependence on their sexual functions alone.

As new forms of natural force are mastered and mechanical appliances perfected, it will be quite possible for the male half of all civilized races (and therefore ultimately of all) to absorb the entire fields of intellectual and highly trained manual labor; and it would be entirely possible for the female half of the race, whether as prostitutes, as kept mistresses, or as kept wives, to cease from all forms of active toil, and, as the passive tools of sexual reproduction, or, more decadently still, as the mere instruments of sexual indulgence, to sink into a condition of complete and helpless sex-parasitism.

Sex-parasitism, therefore, presents itself at the end of the nineteenth century and beginning of the twentieth in a guise which it has never before worn. We, the women of the civilization of the nineteenth and twentieth centuries, stand therefore in a position the gravity and importance of which was not equaled by that of any of our forerunners in the ancient civilization. As we master and rise above, or fall and are conquered by, the difficulties of our position, so also will be the future, not merely of our own class, or even of our own race alone, but also of those vast masses who are following on in the wake of our civilization. The decision we are called on to make is a decision for the race. . . .

In the woman's labor movement of our day, which has essentially taken its rise among women of the more cultured and wealthy classes, and which consists mainly in a demand to have the doors leading to professional, political, and highly skilled labor thrown open to them, the ultimate end can only be attained at the cost of more or less intense, immediate, personal suffering and renunciation, though eventually, if brought to a satisfactory conclusion, it will undoubtedly tend to the material and physical well-being of woman herself, as well as to that of her male companions and descendants.

The coming half-century will be a time of peculiar strain, as mankind seeks rapidly to adjust moral ideals and social relationships and the general ordering of life to the new and continually unfolding material conditions. . . .

It is this fact, the consciousness on the part of the women taking their share in the woman's movement of our age, that their efforts are not, and cannot be, of immediate advantage to themselves, but that they almost of necessity and immediately lead to loss and renunciation, which gives to this movement its very peculiar tone; setting it apart from the large mass of economic movements, placing it rather in a line with those vast religious developments which at the interval of ages have swept across humanity, irresistibly modifying and reorganizing it.

It is the perception of this fact, that, not for herself, nor even for fellow women alone, but for the benefit of humanity at large, she must seek to readjust herself to life, which lends to the woman's most superficial and seemingly trivial attempt at readjustment a certain dignity and importance.

It is this profound hidden conviction which removes from the sphere of the ridiculous the attitude of even the feeblest woman who waves her poor little "woman's rights" flag on the edge of a platform, and which causes us to forgive even the passionate denunciations, not always wisely thought out, in which she would represent the evils of woman's condition as wrongs intentionally inflicted upon her, where they are merely the inevitable results of ages of social movement. . . .

It is this consciousness of great impersonal ends, to be brought, even if slowly and imperceptibly, a little nearer by her action, which gives to many a woman strength for renunciation, when she puts from her the lower type of sexual relationship, even if bound up with all the external honor a legal marriage can confer, if it offers her only enervation and parasitism. This consciousness enables her often to accept poverty, toil, and sexual isolation (an isolation more terrible to her than to any male), and renunciation of motherhood, that crowning beatitude of the woman's existence, which, and which alone, fully compensates her for the organic sufferings of womanhood — in the conviction that, by so doing, she makes more possible a fuller and higher attainment of motherhood and wifehood to the women who will follow her.

It is this consciousness which makes of solemn importance the knock of the humblest woman at the closed door which shuts off a new field of labor, physical or mental: she is convinced that, not for herself, but in the service of the whole race, she knocks.

It is this abiding consciousness of an end to be attained, reaching beyond her personal life and individual interests, which constitutes the religious element of the woman's movement of our day, and binds with the common bond of an impersonal enthusiasm into one solid body the women of whatsoever race, class, and nation who are struggling after the readjustment of woman to life. . . .The fact that without the reaction of interevolution between the sexes, there can be no real and permanent human advance; . . .[that] an arrest in one form is an arrest in both, and in the upward march of the whole human family. The truth that, if at the present day, woman, after her long upward march side by side with man, developing with him through the ages by means of endless exercise of the faculties of mind and body, has now, at last, reached her ultimate limit of growth, and can progress no farther; that, then, here also, to-day, the growth of the human spirit is to be stayed; that here, on the spot of woman's arrest, is the standard of the race to be finally planted, to move forward no more, forever: — that, if the parasite woman on her couch, loaded with gewgaws, the plaything and amusement of man, be the permanent and final manifestation of female human life on the globe, then that couch is also the deathbed of human evolution. . . .

The fact that, at one point, it [the woman's movement] manifests itself in a passionate, and at times almost incoherent, cry for an accredited share in public and social duties, while at another it makes itself felt as a determined endeavor after self-culture; that in one land it embodies itself mainly in a resolute endeavor to enlarge the sphere of remunerative labor for women, while in another it manifests itself chiefly as an effort to reco-ordinate the personal relation of the sexes; that in one individual it manifests itself as a passionate and sometimes noisy struggle for liberty of personal action, while in another it is being fought out silently in the depths of the individual consciousness — that primal battleground, in which all questions of reform and human advance must ultimately be fought and decided; all this diversity, and the fact that the average woman is entirely concerned in labor in her own little field, shows, not the weakness, but the strength of the movement, which, taken as a whole, is a movement steady and persistent in one direction, the direction of increased activity and culture, and towards the negation of all possibility of parasitism in the human female. . . .

## The New Woman

>■—o■—o■—o■—o■—o■—o■—o■—o■—o■—o■—o■—o■—o■—o■—o■—o■—o■—o■—o■—o■—o■—o■—o■—(

### Caroline Bird

Just four years ago, the successful women I interviewed were spending a lot of energy proving that their husbands and children were not neglected, demonstrating their "femininity" by tottering around in frilly clothes, and insisting that they liked men better than women. They could say that they envied this or that privilege of men if they smiled or shrugged when they said it. But not many dared to say that they wished they were male, that they preferred to be single or childless, or that they liked the company of women better than that of men.

Today, a surprising number of women all over the country are daring to say precisely those things. These four years, in fact, have ushered in — almost incredibly — an entirely new era for American women. Consider what has been happening:

New York State has stopped inquiring into a woman's reasons for wanting an abortion and California into her reasons for wanting a divorce. Some colleges have abandoned all responsibility for the private lives of women students. Many newspapers have given up the attempt to classify job ads by sex. Women are admitted to scores of clubs, restaurants, colleges, and jobs formerly closed to them, and every Ivy League college has women students on some basis or other. Congress has removed the legal barrier to women generals and admirals. The venerable Protestant Episcopal Church has abolished its women's division and is presently considering the elevation of women to the priesthood.

Women are also gaining at work. Favorable court decisions are striking down the state labor laws which had "protected" factory women from the hours and duties which led to promotion and competition from union men. The proportion of women in graduate school is rising, and the gap between the starting salaries of men and women college graduates is narrowing.

Quite clearly, too, women are more assertive of their rights. They are filing charges of discrimination on the basis of sex with the Equal Employment Opportunity Commission and Government agencies charged with eliminating discrimination from the civil service. The Equal Rights Amendment forbidding legal distinction of any kind between male and female citizens has attracted support from women who just a little while ago had judged it "too far

From "The New Woman: Out to Finish What the Suffragette Started," THINK, vol. 36, no. 4 (July-August 1970), pp. 7 – 11. Reprinted by permission from THINK Magazine, published by IBM, Copyright 1970 by International Business Machines Corporation.

out" to be worth political effort. When Senator Birch Bayh announced hearings on the amendment, 100 witnesses asked to testify, mostly for it. Virtually everybody in the woman's rights movement has moved to new, more radical ground.

But the most startling innovation since 1966 has been the appearance of a new kind of woman, more alien to American tradition than the flapper of the 1920s, the mansuited, career spinster of the 1930s, or the Rosie who riveted the bombers during World War II. Virtually nonexistent in 1966, the new, liberated woman can today be found on every college campus and in every sizable American city.

The American woman she most resembles is a character successful women had patronized as necessary, perhaps, in her time, but thankfully needed no more: the politically alert, fiercely autonomous, and sometimes man-hating suffragette who won the vote for women at the end of World War I by militant hunger strikes and street demonstrations. Well-educated, privileged, the new liberated woman is often attractive and almost always young — seldom over 25. She is, in addition, idealistic, intense but soft-spoken. And she is furious. Men can't believe her even when they see her. In their book, she's an impossibility: a beautiful or potentially beautiful woman who is deliberately throwing away the advantages of her sex.

She is not fighting to liberate herself from sex repressions. In her privileged circles, her mother and sometimes her grandmother accomplished that. Nor is she out to broaden her horizons to include man's world. The new women scorn requesting, politely or otherwise, that men please move over and give them a piece of the action (the middle-of-the-road New Feminism of the National Organization for Women). They want to remake the world men have created, from top to bottom.

All the new women don't see eye to eye. Still, a majority could probably be mustered for the following platform.

*Love* is the most important human relationship and is available to any two or more individuals of any sex who care deeply for each other and are committed to contributing to each other's personal growth. Love may or may not include sexual relationships and should not be confused with *romantic love*, a put-up job they think is utilized to trap women into giving up their own identities.

*Home and family* (including the cooking, cleaning and shopping) must be an egalitarian institution to which all contribute equally. It can comprise any combination of adults and children, whether related by blood or sexual ties, who find it rewarding to live together. New forms of home and family must be developed by personal experimentation.

*Children* must be a fully optional responsibility for both men and women. Women must have the right to terminate any pregnancy for any reason, and no loss of prestige should attach to any person who chooses not to reproduce.

The rearing of children shall be the equal responsibility of mother and father and shall not be considered a full-time job for anyone, or the source of any woman's identity.

*Divorce* must be available to either partner without fault.

*Alimony* degrades a wife by assuming that she has been supported in return for sexual favors and is entitled to severance pay when she is jilted.

*Jobs* must be available to both sexes on the basis of individually determined capacity, without presumption that the required capacity is more likely to occur in a member of one sex than the other.

*Consumer goods* shall not be promoted as contributors to masculinity or femininity or by exploiting the sexual attraction of women employees or images.

*Media* shall not brainwash women and girls into accepting a limited, domestic role.

*Schools* — ditto.

*Sex differences* in ability and responses which can be proven by objective testing must be ascribed to the way boys and girls are brought up, until they can be specifically attributed to anatomical differences.

*Sex roles* based on a division of labor between men and women are not inevitable in the world of the future just because they have been universal in the past.

*Psychoanalysis* has crippled women by attempting to "adjust" them to a feminine role unacceptable to free human beings.

*Freud* made the mistake of assuming that Victorian marriage and family arrangements which subordinated women to men were inevitable and desirable.

*Marx* saw that the bourgeois family enslaved women by making them the private property of their men.

None of these thoughts is really new. What *is* new is that they have been welded together into a coherent philosophy on the basis of which women can make personal decisions on husbands, jobs, schools, birth control methods, alimony, child-rearing, and politics. The Women's Liberation Movement (WLM), more familiarly known as Women's Lib, is, if anything, overorganized. At the Second Congress to Unite Women held in New York this past May, 600 women represented scores of the shifting new groups which were turning up with names like Bread and Roses, The Feminists, the Media Women, Redstockings, OWL (Older Women's Liberation), SALT (Sisters All Learning Together), as well as WITCH (Women's International Terrorist Conspiracy from Hell).

The movement began with bright, white girls from privileged homes who were free to join the student movement for Negro rights in college because they weren't pushed to marry well or earn money. When they went South for the movement, they found themselves identifying with the blacks more easily than the white boys. They knew how it felt to shut up; take a back seat; accept segregation, exclusion from clubs, restaurants, and meetings; lower their sights to work which was "realistically" open to them; cope with imputations of natural inferiority; and see themselves portrayed in print and picture as stereotypes rather than individuals.

In 1967 it began to dawn on the girls who had gone into the radical movement fulltime after graduation that they were toting coffee and typing, like office girls in business establishments. Those who had joined the movement to escape suburban domesticity found themselves making beds and washing dishes like their legally married mothers. Not taken seriously, refused an opportunity for more substantial participation, these movement women who were "feminists" concluded in 1968 that they couldn't really be liberated unless they did it all by themselves, and while most hoped to rejoin men after their liberation, most excluded men.(The Feminists of New York actually limit to one-third the number of members who may be formally or informally married.)

Women's Liberation made its national debut in September 1968 by halting — if only for a few seconds — the television crowning of Miss America at Atlantic City. They picketed the contest with signs "Let's Judge Ourselves as People." They brought "freedom trash baskets" into which they proposed to dump hair curlers, false eyelashes, girdles, bras, and other devices for making themselves over into the standard sex object. They crowned a live sheep. They threw a stink bomb. They chanted, "We Shall Not Be Used." And some of them got arrested.

Women saw the point, even when they violently, and somewhat defensively, denied that they felt "used." The pageant had long made women feel uneasy, but few had verbalized or even admitted the discomfort they experienced at the spectacle of women parading in a competition to determine which one was most attractive to men. It was hard to say anything against a beauty contest without sounding envious or hostile. The rhetoric of revolution removes this embarrassment by making the notion that women are against each other, a myth perpetrated by men to keep women from joining together against their "oppression."

"ZAP"

The Miss America protest was a model of what the Communists used to call "agit-prop," or the art of making revolutionary capital out of a current event. It was also the proving ground for what they thought was a brilliant new rationale for dealing with a hostile press. The protesting women made the media carry the message by laying down their own ground rules for press coverage. They refused to talk to male reporters. They refused to identify a leader. And they insisted on speaking as an anonymous group. Radicals have sometimes refused to identify their leaders in order to protect them from arrest, but Women's Lib did so in part to refute the notion that women are unable to cooperate. In the revolutionary vocabulary, group action is a "zap."

Zap, used still, is maddening to the media. So too is the attitude of Women's Lib. No group or individual in living memory has ever treated the press so disparagingly. But it has worked. Caught off guard, intrigued, or merely stunned, the print media has given Women's Lib more space than the brassiest press agent could possibly hold out to the most gullible potential client.

Even more innovative is the solution Women's Lib has developed to the gut problems of any social action; how to recruit new members. The technique is "consciousness raising." A consciousness-raising session is informal, intimate. Ideally, a dozen or more women get together to talk about their experiences *as women,* to call to mind the little slights, frustrations and hangups they have put out of mind as inevitable.

There is, say the feminists, a well of anger hidden somewhere inside the gentlest women. Consciousness raising lets the genie out of the bottle. Once a woman admits to herself how she has been victimized, she can never go back to the Garden of Eden. She gets angrier and angrier and she infects the women around her. Every woman who admits she is a victim makes it that much harder for the next woman to pretend she isn't a victim. The anger feeds on itself, and it is contagious. That's what Women's Lib is all about. It is less a movement than a revolutionary state of mind. But is it, really, a revolution?

According to the article on Revolution in the *New Encyclopedia of Social Science*, revolutions are most likely to occur when the old order is breaking down, the despots are reforming themselves, the condition of the oppressed is improving, widening education has created a "revolution of expectations," and a war complicates the work of the ruling class. Read "men" for the powers that be, "women" for the oppressed, and paragraphs of the essay take on new and striking sense.

The old order, the patriarchal system *is* breaking down: more women are single or divorced, more wives are self-supporting, more children are born out of wedlock, more sex is extramarital. The despots *are* reforming themselves: more men, particularly younger men treat women as companions rather than sex objects. The condition of women *is* improving, but perhaps not as fast as widening education is raising expectations. Finally, a war *is* distracting attention from domestic reforms that would improve the status of women, not the least of which is the establishment of publicly-supported child care centers.

THE GREAT DIVIDE

The analogies go even further, to the characteristics of the movement itself. Like political revolutions, Women's Lib is afflicted with schisms, exhausting ideological debate, suspicion of charismatic leaders and experts or professionals who have earned their credentials under the established system. Many of the younger groups are not particularly eager, for instance, to be lectured by authors like Betty Friedan or Caroline Bird. They want and need to speak for themselves, in their own idiom. And like other revolutionaries, they are almost pathologically afraid — as well they might be — that in a general upheaval, some sister (comrade, brother) might feather her own nest. This fear, plus the need for solidarity among the oppressed, explains to some degree why they need consensus decisions.

For all the similarities to classical revolutions, there is one great divide: women can't revolt against society in quite the same way that workers or blacks can revolt. Sex lines cut across class lines. As a bitter feminist has put it, women are the only oppressed class that lives with the master race. They cannot, like the black separatists, really secede from society. For the most part, men are part of the daily lives of even the most fire-breathing feminist.

What is actually happening, I think, is something that carries a wider meaning even than the status of women, trying as that status may be to those concerned about it. The notion of women as an oppressed group has surfaced in every revolution of modern history. The "demands" of the Congress to Unite Women would not have surprised Mary Wollstonecraft, who wrote *A Vindication of the Rights of Women* in 1792, the year they deposed Louis XVI. They would have delighted Elizabeth Cady Stanton, whose Seneca Falls "Declaration of Principles" demanded the vote for women at a time when the issue of slavery threatened the survival of the United States.

Women's Liberation is spreading because American society is in a comparable state of revolution. It reflects not only the revolt of the black separatists, whose rhetoric it follows so closely, but the general loss of credibility in all constituted authority — political, educational, intellectual, religious, even military.

Where will women come out? If previous revolutionary periods are any guide, the answer is: "Better — at least so far as their status as women is concerned." Beyond that, and just as importantly, the answer has to be: "No better than the society as a whole comes out."

# 3. *The Good Provider* ━━━━━━━━━━━━━━━━━━━━━━━━━

> In order to assert ourselves as
> individuals, we relate only to those
> phases of reality which seem to
> promote the attainment of our
> objectives and we remain divorced
> from the rest of it. But the further we
> drive this separation, the deeper grows
> the rift within ourselves.
>
> FRITZ PAPPENHEIM

"We do the world's will," writes George Bernard Shaw, "not our own." For
the weight of social expectation defines us even to ourselves. Such a tendency
in human affairs is today reinforced by a mass society that schematizes the
individual and by a mass communications system that manipulates him to
ingest that scheme as personal identity. So omnipresent are the stereotypes that
even scholars are caught up in them, functional sociologists translating received models into imperatives of prefabricated role.

The consequence is individuals trapped in molds. All women are bounded
by the biological woman; all men are tethered to the economic man. From this
viewpoint, manliness is confirmed only by an unremitting demonstration of the
ability to pay.

In *The Theory of the Leisure Class,* Thorstein Veblen traced the history of
pecuniary repute as the crucial symbol of worth, first in relation to the upper
classes — where leisure and aristocratic patterns are an actual way of life —
and second in the influence of these values on the life styles of other classes.
The selection included here sketches the development of ownership in persons,
the gradual division that came about in categories of service, and the exemption of one group of servants — notably wives — from "industrial employment" (that is, from productive labor). In time, the economy of the leisure class

*Parallel readings for Chapter 3, "The Masculine Mystique."

came to be no longer represented by the busy housewife of the early patriarchal days but by the lady — and the lackey. In this way, says Veblen, there arose a subsidiary or derivative leisure class, whose office was the performance of vicarious leisure for those who could afford such symbols of reputability. This pattern today reaches down to classes that are not leisured, where the ability to pay is demonstrated by vicarious leisure and conspicuous consumption by dependents, especially dependent wives. Veblen's style, "like some wine, is strange, if not distasteful, to the beginner," writes Stuart Chase, "but once familiar, it is heady, bitter and delightful." Here is a sample, which I hope will inspire the reader to study the work from which it is taken.

The next selection, from *The American Male* by Myron Brenton describes the effect of archaic forms on today's life styles. For masculine identity in current terms is narrowly based in the breadwinner role, which occupies the central position of masculine life both physically and psychically. Harking back to the concept of vicarious leisure, self-esteem for the woman derives from enticing a good provider; self-esteem for the man derives from being one. Ability to pay is evidence of success not only in the marketplace but in the private arena of the bedroom. All aspects of personal worth, not excluding sexual potency, are measured by the medium of exchange. Myron Brenton suggests that these ideas and emotions match a society that no longer exists. Since the history of thought is one of continuous revision, he pleads for sexual differentiation appropriate to current forms and emergent novelty — on the basis of individual difference — not arbitrary mechanisms for self-validation.

## Pecuniary Power

*Thorstein Veblen*

There is reason to believe that the institution of ownership has begun with the ownership of persons, primarily women. The incentives to acquiring such property have apparently been: (1) a propensity for dominance and coercion; (2) the utility of these persons as evidence of the prowess of their owner; (3) the utility of their services.

Personal service holds a peculiar place in the economic development. During

From *The Theory of the Leisure Class.* Reprinted by permission of The Viking Press, Inc.

the stage of quasi-peaceable industry, and especially during the earlier development of industry within the limits of this general stage, the utility of their
services seems commonly to be the dominant motive to the acquisition of
property in persons. Servants are valued for their services. But the dominance
of this motive is not due to a decline in the absolute importance of the other
two utilities possessed by servants. It is rather that the altered circumstances
of life accentuate the utility of servants for this last-named purpose. Women
and other slaves are highly valued, both as an evidence of wealth and as a
means of accumulating wealth. Together with cattle, if the tribe is a pastoral
one, they are the usual form of investment for profit. To such an extent may
female slavery give its character to the economic life under the quasi-peaceable
culture that the woman even comes to serve as a unit of value among peoples
occupying this cultural stage — as for instance in Homeric times. Where this
is the case there need be little question but that the basis of the industrial
system is chattel slavery and that the women are commonly slaves. The great,
pervading human relation in such a system is that of master and servant. The
accepted evidence of wealth is the possession of many women, and presently
also of other slaves engaged in attendance on their master's person and in
producing goods for him.

A division of labour presently sets in, whereby personal service and attendance on the master becomes the special office of a portion of the servants, while
those who are wholly employed in industrial occupations proper are removed
more and more from all immediate relation to the person of their owner. At
the same time those servants whose office is personal service, including domestic duties, come gradually to be exempted from productive industry carried on
for gain.

This process of progressive exemption from the common run of industrial
employment will commonly begin with the exemption of the wife, or the chief
wife. After the community has advanced to settled habits of life, wife-capture
from hostile tribes becomes impracticable as a customary source of supply.
Where this cultural advance has been achieved, the chief wife is ordinarily of
gentle blood, and the fact of her being so will hasten her exemption from vulgar
employment. . . .

There results, therefore, a constantly increasing differentiation and multiplication of domestic and body servants, along with the concomitant progressive exemption of such servants from productive labour. By virtue of their
serving as evidence of ability to pay, the office of such domestics regularly tends
to include continually fewer duties, and their service tends in the end to
become nominal only. This is especially true of those servants who are in most
immediate and obvious attendance upon their master. So that the utility of
these comes to consist, in great part, in their conspicuous exemption from
productive labour and in the evidence which this exemption affords of their
master's wealth and power. . . . Hence it comes about that in the economy of

the leisure class the busy housewife of the early partriarchal days, with her retinue of hard-working handmaidens, presently gives place to the lady and the lackey.

In all grades and walks of life, and at any stage of the economic development, the leisure of the lady and the lackey differs from the leisure of the gentleman in his own right in that it is an occupation of an ostensibly laborious kind. It takes the form, in large measure, of a painstaking attention to the service of the master, or to the maintenance and elaboration of the household paraphernalia; so that it is leisure only in the sense that little or no productive work is performed by this class, not in the sense that all appearance of labour is avoided by them. The duties performed by the lady, or by the household or domestic servants, are frequently arduous enough, and they are also frequently directed to ends which are considered extremely necessary to the comfort of the entire household. So far as these services conduce to the physical efficiency or comfort of the master or the rest of the household, they are to be accounted productive work. Only the residue of employment left after deduction of this effective work is to be classed as a performance of leisure.

But much of the services classed as household cares in modern everyday life, and many of the "utilities" required for a comfortable existence by civilized man, are of ceremonial character. They are, therefore, properly to be classed as a performance of leisure in the sense in which the term is here used. They be nonetheless imperatively necessary from the point of view of decent existence; they may be none the less requisite for personal comfort even, although they may be chiefly or wholly of ceremonial character. But in so far as they partake of this character they are imperative and requisite because we have been taught to require them under pain of ceremonial uncleanness or unworthiness. We feel discomfort in their absence, but not because their absence results directly in physical discomfort; nor would a taste not trained to discriminate between the conventionally good and the conventionally bad take offence at their omission. Insofar as this is true the labour spent in these services is to be classed as leisure; and when performed by others than the economically free and self-directing head of the establishment they are to be classed as vicarious leisure.

The vicarious leisure performed by housewives and menials, under the head of household cares, may frequently develop into drudgery, especially where the competition for reputability is close and strenuous. This is frequently the case in modern life. Where this happens, the domestic service which comprises the duties of this servant class might aptly be designated as wasted effort, rather than as vicarious leisure. But the latter term has the advantage of indicating the line of derivation of these domestic offices, as well as of neatly suggesting the substantial economic ground of their utility; for these occupations are chiefly useful as a method of imputing pecuniary reputability to the master or to the household on the ground that a given amount of time and effort is conspicuously wasted in that behalf.

In this way, then, there arises a subsidiary or derivative leisure class, whose office is the performance of a vicarious leisure for the behoof of the reputability of the primary or legitimate leisure class. . . . The leisure of the servant is not his own leisure . . . . The like is often true of the wife throughout the protracted economic stage during which she is still primarily a servant — that is to say, so long as the household with a male head remains in force. In order to satisfy the requirements of the leisure-class scheme of life, the servant should show not only an attitude of subservience, but also the effects of special training and practice in subservience. The servant or wife should not only perform certain offices and show a servile disposition, but it is quite as imperative that they should show an acquired facility in the tactics of subservience — a trained conformity to the canons of effectual and conspicuous subservience. Even today it is this aptitude and acquired skill in the formal manifestation of the servile relation that constitutes the chief element of utility in our highly paid servants, as well as one of the chief ornaments of the well-bred housewife. . . .

With the disappearance of servitude, the number of vicarious consumers attached to any one gentleman tends, on the whole to decrease. The like is of course true, and perhaps in a still higher degree, of the number of dependents who perform vicarious leisure for him. In a general way, though not wholly nor consistently, these two groups coincide. The dependent who was first delegated for these duties was the wife, or the chief wife; and, as would be expected, in the later development of the institution, when the number of persons by whom these duties are customarily performed gradually narrows, the wife remains the last. In the higher grades of society a large volume of both these kinds of service is required; and here the wife is of course still assisted in the work by a more or less numerous corps of menials. But as we descend the social scale, the point is presently reached where the duties of vicarious leisure and consumption devolve upon the wife alone. In the communities of the Western culture, this point is at present found among the lower middle class.

And here occurs a curious inversion. It is a fact of common observation that in this lower middle class there is no pretence of leisure on the part of the head of the household. Through force of circumstances it has fallen into disuse. But the middle-class wife still carries on the business of vicarious leisure, for the good name of the household and its master. In descending the social scale in any modern industrial community, the primary fact — the conspicuous leisure of the master of the household — disappears at a relatively high point. The head of the middle-class household has been reduced by economic circumstances to turn his hand to gaining a livelihood by occupations which often partake largely of the character of industry, as in the case of the ordinary business man of today. But the derivative fact — the vicarious leisure and consumption rendered by the wife, and the auxiliary vicarious performance of leisure by menials — remains in vogue as a conventionality which the demands of reputability will not suffer to be slighted. It is by no means an uncommon spectacle to find a man applying himself to work with the utmost assiduity, in order that his wife may in due form render for him that degree of vicarious leisure which the common sense of the time demands.

The leisure rendered by the wife in such cases is, of course, not a simple manifestation of idleness or indolence. It almost invariably occurs disguised under some form of work or household duties or social amenities, which prove on analysis to serve little or no ulterior end beyond showing that she does not and need not occupy herself with anything that is gainful or that is of substantial use. As has already been noticed under the head of manners, the greater part of the customary round of domestic cares to which the middle-class housewife gives her time and effort is of this character. Not that the results of her attention to household matters, of a decorative and mundificatory character, are not pleasing to the sense of men trained in middle-class proprieties; but the taste to which these effects of household adornment and tidiness appeal is a taste which has been formed under the selective guidance of a canon of propriety that demands just these evidences of wasted effort. The effects are pleasing to us chiefly because we have been taught to find them pleasing. There goes into these domestic duties much solicitude for a proper combination of form and colour, and for other ends that are to be classed as aesthetic in the proper sense of the term; and it is not denied that effects having some substantial aesthetic value are sometimes attained. Pretty much all that is here insisted on is that, as regards these amenities of life, the housewife's efforts are under the guidance of traditions that have been shaped by the law of conspicuously wasteful expenditure of time and substance. If beauty or comfort is achieved, — and it is a more or less fortuitous circumstance if they are, — they must be achieved by means and methods that commend themselves to the great economic law of wasted effort. The more reputable, "presentable" portion of middle-class household paraphernalia are, on the one hand, items of conspicuous consumption, and on the other hand, apparatus for putting in evidence the vicarious leisure rendered by the housewife.

The requirement of vicarious consumption at the hands of the wife continues in force even at a lower point in the pecuniary scale than the requirement of vicarious leisure. At a point below which little if any pretence of wasted effort, in ceremonial cleanness and the like, is observable, and where there is assuredly no conscious attempt at ostensible leisure, decency still requires the wife to consume some goods conspicuously for the reputability of the household and its head. So that, as the latter-day outcome of this evolution of an archaic institution, the wife, who was at the outset the drudge and chattel of the man, both in fact and in theory, — the producer of goods for him to consume, — has become the ceremonial consumer of goods which he produces. But she still quite unmistakably remains his chattel in theory; for the habitual rendering of vicarious leisure and consumption is the abiding mark of the unfree servant.

This vicarious consumption practised by the household of the middle and lower classes can not be counted as a direct expression of the leisure-class scheme of life, since the household of this pecuniary grade does not belong within the leisure class. It is rather that the leisure-class scheme of life here comes to an expression at the second remove. The leisure class stands at the head of the social structure in point of reputability; and its manner of life and its standards of worth therefore afford the norm of reputability for the community. The observance of these standards, in some degree of approximation, becomes incumbent upon all classes lower in the scale. In modern civilized communities the lines of demarcation between social classes have grown vague and transient, and wherever this happens the norm of reputability imposed by the upper class extends its coercive influence with but slight hindrance down through the social structure to the lowest strata. The result is that the members of each stratum accept as their ideal of decency the scheme of life in vogue in the next higher stratum, and bend their energies to live up to that ideal. On pain of forfeiting their good name and their self-respect in case of failure, they must conform to the accepted code, at least in appearance.

The basis on which good repute in any highly organized industrial community ultimately rests is pecuniary strength; and the means of showing pecuniary strength, and so of gaining or retaining a good name, are leisure and a conspicuous consumption of goods. Accordingly, both of these methods are in vogue as far down the scale as it remains possible; and in the lower strata in which the two methods are employed, both offices are in great part delegated to the wife and children of the household. . . .

The exigencies of the modern industrial system frequently place individuals and households in juxtaposition between whom there is little contact in any other sense than that of juxtaposition. One's neighbors, mechanically speaking, often are socially not one's neighbors, or even acquaintances; and still their transient good opinion has a high degree of utility. The only practicable means of impressing one's pecuniary ability on these unsympathetic observers of one's everyday life is an unremitting demonstration of the ability to pay.

New Ways to Manliness

*Myron Brenton*

### THE BREADWINNER

When sociologist Helena Lopata of Roosevelt University queried more than 600 women in the Chicago area to find out how they viewed their roles in life, in order of importance, she discovered that they considered themselves mothers first of all. When she asked them to do the same for their husbands, their replies were an even greater revelation. Did these women—suburban wives in their thirties, with a family income between $6,000 and $10,000; urban wives with a median age of forty-nine and a family income from $5,000 to more than $16,000—see their mates primarily as husbands? As fathers? Or as breadwinners? The answer, startling though it is, isn't difficult to guess. Nearly 65 percent of the wives in both groups stated unequivocally that the most important role of the man of the family is, in their eyes, his breadwinning one. Father came in second; husband, a poor third.

These statistics lend themselves to a very plausible explanation. Since the American male bases his masculine identity so narrowly on the breadwinning role, since it occupies—both psychically and physically—the central position in his life, his wife naturally is inclined to see him in the same utilitarian way. If one leaves aside the implications this has for the emotional relationship between husband and wife, the fact is that by depending so heavily on his breadwinning role to validate his sense of himself as a man, instead of also letting his roles as husband, father, and citizen of the community count as validating sources, the American male treads on psychically dangerous ground. It's always dangerous to put all of one's psychic eggs into one basket.

This is not to deny the meaning and importance of work in a person's life. Ideally, work is an outlet for creative energy, a way of channeling aggression, a tie with reality, and what Erik H. Erikson has called the backbone of identity formation. What is suggested here is this: (1) The other roles a man plays in life may also be very valuable in these respects; (2) present-day working conditions do not permit fulfillment of the traditional psychological aims of work to any significant degree; and (3) a narrow concentration of work in terms of his identity does not allow the male enough scope and flexibility to deal with the complexities of the times.

In a bureaucratic, technological society with its insistence on rote and specialization the psychological meaning of work undergoes considerable reduction. With roughly 80 percent of the working population of the United States employed by someone else, most breadwinners are to some extent alienated from their work. Sociologist Robert Blauner defines alienation along four principal lines:

1. The breadwinner feels a sense of powerlessness because he has no say over the end result of his efforts, no control over his actions, is at the mercy of the machine or the front-office brass.

2. The breadwinner feels a sense of meaninglessness because all he knows are his specialized little tasks, which he can't relate to the various other departments, to the organization as a whole.

3. The breadwinner feels a sense of isolation because he can't really identify with the firm or its goals.

4. The breadwinner feels a sense of self-estrangement because there's little or no integration between his work and other aspects of his life.

Although Blauner was referring principally to industrial workers, it's clear that his definitions are—to a greater or lesser degree—applicable at all levels of the working world. There aren't too many men who have the autonomy or the freedom to make decisions that is the hallmark of individual initiative. Nor are there many people—whether in business, industry, or even the professions —who can fully escape the feeling that they are cogs in some impersonal machine. Furthermore, the more work is fragmented, the less able a man is to relate to people not in his immediate specialty. To be sure, many breadwinners are interested in their work, but on a comparatively narrow level. For the most part, what challenges there are lack real dimension. Truly creative jobs —those in which the individual feels a sense of autonomy, a call for his best efforts, a solid sense of accomplishment, a real recognition of his particular services, and a knowledge that what he's doing is truly a worthwhile contribution to the world—are relatively few in number. On the whole, men are more acceptant of their jobs than actually caught up in them. Thus, for the tremendous ego investment a man makes in his job, the great emphasis he places on it in terms of his masculinity, the work he does will not, generally speaking, reward him commensurately. And he shows it. The growing problems of pilferage, restriction of output, malingering, "putting something over" on the company, expense-account cheating, and heavy drinking at lunch or after work—all are, in part at least, manifestations of job alienation. It may well be that in some instances strikes are also a manifestation of the psychic distancing between a man and his job.

Actually, these days it is not the task itself that the majority of American males are primarily involved with when it comes to their breadwinning role. The fruits of work are what the male considers more meaningful to him in terms of his manliness: the pay he gets, the prestige the job has, the status it gives him in the community, the possessions it allows him to buy, and the better life it enables him to give his family. His wife views his breadwinning role the same way; many wives have little comprehension of what their mates actually do for a living.

As Vance Packard put it, "Ever more people . . . find their main life satisfactions in their consumptive role rather than their productive role." In such circumstances the work itself becomes "instrumental," to use sociologist Harold L. Sheppard's description of the phonomenon. It "becomes the means by which a man is able to achieve valued goals unrelated to the job. A 'good job' thus is one that allows the maximization of these goals with a minimum of effort and with as good physical conditions as possible."

Here may be one very good reason that so often and so justifiably is heard the complaint "Men don't take pride in their workmanship any more." Whatever rewards a highly affluent consumer society has to offer, pride of workmanship isn't one of them. There are other things that make the man.

Here, too, is one reason that so often these days one hears the comment "People are afraid to stick their necks out on the job, to make decisions, to rock the boat." With the intrinsic rewards of the tasks one performs much less important than the extrinsic rewards they provide, it behooves one not to rock the boat. This doesn't mean less competition; it means, for many men, intense competition of a different sort: they play it safe; they "play it cool"; they become more adept at manipulating the environment than in pursuing excellence or even, on an overt level, the other man's job. They develop the skill of fending off the competition—the younger men under them on the way up, the eager beavers on their own level. They learn the art of being present without being seen, of doing nothing that would make their superiors really take notice of them. Such men are trying to create an anxiety-free environment for themselves, but they wind up with the worst possible case of anxiety. A therapist in Connecticut told me about one such patient, a man working for I.B.M.:

> He's under constant fear and tension. He's constantly worried about whether he's going to get ahead or isn't he? He's not worried about being dropped, but he's very worried about what people are thinking about him. He's been with I.B.M. for something like eight years, and he hasn't moved ahead. He's putting the pressure on himself. It's him in relation to the society of I.B.M. He's afraid of taking the risk of getting a promotion, afraid he might not be able to handle the new responsibilities. He's also afraid of the competition. His idea is that if he fails, he'll look worse than if he didn't try at all. So he doesn't try. The failure becomes much more difficult for him to handle.

One of the most important things a democracy has to offer is the freedom for a man to choose his own line of work. Economics, lack of training, or other factors of this kind limit his choice, of course; often he has to take the first thing that comes along. But at least there's no government agency to tell him what he must do or where — no one shipping him off to pick crops in California, say, or putting him to work on space projects in Houston when the need arises. Yet the masculine stereotypes themselves serve to delimit job choice. This is especially the case with occupations having a feminine or an artistic connotation. When masculinity is closely bound up with job status, as is so very much the case today, there's even more constriction of job choice. A study of middle-class fathers and sons shows that such fathers usually say that their sons are free to take any jobs they want, although further probing elicits the fact that what they really mean is that their boys are free to take any jobs that are safely middle-class. So many a middle-class boy who loves to get his hands dirty working on cars and who would make a skilled mechanic winds up in the pristine surroundings of an office, working on a job really not much to his liking. This also works in reverse: Some blue-collar workers who would otherwise enjoy their jobs can't allow themselves to do so because these jobs don't have middle-class status.

The rating of jobs in terms of prestige is probably inevitable; it occurs in all industrial nations. But its built-in hazards are intensified when the society is very competitive. It isn't the job that really goes on the rating scale; it's the man who holds it. This automatically creates a lot of losers. By definition, any rating scale can only accommodate X number of prestige positions; this means that about 80 percent of the working population is more or less disqualified. Dr. Marvin Bressler, professor of sociology at Princeton University, pointed out that when there's a hierarchical system in which the bulk of the population holds positions which aren't highly esteemed "the occupational structure itself systematically generates a sense of failure in many men. A janitor who does his work with skill and fidelity nevertheless remains a janitor and he may convert the low prestige attached to his job into a generalized estimate of his own self-worth. Men are peculiarly vulnerable to this process. Women may escape harsh self-judgment by invoking the durable symbols of feminine virtue—wife and mother — that by public and private consent still redeem their lives. The alternative of shrinking the universe to family size is not now a viable male option."

Even if the job carries a goodly measure of prestige — or, at any rate, enough to satisfy the man who has it — he isn't off the hook. The trouble is that prestige isn't a stable element. Once achieved, it has to be maintained, leaving the man who banks on it at the mercy of all kinds of competitive pressure and changing circumstances. For instance, Walter Buckingham, a specialist in automation, makes the point that in the past workers were dirty while managers were clean. This gave managers a prestige that automation has done away with, and they don't like it. He tells of a U. S. Bureau of Labor Statistics survey of an insurance company that was in the process of installing computers— machines that would displace many of the white-collar workers. The survey showed that it wasn't the workers who objected. Dissent came from the vice-presidents, who felt their own status would be diminished. On every level of the executive pyramid in the larger corporations there has evolved what Vance Packard calls the "intense preoccupation" with "symbols of status." He quotes the comment of a Cleveland corporation president that "often the little privileges that go with an office are more important to an executive than a raise. You'd expect executives to be more mature, but they frequently aren't." In effect, competition these days doesn't necessarily mean climbing up the ladder of success. It can also mean making one's particular rung as safe and plush and comfortable as possible.

The American male looks to his breadwinning role to confirm his manliness, but work itself is fraught with dehumanizing — *i.e.,* unmanning — influences. With the growing impact of automation, they're bound to increase. The very fact that leisure time is already becoming a social problem in America, a problem getting a great deal of expert scrutiny (several major universities have centers for the study of leisure, and the American Psychiatric Association has a standing committee on leisure), is a manifestation of how an overemphasis on work in terms of identity has a boomeranging effect. Most factory workers don't want more free time; this is reflected in the fact that the majority of unions have stopped bargaining for a shorter workweek. It's the threat of being displaced, however, that makes automation a major threat for most people. That threat is felt not only by low-level workers but also by white-collar workers and junior executives. A contributor to *Mass Society in Crisis* observes in discussing the new computers:

> [They] combine high technical competence with just enough of an I.Q. to keep them tractable. They do precisely the kind of work to which junior executives and semi-skilled workers are usually assigned. . . . Many middle management people in automated companies now report that they are awaiting the ax, or if more fortunate, retirement.

Scientists themselves are becoming obsolete in terms of their present skills. Many scientists—especially those in government defense work—are over-trained in one specialty. As their jobs are being eliminated, these Ph.D.'s and technicians face serious adjustment problems, for circumstances require them to retrain so as to put their expertise to work in a new field

Eventually, automation is expected to make some profound changes in the work role. Depending on which expert you talk to and which crystal ball he uses, everybody will work, but only a few hours a day or week; or most people will only be occupied in research and services; or every person will acquire several different skills and jobs in his lifetime; or one-third of the population will always be in school; or the definition of work itself will undergo radical changes, encompassing some of the activities we now call leisure-time activities. Such changes, however, won't come about in the very near future. As for now, the man who invests his entire identity in the work role is rendered extremely vulnerable. Dr. Bressler summed it up this way:

Many people invest too much of their psyches in work. A wide variety of circumstances — limited native capacity, skills that become obsolescent, impersonal socio-economic forces, capricious judgments by superiors — make the prediction and control of occupational success very hazardous. Accordingly, a prudent man would do well to develop other sources of ego-gratification.

DEALING WITH ADVERSITY

The more flexible a person is in terms of his life roles — that is, the greater his ability to commit himself to a wide repertoire of roles—the less vulnerable he is to temporary setbacks in the playing of any one of them. The more flexible a person is in his relationships with other people — that is, the fewer preconceived notions about appropriate male and female behavior he has — the greater his ability is to deal with adversity.

A personal crisis — sudden unemployment, for example — demonstrates clearly and dramatically the stunting effects of inflexibility, of a rigidly patriarchal outlook. If further evidence is needed that for the majority of American males, work is at the center of their conception of themselves as men, their reaction to the abrupt loss of their jobs proves it amply. Often their immediate reactions are remarkably like those of war casualties or victims of sudden accidents. Almost everything on which they have based their inner security is shattered. They're bereft.

When the Packard automobile plant shut down in 1956, for instance, many of the workers showed "stupefaction, bewilderment, a feeling of being 'lost.' " One employee said, "I felt like a bomb hit me . . . no place to go." Another commented, "I felt like someone had hit me with a sledge hammer." And a third told an interviewer, "I felt like jumping off the Belle Island Bridge in the river — put that down, you put that down." When news broke in the closing months of 1964 that the New York Naval Shipyard, in Brooklyn, would be shut down, one worker told a *Herald Tribune* marine reporter, expressing what many of the workers felt, "We've been bombed out." When sociologists looked at the dislocations caused by the Studebaker automobile plant shutdown a year earlier, they found a high number of suicides taking place among the former workers — a rate far higher than would be the case in the total population with people having the same characteristics.

According to Dr. Harold L. Sheppard, of the W. E. Upjohn Institute for Employment Research, many former workers shut themselves inside their houses after the Studebaker plant had closed down. They never went out. "It was," Dr. Sheppard told me, "like a sudden, unexpected death in the family." He pointed out that not only had these men banked so heavily on the breadwinning role in terms of their image of themselves, but they also had a unidimensional view of that role:

When a man has been an auto worker or a miner for twenty or thirty years, he can't picture himself as being anything else. We need some new counseling techniques to shake these men up, get them out of the rut, get them started thinking of new possibilities.

This pattern of a man who has lost his job shutting himself up in his house for days or weeks at a time, shutting out the world, is by no means an unusual one. It occurred in California when a Lockheed Aircraft Corporation plant laid off 500 engineers. Many of the men — who had worked at Lockheed for eight years or more, who had nice houses, expensive furniture, and several cars, but who hadn't yet consolidated their gains — could not handle the stress situation. One man left his house and came back home at the normal times each day, just as though he were still working, but he spent those eight or nine hours sitting in the park. This went on for two weeks. As luck would have it, a friend of his learned of a fine job opportunity, something the man was ideally suited for, but didn't tell him because he assumed from this going-to-work-as-usual pattern that he was in fact still working.

Dr. Gertrude Hengerer told me that financial counselors in her area, Palo Alto and Los Altos, California, become swamped with work when there are mass layoffs. One reason is that many of the people who lose their jobs are bogged down with debts, frequently in order to keep up, to buy the essentially unneeded home, cars, expensive vacations, and the like that become very much needed as a result of an overemphasis on the fruits of work. Wives may have to go to work precipitously to bring in some money. The whole family, including the children, become anxiety-ridden. The man who was laid off watches others still on the job, and the overriding question in his mind becomes, "Why me?" The men still on the job become terribly anxious, too. Their fear is, "Will I be next?" Dr. Hengerer said, "You can't get away from that question, 'Why me?' It really hits at your sense of self-worth, of masculinity."

Dr. Sheppard pointed out that the loss of job or even a sharp cut in pay is apt to be far more traumatic today than it was in Depression times. Then, nobody was asking, "Why me?" It was happening to everyone, and this took some of the psychological sting out of the stress situation.

The loss of job is obviously never a cause for rejoicing. In a youth-oriented culture it's especially agonizing for a man over the age of forty, who not infrequently is made to feel as though he has reached the extremes of decrepitude as he goes job hunting. But men vary widely in their ability to deal with adversity, and it has been demonstrated time and again that men who see their identity in the narrowest of terms, see it based principally in their breadwinning role, are in the greatest psychological trouble when they are suddenly deprived of this role.

The Depression is a relevant phenomenon to explore in this connection for a number of depth studies — both psychological and sociological — were made in those bleak times. In study after study what keeps showing up is that the experience of a sudden job loss was far more of a shock to the men than to the women, although the loss of income would affect both equally. It was the men who had been primarily making money. It was the men, now out of work, whose main role had disappeared, who lacked anything to involve themselves in, both physically and psychically. Revisiting Middletown during the Depression, about a decade after their initial trip there, sociologists Robert and Helen Lynd noticed that for women the reverse often held true. The women's roles didn't contract; they expanded. Not only did the wife have to go on with the household routine—cooking, cleaning, taking care of the children—but frequently the wife was also the one who held the family together when her husband was prone to go to pieces.

Paul Lazarsfeld, another noted sociologist, found somewhat the same situation when, in 1931, he scrutinized a small Austrian village that two years earlier had lost its one and only industry, a textile plant. Of a population of 1,486, 80 percent were out of work. Again, it was the men who were hardest hit psychologically, the ones who now had nothing to do and nothing to invest themselves in. They drifted helplessly and apathetically in the streets, looking dully for some means of rescue. On the other hand, the woman's world — the world of cooking, cleaning, mending, and childrearing — remained intact.

Since the women weren't deprived of their principal roles in life, it stands to reason that they would be less shattered than the men. Possibly if they were suddenly unable to fulfill their housewife-mother roles, they would also tend to fall apart, although I suspect that the very roles women concentrate on — the expressive, emotional ones, in terms of temperament—render them more adaptable. But there remains the point that a narrow concentration on role poses considerable psychological danger.

The subjects of the Lynds' study, and Lazarsfeld's, had strong patriarchal orientations. They conceived themselves as men principally in terms of being their families' breadwinners. When no bread was there to be won, they lacked the ability to make a shift, to obtain greater psychic rewards from their roles as husbands and fathers. On the contrary, since his supremacy was structured by externals, often an unemployed man's prestige as husband and father, as head of the household, deteriorated badly. "I still love him, but he doesn't seem as big a man," says a Depression wife about her husband in Dr. Komarovsky's classic study of *The Unemployed Man and His Family.* Dr. Komarovsky gives a poignant description of such a man's loss of power and prestige at home:

> The general impression that the interviews make is that in addition to sheer economic anxiety the man suffers from deep humiliation. He experiences a sense of deep frustration because in his own estimation he fails to fulfill what is the central duty of his life, the very touchstone of his manhood — the role of family provider. The man appears bewildered and humiliated. It is as if the ground had gone out from under his feet. He must have derived a profound sense of stability from having the family dependent on him. Whether he had considerable au-

thority within the family and was recognized as its head, or whether the wife's stronger personality had dominated the family, he nevertheless derived strength from his role as provider. Every purchase of the family — the radio, his wife's new hat, the children's skates, the meals set before him — all were symbols of their dependency on him. Unemployment changed it all. It is to the relief office, or to a relative, that the family now turns. It is to an uncle or a neighbor that the children now turn in expectation of a dime or a nickle for ice cream, or the larger beneficences such as a bicycle or an excursion to the amusement park.

When there is prolonged unemployment, as in depressed areas, the erstwhile breadwinner's reaction can take a different turn. Witness what the unavailability of jobs over a protracted period has brought about in Appalachia. With unemployed miners unable to get other work — and unwilling to work in nearby textile mills because they considered what they would have to do woman's work — their wives have become the chief breadwinners in the family. But according to Dorothy Cohen, executive director of the Family Service Association of Wyoming Valley, Pennsylvania, there's no real role reversal:

> In many instances, the women are faced with carrying the responsibility for home and children in addition to their jobs. Often, the care of the children is haphazard. Sometimes, relatives help. Day-care facilities are almost completely lacking in Wyoming Valley.

Some of the unemployed miners have fallen victim to what observers in the area call the depressed-area syndrome. They no longer feel degraded by their lack of employment. They don't involve themselves in home responsibilities. They congregate and drink together, while their wives work.

But it doesn't take as traumatic and explosive an experience as sudden unemployment to demonstrate the hazards of a firm belief in rigid patriarchal standards. Retirement also proves the point. There are, in fact, some strong similarities between retirement and unemployment. Retirement too brings out different reactions in men and women. The woman has already had her functions reduced when the children left home, but she never really completely retires; she must still cook the meals, clean the house, and take care of her husband. It may have been a very difficult moment for her when her last child departed for a life of his own, but she still has a somewhat familiar routine to pursue.

> As she goes about her daily routines [observes Donald E. Super, an expert on the psychology of careers], the husband is occasionally in her way, and both of them become uncomfortably conscious of the fact that she belongs there, that — whereas she has a role to play and ideas as to how she should play it — he does not belong there, he has no role to play. His role has changed from that of breadwinner to that of do-nothing, while his wife is still a homemaker. The self-concept which goes with the role of do-nothing is not a comfortable one to try to adopt after thirty-five years of working and of being a good provider.

Thus, the man who adjusts least well to retirement is the one who identifies himself — as a man — most closely with the breadwinning role. Conversely, the man who adjusts best is the one whose psychic investments have throughout the years been multidimensional:

> The physician-artist finds it easy to keep on painting, for he took up painting in the first place because of his interest; medical and artistic interests have been shown to tend to go together. Indulging these interests is purely avocational; it contributes nothing to his status as a physician; it brings him no fame or fees, merely satisfaction and friends. On the other hand, the executive does not find it easy to keep up his golf, his yachting or his cards, for he took these up originally not so much out of interest in the activities themselves as for the associations they would bring him. Mixing with the right people at the club brings clients, customers, contracts, and the right people are glad to mix with him for the same reasons. Once the business motivation is removed the association no longer has the same mutual appeal, and the activity itself loses point. There are exceptions, of course; businessmen have real friendships, as well as friendships of convenience, and some businessmen like golf, yachting or cards for their own sakes. But these are probably the exceptions.

If avocations help the male adjust to retirement, it stands to reason that a flexible view of what it is that constitutes musculinity, a fundamentally equalitarian approach to the marital interaction, will also help enormously. The husband who doesn't look at himself or his wife in terms of roles, who's neither demasculinized by doing the dishes or by having a working wife or by showing tenderness and love — the man who in his conception of himself finds genuine rewards in being a successful husband and father, as well as breadwinner — is hardly going to feel, after he retires, that he doesn't belong at home.

EQUALITY, FLEXIBILITY, AND MARITAL HAPPINESS

The functional psychiatrists and sociologists don't quite see it like this. They don't approve of the loose-knit equalitarian marriage. Their way is to pigeon-hole men and women into neat categories. They envision the ideal family, from the mental-health viewpoint, operating on the basis of clear-cut role differentiation. The man is the instrumental or task leader, the breadwinner, the authority figure, the one who gets things done, the parent who offers conditional love. The woman is the emotional or expressive-integrative leader, the one who keeps house and raises the children, the one solely responsible for binding the family's psychic wounds, the parent who offers unconditional love.

Such an inflexible division of roles rides roughshod over any individual characteristics. Task division is sharp — people know exactly what their roles are and no mistake about it — but focus on the uniqueness of individual personality is very blurred.

Moreover, in today's world, it isn't even really functional. It isn't functional because the way the American pattern is going — especially in terms of ecological shifts — the American family absolutely needs strong, flexible men and strong, flexible women to get things done. Most middle-class people and a growing number of working-class families are fleeing the cities, establishing themselves in the suburban way of life. In the suburbs a great deal of reliance must be placed on the wife. If something goes wrong, who's to see that it's taken care of? The husband is fifteen or twenty miles away at his job and is possibly working late. As Dr. James A. Peterson points out, if the wife is weak, if she can't get things done, if she can't handle situations, the family is in real trouble. Of course, a city wife has to be strong, too: few husbands can take off from work to handle every domestic crisis that comes along.

Studies at the University of Southern California, Dr. Peterson's bailiwick, show that when marriages have a strict division of roles in the traditionally functional pattern — that is, when the husband is solely the task leader; the wife, solely the expressive leader — the family as a functioning unit ceases to function. He explains:

> Unless there's an interpenetration of roles, the whole thing doesn't work — that is, if the wife cannot play the instrumental role, can't do the tasks that previously the man would insist on doing, the family breaks down. But likewise, if the husband is not an expressive leader, emotional leader, and gives his wife these things, the family breaks down, so that the roles not only become confused in our day, compared to earlier days, they've also shifted somewhat.

To be sure, society may insist that a man who responds emotionally enough to give this kind of leadership has a considerable feminine component in his personality. It may insist on a whole sequence of elaborate rules and standards for what constitutes appropriate masculine and feminine response, for the most part erroneously and arbitrarily connecting them to innate sex-linked traits. But to the extent to which such elaborations require demonstration as proof of sexual identity, to this extent many individuals will suppress portions of their personalities, or they will try to conform to the rules and standards but feel insecure because not all aspects of themselves really fit in with what is expected.

However, gaining a feeling of security about one's sexual identity doesn't really require such heavy reliance on any superficial or narrow set of standards or such great emphasis on the tasks one performs. Secure sexual identity depends far more on how fully one incorporates the notion that one is a male (or female) — how confortable one feels in one's sex, how acceptant one is of it. This incorporation and this acceptance in turn depend very much on how fully the individual's family of origin accepted him, accepted his sex, and allowed him to develop at his own rate of speed.

Discussing this vital point at a symposium conducted by the Child Study Association of America, Dr. M. Robert Gomberg noted:

> We are moving towards an era when it will be progressively less important to distinguish between male and female on the basis of social activity and responsibility. When the emphasis is put on inner personal fulfillment, it will be less

important whether the social roles are diametrically opposed or overlap than that the inner image of oneself be that of a person who is respected, loved, wanted. If a small child in his littleness feels wanted and respected, it is natural for him as he grows to know himself as a loved male child, protected by a family that supports his values, even if society is in transition and is confused in some of its dictates. He will find the strength from within, buttressed by the family, to find his own way and to play out his own role. Conversely, an individual may learn the stereotypes of masculinity. But if he has acquired them in a family that is angry, frightened, and competitive, though he sounds assertive and male, he may be inwardly frightened and need the loud sound of yesterday's maleness to disguise an inner hollowness.

The person who has grown up learning to accept himself and his sex — who learned this acceptance without pressure or compulsion — is the one best able to deal with the demands of a society that has worked out a whole sequence of sex-role elaborations. He's the one best able to take it and leave it, to conform to sex-role demands when conformity is in accord with his personality or does no violence to it and to reject the rest without feeling threatened.

If a man is real — if he is fundamentally secure in his manhood — women do not threaten him; nor does he need to confirm his masculinity at their expense. If his manhood is secure, then, as one young woman writes, "there is nothing the destructive part of me can destroy or hurt, so I can relax and enjoy being a complete woman, revel in my femaleness and enjoy his complete maleness." If he's secure, he can live his equalitarian life in an equalitarian marriage without fear of having his sexual identity shattered because roles merge or overlap. The secure man is warm, expressive, tender, and creative, yet quite capable of showing a sufficient amount of assertiveness when assertiveness is called for. The secure man can wash a dish, diaper a baby, and throw the dirty clothes into the washing machine — or do anything else women used to do exclusively — without thinking twice about it.

It's only when a man depends on arbitrary mechanisms outside himself to determine whether he's appropriately masculine, when he uses the stereotypes as strict guidelines to his identity, that he comes to feel somewhat beleaguered by the changes taking place in the roles of men and women. He reacts by belittling the female or by surrendering his autonomy to her. It's true that the blurring of the roles creates a great deal of identity confusion in both men and women at present, but it's a confusion brought on by the fact that neither sex has actually been assimilating the continuing changes in the condition of — and relationship between — the sexes. Nor may this assimilation be expected to come easily. For centuries woman's place was in the home, whereas her relative emancipation has existed for a comparatively small fraction of time.

Many people fear the phenomenon of role blurring because they earnestly believe that it will eventually spell the complete eradication of sex differentiation in role and in personality. This seems a needless fear. The biological differences between the sexes will, after all, remain. So will the psychological drives rooted in biological structure. In fact, sex differentiation may in one sense be more acute when it's not camouflaged by the stereotypes. Robert Sunley, assistant director of the Family Service Association of Nassau County, New York, noted:

> My impression is that the more the roles are blurred, the more the superficial functional differences are eliminated, actually the more essential sexual differentiation occurs. In other words, your more truly masculine and feminine attributes emerge. I think the artificial distinctions don't really fit the people's personalities, and they also don't really fit the essential sexuality involved. It confuses it, if anything. I think if you eliminate the arbitrary kinds of role distinctions, then the real sexual attraction — if there is any — emerges.

We may also surmise that the wonderful human diversity in temperament and in total personality structure will itself ensure the maintenance of many traditional psychosocial patterns of masculinity and femininity, as well as the patterns truly grounded in biology. The breakdown of the stereotypes therefore doesn't necessarily mean that the patterns behind them will eventually disappear. What it means is that they will not pose a threat. They will exist for people, rather than have people existing for them. This would put sex differentiation on the basis of the individual, not an indiscriminate mass.

To be sure, sex differences are much narrower in the United States at present than they are — or have been — in patriarchal cultures. Although this may be seen as a loss by some people, it should be recognized that this narrowing enables the sexes to be more friendly and companionable with each other than in the past. Only when each sex accepts the fact that it has components of the other in its personality, only when each individual of either sex learns, in a sense, to act out the other's roles, can the two sexes really and essentially communicate with each other. In fact, identity is built up in part by one's ability to master not only one's own roles, whatever they may be, but the roles of others as well. Furthermore, the very process of learning the roles of the opposite sex enables a person, if he is not threatened by it, to be more comfortable with his own sex — hence, with himself. Dr. Reuben Hill, the prominent University of Minnesota sociologist, explained:

> I happen to think that a family functions best that is able to communicate rather fully. That does not deny the opportunity to communicate at all levels. This permits a much wider repertoire of roles because you can discover what it's like to be a woman from a communicating mother, sister, and, later, girl friend. If you're a young man growing up, it's not as much of a mystery. You make fewer *faux pas* in anticipating their responses and are known as a man who is at ease with women. And similarly, with respect to men, you feel more at home with men because the communication bars that would separate you from womankind are not up but down. Because you can understand what the other's roles are, you can better understand what your own may be.

# 4. *So Dearly Joined* ━━━━━━━━━━━━━━━━━━━━━━━━━━━━━━━━━━━━━━

> The whole range of human error is essentially due to defective communication from mind to mind.
>
> SIR ROBERT WATSON-WATT

Marriage is still the most popular profession for women in America today, and judicious mating is still the surest path of vertical mobility. For if a woman is effective in turning *his* head, she can go farther than if she endeavors to use *hers,* Social models still reinforce the traditional indicia of femininity: development gap and dependency syndrome. Even the campus coed continues to be pressured to hitch her wagon to a mate, not a star; to consider her sex function as her salient marketable skill; to suspend her universe from a little gold ring. The pattern is still that of gaining a living through wedlock, of fulfillment through others, of affirmation by being. Spouses live in two communities, that of partners and that of peers; diminished women and harassed men have difficulty communicating with one another across the distances that separate their orbits.

In the first selection that follows, Cicely Hamilton describes much the same design for living in a work published in 1909. The terms she uses for the dependency syndrome are "supplication, abasement, compliance," and for the development gap, "narrowness of mind, stupidity, subservience." These qualities may promote the comfort of a husband, but they do not, by and large, generate his respect. Nor are the duties of wife and mother exalted when they stem not from free choice, but from the need to earn a living. And esteem is

*Parallel readings for Chapter 4, "Marriage à la Mode."

rarely accorded to anyone for the performance of purely animal functions: "If a woman is reverenced only because she reproduces her kind, a still higher meed of reverence is due to the rabbit."

In other fields of human endeavor, women have become amateurs. With sound business instinct, they develop professional expertise only in the area of attractiveness, for that is the prerequisite of success in the mating trade — where engagement follows the desire for possession, and where the living wage is not related to competence. Woman may be compared in all else to the odd-job laborer, for through isolation (like the lighthouse keeper or the shepherd in a mountainous district) she is cut off from significant experiences of social existence. As the Disney case (cited in "Marriage à la Mode," Chapter 4) explicitly illustrates, conventional wisdom assumes that wifehood is a service industry for the comfort and convenience of husbands.

Talcott Parsons, writing in 1942, also documents the development gap and the dependency syndrome, focusing, however, on the other side of the compact, the role of the husband as a good provider. Both the social and financial status of the wife are derivative, suspended from the husband's job in terms of prestige and earning power. There are then three roles available to dependent wives: the domestic, the glamorous, and the good companion. All are, however, pseudo-occupations, with elements of insecurity. Feminine emancipation has released inhibitions, but its ironic consequence is the separation of sex from personality (woman as sex object) and the segregation of sex roles (seductive product bonded to ability to pay). The range of mutuality between man and wife is thus limited by the specialized nature and instrumental character of their *apartheid*.

## Marriage as a Trade

*Cicely Hamilton*

For, be it noted, respect is a tribute to be commanded; not a reward to be won by supplication, by abasement, or compliance with the wishes of others. We do not necessarily like what we respect — for instance, the strength, the skill, and the resources of an enemy; and we do not necessarily respect in other

From *Marriage as a Trade* (London: Chapman & Hall, Ltd., 1909), pp. 144–168.

people qualities which, in our own interests, we should like them to possess — qualities of subservience, submission, and timidity, which we are quite willing to make use of even while we despise them.

This latter attitude, it seems to me, is the attitude of man to woman. For generations the training of woman has been directed towards the encouragement in her of certain qualities and characteristics — such as subservience, narrowness of mind, stupidity — all of them designed to promote the comfort and well-being of her owner, but none of them calculated to arouse in him a sensation of esteem. One may be kind to a person who is subservient, narrow-minded, and stupid; but one does not respect that person. It is no reproach whatever to a man to say that he does not respect women so long as he believes (and is encouraged to believe) that their only interests in life are the interests represented in a newspaper by the page entitled *Woman's World,* or the *Sphere of Woman* — a page dealing with face-powder, frilled nightgowns, and anchovy toast. No sane and intelligent man could feel any real respect for a woman whose world was summed up in these things. If the face-powder were applied with discretion and the directions on the subject of anchovy toast carried out with caution, he might find her an ornament as well as a convenience in his home; but it would be impossible for him to respect her, because she would not be, in the proper sense of the word, respectable. If he encourages the type, it is not because he respects it.

It may, of course, be urged that woman's claim to reverence and respect is based on far higher and surer ground than mere intelligence, or even character — on the fulfillment of her duties as wife and mother. Personally, I fail to see that any very great measure of respect or reverence is dealt out to her on this or any other ground — except, perhaps, now and again on paper; and even if it were, I should not, under present conditions, consider it justified. As long as the fulfilment of those duties is not a purely voluntary action on the part of woman, it gives her no claim upon any one's respect. Heroism under pressure is not heroism at all; and there is, to my mind, nothing the least exalted or noble in bringing up children, cooking chops, and cleaning doorsteps merely because very few other ways of earning a decent living happen to be open to you. And so long as marriage and motherhood are not matters of perfectly free choice on the part of the majority of women, so long will the performance of the duties incurred by marriage and motherhood, however onerous and however important, constitute no particular title to respect.

In so far as men do respect women, and not despise them, it seems to me that they respect them for exactly those qualities which they esteem in each other — and which, paradoxically enough, are for the most part exactly those qualities which they have done their best to erase and eradicate from the feminine character. The characteristics which make a man or a woman "respectable" are not the characteristics of subserviency and servility; on the contrary, those particular characteristics, even when encouraged for interested reasons, are rightly and naturally regarded with contempt. They may be more comfortable to live with — man evidently thinks so — but, comfortable or not, they are despised instinctively. They have their reward, no doubt; but that reward is not reverence and respect — since reverence and respect must be commanded, not coaxed or cringed for. A woman who insists on flinging aside the traditions of her early training, standing on her own feet, fighting her own battle, and doing that which is right in her own eyes, may not get from man anything more than respect, but, in the long run, she will certainly get that. It may be given grudgingly, but it will be given, all the same; since courage and independence of thought are qualities respectable in themselves. And, on the other hand, and however much he may desire to do so, it is, I should say, quite impossible for any thinking man to entertain a real reverence and esteem for a section of humanity which he believes to exist solely in order to perform certain animal functions connected with, and necessary to, the reproduction of the race. After all, it is not upon the performance of a purely animal function that a human being should found his or her title to respect; if woman is reverenced only because she reproduces her kind, a still higher meed of reverence is due to the rabbit.

And in this connection it is interesting to note that the mediaeval institution of chivalry, with its exalted, if narrow, ideal of reverence for, and service of, womanhood, took its rise and flourished in times when the housekeeping and child-bearing trade was not the only occupation open to women; when, on the contrary, they had, in the religious life, an alternative career, equally honoured with, if not more honoured than, marriage; and when it was not considered essential to the happiness and well-being of every individual woman to pair off, after the fashion of the animals going into the ark. Whatever the defects and drawbacks of conventual life, it stood for the principle, denied before and since, that woman had an existence of her own apart from man, a soul to be saved apart from man. It was a flat defiance of the theory that she came into the world only to marry and reproduce her kind; it acknowledged and admitted the importance of her individual life and conduct; in short, it recognized her as something besides a wife and a mother, and gave her other claims to respect than that capacity for reproduction which she shared with the lower animals. Further, by making celibacy an honourable instead of a despised estate, it must have achieved an important result from an economic point of view; it must have lessened the congestion in the marriage market by lessening the number of women who regarded spinsterhood as the last word in failure. It enhanced the value of the wife and mother by making it not only possible, but easy, for her to become something else. It opened up a career to an ambitious woman; since, in the heyday of the Church, the head of a great community of nuns was something more than a recluse — a power in the land, an administrator of estates. None of these things, of course, were in the minds of those who instituted the celibate, conventual life as a refuge from the world; they were its unforeseen results, but none the less real because unforeseen. They followed on the institution of the conventual life for woman because it represented the only organized attempt ever made to free her from the necessity of compulsory marriage and child-bearing.

I have no bias, religious or otherwise, in favour of the conventual life, which, as hitherto practised, is no doubt open to objection on many grounds; but it seems to me that any institution or system which admits or implies a reason for woman's existence other than sexual intercourse and the reproduction of her kind must tend inevitably to raise the position not only of the celibate woman, but, indirectly, of the wife and mother. In its palmy days, when it was a factor not only in the spiritual life of a religious body, but in the temporal life of the State, the convent, with all its defects, must have stood for the advancement of women; and if it had never come into existence, I very much doubt whether the injunctions laid upon knighthood would have included respect for and service of womanhood.

The upheaval which we term the Reformation, whatever its other merits, was distinctly anti-feminist in its tendencies. Where it did not sweep the convent away altogether, it narrowed its scope and sapped its influence; and, being anti-feminist, evolved no new system to take the place of that which it had swept away. The necessity of replacing the monk by the schoolmaster was recognized, but not the necessity of replacing the nun by the schoolmistress; the purely physical and reproductive idea of woman being once again upper-most, the need for training her mind no longer existed. The masterful women of the Renaissance had few successors; and John Knox, with his *Monstrous Regiment of Women,* was but the mouthpiece of an age which was setting vigorously to work to discourage individuality and originality in the weaker sex by condemning deviations from the common type to be burnt as witches.

This favourite pastime of witch-burning has not, I think, been sufficiently taken into account in estimating the reason for the low standard of intelligence attained by women at a time when men were making considerable progress in social and intellectual fields. The general impression appears to be that only old, ugly, and decrepit hags fell victims to popular superstition or the ingenuity of the witch-finder; but, as a matter of fact, when the craze for witch-finding was at its height, any sort of peculiarity, even beauty of an unusual and arresting type, seems to have been sufficient to expose a woman to the suspicion of secret dealings with the Prince of Darkness. At first sight it seems curious (since the religious element in a people is usually the feminine element) that the Prince of Darkness should have confined his dealings almost exclusively to women — it has been estimated that wizards were done to death in the proportion of one to several thousand witches; but on further consideration one inclines to the belief that the fury of witch-burning by which our ancestors were possessed must have been prompted by motives other than purely devo-tional. In all probability those motives were largely unconscious; but the rage of persecution against the witch has so much in common with the customary masculine policy of repressing, at any cost, all deviations from the type of wife-and-mother-and-nothing-else, that one cannot help the suspicion that it was more or less unconsciously inspired by that policy.

So far I have treated of the various influences which have been brought to bear upon women with the object of fitting them for the trade to which the male half of humanity desired to confine them; and I have, I hope, made it clear that, to a certain extent, these influences have defeated their own ends by discouraging the intelligence which ought to be a necessary qualification for motherhood, even if it is not a necessary qualification for wifehood. It remains to be considered what effect this peculiar training for one particular and peculiar trade has had upon woman's activity in those departments of the world's work which are not connected with marriage and motherhood, how it has acted upon her capacity for wage-earning and bread-winning on her own account, how it has affected her power of achievement in every other direction; what, in short, has been its effect upon woman in the life that she leads apart from man. (I must ask the male reader to be good enough to assume, even if he cannot honestly believe, that woman can, and occasionally does, lead a life apart from man.)

And one notes, to begin with, that the customary training, or lack of training, for marriage tends almost inevitably to induce that habit and attitude of mind which is known as amateurishness. And particularly, I should say, in the large class of society, which we describe roughly as the middle class; where the uncertainty with regard to the position, profession and consequent manner of living of the probable husband is so great as to make a thorough and businesslike training for the future nearly an impossibility. The element of chance — an element which plays such a very large part in the life, at any rate, of the average married woman — may upset all calculations based on the probable occupation and requirements of the husband, render carefully acquired accomplishments useless or unnecessary, and call for the acquirement of others hitherto unwanted and even undreamed of. Two sisters brought up in exactly the same surroundings and educated in exactly the same manner may marry, the one a flourishing professional or city man, who expects her to dress well, talk well, give good dinners and generally entertain his friends; the other a man whose work lies on the frontier of civilization where she will find it necessary to learn something of the management of horses and to manufacture her own soap and candles. While a third sister in the same family may never marry at all, but pass her life in furnished apartments, being waited on by landladies. These may be extreme, but they are not very unusual instances of the large part taken by sheer chance in the direction of a woman's life and the consequent impossibility of mapping out and preparing for the future. Hence a lack of thoroughness and an attitude towards life of helplessness and what I have called amateurishness. (The corresponding male attitude is found in the unskilled labourer of the "odd job" type.) Hence also the common feminine habit of neglecting more solid attainments in order to concentrate the energies on an endeavour to be outwardly attractive.

This concentration of energy on personal adornment, usually attributed to vanity or overflowing sexuality, is, so far as I can see, largely the outcome of a sound business instinct. For, be it remembered, that the one solid fact upon which an ordinary marriageable girl has to build the edifice of her life is the fact that men are sensitive to, and swayed by, that quality in woman which is called personal charm. What else her future husband will demand of her is more or less guess-work — nothing upon which to raise a solid foundation of preparation for his requirements and her own. He may require her to sit at the head of his table and talk fashionable gossip to his friends; he may require her to saddle horses and boil soap; the only thing she can be fairly certain of is that he will require her to fulfil his idea of personal attractiveness. As a matter of business then, and not purely from vanity, she specializes in personal attractiveness; and the care, the time and the thoroughness which many women devote to their own adornment, the choosing of their dresses and the curling of their hair is thoroughly professional and a complete contrast to their amateurishness in other respects.

The cultivation of personal charm, sometimes to the neglect of more solid and valuable attainments, is the more natural, because, as I have already pointed out, the material rewards of wifehood and motherhood have no connection at all with excellence in the performance of the duties of wifehood and motherhood — the wage paid to a married woman being merely a wage for the possession of her person. That being the case, the one branch of woman's work which is likely to bring her a material reward in the shape of an economically desirable husband is cultivation of a pleasing exterior and attractive manners; and to this branch of work she usually, when bent on marriage, applies herself in the proper professional spirit. A sensible, middle-class mother may insist on her daughter receiving adequate instruction in the drudgery of household work and cookery; but if the daughter should be fortunate enough to marry well such instruction will be practically wasted, since the scrubbing, the stewing, the frying and the making of beds will inevitably be deputed to others. And the sensible, middle-class mother is quite aware that her daughter's chance of marrying well and shirking disagreeable duties does not depend on the excellent manner in which she performs those duties, but on the quality of her personal attractions. The cultivation of her personal attractions, therefore, is really a more important and serious business for the girl who desires to marry than the acquirement of domestic accomplishments, which may, or may not, be useful in her after life, and which in themselves are unlikely to secure her the needful husband. This state of things is frankly recognized in the upper or wealthier ranks of society. There the typical domestic arts find practically no place in a girl's scheme of training which is directed solely towards the end of making her personally attractive and therefore desirable. Which means, of course, that those women who are in a position to do so concentrate their energies on the cultivation of those particular outward qualities by which alone they can hope to satisfy their ambition, their need for comfort, luxury, etc., or their desire to bring children into the world. They recognize that however much man may profess to admire the domestic and maternal qualities in woman, it is not that side of her which arouses in him the desire for possession, and that the most effective means of arousing that desire for possession is personal charm. We have been told that every woman is at heart a rake; it would, I think, be more correct to say that every woman who desires to attract some member of the opposite sex so that she may marry and bear children must, whatever she is at heart, be something of a rake on the surface.

With girls of the working-class, of course, a certain amount of training in domestic work is usually gone through, since it is obvious that domestic work will be required of them in after life; but even in the humblest ranks of society the rule holds good that it is personal attractiveness and not skill in the duties required of a wife and mother which makes a girl sought after and admired by the opposite sex. Consequently even working-class wives and mothers, women who have no chance of deputing their duties to paid servants, are frequently nothing but amateurs at their trade — which they have only acquired incidentally. In practically all ranks of society the real expert in housekeeping or in the care and management of infants is the "unattached" woman who works in other people's houses and attends to other people's children. She is the professional who knows her business and earns her living by it; the wife and mother, as often as not, being merely the amateur.

Human nature, and especially male human nature, being what it is, I do not know whether it is possible or even desirable that this state of things should be altered. My object in calling attention to it is not to suggest alteration (I have none to suggest), but simply to point out that women who are brought up in the expectation of marriage and nothing but marriage are almost of necessity imbued with the spirit of amateurishness which makes for inefficiency; and that this spirit has to be taken into account in estimating their difficulties where they have to turn their attention to other trades than marriage.

There are several other respects in which the marriage tradition (by which I mean the practical identification during many generations of womanhood with wifehood and motherhood) acts as a drag and a hindrance to the woman who, married or unmarried and with or against her will, has been swept out of the sacred and narrow sphere of home to compete for a wage in the open market. (Be it remembered that she is now numbered not by hundreds or thousands, but by millions.) As I have already pointed out, the trade of marriage is, by its very nature, an isolated trade, permitting of practically no organization or common action amongst the workers; and consequently the marriage-trained woman (and nearly all women are marriage trained — or perhaps it would be more correct to say marriage expectant) enters industrial or commercial life with no tradition of such organization and common action behind her.

I do not think that the average man realizes how much the average woman is handicapped by the lack of this tradition, nor does he usually trouble to investigate the causes of his own undoubted superiority in the matter of combination and all that combination implies. In accordance with his usual custom of explaining the shortcomings of womanhood by an inferiority that is inherent and not artificial and induced, he assumes that women cannot combine for industrial and other purposes because it is "natural" for them to be jealous and distrustful of one another. (This assumption is, of course, an indirect compliment to himself, since the jealousy and distrust of women for each other is understood to be inspired solely by their overpowering desire to attract the admiration of the opposite sex.)

This simple and — to man — flattering explanation of woman's inferiority in this respect completely fails to take into account the fact that the art of combination for a common purpose has been induced in one half of humanity by influences which have not been brought to bear upon the other half. I do not suppose that even the firmest and most hardened believer in woman's essential disloyalty, treachery and incapacity for common action, would venture to maintain that if all the men of past generations had been compelled to earn their living at isolated forms of labour — say, as lighthouse-keepers or shepherds in mountainous districts — the faculty of united action for common ends would be very highly developed amongst them. As I have already tried to show, in the division of labour between the two sexes man has almost invariably reserved for himself (having the power to do so, and because he considered them preferable) those particular occupations which brought him into frequent contact with his fellows, which entailed meeting others and working side by side with them; and this frequent contact with his fellows was, in itself, a form of education which has been largely denied to the other half of humanity. Woman's intercourse with her kind has been much more limited in extent, and very often purely and narrowly social in character. Until comparatively recent years it was unusual for women to form one of a large body of persons working under similar conditions and conscious of similar interests. It is scarcely to be wondered at that the modern system of industrialism with its imperative need for cooperation and common effort should have found her — thanks to her training — unprepared and entirely at a disadvantage.

It must be remembered also that the generality and mass of women have never come under the direct influence of two of the most potent factors in the social education and evolution of man as we know him — war and politics. However decivilizing an agency war may appear to-day, it has not been without its civilizing influence, since it was through the necessity of standing side by side for purposes of offence and defence that man first learned the art of combining for a common end, and acquired the virtues, at first purely military, that, in course of time and under different circumstances, were to develop into civic virtues. The camp was the state in embryo, the soldier the citizen in embryo, and the military tradition the collective and social tradition of organization for a common purpose and common interests. In the face of a common peril, such as war, men readily forget their differences and work shoulder to shoulder. Hence an appeal to the fears or the warlike spirit of a discontented people is the instinctive refuge of a government in difficulties, since there is no means so effective for producing at least a passing phase of unity amongst the jarring elements of a nation.

Woman, so far as one can judge, is, when occasion arises, just as much influenced by that necessity of common action in a common danger which first produced unity of effort and public spirit in man; but for her, as a rule, occasion has not arisen. Now and again under exceptional circumstances, such as a desperate and hard-fought seige, she has shown that the sense of peril acts upon her in exactly the same way as it acts upon her brethren; but the actual waging of battle has not often, even in the most turbulent of ages, entered into her life to teach her (along with other and less desirable lessons) the lesson of united effort and subordination of individual interest to the common weal.

The exclusion of woman from the arena of politics has barred to her another method of acquiring the art of combination and the strength that inevitably springs from it; an exclusion based upon the deep-rooted masculine conviction that she exists not for her own benefit and advantage, but for the comfort and convenience of man. Granted that she came into the world for that purpose only, the right of effective combination in her own interests is clearly unnecessary and undesirable, since it might possibly lead to results not altogether conducive to the comfort and convenience of man. The masculine attitude in this matter seems quite logical.

## Sex in the Social Structure

*Talcott Parsons*

It is of fundamental significance to the sex role structure of the adult age levels that the normal man has a "job" which is fundamental to his social status in general. It is perhaps not too much to say that only in very exceptional cases can an adult man be genuinely self-respecting and enjoy a respected status in the eyes of others if he does not "earn a living" in an approved occupational role. Not only is this a matter of his own economic support but, generally speaking, his occupational status is the primary source of the income and class status of his wife and children.

In the case of the feminine role the situation is radically different. The majority of married women, of course, are not employed, but even of those that are a very large proportion do not have jobs which are in basic competition for status with those of their husbands. The majority of "career" women whose occupational status is comparable with that of men in their own class, at least in the upper middle and upper classes, are unmarried, and in the small proportion of cases where they are married the result is a profound alteration in family structure.

This pattern, which is central to the urban middle classes, should not be misunderstood. In rural society, for instance, the operation of the farm and the attendant status in the community may be said to be a matter of the joint status of both parties to a marriage. Whereas a farm is operated by a family, an urban job is held by an individual and does not involve other members of the family in a comparable sense. One convenient expression of the difference lies in the question of what would happen in case of death. In the case of a farm it would at least be not at all unusual for the widow to continue operating the farm with the help of a son or even of hired men. In the urban situation the widow would cease to have any connection with the organization which had employed her husband and he would be replaced by another man without reference to family affiliations.

In this urban situation the primary status-carrying role is in a sense that of housewife. The woman's fundamental status is that of her husband's wife, the mother of his children, and traditionally the person responsible for a complex of activities in connection with the management of the household, care of children, etc.

For the structuring of sex roles in the adult phase the most fundamental considerations seem to be those involved in the interrelations of the occupational system and the conjugal family. In a certain sense the most fundamental basis of the family's status is the occupational status of the husband and father. As has been pointed out, this is a status occupied by an individual by virtue of his individual qualities and achievements. But both directly and indirectly, more than any other single factor, it determines the status of the family in the social structure, directly because of the symbolic significance of the office or occupation as a symbol of prestige, indirectly because as the principal source

From "Age and Sex in the Social Structure," *American Sociological Review,* vol. 7 (October 1942), pp. 608 – 614.

of family income it determines the standard of living of the family. From one point of view the emergence of occupational status into this primary position can be regarded as the principal source of strain in the sex role structure of our society since it deprives the wife of her role as a partner in a common enterprise. The common enterprise is reduced to the life of the family itself and to the informal social activities in which husband and wife participate together. This leaves the wife a set of utilitarian functions in the management of the household which may be considered a kind of "pseudo-" occupation. Since the present interest is primarily in the middle classes, the relatively unstable character of the role of housewife as the principal content of the feminine role is strongly illustrated by the tendency to employ domestic servants wherever financially possible. It is true that there is an American tendency to accept tasks of drudgery with relative willingness, but it is notable that in middle class families there tends to be a dissociation of the essential personality from the performance of these tasks. Thus, advertising continually appeals to such desires as to have hands which one could never tell had washed dishes or scrubbed floors.[1] Organization about the function of housewife, however, with the addition of strong affectional devotion to the husband and children, is the primary focus of one of the principal patterns governing the adult feminine role — what may be called the "domestic" pattern. It is, however, a conspicuous fact, that strict adherence to this pattern has become progressively less common and has a strong tendency to a residual status — that is, to be followed most closely by those who are unsuccessful in competition for prestige in other directions.

It is, of course, possible for the adult woman to follow the masculine pattern and seek a career in fields of occupational achievement in direct competition with men of her own class. It is, however, notable that in spite of the very great progress of the emancipation of women from the traditional domestic pattern only a very small fraction have gone very far in this direction. It is also clear that its generalization would only be possible with profound alterations in the structure of the family.

Hence it seems that concomitant with the alteration in the basic masculine role in the direction of occupation there have appeared two important tendencies in the feminine role which are alternative to that of simple domesticity on the one hand, and to a full-fledged career on the other. In the older situation there tended to be a very rigid distinction between respectable married women and those who were "no better than they should be." The rigidity of this line

---

1. This type of advertising appeal undoubtedly contains an element of "snob appeal" in the sense of an invitation to the individual by her appearance and ways to identify herself with a higher social class than that of her actual status. But it is almost certainly not wholly explained by this element. A glamorously feminine appearance which is specifically dissociated from physical work is undoubtedly a genuine part of an authentic personality ideal of the middle class, and not only evidence of a desire to belong to the upper class.

has progressively broken down through the infiltration into the respectable sphere of elements of what may be called again the glamor pattern, with the emphasis on a specifically feminine form of attractiveness which on occasion involves directly sexual patterns of appeal. One important expression of this trend lies in the fact that many of the symbols of feminine attractiveness have been taken over directly from the practices of social types previously beyond the pale of respectable society. This would seem to be substantially true of the practice of women smoking and of at least the modern version of the use of cosmetics. The same would seem to be true of many of the modern versions of women's dress. "Emancipation" in this connection means primarily emancipation from traditional and conventional restrictions on the free expression of sexual attraction and impulses, but in a direction which tends to segregate the element of sexual interest and attraction from the total personality and in so doing tends to emphasize the segregation of sex roles. It is particularly notable that there has been no corresponding tendency to emphasize masculine attraction in terms of dress and other such aids. One might perhaps say that in a situation which strongly inhibits competition between the sexes on the same plane the feminine glamor pattern has appeared as an offset to masculine occupational status and to its attendant symbols of prestige. It is perhaps significant that there is a common stereotype of the association of physically beautiful, expensively and elaborately dressed women with physically unattractive but rich and powerful men.

The other principal direction of emancipation from domesticity seems to lie in emphasis on what has been called the common humanistic element. This takes a wide variety of forms. One of them lies in a relatively mature appreciation and systematic cultivation of cultural interests and educated tastes, extending all the way from the intellectual sphere to matters of art, music and house furnishings. A second consists in cultivation of serious interests and humanitarian obligations in community welfare situations and the like. It is understandable that many of these orientations are most conspicuous in fields where through some kind of tradition there is an element of particular suitability for feminine participation. Thus, a woman who takes obligations to social welfare particularly seriously will find opportunities in various forms of activity which traditionally tie up with women's relation to children, to sickness and so on. But this may be regarded as secondary to the underlying orientation which would seek an outlet in work useful to the community following the most favorable opportunities which happen to be available.

This pattern, which with reference to the character of relationship to men may be called that of the "good companion," is distinguished from the others in that it lays far less stress on the exploitation of sex role as such and more on that which is essentially common to both sexes. There are reasons, however, why cultural interests, interest in social welfare and community activities are particularly prominent in the activities of women in our urban communities.

On the one side the masculine occupational role tends to absorb a very large proportion of the man's time and energy and to leave him relatively little for other interests. Furthermore, unless his position is such as to make him particularly prominent his primary orientation is to those elements of the social structure which divide the community into occupational groups rather than those which unite it in common interests and activities. The utilitarian aspect of the role of the housewife, on the other hand, has declined in importance to the point where it scarcely approaches a fulltime occupation for a vigorous person. Hence the resort to other interests to fill up the gap. In addition, women, being more closely tied to the local residential community are more apt to be involved in matters of common concern to the members of that community. This peculiar role of women becomes particularly conspicuous in middle age. The younger married woman is apt to be relatively highly absorbed in the care of young children. With their growing up, however, her absorption in the household is greatly lessened, often just at the time when the husband is approaching the apex of his career and is most heavily involved in its obligations. Since to a high degree this humanistic aspect of the feminine role is only partially institutionalized it is not surprising that its patterns often bear the marks of strain and insecurity, as perhaps has been classically depicted by Helen Hokinson's cartoons of women's clubs.

The adult roles of both sexes involve important elements of strain which are involved in certain dynamic relationships, especially to the youth culture. In the case of the feminine role marriage is the single event toward which a selective process, in which personal qualities and effort can play a decisive role, has pointed up. That determines a woman's fundamental status, and after that her role patterning is not so much status determining as a matter of living up to expectations and finding satisfying interests and activities. In a society where such strong emphasis is placed upon individual achievement it is not surprising that there should be a certain romantic nostalgia for the time when the fundamental choices were still open. This element of strain is added to by the lack of clear-cut definition of the adult feminine role. Once the possibility of a career has been eliminated there still tends to be a rather unstable oscillation between emphasis in the direction of domesticity or glamor or good companionship. According to situational pressures and individual character the tendency will be to emphasize one or another of these more strongly. But it is a situation likely to produce a rather high level of insecurity. In this state the pattern of domesticity must be ranked lowest in terms of prestige but also, because of the strong emphasis in community sentiment on the virtues of fidelity and devotion to husband and children, it offers perhaps the highest level of a certain kind of security. It is no wonder that such an important symbol as Whistler's mother concentrates primarily on this pattern.

The glamor pattern has certain obvious attractions since to the woman who is excluded from the struggle for power and prestige in the occupational sphere it is the most direct path to a sense of superiority and importance. It has, however, two obvious limitations. In the first place, many of its manifestations encounter the resistance of patterns of moral conduct and engender conflicts not only with community opinion but also with the individual's own moral standards. In the second place, it is a pattern the highest manifestations of which are inevitably associated with a rather early age level — in fact, over-whelmingly with the courtship period. Hence, if strongly entered upon, serious strains result from the problem of adaptation to increasing age.

The one pattern which would seem to offer the greatest possibilities for able, intelligent, and emotionally mature women is the third — the good companion pattern. This, however, suffers from a lack of fully institutionalized status and from the multiplicity of choices of channels of expression. It is only those with the strongest initiative and intelligence who achieve fully satisfactory adaptations in this direction. It is quite clear that in the adult feminine role there is quite sufficient strain and insecurity so that widespread manifestations are to be expected in the form of neurotic behavior.

The masculine role at the same time is itself by no means devoid of corresponding elements of strain. It carries with it, to be sure, the primary prestige of achievement, responsibility and authority. By comparison with the role of the youth culture, however, there are at least two important types of limitations. In the first place, the modern occupational system has led to increasing specialization of role. The job absorbs an extraordinarily large proportion of the individual's energy and emotional interests in a role the content of which is often relatively narrow. This in particular restricts the area within which he can share common interests and experiences with others not in the same occupational specialty. It is perhaps of considerable significance that so many of the highest prestige statuses of our society are of this specialized character. There is in the definition of roles little to bind the individual to others in his community on a comparable status level. By contrast with this situation, it is notable that in the youth culture common human elements are far more strongly emphasized. Leadership and eminence are more in the role of total individuals and less of competent specialists. This perhaps has something to do with the significant tendency in our society for all age levels to idealize youth and for the older age groups to attempt to imitate the patterns of youth behavior.

It is perhaps as one phase of this situation that the relation of the adult man to persons of the opposite sex should be treated. The effect of the specialization of occupational role is to narrow the range in which the sharing of common human interests can play a large part. In relation to his wife the tendency of this narrowness would seem to be to encourage on her part either the domestic or the glamorous role, or community participation somewhat unrelated to the marriage relationship. This relationship between sex roles presumably introduces a certain amount of strain into the marriage relationship itself since this is of such overwhelming importance to the family and hence to a woman's status and yet so relatively difficult to maintain on a level of human companionship. Outside the marriage relationship, however, there seems to be a notable inhibition against easy social intercourse, particularly in mixed company.[2] The man's close personal intimacy with other women is checked by the danger of the situation being defined as one of rivalry with the wife, and easy friendship without sexual-emotional involvement seems to be inhibited by the specialization of interests in the occupational sphere. It is notable that brilliance of conversation of the "salon" type seems to be associated with aristocratic society and is not prominent in ours.

Along with all this goes a certain tendency for middle-aged men, as symbolized by the "bald-headed row," to be interested in the physical aspect of sex — that is, in women precisely as dissociated from those personal considerations which are important to relationships of companionship or friendship, to say nothing of marriage. In so far as it does not take this physical form, however, there seems to be a strong tendency for middle-aged men to idealize youth patterns — that is, to think of the ideal inter-sex friendship as that of their pre-marital period.[3]

2. In the informal social life of academic circles with which the writer is familiar there seems to be a strong tendency in mixed gatherings — as after dinner — for the sexes to segregate. In such groups the men are apt to talk either shop subjects or politics whereas the women are apt to talk about domestic affairs, schools, their children, etc., or personalities. It is perhaps on personalities that mixed conversation is apt to flow most freely.

3. This, to be sure, often contains an element of romantization. It is more nearly what he wishes these relations had been than what they actually were.

# 5. Domestic Relations━●━●━●━●━●━●━●━●━●━●━●━●━

> Ye must know that women have
> dominion over you: do ye not labor and
> toil, and give and bring all to the
> woman?
>
> THE APOCRYPHA

The law is a museum of mummies in which the past is preserved in amended
layers of the present. One of those mummies is the institution of marriage,
which is founded in the fiction of husband and wife as one person — the reality
being that the husband becomes that person. This situation persists despite
Married Women's Property Acts and other legislation adopted to accommodate the challenging view. Domestic relations doctrine is consequently still
framed to fit the model of the traditional woman who is psychologically and
financially dependent. Although the rationale for the obligation of men to
support their wives is the latter's reproductive role, no legal distinction is made
between childbearing wives and other wives, between wives responsible for
rearing minor children and wives whose children are grown, between wives
who do the housekeeping chores and those whose services consist of symbolic
courtesies. For this reason, marriage for a woman continues to be what it was
in Jane Austen's day, "the pleasantest preservation from want." The problem
on the property side parallels that on the emotional one: in both, contradictions
arise from the circumstance that love and money are entangled in the same
relationship. And the inherent difficulties latent in such an "honorable estate"
are even more evident on its dissolution.

Leo Kanowitz, in the first selection that follows, takes up the crucial element

*Parallel readings for Chapter 5, "Law the Laggard."

in the conjugal equation: the obligation of support and its significance in the relationship between the spouses, in the family unit's relationship with the outside world, notably creditors, and in the dissolution of the compact.

Regarding the obligation of support, the biological argument, founded in the patterns of rudimentary societies, is classically cited as the basis of the asymmetrical arrangement. The legal consequence is that the husband is decision-maker, on the theory that "he who pays the piper calls the tune." Marriage as partnership is thus reduced to a fiction similar to the feudal definition of man and wife as one person. The dilemmas of reformers seeking to deal with the anomalies of the current situation unwittingly expose the underlying structural nature of the problem, but so far, most official bodies are not ready to open that Pandora's box. This means that alimony is still meted out in most states to the unemployed wife and that creditors look to the husband as the principal payer of family indebtedness.

This is revealed by the *Report of the Task Force on Family Law and Policy,* the second selection that follows. Here the recommendations are in favor of a legally defined right of each spouse in the property of the other. Since it is usually the good provider who has such property, the tendency of such proposals is to make marriage a source of greater security for the wife. The underlying reasoning is, however, a mosaic of the philosophies of both the traditional approach and the challenging view. The rationale is not entirely the biological, based in woman's reproductive helplessness, but rather the contractual one, based in her active partnership as contributor of separate but equal services to the marriage. One of the new extenuations of alimony goes so far as to suggest it should be awarded as recompense for interruption of the woman's career to take up homemaking and child rearing duties. Although there is recognition of the fact that husbands can be hard-pressed, there is also acute awareness that wives walk the new roads with bound feet. On the one hand, thought is given to the idea that the obligation of support should be reciprocal, while on the other there is recommendation that the woman be charged with such obligation only if she has the means. Similarly, in stating that adults should not be required to support other adults, the Task Force specifically exempts "spouses" (read "wives"). Thus mummified legal systems preserving yesterday's antique verities continue to distort our lives even when they are carefully wrapped in layers of social relevance.

# Married Women and the Law of Support

*Leo Kanowitz*

The details of the legal rules governing the financial support obligations and rights of husband and wife are as complex as those in any other field of law. Their basic principles, on the other hand, are relatively simple. Except for some states that impose a duty upon the wife to support the husband "under certain circumstances,"[1] the universal rule is that the primary obligation to provide financial support to the family rests upon the husband. This fundamental rule finds expression in a variety of situations. First, it has meaning— although precisely what that meaning is may often be difficult to determine — with regard to the relations between husband and wife in an ongoing marriage. Secondly, the rule is important to creditors, *i.e.* those who have supplied goods or money on credit to the husband, the wife, or to the family as a single entity. And thirdly, the rule plays a decisive role in fixing the nature, extent, and allocation of financial obligations when marriages are disrupted by judicial separation or dissolved by divorce.

Failure to distinguish these various functions served by rules about support may account in part for what commentators have generally agreed are their anachronistic character. In the light of fundamental changes in the husband-wife relationship worked by the Married Women's Acts and other emancipatory legislation, the legal rules about support often appear to have been left behind by social developments.[2]

From *Women and the Law: The Unfinished Revolution* (Albuquerque: University of New Mexico Press, 1969), pp. 69–75. Copyright by the author.

1. VERNIER, AMERICAN FAMILY LAWS 109 (1935). In 1935, Professor Vernier had found such legislation in 17 jurisdictions. *Id.* Professor Paulsen has grouped those statutes into 3 types: "(1) Those that provide that husband and wife contract toward each other obligations of mutual respect, fidelity and support; (2) those which provide that the wife shall support her husband if he is unable because of infirmity to do so; and (3) those which require a wife to support a husband who is likely to become a public charge." Paulsen, *Support Rights and Duties Between Husband and Wife*, 9 VAND.L. REV. 712 (1956). Since "statutes of the first type set forth a moral duty only," *Id.*, one may heartily endorse Professor Paulsen's observation that "the creation of a duty in the wife only when disaster strikes the husband falls a good deal short of treating the sexes equally."

2. *See* Brown, *The Duty of the Husband to Support the Wife*, 18 VA.L. REV. 823 (1932): "No part of the law has been more completely transformed in the past century than that relating to husband and wife . . . But certain phases of even this branch of law remain substantially unchanged, and of these one of the most conspicuous examples is that relating to the duty of the husband to support the wife. It is entirely clear that the married women's acts in the various states have not substantially affected the binding force of this obligation." *See also* Sayre, *A Reconsideration of Husband's Duty to Support and Wife's Duty to Render Services*, 29 VA.L.REV. 857 (1943) in which the husband and wife's respective common law duties of support and to render services are described as "fantastically unchanged, through succeeding generations when the nature of the family and the other rights and duties of husbands and wives apart from their families have clearly changed. *See also* Paulsen, *Support Rights and Duties Between Husband and Wife*, at 710: "It is startling that the great nineteenth century movement toward the legal equality of the marriage partners has left the duty of the husband to support his wife so little changed."

The effects of the basic rule upon the marital relationship itself are complex. In common law marital property jurisdictions, the husband's legal obligation to support the family is not an unmixed blessing for the wife. That obligation has been cited, for example, as justifying his right to choose the family home. It has no doubt also played an important part in solidifying his legal role as head and master of the family. For in according the husband this position within the family, the law often seems to be applying on a grand scale the modest principle that "he who pays the piper calls the tune." However, even in the community property states, in which a wife's services in the home are theoretically viewed as being equal to or exceeding in monetary value the husband's earnings outside of the home, husbands have generally been given the rights to manage and control the community property, along with other superior rights and interests in it.

Not unlike the rules that accord the husband the right to choose the family home, those requiring him to support his wife may have only limited practical significance in an ongoing marriage. True, a husband's willful failure to satisfy that obligation may in almost all jurisdictions constitute a crime. But though the wife's institution of criminal proceedings can lead, indirectly, to her receiving money from the husband (as where he is placed on probation on condition that he make certain payments to her), such a course of action, like the husband's insistence upon his right to locate the family home, would in most instances soon lead to a complete dissolution of the marriage by divorce. Similarly, if a wife should rely upon her husband's failure to support her as a reason for leaving him or divorcing him — which she may do almost everywhere—this too would, by definition, be something altogether different from the fulfillment of the husband's support obligation while the spouses are living together. Indeed, as Professor Paulsen has demonstrated,

> [A] wife living with her husband has almost no remedy to *enforce* her right to support except her personal persuasiveness. . . . "[A]lmost" because both self help and pledging the husband's credit for necessaries are, theoretically, means of enforcing a wife's rights against a spouse with whom she lives.

The precise nature of the husband's legal duty to support his wife is, therefore, rarely ever articulated while the marriage is in progress and the spouses are living together. In fact, its exact details are normally spelled out by the law only in cases of marital breakdown—when the marriage has been disrupted or dissolved by a judicial separation, a decree of annulment, an interlocutory or final decree of divorce, or a preliminary proceeding relative thereto. Not until one of these events has occurred does a court usually decide how much support a husband (or more accurately, in most cases, a former husband) is required to contribute for the maintenance of his spouse (or former spouse), and issue an effective order assuring a wife that the power of the state will be applied on her behalf in collecting the payments ordered.

One explanation for the lack of definition or enforceability of the husband's support liability while the spouses are living together has been proffered by Blanche Crozier. In her view, the "peculiar" rule that the husband has the legal duty to support the wife was founded upon the concept that the wife was, in many important respects, the husband's property. Though the sweeping nature of this generalization renders it of doubtful validity, it is clear that at common law, the wife's labor, at least, was owned by the husband.[3] For Blanche Crozier, however, the wife's status as the husband's property accounted for her inability to get a court to enforce the husband's support obligation while they were living together. "This is precisely the situation in which property finds itself," she wrote, "it may be overworked and underfed, or it may be petted and fed with cream, *and that is a matter for the owner to decide.*"

A more satisfactory explanation of this principle may lie in the fact that the law, in applying it, appears to be giving at least tacit recognition to some obvious facts of life: 1) that marriage is based upon mutual affection; 2) that husband and wife abide by "legal" obligations toward each other not because the law tells them that they must but because they wish to do so; and 3) that if those obligations require enforcement by the courts, the marriage in all likelihood consists of not much more than an empty shell. These, in fact, may be implicit in Professor Paulsen's analysis of the rules about support, when he suggests that those rules "often give a kind of reality to cherished myth."

Still another explanation for the rules about support can be found in the field of cultural anthropology. George Murdock, the American anthropologist, has described the functions and relations of the "nuclear family" (presumably without regard to time or place) in the following terms:

> By virtue of their primary sex differences, a man and a woman make an exceptionally efficient cooperating unit. Man, with his superior physical strength, can better undertake the more strenuous tasks, such as lumbering, mining, quarrying, land clearance, and housebuilding. Not handicapped, as is woman, by the physiological burdens of pregnancy and nursing, he can range farther afield to hunt, to fish, to herd, and to trade. Woman is at no disadvantage, however, in lighter tasks which can be performed in or near the home, e.g. the gathering of vegetable products, the fetching of water, the preparation of food, and the manufacture of clothing and utensils. *All known human societies have developed specialization and cooperation between the sexes roughly along this biologically determined line of cleavage.* It is unnecessary to invoke innate psychological differences to account for the division of labor by sex; the indisputable differences in reproductive functions suffice to lay out the broad lines of cleavage.

Thus, if Murdock's view were adopted the biological differences between the

---

3. But *cf.* Lippman, *The Breakdown of Consortium,* 30 COLUM. L. REV. 651, 658 (1930), in which the husband's common law cause of action for criminal conversation is described as resting upon "the *proprietary* interest of the husband in the *body* and services of the wife." (Emphasis supplied.)

sexes, and especially the incapacitating effects of pregnancy upon women, would account in large part for the universal division of labor between the sexes in all societies.

There is no doubt that ideas of a natural division of labor between husband and wife have played a significant part in shaping our legal rules about the rights and duties of support within the family. Still, it is important to distinguish those factors that are strictly biological and that can scarcely be altered in the foreseeable future from others that are primarily of a cultural or sociological character. That it is the wife rather than the husband, for example, who actually gives birth to the child is, for the moment, a controlling circumstance militating in favor of social and legal policies imposing the exclusive or primary support obligation upon a husband rather than a wife. But the fact that homemaking has in the past been such a time-consuming occupation has no doubt also contributed to the development of those policies. In an era of technological revolution, however, the time may not be far off—and in some families may have already arrived—when homemaking functions (including child care) can be dispatched with a minimum of effort and in a very short time. The prospect of new labor-saving inventions, along with the greater employability of women resulting from changed social patterns and the availability of law-enforced penalties for those who would discriminate against women in hiring, may require American lawmakers to begin devising new modes of regulating support rights and duties within the family.

That the time has not yet arrived for such a restructuring of family support rights and duties may explain the qualified position on this question assumed by the Committee on Civil and Political Rights of the President's Commission on the Status of Women. Though a doctrinaire feminism or a fascination with symmetry might lead some persons to insist that the principle of true equality of the sexes requires that, at the very least, both husband and wife should now share equally in the obligations of family support, the Committee has refused to take such a stand. Instead, it has limited its action on the problems of family support to the following recommendation:

> The husband should continue to have the primary responsibility for the support of his wife and minor children, but in line with the partnership view of marriage, the wife should be given some legal responsibility for sharing in the support of herself and the children to the extent she has sufficient means to do so.

While this recommended rule would, in some instances, affect the spouses in an ongoing marriage (as where the wife was possessed of a substantial estate at the time she was married), it is clear that in the vast majority of cases, the rule would be much more important to third parties, such as creditors of the family, than to the spouses themselves. Significantly, the recommendation does not require the wife to acquire "sufficient means" in order to be able to share in the support of herself and the children. It is by no means suggested, for example, that she must seek gainful employment — which, after all, is the most common way for a married woman to acquire separate funds. Only where the wife has already done this is she given some responsibility for family support.

But this rule would be generally superfluous — at least to the extent that only the spouses themselves are concerned. It is the rare marriage in which a wife uses her separate earnings for purposes entirely unrelated to family needs. If adopted, therefore, the rule's major effect would be to create an additional fund to which family creditors could look for satisfaction of outstanding obligations.

That creditors may need such assistance is not unlikely. Though in a few states, family expense statutes render a wife liable for certain family items furnished on credit, in most states it is the husband alone who is liable.

In the areas of divorce and alimony, the Committee's recommendation would again appear to have a limited effect upon present law. Though a wife's claim to alimony may be denied if the divorce is decreed because of her "fault," it is still the general rule that in the absence of fault on her part or upon a showing of lesser fault than her husband's, she may be awarded alimony. That award is often based on other factors than those entitling a wife to be supported during the marriage. Alimony may represent a continuation of that basic support obligation, compensation for the loss of reasonably anticipated economic benefits from the marriage, an effort to prevent the wife from becoming a public charge, or — as is demonstrated by the practice of courts' granting a higher alimony award when the husband's fault has been especially reprehensible — as a means of punishing him for his marital misconduct.

In any event, to the extent that alimony awards are based on the same considerations as support obligations during marriage, the Committee's recommendation, conditioning a wife's responsibility for sharing in the family support on her having "sufficient means to do so" while not insisting that she acquire those means, would leave present law relatively unchanged.

Support obligations within the family cannot be considered in complete isolation from other legal and social phenomena. They are, for example, inextricably bound up with the matter of general employment opportunities for a married woman. These, in turn, may depend upon her age, the length of her marriage, and the number of years she has been absent from the labor market. The allocation of support obligations within the family is also profoundly influenced by the level of technological development within any country — since it may directly affect the time required to perform, and thus the monetary value of, household tasks. Still other factors that are relevant in establishing present support rights and duties between husband and wife are the biological fact that women, and not men, bear children, and the sociological presumption that young children, and therefore society as a whole, are better served if those children are cared for at home by their mothers rather than their fathers. This presumption, as we have seen, is expressed in the rule that gives a divorced mother rather than a father superior rights to the custody of a child of tender years.

Except for the childbearing principle (which may not itself be immutable), all of these other factors are now in the process of rapidly accelerating change. Though the time may not be ripe for fundamental alterations in the family support laws, lawmakers should begin to pay closer attention to developments that affect this issue, with the aim of taking measures that reach beyond the restrained recommendations of the President's Commission at the earliest opportunity. True legal equality of the sexes cannot be achieved until support rights and duties between husband and wife are drastically altered. But before that is done, and in order to avoid a state of affairs in which more problems are created than solved, it is probably best to postpone fundamental changes in the rules about support until meaningful changes have occurred in most of the other areas of legal regulation considered in these pages.

## Marriage and Family Support

### Task Force on Family Law and Policy

### I. Marriage as an Economic Partnership

In March, 1966, one third of married women living with their husbands worked outside the home, contributing to the economic support of their families.[1] A much larger proportion of married women, of course, are employed at some time during their married lives. On the other hand, in many families the mother spends almost all of her married life in homemaking and child rearing.

State laws dealing with property rights as between the spouses must be examined in light of the varied family patterns in existence today; the law should operate fairly on both spouses, whether the work of the wife is as homemaker or in a paid job or both.

There are two types of property systems in the United States — "common law" and community property. In the 42 common law States and the District of Columbia, income and property acquired by each spouse during marriage is owned separately by the spouse who acquires it. In the remaining eight "community property" States (Arizona, California, Idaho, Louisiana, New

*Report* of the Task Force on Family Law and Policy to the Citizens' Advisory Council on the Status of Women, April 1968 (Washington, D.C.: U.S. Government Printing Office: 1968), 0-315-943.
1. *Working Wives — Their Contribution to Family Income,* Women's Bureau, U. S. Department of Labor, 1967.

Mexico, Nevada, Texas and Washington) income and property acquired by each spouse during the marriage is generally owned in common by husband and wife.

## A. MANAGEMENT OF JOINTLY OWNED PROPERTY IN COMMUNITY PROPERTY STATES

In community property States, even where the wife works all or part of her married life as a housewife and mother, rather than as a wage earner outside the home, her contribution to the family is recognized since she has an equal interest in the family income and property. However, the Civil and Political Rights Committee Report of the President's Commission on the Status of Women pointed out that management control of community property, acquired by either husband or wife, generally vests in the husband.

The income of a working wife as well as that of the husband becomes part of the community property and, under the traditional community property system is managed by the husband, with the wife having no say in how her income is to be spent.

Texas has recently eliminated this inequity to working wives by amending its community property laws to provide that "each spouse shall have sole management, control and disposition of that community property which he or she would have owned if a single person," and if community property subject to the management of one spouse is mixed or combined with that of the other spouse, it is subject to joint management unless the spouses agree otherwise. (*Texas Rev. Civ. Stats.*, Art. 4621). This system of separate control of community property is similar to the system for management of matrimonial property adopted in Norway and Denmark.

## B. DIVISION OF PROPERTY AT DEATH OF A SPOUSE IN COMMON LAW STATES

Unlike the traditional community property system which gives the husband power to manage his wife's income, the common law system of separate ownership allows each spouse to manage his own income and property. However, the principle of separate ownership of property by each spouse generally does not adequately recognize the contribution to the family made by a wife who works only in the home. In such case a wife does not have an opportunity to acquire earnings and property of her own.

The Report of the President's Commission on the Status of Women (*American Women,* page 47) directs the attention of State legislatures and other groups concerned with improving family law to the following statement:

"Marriage as a partnership in which each spouse makes a different but equally important contribution is increasingly recognized as a reality in this country and is already reflected in the laws of some other countries. During marriage, *each spouse should have a legally defined substantial right* in the earnings of the other, in the real and personal property acquired through those earnings, and in their management. Such a right should be legally recognized as surviving the marriage in the event of its termination by divorce, annulment, or death. Appropriate legislation should safeguard either spouse and protect the surviving spouse against improper alienation of property by the other. Surviving children as well as the surviving spouse should be protected from disinheritance." (emphasis supplied)

Upon termination of marriage at the death of a spouse, the property of both spouses could be divided according to a statutory formula. For example, there could first be deducted from each spouse's property, any of his or her debts. There could also be deducted certain types of property — the value of property owned at the time of marriage, gifts from third persons and inheritances, and any other property which the spouses agreed to have deducted by a marital property contract. The remainder, after these deductions are made from each spouse's property, could be added together and divided equally between husband and wife. Similar formulae have been adopted in Sweden and the Federal Republic of Germany for equitable division of the spouses' property upon termination of the marriage. The task force believes that such a formula for property division upon termination of marriage by death would help to implement the above-quoted statement from *American Women* and could be adapted to the separate property systems in the 42 common law States and the District of Columbia.

The foregoing discussion outlining a 50-50 formula for property division at the death of a spouse in common law States should not be confused with *inheriting* property from a spouse. If a State provided for such a property division upon the death of a spouse it would mean that the surviving spouse would own outright 50 percent of the marital property. After the division is made the inheritance laws would apply, but only to the deceased's 50 percent, of course.

C. PROPERTY DIVISION UPON DIVORCE IN COMMON LAW STATES[2]

At the present time, the laws of some States (*e.g.,* New York and New Jersey) do not authorize courts to divide property of the spouses upon divorce. Other States give the courts discretion to make a property division between the spouses. See, for example, *Wisconsin Statutes Annotated,* Sec. 247.26.[3]

2. Under some circumstances the discussion in this section might also be relevant to cases of annulment and separate maintenance proceedings.

3. However, the Wisconsin law does not apply equally to the spouses. In addition to providing for alimony for the *wife,* the court is authorized to "finally divide and distribute the estate, both real and personal, of the husband, and so much of the estate of the wife as has been derived from the husband, between the parties and divest and transfer the title of any thereof accordingly, after having given due regard to the legal and equitable rights of each party, the ability of the husband, the special estate of the wife, the character and situation of the parties and all the circumstances of the case; . . ."

The task force considered the question of whether the application of a statutory formula for dividing property of the spouses, such as described above . . .with respect to termination of marriage by death, would·be desirable in cases of termination of marriage by divorce. For example, deductions of certain types of property (such as property owned by a spouse before marriage, gifts and inheritances) might be made from each spouse's property, the remainder added together and divided 50-50 between husband and wife. The laws of Germany and the Scandinavian countries provide for a system of property division upon divorce along these lines.

Some task force members believed that a fixed equal division of property upon divorce would not operate fairly in some cases, and that divorce courts should be given discretion to determine a different proportion for each spouse, based on consideration of such factors as the respective contributions (not limited to financial) each spouse made to the marriage, duration of the marriage, economic dependency and age of the spouses. On the other hand, with respect to property division at the death of a spouse, a fixed 50-50 formula would have some advantages. Unlike the case of death, a divorce proceeding is a two-party action with both spouses having an opportunity to show the respective contributions they have made to the marriage. Moreover, if a probate court had to consider and make a determination based on various factors in the marriage of a deceased person, it would delay the settling of estates.

## D. PROTECTION AGAINST DISPOSITION OF PROPERTY TO DEFEAT SPOUSE'S RIGHTS

If a legally defined right such as this equal division of the combined property of the spouses at the death of one spouse is given to each spouse, some legal control of disposing of property during the lifetime of the spouses would be necessary so the husband (or wife) could not defeat the rights of the other by selling or giving away all his property while living. In order that restrictions on the freedom to manage and dispose of one's property be kept at a minimum, this legal control over disposing of property could be limited to requiring the consent of the other spouse or of the court (1) to the sale by the owner-spouse of the home, and (2) to the excessive gifts made from the kind of property which would be combined and divided equally under the above formula (*i.e.,* this would not apply to gifts from property owned before marriage or inherited property).

## E. RECOMMENDATIONS

In view of the foregoing problems under present law, and some of the possible solutions adverted to, as well as the need for further careful study of these complex issues, the task force recommends that the Council request some appropriate agency (such as the American Law Institute, the American Bar Foundation or the Commissioners on Uniform State Laws) to undertake a fundamental study of family property interests. Pending the completion of such a study, we recommend the following interim steps:

(1) The Council bring to the attention of State Commissions on the Status of Women and other appropriate organizations in community property States the recent Texas legislation described [earlier in] this report.

(2) The Council bring to the attention of State Commissions and other appropriate organizations the desirability of empowering their courts to make discretionary divisions of the property of the spouses in matrimonial status actions (such as separation, divorce or annulment), it being left to local determination what types of property are to be subject to such division and the criteria which are to govern.

## II. Family Support

### A. THE QUESTION OF ALIMONY

Some State laws permit divorce courts to grant alimony to the wife but not to the husband. More than one-third of the States permit alimony to be awarded to either spouse. The amount of the alimony, if any, awarded to a spouse is ultimately a question for determination by the court in light of the circumstances of the particular case, such as the economic needs of the spouses, duration of marriage and relative contributions to the marriage.

Consultations with experienced practitioners indicated that in the great majority of divorce cases, the amount of alimony and child support is determined by negotiation between the parties, with the court simply confirming the agreement. Often *child* support payments are camouflaged as alimony because of the impact of Federal income tax laws; taxes on alimony payments to an ex-wife are payable by her not the ex-husband, *i.e.,* the total amount of alimony is subtracted from the ex-husband's income. The party which contributes more than one-half the support of a child may take the $600 dependency exemption for the child. In most cases the wife's income is less than that of the husband and she therefore pays taxes at a lower rate. As a result of lumping child support payments together with alimony and designating the total sum as alimony, the husband has a tax advantage and the wife may be able to negotiate a larger total payment. Because of these factors, although the laws on the books in some States favor women by permitting alimony for wives but not for husbands, this seeming inequity to men may be somewhat tempered by the law in practice.

If a system for division of property between husband and wife upon divorce such as outlined above were adopted, and if the family has sufficient property to divide, it would be possible to drastically reduce or eliminate alimony as continued support for an ex-spouse.

Whether, how much, and for how long alimony should be paid in a given case necessarily involves consideration of a variety of factors. The task force suggests the following as being among the criteria which are consistent with the economic partnership view of marriage.

1. In the traditional family, where the husband has been the chief source of income, the contribution of the wife to the economic partnership of marriage may have been great, as in a marriage of many years in which she was devoted to her family's well-being, or it may have been minimal, as in a marriage of brief duration. Alimony should recognize a contribution made by a spouse to the family's well-being which would otherwise be without recompense.

2. Alimony should provide recompense for loss of earning capacity suffered by either spouse because of the marriage. For example, where a wife interrupts her career because of homemaking and child rearing.

3. If either spouse upon divorce is in financial need, some continuing responsibility on the part of the other spouse to meet such need may be recognized for a period of time after the dissolution of a marriage. One of the determinants of the proper period may be the duration of the marriage; another might be whether the dependent spouse can or should establish some other means of support, and if so, the time likely to be required to do so.

Alimony payments are sometimes used as a means of redressing wrongs suffered by either spouse at the hands of the other. The spouse who is found at fault may be required to pay more or to accept less. This encourages actions for divorce or separation to explore the relative faults of the parties and is virtually certain to have undesirable consequences for any future relations between the couple. Alimony should not be used as a way of awarding compensation for damages.

B. OBLIGATIONS FOR SUPPORT

1. *Spouse-spouse liability.* If marriage is viewed as a partnership between a man and a woman, then each spouse should be responsible for the other in accordance with need and ability to support. This general principle should be reflected in State laws dealing with support obligations for spouses. Some of the task force members believed that a husband should only be liable for the support of a wife who is unable to support herself due to physical handicap, acute stage of family responsibility or unemployability on other grounds. Other task force members believed that other factors may need to be considered in light of the general equities of the situation. A wife should be responsi-

ble for the support of her husband if he is unable to support himself and she is able to furnish such support.

The Council of State Governments list of "Basic Duties of Support Imposed by State Law"[4] indicates that the following jurisdictions do not impose an obligation on the wife to support a husband unable to support himself: Alabama, Colorado, Florida, Georgia, Hawaii, Indiana, Iowa, Kentucky, Maryland, Massachusetts, Mississippi, Missouri, Rhode Island, South Carolina, Tennessee, Texas, Virginia, Washington, and Wyoming. All jurisdictions make a husband liable for the support of his wife, but without regard to the ability of the wife to support herself.

2. *Parent-child liability.* As an extension of the equal partnership principle of marriage, both parents should be liable for the support of their offspring, not merely the father. No distinction should be made in the rights of legitimate and "illegitimate" children to parental support. The Council of State Governments lists Colorado, Montana, Ohio, and Rhode Island as requiring the father alone to support legitimate children, and Alaska, Colorado, Minnesota, Mississippi, Ohio and Rhode Island as requiring the father alone to support illegitimate children.

No distinction should be made in the rights of boys and girls to parental support. The Council of State Governments lists Arkansas, Idaho, Nevada, North Dakota, Oklahoma, South Dakota and Utah as giving girls a right to support up to age 18, and boys to age 21.

The age at which a child's right to parental support terminates varies from State to State; ages 18 or 21 are most often specified. The task force believes that in general an adult should not be *legally* liable for the support of other adults (other than spouses) and that the age at which legal liability for the support of a child terminates should be no older than 21. However, with respect to a handicapped child over the legal age (or at any age), further study is needed on the question of whether the financial burden for providing proper treatment and care for such a child should be on the parents or whether the State should assume all or part of this responsibility. Proper care for mentally or physically defective children is often extremely expensive and seriously affects the standard of living of middle income, as well as poor, families.

Further study is also needed on the question of whether children should be obligated by law to support their parents. Requiring a person to support a parent can aggravate family hostilities and can depress family income levels to the detriment of his own children. A majority, but not all, of the task force members favored repeal of laws requiring children to support their parents.

The Council of State Governments lists the following jurisdictions as impos-

4. Information Manual on *Reciprocal State Legislation to Enforce the Support of Dependents* (1964 edition).

ing legal obligations on children to support their parents . . .: Alabama, Alaska, California, Connecticut, Delaware, District of Columbia, Guam, Hawaii, Idaho, Illinois, Indiana, Iowa, Louisiana, Maine, Maryland, Massachusetts, Michigan, Montana, Nevada, New Hampshire, New Jersey, North Carolina, North Dakota, Ohio, Oregon, Pennsylvania, Puerto Rico, Rhode Island, South Dakota, Utah, Vermont, Virginia, Virgin Islands, and West Virginia.

3. *Liability beyond the nuclear family.* The basic unit in modern society consists of a man and a woman and their dependent offspring. We are increasingly an urban, mobile, technological society and have witnessed over the past thirty years of social security and welfare legislation a gradual recognition of the changed nature of our family system. Unemployment compensation, old age and retirement benefits under social security are contemporary substitutes for responsibility that was once defined as a "family matter," sometimes generously offered, sometimes with considerable reluctance and hardship.

Religious and moral values often guide individuals to assume voluntarily varying degrees of responsibility for parents, grandparents, siblings, nieces and nephews. Where these obligations to their kinsmen are voluntarily accepted by adults without undue hardship to their primary obligations to spouse and dependent children, these are admirable social acts of generosity. However, such support should be just this — voluntary. If individuals are not themselves committed to a value that extends obligations outside the primary family, or if individuals cannot afford to lend financial support to kinsmen, they should not be subject to legal pressure to assume such responsibilities.

The task force recommends that laws which require individuals to accept financial responsibility for the support of siblings, grandparents, grandchildren or other extended kin be repealed.

The Council of State Governments list . . . indicates the following jurisdictions as imposing legal obligations to support extended kin:

*Sibling support*—Alabama, Alaska, Colorado, Illinois, Massachusetts, Montana, Nevada, Puerto Rico, Utah, Virgin Islands, West Virginia.

*Grandparents for grandchildren* — Alabama, Alaska, Colorado, Iowa, Louisiana, Montana, New Jersey, Rhode Island, Utah, Virgin Islands.

*Grandchildren for grandparents* — Alabama, Alaska, Colorado, Iowa, Louisiana, New Jersey, Puerto Rico, Utah.

The task force recommends that the Council invite the attention of State Commissions on the Status of Women and other interested groups to the foregoing principles and recommendations with a view to reexamination and appropriate revision of laws pertaining to family support obligations.

C.   INTERSTATE ENFORCEMENT OF FAMILY SUPPORT OBLIGATIONS

All of the States, the organized territories and the District of Columbia have enacted the Uniform Reciprocal Enforcement of Support Act or a similar law providing for both civil and criminal enforcement of support obligations across State lines.

Support obligations imposed by one State may be enforced against a parent in another State through reciprocal court proceedings in the two States. By far the greatest number of reciprocal actions involve cases where the mother and children reside in one State and the mother is seeking financial assistance for the children's support from the father who resides in another State. The parents may or may not be divorced.

The procedure is as follows: The mother may file a complaint in a court in the State where she resides. The county or city prosecuting attorney generally represents the complainant, at the request of the court. The complaint must state the name, and so far as known to the complainant-mother, the address and circumstances of the father and the children for whom support is sought. If the court finds that the complaint sets forth facts from which it may be determined that the respondent-father owes a duty of support and that the court of another State may obtain jurisdiction over the father, the court transmits copies of the complaint and other pertinent papers to the court of the father's State.

When the clerk of the latter responding court receives the documents, he dockets the case and notifies his county's (or city's) prosecuting attorney. The prosecuting attorney is required to use all means at his disposal to locate the respondent or his property.

If the responding court finds a duty of support, it may order the father to furnish support and subject his property to the support order.

The Uniform Act also provides for extradition of persons charged with the crime of failing to provide for the support of a dependent. In some States the law provides that civil proceedings such as described above must first be tried, or that it be shown that such civil proceedings would not be effective, before the Governor will turn over the respondent-father to the authorities in the mother's State.

The latter provision was added by 1958 amendments to the Uniform Act. The 1958 amendments also provided an additional civil procedure for cases in which the mother has previously obtained a support order, such as a child support order as part of a divorce decree. In such a case, she may simply register the support order directly in the court of the State where the father resides. The latter court may confirm the support order and enforce it as if it were an original order of that court. However, more than half the States have not yet adopted the 1958 amendments. The 1958 amendments also provide that the Uniform Act may be used when the parties are in the same State, but in different counties.

Proceedings under State reciprocal enforcement of support laws do not always result in child support payments. Some of the reasons for lack of success under the laws are: (1) the father cannot be located; (2) officials, particularly in the responding State where the obligor resides, are not diligent in enforcing the law; (3) the obligor-father simply does not have the money to pay and perhaps has acquired a second family.

1. *Locating missing parents.* The Council of State Governments' *Handbook of Administrative Procedures under the Uniform Reciprocal Enforcement of Support Act* includes an appendix listing techniques and sources of information as to the whereabouts of missing parents. To some extent, certain Federal records may be used. For example, regulations of the Secretary of Health, Education, and Welfare permit disclosure of information from Social Security records to local public welfare officials about the whereabouts of parents who have deserted their children. However, this applies only to cases where the children are eligible for assistance under the aid to families with dependent children program.

District Directors of Internal Revenue are permitted to advise whether or not a person has filed an income tax return and, if so, the name and address appearing on the return. (See 26 U.S.C. 6103 [f].) Veterans' Administration regulations permit addresses of VA claimants to be furnished only to police or court officials and only in cases where there is an indictment against the claimant or a warrant for his arrest. (38 CFR 1.518.)

One of the requirements of State plans for aid to families with dependent children is that provision be made for prompt notice to law enforcement officials in cases where children have been deserted or abandoned by a parent. (42 U.S.C. 602.) The Department of Health, Education, and Welfare requires State welfare departments to establish location services to assist in locating persons liable for support in cases involving aid to families with dependent children funds.

A New York law provides that the State Department of Social Welfare shall establish a central registry of records for location of deserting parents of children who are recipients of public assistance or likely to become in need of assistance. The Department is authorized to obtain information concerning the identity and whereabouts of deserting parents from other agencies of the State or political subdivisions (*e.g.,* motor vehicle and tax records). Information is available only to welfare officials and law enforcement officials and agencies having jurisdiction in support or abandonment proceedings. (*McKinney's Consol. Laws of N.Y.,* Soc. Wel. Law, sec. 372-a.) Similar central location units have been set up in a number of other States and some provide interstate assistance in locating deserting parents.

With respect to families receiving aid to dependent children funds, section 211 of the Social Security Amendments of 1967 (P.L. 90-248; 81 Stat. 821, 896) provides that the State agencies are to report to the Department of Health, Education, and Welfare names of missing parents who are not complying with a support order or against whom a petition for support has been filed. The names are then to be furnished to the Department of the Treasury which endeavors to ascertain the address of such parent from Internal Revenue Service files.

2. *Failure to enforce the law.* In some cases officials in the responding State simply do not follow through on reciprocal actions. This may be due to lack of appreciation of the importance of enforcing child support or a belief that efforts to enforce the parent's child support obligations would not result in payments and would be a waste of time. The Council of State Governments suggests that a district attorney in a State where an action is initiated who is not able to ascertain the status of a case in a court of the responding State should write to the "State information agent" of the responding State for assistance. The agency designated under the State reciprocal laws is usually either the State Welfare Department or the Attorney General's Office.

For a number of years, bills have been introduced in Congress to provide for enforcement of support orders in Federal courts and to make it a crime to move in interstate commerce to avoid compliance with support orders. See for example, H.R. 11633, 90th Cong., 1st Sess. (1967), a proposed "Federal Family Support Act." That bill would permit an obligee (usually the mother) to register her support order in a State or Federal court which has jurisdiction over the obligor (usually the father). The court could then bring contempt proceedings against the obligor in the same manner as if the original support order were its own order. In addition, each Federal district court would have original jurisdiction, concurrent with the State courts, of civil actions brought by a citizen of another State to order a citizen of the State in which the court is located to make support payments. However, the complainant would have to show that she had first exhausted remedies available in the State courts. The bill would also provide a criminal penalty of a fine of $2500 or imprisonment for three years or both for moving in interstate or foreign commerce from a State in which proceedings had been begun under the "Federal Family Support Act."

Whether or not such legislation would benefit mothers in obtaining financial assistance from fathers for the support of their children would depend in part on: (a) the extent to which procedures under the Uniform Reciprocal Enforcement of Support Act fail to result in adequate support payments for children; (b) the extent to which lack of diligence on the part of State and local officials is responsible for such failure; and (c) whether Federal officials (U.S. attorneys, U.S. marshals and F.B.I.) would likely be more diligent in enforcing child support obligations.

## D.  INABILITY TO PAY

The mother more often has custody of the children by court order or by the fact of desertion of the family by the father. This means the mother not only has the responsibility for the care and upbringing of the children, but the entire burden of their financial support as well. When she faces the added obstacle of sex discrimination (and in the case of nonwhite mothers, racial discrimination) in employment and in job training, she may well find herself one of the 42% of families headed by women with annual incomes of less than $3000.

But where the father simply does not have the means to provide support, enforcement of support laws is no solution to the problem. A lower-income father may find himself in jail for being delinquent in making child support payments. This does not help the mother of the children and gives an otherwise law-abiding father a criminal record. Some public assistance agencies require an applicant for Aid to Families with Dependent Children to declare her willingness to file criminal non-support charges against the father. This is a degrading experience for both mother and father and creates further hostilities and bitterness between them, often to the detriment of the children.

The tast force recommends the following:

1. That criminal enforcement of support should not be resorted to until after exhaustion of civil remedies. (The Uniform Reciprocal Enforcement of Support Act contains a provision to this effect.)
2. Public assistance agencies should not require that the granting of an application for AFDC assistance be conditioned upon willingness on the part of a parent to file a criminal non-support charge.
3. Such agencies should attempt wherever possible to negotiate support agreements rather than resort to court action.
4. The responsibility for enforcing the obligations of a spouse for child support should be the public assistance agency's or the appropriate law enforcement officer's, rather than the other spouse's. In particular, a woman should not be required to appear in court as complainant against the father of her children should the latter fail to satisfy a court order to reimburse a public assistance agency. This task should be assumed by the agency.

The responsibility of child support should be shared by the parents. The amount of child support required of the parent who does not have custody should reflect this, as well as the capacity to furnish support, and the earnings and financial situation of the spouses. The level of child support and alimony together should take into consideration the principle that it is desirable for both husband and wife to maintain a reasonable standard of living. The level should also be such that it would enable both the parent having custody and the parent paying child support to remarry.

Where the income level of both families would be reduced below subsistence level, it should be supplemented by the government.

The task force supports the current study of the various possible methods of family income maintenance. The need for some system of insuring a minimum family income level, whether through the social security system, negative income tax or other legal machinery, is particularly acute in cases of broken families.

The task force recommends that the Council bring the foregoing principles and recommendations to the attention of the State Commissions on the Status of Women, State agencies administering Aid to Families with Dependent Children, appropriate law enforcement officials and other interested persons and groups.

# 6. *Woman's Place* ━●━●━●━●━●━●━●━●━●━●━●━●━●━●━●━●━●━●━●━●

> Shall the home be our world . . . or the
> world our home?
>
> CHARLOTTE PERKINS GILMAN

We think in one world and live in another. On the one hand, we have inherited
the dogma of individual autonomy, with its picture of the family as a free-
standing, self-contained unit, with significant productive functions, patriarchal in character, and rural and rooted in design. On the other hand, the actual
conditions of life for families in an industrial setting make the mythic models
unattainable. Some authorities, conscious of the inability of today's family to
perform the functions of the past, applaud changed patterns as opportunities
for the performance of more intimate functions. The problem is that the family
continues to be an economic unit; moreover, in a nation of employees it is a
*dependent* economic unit which, far from standing alone, swings like a pendulum suspended from the social rafters. It can only concentrate on love and
development when it has practical security; when it is not faced with failure
or inadequacy of income to meet crises of sickness, accident, or death. For we
no longer *make* a living, we *buy* it. And that means we must have the
wherewithal. Yet the myths of self-sufficiency persist, the dream is constant,
and each family sees itself guiltily as deviant.

Mirra Komarovsky, in the first selection, indicates the character of this
ambivalence with respect to the status of women. "The old and the new
moralities exist side by side," she writes, "dividing the heart against itself."

*Parallel readings for Chapter 6, "A House Is Not a Homestead."

The reverse of the American dream is the disharmony of its reality, the contradiction between vaunted individualism and intransigent social structure.

This contradiction is explored in the second reading in terms of the individual and in terms of the quality of life in the contemporary home. The new material culture, Lawrence Frank notes, is readily assimilated, but we are more resistant to change in our mores. *Earning* a living signifies an entirely different way of life than *making* a living, for it suggests individual helplessness, closing former avenues to personal enterprise and initiative. At the same time, the home has been stripped of its former functions and responsibilities. The discrepancy between patterns offered by tradition and those implied by present circumstances gives rise to acute anxiety in the individual man and the individual woman. For both sexes, the overriding need is to realize mutual uncertainties and to face the task of working out the future, of searching together for stable means to match enduring human needs.

The third selection specifies certain of these means. The President's Commission on the Status of Women first emphasizes the importance of child care centers for the family in an industrial society. Additionally, it recommends agencies to help families in crisis, homemaker services for emergencies, health services, and designs for household maintenance.

The final reading is part of a letter written to the editor of *The Washington Post,* describing arrangements in other industrial societies that help to bring security to the family. It reflects the underlying philosophy of some of these programs: that all children are our children.

## Women as a "Social Problem"

>=•=•=•=•=•=•=•=•=•=•=•=•=•=•=•=•=•=•=•=•=•=•=•=•=•=•=•=•=•=•=•=•=•=•=•=•=<

*Mirra Komarovsky*

Women became a "social problem" because technological and social changes over the past century and a half have disturbed an old equilibrium without as yet replacing it with another. As a result, our society is a veritable crazy quilt of contradictory practices and beliefs. Some old attitudes persist stubbornly in the face of a new reality which has long since rendered them meaningless. New conditions have arisen which have not as yet been defined by public opinion

From *Women in the Modern World:Their Education and Their Dilemmas* (Boston: Little, Brown, 1953), pp. 48–52. Copyright 1953 by Mirra Heyman.

—leaving human beings without guidance and protection. New goals have emerged without the social machinery required for their attainment. The old and the new moralities exist side by side dividing the heart against itself. The present disharmony has a myriad of facets. Here a widow goes to work, leaving her children unattended because society still assumes that all mothers can stay home and take care of their children. There, a successful homemaker says apologetically, "I am just a housewife," thus reflecting the new demands upon women to be also achievers in the outside world. Again a woman, doing a man's job and supporting her aged parents, gets a lower wage on the old theory that women work for pin money. "What to do with the remaining third of my life?" asks a middle-aged woman whose housekeeping duties have been reduced by smaller families and modern inventions. "Was it worth it?" wonders a career woman who accepted her society's challenge to succeed in her career only to discover that success endangered her marriage. Economic forces drive a wife to take a factory job but, having done a day's work, she returns to her full round of washing, cleaning, and cooking. One can go so far as to say that whatever the woman does, whether she is single or married, a homemaker or a career woman, childless or a mother — each design for living has its own pattern of frustrations. This observation does not refer to the obvious fact that life, in general, is no bed of roses. Quite the contrary; the frustrations here stated are precisely those which are not inherent in human life but are due to inconsistent social changes of the past century and are, it is hoped, amenable to social control.

The pre-industrial English and American societies were, despite their differences, both relatively consistent with respect to the status of women. The elements which went to make up the position of women in the family and in society were relatively well geared to one another. The economic functions of women, their legal status, the ideal of femininity presented to the growing girl, the education given her for adult life, the definition of her role as wife and mother, the mores regulating the relations between the sexes, the conception of the feminine personality — all these were of a piece, each relatively well meshed into the other.

It was to be expected that the confusion of our own era should give birth to nostalgic longings for that relatively unambiguous and consistent past. Human beings tend to take for granted their current blessings and, in comparing their present situation with the past, to think only of the advantages that the past had over the present. They overlook the fact that the past had its own share of troubles. We must not forget that harmony and order (alluring as these words sound to modern ears) are not necessarily good. Harmony may be too dearly paid for; order may be based on tyranny. We shall probably never know, though some writers presume to tell us, just how happy our great-great-grandmothers were. There were no Kinseys to record their sexual frustrations, no psychiatrists to unravel their neuroses, no novelists to indict them for momism. But of what avail would it be to know? We can't bring back the past even if we desire it. We might as well talk of returning the loom to the home.

The old system began to change not because a group of emotionally disordered feminists succeeded in hoodwinking or bullying the Western world, but because the Industrial Revolution radically reorganized the whole of our society. We think of our historic past as a period of clear-cut division of labor between the sexes: man the provider, woman the homemaker. Actually women were also economic providers through the multitude of goods and services supplied by home industry. Once economic production moved to the factory, women were forced to follow their work beyond the confines of their homes.

In the wake of the French and the American Revolutions, with their ideals of equality and political democracy, certain other changes in the status of women were bound to follow. It was no accident that the Seneca Falls Convention in 1848 couched the first public demand for women's suffrage in the words of the Declaration of Independence, faintly ridiculous as the transposition sounded. "No taxation without representation" was too deeply felt a principle not to be applied, eventually, to women also. Sooner or later, for a working woman to have no part in the control of her earnings was bound to appear unfair, and other legal rights of married and single women were, likewise, modified. The demands for educational opportunities for women grew apace.

Changes in the mode of life were influencing women in other ways. No chaperons could daily escort the teacher or the saleslady to her job, and the convention forbidding a lady to appear unaccompanied at a public place could not long endure under new conditions. With new occupations came new demands upon personality. To be "delightfully illogical" is no asset for a teacher and "cuteness" is not what an employer needs in a department store buyer.

These changes in ways of living and of thinking did not actually occur in the orderly fashion the foregoing paragraphs suggest. The pattern of social change is much more haphazard. Some new invention is quickly adapted with no awareness of the many unintended dislocations it will produce in other areas of life. Even when the need for them is recognized, adjustments are long delayed, whether by vested interests or by irrational attachments to the past. An adjustment of one difficulty sometimes creates an unexpected pinch elsewhere.

The changes in the position of women here described have not exhausted their momentum and we find ourselves in the mesh of contradictions. . . . One word of caution. . . . Not every woman experiences these problems with equal intensity, if at all. Indeed, a social order can function only because the vast majority have somehow adjusted themselves to their place in society and perform the functions expected of them. This applies to women too. But there are many and poignant signs of discontent and if the picture should appear unduly dark it is because its purpose is precisely to portray the disturbed areas of life.

# Social Change and the Family

>=•=o=•=o=•=o=•=o=•=o=•=o=•=o=•=o=•=o=•=o=•=o=•=o=•=o=•=o=•=o=•=o=•=o=•=<

*Lawrence K. Frank*

If we are to understand the rather bewildering situation in family life today, we shall have to go behind the social and economic situation and attempt to reveal what is happening to men and women. It is not enough to repeat the catalogue of economic and industrial changes if we do not go further and ask what they imply for the conduct of men and women generally, and more especially in the association we call marriage.

From many discussions of the home and the family, one might gather the impression that there were grave difficulties in altering our traditional domestic economy over to the new. It is frequently suggested that living in a multiple-family dwelling, buying bread, cooked food, and canned goods, sending out the washing to the laundry, using gas and electric power, riding in automobiles, using rapid transit, and otherwise utilizing the manifold conveniences and comforts of urban life were so baffling that the home and the family could not cope with them.

Again, it is often asserted that technical changes in industry and business, the growing size of establishments, the use of power machinery, the operation of chain stores, and other aspects of the contemporary industrial development have revolutionized social life; but just how those changes react upon the family is less clearly indicated.

## MATERIAL CHANGES EASILY ACCEPTED

If one reflects upon the situation and reviews his or her own recent experience, it is readily seen that no great difficulty is encountered in adopting modern

From "Social Change and the Family" in *Modern American Family,* ed. by D. Young, Annals of the American Academy of the Social and Political Sciences, vol. 160 (March 1932), pp. 94-102.

ways of living, with their conveniences and inconveniences, their gadgets and their refinements. Indeed, it is so easily accomplished that a family or an individual from the back woods may come to the big city and be thoroughly urbanized in a few months' time, so far as acceptance of modern urban living is involved.

What we are prone to forget or ignore is that the material culture — as the anthropologists term this array of tools and equipment, techniques and skills — is readily changed, but the non-material culture of custom, tradition, codes of behavior, ethics and morals, and the *mores* or folkways of behavior, is less plastic. Long after the material culture has changed, the patterns of conduct which governed man's behavior in that former material culture will still be observed, producing confusion and dismay and often misery and distress as he struggles to reconcile the old with the new. An illustration of the cultural lag can be found in the industrial situation. The introduction and widespread adoption of machinery and modern technology in factories displaced the older handicraft; yet the customs of the older culture persisted in the law of master and servant and in a variety of traditions and ancient standards of conduct which we see today in many problems of industrial relations.

If we are to gain some insight into family life and the marriage situation today, we must address ourselves to these less apparent aspects of the situation and, if possible, discover how far the traditional folkways and patterns of conduct for men and women, for parents and children, are being frustrated and distorted by these changes in the material culture we are witnessing. In other words we must attempt to reveal the impact of the changing economic life upon personality and mating.

EARNING A LIVING

Perhaps the most direct evidence of the effect of the changing social-economic situation upon the individual is to be seen in earning a living. At the outset it is well to remind ourselves that today it is largely a question of *earning* a living, while a few generations ago it was a question of *making* a living. Then, the individual man and woman was for the most part engaged in agriculture or handicrafts in which strength, skill, patience, and endurance bulked large. Money, as income and as expenditure, played a relatively small role, as the following extract from the diary of a New England farmer clearly shows:

> My farm gave me and my whole family a good living on the produce of it and left me, one year with another, one hundred and fifty silver dollars, for I never spent more than ten dollars a year, which was for salt, nails and the like. Nothing to eat, drink or wear was bought, as my farm produced it all.

The family was the industrial and economic unit, and to make a living a man had before him the example of his father and his neighbors, with a body of lore and custom to guide him in growing food and raw materials and fabricating them into needed articles. The young woman also had her guides and teachers in her mother and other older women, who taught her the arts and crafts needed in her activities as a housewife or a spinster.

Today the situation has changed completely, and even in the rural sections, few farmers are engaged in *making* a living; for the most part they are occupied in raising cash crops to sell in order to *earn* a living. Moreover, where formerly only the most enterprising and courageous (and perhaps also the black sheep) went out to seek new occupations and livings, today, with the decline of the rural population and the growth of the urban, almost every one is being forced out to seek a job and to face new and unfamiliar conditions. Thus we see how, for the majority of persons, no longer are there safe and comfortable refuges of traditional occupations and ways of life; all are faced with uncertainty, often anxiety, and are called upon to exert themselves in strange surroundings with few guideposts and traditions. How much this has to do with the current mood of anxiety and restless uneasiness, we can only speculate.

Money income is the focus of endeavor and the only means to a livelihood, in earning which not only men but increasingly women, unmarried and married, are engaged. The conditions affecting gainful occupations are therefore of prime significance for the family life and the home, since the individual man and woman is subject to their governance.

INDIVIDUAL HELPLESSNESS

The helplessness of the individual is perhaps the outstanding characteristic of these conditions. Whatever may be the individual's capacity and skill, his employment is subject to abrupt termination or limitation by business depression, which closes down not only his place of employment but also others, to a greater or less extent, thus preventing him from seeking another job in a different location or in another industry or business. When times are good, he is subject to loss of his job through technical changes which render his work obsolete or his particular factory uneconomical to operate. The person who escapes these threats may be laid off or discharged because he is too old — at forty.

These large and intangible factors creating the worker's helplessness are reenforced by more direct limitations upon his activities. The control of wages, hours, and output by trade unions and other forms of collective bargaining has deprived the individual of any but an indirect participation in determining his earnings, whatever may be his capacity or skill.

Again, the growth of large-scale industrial processes, demanding ever larger capital investment; the rise of chain stores and other forms of productive or distributive activities, requiring incorporation, strong resources, and connections increasingly beyond the reach of the individual — all have conspired to close the former avenues to personal enterprise and initiative. Earning a living is being restricted to wage earning and salary earning under conditions but little amenable to influence or modification by the ordinary worker.

Within the larger corporations, promotion is fairly slow and restricted, and the routine demands a conformity that gives little room for individual activities except for a few at the top. In the professions — law, medicine, and engineering — the overcrowding is notorious; and for one or two brilliant successes there are thousands who barely earn a living in the practice of their profession, while many, after undergoing the prolonged training required, enter upon other occupations as the only way to earn a living.

With the growth of child-labor laws and compulsory school attendance, the age for beginning to earn an income has been progressively postponed. In this present period of acute unemployment, the school authorities are urging pupils to continue their schooling and to defer seeking a job.

The foregoing description of the economic situation is intended to show the direction of social change. In some sections of the country the old conditions still obtain, and many small shops and factories are still in operation; but it is clear that the drift is away from those former conditions, and impending changes are already at work upon the attitudes and beliefs of men and women. Lest the reader be led into despondence over this seemingly gloomy picture, he should be reminded that the introduction of the factory system and the elimination of handicraft, a century or so ago, brought as great if not greater changes of a similar character to the artisan and craftsman. The industrial revolution is still in process.

While the individual has been rendered ever more helpless in this matter of earning a living, he has also been progressively relieved of the frequent claims upon him for immediate or future contingencies. Through widows' pensions, old-age pensions and retirement allowances, accident compensation and often sickness allowances, industrial or governmentally supplied medical care and the succor of family welfare societies, a large portion of the former responsibilities and anxieties has been lifted from the shoulders of the wage earner. These provisions reflect fairly accurately the helplessness and inability of the individual today to make provision for such contingencies, and the disappearance of the older arrangement of family and neighborhood assistance.

TRANSFER OF HOME FUNCTIONS

When we turn to the question of what is this living for which an income must be earned, we again see a large shift in process. The functions of the home upon which the family life was focused are being transferred to other agencies and organizations. Food, as we know, is to be found increasingly in restaurants and cafeterias, and that which is consumed in the home is prepared by canning factories, bakeries, ice cream factories, and so on.

The care of the sick and the maintenance of health has become institutionalized in hospitals, sanatoria, and clinics, aided by visiting nurses and related personnel who render the care formerly given by members of the family.

Childbirth is increasingly taking place in hospitals, and the care and nurture of the child is likewise moving outside of the home to clinic, nursery school, kindergarten, school, summer camp, playground, and youth organization. The young adult who formerly lived at home is now living in dormitories and bachelor hotels, thus leaving the family group as soon as wage earning begins, instead of waiting until marriage. With the prolongation of schooling, however, the economic dependence of the child is continuing into the years when the maintenance of the child is probably most costly.

The making of clothes for men and now for women is being industrialized, as is their cleaning and laundering, which marks another transfer of home functions.

For recreation and leisure-time activities, the home has already yielded to the theater for plays and moving pictures, to clubs and associations and commercialized amusements of all kinds. On the other hand, the radio is bringing entertainment into the home, with the possibility of television as a further addition to home life.

The provision against the proverbial rainy day, as already discussed, is being cared for by social and governmental schemes of pensions, allowances, and tax-supported services.

In the religious sphere, the home and the family are becoming an increasing object of concern on the part of the church leaders, while the old-time intimate religious life of the family appears to be fading out or losing much of its former importance and significance.

These transfers and losses of home functions are being met by changes in housing. We are rapidly becoming residents of congregate dwellings, or apartment houses as we call them, where we live as tenants, paying rent. The home as a secure haven and as a symbol of solid achievement and status, is passing, so that we may in truth refer to the homeless millions, who occupy a house or an apartment only so long as the rent is forthcoming. This homelessness is reflected in the frequent moving from one apartment to another, since our complete lack of responsibility or concern, save for the rent, prevents the formation of ties to the particular dwelling we inhabit. In this connection it should be remembered that by paying rent we are provided with all the services which members of the family once performed, such as maintaining the heating and hot water, removal of garbage and trash, cleaning the premises, repairing equipment, and the like, not forgetting the use of gas for cooking and electric power for lighting, and the innumerable household chores they have wiped out.

FORMER GOALS ARE PASSING

Thus stripped of its functions and responsibilities, the home no longer is a focus of human endeavor and interest, but is becoming rather a place at which various services are rendered, for which the payment of a money income is necessary. Home ownership is ceasing to be the goal of striving it once formed for the family; houses are purchased or built for financial reasons, and mortgages are not reduced except when required.

Other goals are being relinquished in this shift of home functions. To own property, especially land and a house, was once the chief aim of a family and the mark of its solid worth in the community. Various furnishings also occupied a special position in the family aspirations and were objects to be sought through thrifty saving. But installment purchasing has changed that, and as the automobile and the radio have superseded the piano and other prized items of furniture, the need for waiting and saving has passed. The car and the radio are not goals, they are necessities and are purchased as such, to be paid for "on time."

Status in the community has long been the goal of endeavor, but today has a limited appeal. The restrictions upon small enterprise and industry have closed the door to the usual route to respectable competence and a dignified position in the community, and the frequency of moving about in large cities has rendered the neighborhood of little account except to the children. The prestige of the competent housekeeper and mother of a family has diminished with the simpler function of the household and the decrease in number of children.

Children have been both a goal and the focus of family endeavor; but with the declining birth rate they are playing a somewhat altered role in the family. Today economic insecurity and conditions of urban life unfavorable to child care are both to be considered before childbearing is undertaken. When and if a couple has children, the number is less frequently four or five, as formerly, and more often one or two. The multiplication of child-caring techniques, each calling for additional expenditures of energy and money, has enhanced the cost of child rearing for the conscientious parents who are anxious to provide the best available care and treatment for their children.

THE CHANGING WAY OF LIFE

While we rapidly note the passing of these different goals and enumerate the loss of home and family functions, we cannot too much emphasize that the disappearance of these various activities and strivings marks the passing of a *way of life,* To marry, have children, acquire property, gain a position of respect and dignity in the community, share in the common body of beliefs and affirmations about the universe and man's place therein — these made up a way of life to which the teachings of family, school, and church and the sanction of government and religion were all directed. Young people grew up in a society where the patterns appropriate to this way of life were ready-made, and, while they often criticized their stodgy parents and revolted against their demands, middle age found them more or less settled into the ruts of conformity, since there were no socially sanctioned alternatives.

The patterns for this older way of life remain, but the social-economic situation to which they were addressed has altered. Young men and women face either frustration in their efforts to conform to the older patterns, or confusion and anxiety as they explore for new patterns of conduct. These frustrations and anxieties are the dominant aspect of home and family life today.

The young man who would fulfill the older conception of a competent male, ambitious, enterprising, prepared to support a wife and family, faces a most perplexing situation. What kind of a job shall he seek, what career shall he undertake, what scale of income shall he adopt as his goal? The young men of today, coming out of high school or college, are beset with such questions, since they must have some program or aim by which to guide their efforts and to measure their achievements. No less is the young woman bewildered and adrift or acutely miserable under the authority of tradition and the impulsion of present-day movements.

There are a few fundamental patterns and needs which determine in large measure the conduct of the individual and his mating. These touch his security, his reassurance, and his sex functioning; and if we are to understand how social and economic changes are affecting men and women, we must seek some illumination on these fundamentals and their fate today.

THE PERSONAL GOAL

Security for an individual is relative — not absolute; it is defined by the reach of the individual's aspirations and ideals. As he pictures himself, as a man, as a worker, as a husband, as a father, in the various other roles which as a male he must play immediately or in the future, he creates an ideal self — the kind of man he would like to be. This is compounded of all the images and experiences he has had of real and imaginary men, in books and plays, and it becomes the secret goal and ambition of his life. To the extent that this ideal self is congruous with and sanctioned by the social-economic life around him and is within the reach of his real abilities and talents, it may be thoroughly realistic and desirable, giving to the man who cherishes it an admirable purpose and stability. Until he does achieve those purposes and fulfill those ambitions, he must remain anxious, apprehensive of check or defeat — in a word, insecure.

This insecurity, however, is of the man's own making, for it represents what tasks he has measured off for himself against the world. To his aid he may summon mighty forces of religion to give him a feeling of relatedness to the visible and the invisible universe and a belief in his own importance to whatever power lies behind the universe. He may invoke the strength of his family position and status to reenforce his own immature prowess and win for him the opportunities to show his ability. He may call upon his age and sex mates for assurance of his fitness and comparative capacities. Within himself he may find a large resource of quiet confidence in his readiness to meet life and its demands, if he has been fortunate enough to grow up in an atmosphere favorable to such inner peace. Beyond these ministrations to his security he may have access to affectionate intimacy in the love of his parents and later of his own mate and children, which will give him the most potent of all reassurance to meet the world.

But if one builds up for himself an ideal that is beyond his actual abilities, that is torn with internal conflicts or is irreconcilable with the actual social, economic, and political life in which he must live, then his aspirations and ambitions will betray him into endless anxiety and fear, leading him into vain endeavors for a security he can never achieve. The resources of religion, of family status, and of contemporary regard will avail little in this struggle, for he bears within himself the real source of his insecurity, for which no external reassurance will avail.

THE YOUNG MAN'S OUTLOOK ON LIFE

This is in large measure the situation of the young man today, for the discrepancy between the patterns offered him by a tradition (an older way of life) and the changing social-economic conditions, gives rise to acute anxiety and perplexity. There is no security either in himself or in the social life around him, and the sources of reassurance have been depleted if not eliminated through the very process of change, undermining religious beliefs, family status and position, and the power of contemporary associations. This anxiety and dismay have infected the older men and women too, so that their affection is troubled and they can give little intimacy to their children.

What, asks the young man, can I do? What should I do? What is worth striving for, amid all this confusion and turmoil? What picture of myself can I construct as an ideal to be achieved with all the abilities and energies I can command? To these questions the young man receives dubious answers, since the old patterns are not applicable to the new organizations, the new operations, and the new set of economic, pecuniary arrangements now emerging from our obsolescent institutions. As yet, the new patterns which will guide the young man of tomorrow have not been created. In endless experiments and many futile efforts this generation is seeking them, but it has not clarified or stabilized them or given the sanctions needed for authoritative use.

According to the once popular view, a man's love was "a thing apart" from his work and position, and his marriage and family life were quite removed from his occupation. But this view will scarcely survive against the contrary evidence today. The man looks to his wife for recognition of the man he hopes to be, seeking from her the reassurance he needs to achieve his ambitions. He must have aspirations and ideals to lay before her as an earnest of the true self he hopes to attain and as a touchstone of her faith and love for that self. If his ideals are shaky or dubious and he is filled with anxiety, he has little to offer or to gain in his mating. Or if his ambitions are high but incompatible with the new conditions of life, then he is threatened with heightened anxiety from without and from his wife's too trusting faith in him. If he has overrated his prowess before marriage, he faces his wife's reproaches or her silent disappointment, even when he has fought the good fight against overwhelming odds — changed conditions making that kind of success impossible. If he has too modestly pitched his hopes, while another succeeds, often by fortuitous circumstances, he may feel inferior and lose her esteem. These mischances and dismays are not so much the failing of the man as they are unavoidable situations of a changing social life, wherein the young man can find no unequivocal patterns to guide him.

There is no need for elaborating upon this theme. Any one with insight and awareness can see on all sides the tragedy of marital discord engendered by this insecurity and the lack of a compelling way of life.

The ego ideal, or *persona,* of an individual, the picture of himself as he hopes to be, is the most important aspect of an individual, and when it is confused and weakened, his whole self and all his relations are disturbed. Especially are his marital relations disturbed, since the need for recognition of the ego ideal and for reassurance are as important as, if not more so than, sex needs. Indeed, sex compatibility is scarcely possible unless a man and a woman have faith in each other's personality and integrity. Moreover, the man who lacks security is scarcely able to fulfull the role of a competent husband, for which psychological potency is as essential as physiological potency.

New patterns in mating, especially for the male, are imperatively needed, since successful mating has become so much more important in marriage faced with the loss of family functions and responsibilities. Men and women require more affection and fuller sex realization to compensate for the loss of other activities and satisfactions, and to sustain them under strain and anxiety.

THE WOMAN'S BEFOGGED CONDITION

Woman, in these changing social conditions, is no less insecure and troubled with doubt. Her traditional goals and patterns are gone and she faces the necessity not merely of finding substitutes, as does the man, but also of discovering patterns for new activities and functions never before attempted by women. The conflict of competing loyalties is terrific and her sources of security are more depleted than are those of the man. Indeed, parents, education, religion, and art have only intensified her problems by their conservative refusal to recognize the change or help her to find some way of life compatible with her needs and new responsibilities.

It would take several volumes to outline the perplexities of the woman today, their source, and the frustrations they are imposing upon her. In the field of gainful employment into which women have been entering more rapidly than men, various obstacles and the disillusionment about men are productive of attitudes and emotional conditions of serious import for marriage, especially marriage of the old pattern. We can but indicate here how woman is fumbling for ego ideals into which she can pour her hopes and dreams and for which she can employ her immense energies and capacities; how she might clarify her aspirations but dare not because men are not ready to accept her vision and her hopes — not prepared to receive the new woman who will displace the creature of masculine tradition.

We have today the high tragedy not only of bewildered men and women unable to find their way through these novel situations and circumstances, but of tortured personalities yearning for reassurance and intimacy and full mating, but doomed to rend each other through lack of insight into themselves and their mates and the patterns of conduct needed for their realization.

What men and women are doing to each other, they are doing to their children, but in different ways. The child, above all, needs security, reassurance, and the warmth of affection and peace which his parents, preoccupied with their anxieties and frustrations, can rarely give him. Nor can the father and the mother who are apprehensive over their own way of life offer tolerance and sympathy for the child's bewildering experiments.

## THE FORWARD LOOK

We cannot stand still nor go back to the older ways of life, since belief in their authority and the sanctions are gone. We must go forward in faith and hope, trying to gain some real insights and a more sympathetic awareness of the personality needs of one another. No one is untouched by these situations, and no one is free from the anxieties and the poignant need of reassurance and intimacy. Perhaps the largest step in the working-out of the new home and family life will be taken when men and women realize their mutual uncertainties and needs, and together face the task of working out the future.

When we seek to understand the influence of changing social and economic conditions upon the home and the family, let us remember to go behind the housing, the conveniences, and the thousand-and-one changes of material culture. Let us try to envisage the groping man and woman who, amidst these changes, are seeking something stable and effective for those enduring human needs that will, some day, we hope, find a new fruition in the good society which all this turmoil and confusion will produce.

## Home and Community

*President's Commission on the Status of Women*

Not so long ago, and not only in rural areas, family tasks were shared by members of two or more generations — by grandmothers, mothers or mothers-in-law, and maiden aunts, as well as by women with young children. Sisters and sisters-in-law often lived under the same roof or closeby.

Now, though fathers often take a larger share in the performance of household tasks than they used to and the older children help in many ways, in most families the mother is the only grown person present to assume day-to-day responsibility in the home. And the family is more than likely to be an anonymous newcomer among strange neighbors in an urban or suburban setting. These simultaneous changes in the composition of families and communities have altered the very nature of family life.

CHILD CARE AND FAMILY SERVICES

Child care services are needed in all communities, for children of all kinds of families who may require day care, after-school care, or intermittent care. In putting major emphasis on this need, the Commission affirms that child care facilities are essential for women in many different circumstances, whether they work outside the home or not. It is regrettable when women with children are forced by economic necessity or by the regulations of welfare agencies to seek employment while their children are young. On the other hand, those who decide to work should have child care services available.

The gross inadequacy of present child care facilities is apparent. Across the country, licensed day care is available to some 185,000 children only. In nearly half a million families with children under 6 years, the mother is frequently the sole support. There are 117,000 families with children under 6 with only a father in the home. Almost 3 million mothers of children under 6 work outside the home although there is a husband present. Other mothers, though not at work, may be ill, living in overcrowded slum conditions with no play opportunities for children, responsible for mentally retarded or emotionally handicapped children, or confronting family crises. Migrant families have no fixed homes.

In the absence of adequate child care facilities, many of these mothers are forced to resort to makeshift arrangements or to leave their children without care. A 1958 survey disclosed no less than 400,000 children under 12 whose

From "Home and Community," *Report of the President's Commission on the Status of Women,* 1963 (Washington, D.C.: U.S. Government Printing Office, 1936), 0-693-825, pp. 19- 24 (abridged).

mothers worked full time and for whose supervision no arrangements whatsoever had been made. Suitable afterschool supervision is especially crucial for children whom discrimination in housing forces into crowded neighborhoods.

Plans for housing developments, community centers, urban renewal projects, and migratory labor camps should provide space for child care centers under licensing procedures insuring adequate standards.

Localities should institute afterschool and vacation activities, in properly supervised places, for schoolage children whose mothers must be away from home during hours when children are not in school.

Failure to assure such services reflects primarily a lack of community awareness of the realities of modern life. Recent Federal legislation offering assistance to communities establishing day care is a first step in raising its provision to the level of national policy. As a number of localities have discovered, child care can be provided in many ways as long as proper standards are assured: cooperatively by groups of parents; by public or private agencies with fees on a sliding scale according to ability to pay; or as a public undertaking.

Where group programs serve children from a cross section of a city, they provide training grounds for democratic social development. Their educational possibilities range from preparing underprivileged children for school, to providing constructive activities for normal youngsters, to offering especially gifted children additional means of development.

For the benefit of children, mothers, and society, child care services should be available for children of families at all economic levels. Proper standards of child care must be maintained, whether services are in homes or in centers. Costs should be met by fees scaled to parents' ability to pay, contributions from voluntary agencies, and public appropriations. . . .

Family services under public and private auspices to help families avoid or overcome breakdown or dependency and establish a soundly based homelife, and professionally supervised homemaker services to meet emergency or other special needs should be strengthened, extended, or established where lacking. . . .

Community programs under public and private auspices should make comprehensive provisions for health and rehabilitation services, including easily accessible maternal and child health services, accompanied by education to encourage their use. . . .

The reorganization of ordinary home maintenance service is long overdue. That many of the women employed in household work remain in it only because they have no alternative became apparent when other opportunities opened up during World War II. In 1940, almost 18 percent of all employed women were household workers; by 1950, the percentage had gone down to 8. Slightly more than 2 1/4 million women are employed in household work at present.

Household workers have, historically, been low paid, without standards of hours and working conditions, without collective bargaining, without most of the protections accorded by legislation and accepted as normal for other workers, and without means and opportunity adequately to maintain their own homes.

Few families can now afford to employ such workers full time at decent wages, but many families can pay rates in line with modern labor standards for special services as they need them. Privately run placement organizations to market such special services can operate to the mutual benefit of employer and employee, and are doing so in some communities. They can conduct training programs and insure standards of job performance, and they can monitor conditions of work and wages paid. The public employment offices should review their treatment of household service, encouraging the development of specialties and conducting placement on that basis.

## Children of Mankind

*Letter to the Editor*

I have lived as a mother of three children in Belgium. Every month I went, with dignity, to the Post Office and drew out a family allowance for each of my three children. No one asked whether my children were black, white, yellow, legitimate or illegitimate.

I have lived in England as a widow with three children. Every month I received my family allowance. No one queried the color or legitimacy of my children. Each town had free prenatal and post natal care. I received milk at half price and orange juice and vitamin pills for the children at a very low cost.

I had the National Health Scheme. If my children were sick or needed dental treatment, I took them to the doctor or dentist of my own choice and they received treatment. I did, too. This treatment was free.

I now live in the United States with my three American children. Only in the gravest emergency dare I call a doctor or go to a dentist.

I have watched the heartrending TV programs about the children and people living in Mississippi and Appalachia. I have read of riots and the

From a "Letter to the Editor," *The Washington Post* (Summer 1967), as quoted by Daniel P. Moynihan in Foreward to *Children, Poverty and Family Allowances,* ed. by James C. Vadakin (New York and London: Basic Books, 1968.)

incredible poverty in the slums. I have read of the poverty programs, the food stamp programs, etc., all very worthy, and I am sure they have done much good. But have they done enough and are they reaching the children suffering from malnutrition and rat bites?

Why cannot America, the richest country in the world, come up with a family allowances scheme whereby every mother of children under eighteen could collect, with dignity, and without feeling it was charity, an allowance for each child in her care, whether the child was black, white, yellow, legitimate or illegitimate? The wealthy mothers could collect it if they wanted to, the working mothers could collect it, and the mothers unable to work could collect it.

Would the cost be so much greater than all the schemes which are being tried, and which are not reaching the children in the Appalachians, nor the children in Mississippi, nor the children in the slums?

# 7. Fair Trade

> It has been bitterly said that in the markets of the world there is nothing so cheap as womanhood, and it is literally true. Place that saying beside this other, that woman is today paid for her dishonor better than for anything else.
>
> LILLIE DEVEREUX BLAKE

To advantaged women, the word *toil* has been the symbol of social integration; to ordinary women, it has meant, simply, a necessary burden. In earlier periods of agitation, while rebels of the middle class demanded full participation in the world of work, rebels of the working class sought only protection from the sweatshops. This dichotomy has been present throughout the history of feminism. The goals of both groups have, however, been consistently frustrated by the marginal status of all women in the marketplace. And both groups have suffered the consequences of being cast as classical wage cutters. These conditions persist today, intensified by the circumstance that computer technology increasingly makes even cheap labor redundant. Woman's economic place continues perilous.

Eleanor Flexner, in the first reading, describes the position of laboring women in the United States from the Civil War to the onset of World War I, tracing their efforts to enter existing trade unions and to form their own protective leagues. The virtual exclusion of women from the mainstream of the labor movement goes far to explain why they were forced to seek through legislation the safeguards that men attained through association.

The second reading, part of a 1963 *Report* by the Commission on the Status of Women appointed by President John F. Kennedy, presents a picture of the

*Parallel readings for Chapter 7, "In the Marketplace."

contemporary situation: woman still disadvantaged and subject to discriminatory practice. The reasons offered by employers for differential treatment provide an interesting sidelight. Also noteworthy is a description of the various categories of protective legislation and the Commission's recommendations respecting them.

In the third reading, Leo Kanowitz notes the negative effect of rising female employment upon the relationships between men and women, exaggerating culturally determined distinctions. This is seen as a consequence of two economic factors: differentials in wage scales, and classification of jobs by sex. He then discusses landmark legislation affecting the status of women in the marketplace: the federal Equal Pay Act of 1963 and Title VII of the Civil Rights Act of 1964, new efforts to deal with old inequities as opposition to sex discrimination in employment becomes official national policy. The weakness of these measures is also suggested in relation to enforcement procedures, existing state laws, and evasionary devices.

Sonia Pressman Fuentes, in the final reading in the section, focuses particularly on the most vulnerable contingent in the labor force, the black female worker. Such women, at the same time that they carry a significant burden of family responsibility, must cope with a lower income and a higher rate of unemployment than any other group. Mrs. Fuentes, Senior Attorney in the Office of the General Counsel of the Equal Employment Opportunity Commission, the administrative arm of Title VII, then outlines the functions of that agency and summarizes some of its rulings.

## Women and Labor

*Eleanor Flexner*

### Women in the Trade Unions, 1860–1875

Industrial development in the northern states, already under way before the Civil War, was tremendously accelerated by the four-year conflict. Equipping and maintaining large armies, in addition to steadily increasing westward expansion, brought about large-scale capital growth, which was further stimulated by the outcome of the war — the victory of free over slave labor. The maturing of the American business and industrial giant had begun . . . .

From *Century of Struggle: The Woman's Rights Movement in the United States* (Cambridge, Mass.: Belknap Press of Harvard University Press, 1959), chapters IX, XIV, XVIII (abridged). Reference notes have been omitted due to space requirements, but all sources are indicated in the original. [E. F.]

Women factory workers were increasing steadily in numbers. The 225,922 shown in the 1850 census rose to 270,987 by 1860 and to 323,370 by 1870. Thousands of women were forced into the labor market when their menfolk joined the Federal armies, came back crippled, or died in action. Most of them, with no other skills to fall back on, glutted the sewing trades, where their situation was desperate. Early in 1865 a group of sewing women in Cincinnati petitioned President Lincoln to end the system of subcontracting for army uniforms since it reduced their earnings below the level of subsistence. Protesting their patriotism and their wish to do the work needed by the army, they pointed out that

> we are unable to sustain life for the price offered by contractors, who fatten on their contracts by grinding immense profits out of the labor of their operatives. As an example, these contractors are paid one dollar and seventy-five cents per dozen for making gray woolen shirts, and they require us to make them for one dollar per dozen. . . . The manufacture of pants, blouses, coats, drawers, tents, tarpaulins, etc., exhibits the same irregularity and injustice to the operative.

Women in such dire straits were available to employers looking for cheap labor and constituted a threat, in any trade they entered, to the men's attempts to better their standards by organizing. The first two national unions to admit women to membership because so many of them were entering their industries were the cigarmakers in 1867, and the printers in 1869. Similarly, the increase of women in various trades lay behind the concern for them shown by the National Labor Union, a short-lived, loosely knit federation of national unions led by William Sylvis. Sylvis was president of the Ironmolders Union, a man of radical sympathies who gave support to the woman's rights movement and who saw that in the last analysis the interests of men and women workers were indivisible. At its first convention in 1866, the National Labor Union resolved that

> we pledge our individual and undivided support to the sewing women and daughters of toil in this land, and would solicit their hearty cooperation, knowing, as we do, that no class of industry is so much in need of having their condition ameliorated as the factory operatives, sewing women, etc., of this country.

The organization of working women at this time took several forms. One was that of the bona fide trade union, either an independent group limited to the women in a particular industry, or part of an existing union to which women were admitted. Another form was the Working Woman's Association which took in any and all women who worked for their livelihood. A third was the Protective Association, which also took in women regardless of trade or occupation, but which confined itself to such welfare problems as legal aid or finding reputable employment. . . .

During the two years [Susan B. Anthony] was publishing her own weekly newspaper, *The Revolution,* [she] devoted considerable time and effort to helping such women organize, especially during the latter part of 1868.

Typical of the items it often carried was the following: "A meeting of ladies was held on September 17 at noon, in the offices of *The Revolution* newspaper, 37 Park Row, for the purpose of organizing an association of working-women, which might act for the interests of its members, in the same manner as the associations of workingmen now regulate the wages, etc., of those belonging to them."

The gathering, which formed a Working Women's Association, represented a cross-section of the currents of thought then emerging among women. There was Mrs. Stanton, convinced that women could never engage in the pursuits of their choice unless they won the ballot, urging the young organization to take a position endorsing woman suffrage. Also present were several women engaged in the novel occupation of setting type, among them Miss Augusta Lewis ("a brunette lady with pleasing dark eyes") who knew her fellow typographers well enough to declare that identifying the organization with woman suffrage would also label it in their minds with "short hair, bloomers and other vagaries"; it would be better to call the women typesetters together for "business purposes" first, and educate them on the suffrage question later. Miss Lewis had her way on this point. However she herself had illusions which she had to unlearn in the course of the next two years. One of them was the belief that the chief obstacle to women's being paid as much as men for the same amount of work was their failure to learn their craft or trade as thoroughly as the men did, because they expected to get married. Miss Lewis was also certain, at the start, that men would be open to conviction on the matter of equal pay, "if it were put to them properly." She was to learn otherwise.

Miss Lewis was an educated woman who had written newspaper articles and who lived up to her own principles by mastering the art of typesetting so well that she was known for her ability to set the entire text of *Rip Van Winkle* (consisting of 24,993 ems of solid agate type) in six and a half hours. When Women's Typographical Union No. 1 sprouted from the Working Women's Association, Miss Lewis became its president. The new union received encouraging support from the established men's printing union in New York, Local No. 6. At its very first meeting the corresponding secretary of Local No. 6 read a letter in which the latter pledged itself to

> aid you all we can in your movement, knowing that your interests are identical with our own. We have agreed to hire a hall for your meetings, furnish you with books, stationery, etc. and assume all other expenses which it may be necessary for you to incur in getting your Association into working order, and to continue to do so until your Union shall be in a condition to support itself.

Never before had working women received such assurances and encouragement. No wonder Miss Anthony, who was present to see her fledglings get underway, took fire and urged them on to greater efforts:

> Girls, you must take this matter to heart seriously now, for you have established a union, and for the first time in woman's history in the United States, you are placed, and by your own efforts, on a level with men, as far as possible, to obtain wages for your labor. I need not say you have taken a great, a momentous step forward in the path to success. Keep at it now, girls, and you will achieve full and plenteous success.

For a time matters looked promising. In June 1869 at the national union's convention in Albany, the delegation of Local No. 6 presented a petition from Women's Local No. 1 applying for a charter. Miss Lewis and the local's treasurer, Eva B. Howard, attended all sessions of the convention, working hard for the recognition of their organization, and Miss Lewis addressed the convention. The charter was granted after the national president pointed out that the women had certainly earned it:

> Though most liberal inducements were offered to women compositors to take the places of men on strike, not a single member of the women's union could be induced to do so. Offers have been made to the president of their organization to furnish women compositors to other cities for the purpose of reducing the wages of men, and in every instance have been declined.

When Augusta Lewis appeared at the convention of 1870 as a delegate from Women's Local No. 1, she received the distinction of being elected corresponding secretary of the national union for the ensuing year. This post was no sinecure: of greater importance than the honor paid to her was the fact that she filled it with singular ability. Her report to the union's 1871 convention, presenting a comprehensive picture of the printing industry, including employment conditions and wage scales in a dozen cities, is the first such document to emanate from a woman in American labor history. Her information was amassed through correspondence with men who were unaccustomed, in that day and age, to dealing with a woman in such a capacity; that Miss Lewis was able to elicit their cooperation is in itself a tribute. Said the President in his annual report to the convention:

> The distrust of her abilities expressed by Miss Lewis upon accepting the position of corresponding secretary has not been sustained by the facts. She has displayed industry, zeal and intelligence in the position rarely met with. . . . The details of the state of the trade in the various localities in our jurisdiction are so fully and clearly set forth by her, that I have only to refer you for information on that head to her very comprehensive report.

Nor did the corresponding secretary overlook in her work the principal reason which had led her to overcome her hesitations and accept the post: "to add a link to the chain that would span the chasm that has heretofore divided the interests of the male and female printers." Through personal interviews and by correspondence, Miss Lewis tried to widen the opportunities for women printers already in the union, and to help others to organize. Unfortunately the hopes with which she herself had joined the union, that the men in the trade might see the reasonableness of women's demands for equal pay, and their common interest in such a goal, were not realized. The objectivity of her report to the convention of 1871 does not obscure its bitterness:

> We refuse to take the men's situations when they are on strike, and when there is no strike if we ask for work in union offices we are told by union foremen "that there are no conveniences for us." We are ostracized in many offices because we are members of the union, and although the principle is right, disadvantages are so many that we cannot much longer hold together. . . . It is the general opinion of female compositors that they are more justly treated by what is termed "rat" foremen, printers and employers than they are by union men.

. . .The women's union which became best known throughout the labor movement during its brief history was that of the collar makers and laundry workers of Troy, New York. . . .

We first learn of the women in the laundries, where they worked long hours in temperatures near one hundred degrees "while the implements with which they work are throwing out an equal amount of heat with increasing intensity." In 1863 they banded together, went on strike, and won a wage increase. Three years later their organization was sufficiently substantial to donate the phenomenal sum of $1,000 to aid the locked-out and striking Iron Molders Union, a gesture which neither the union nor its leader, William Sylvis, forgot. In 1868 they won further increases in pay, and their leader, Kate Mullaney, was chosen by Sylvis as assistant secretary of the National Labor Union.

Beyond this fact, and that she was known to Susan Anthony and other outstanding women of the day, we know nothing of what must have been a dynamic and indomitable woman beside the bare facts of the rise of the Laundryworkers Union and its eventual defeat. In the spring of 1869 the collar ironers demanded a raise of one-half, one, one-and-a-half, and two cents per dozen pieces "according to the size of the article"; when their demand was refused they went out on strike again, and the starchers, although making no wage demands themselves, went out with their sister unionists, to the number of 430 in all. The *Troy Whig,* usually liberal in tone and in its support of unions, termed it an "unfortunate and ill-timed strike," but support flowed in from a long list of unions in printing, the building trades, iron work, shoemaking, etc., the individual sums ranging from $25 to $250; in one week alone $558 was received.

A mass meeting on the steps of the town court house was addressed by prominent union men; plans were announced for a cooperative laundry which hoped to take the patronage of working people away from the established firms. A picnic held on July 19 was highly successful — the conservative *Troy Times* called it "a monstrous affair" and the *Whig* reported that the streets of neighboring villages were deserted because everyone had gone to the picnic; it netted the strikers $1,200.

Yet on July 23 another large meeting which was to have been addressed by Richard Trevellick, a national labor leader, was canceled without explanation. Just one week later on July 31 a meeting of the union voted not merely for its members to return to work, but to dissolve the organization.

The most logical explanation for the debacle lies in the sudden death of William Sylvis after a brief illness, which threw the entire labor movement into near panic, and diverted further aid from the collar workers. The employers were not slow to press their unexpected advantage. On July 30, the day before the union meeting, the *Troy Times* ran four prominently displayed advertisements of a new *paper* collar, developed "for the accommodation of the growing demand among our citizens for this celebrated goods," a threat to the jobs of the laundry workers. The employers also met to confer on a common policy of re-employing the "old hands," many of whom were offered positions in a large new plant. These onslaughts, coupled with the demoralization resulting from Sylvis' death, had the desired results. The union vanished overnight, and the cooperative laundry it had launched lasted only a few weeks longer.

Another brief chapter in the organization of women workers was written in Lynn, Massachusetts, long the center of the shoe industry. Like Troy, Lynn had not yet been reached by recent waves of immigrant labor; the women who stitched shoe tops, which they had previously done in their own homes but did now in factories, were largely of Irish-Scotch and English extraction but Americans for several generations. Out of their discontent over low pay and long hours developed a short-lived but unique trade union which spread to other growing centers of shoe manufacturing, and became a national organization — the Daughters of St. Crispin, patterned on the union of men shoe workers, the Knights of St. Crispin, and occasionally aided by it.

Like all these earlier women's organizations (with the exception of the Lowell textile operatives) they left no records, and what is known of their history is scattered in the labor press of the period. The founding convention was held on July 28, 1869 (just at the time the Troy collar workers union collapsed), and two Lynn women — Miss Carrie Wilson and Miss Abbie Jacques — were elected president and secretary, respectively. Within a few months the organization had grown to twenty-four lodges, fourteen in Massachusetts, the others scattered in Maine, New York, New Hampshire, Pennsylvania, Ohio, Illinois, Wisconsin, and California.

Annual conventions were held until 1872, and two officers were present as delegates at the 1870 convention of the National Labor Union. That year the Daughters of St. Crispin passed a resolution demanding "the same rate of compensation for equal skill displayed, or the same hours of toil, as is paid other laborers in the same branches of business; and we regard a denial of this right by anyone as a usurpation and a fraud." Then, perhaps feeling that such strong language might cost them the support of opponents of equal rights for women, they added a conciliatory note: "Resolved, that we assure our fellow-citizens that we only desire to so elevate and improve our condition as to better fit us for the discharge of those high social and moral duties which devolve upon every true woman."

In 1872 the shoe manufacturers of Lynn attempted to cut wages and compel every worker to sign a pledge that she would give two weeks' notice before leaving her position, or else forfeit five dollars of her pay. A meeting of nine hundred women voted unanimously not to comply with such a demand and adopted a set of resolutions which deserve quotation in full:

> We, the Workingwomen, in convention assembled, do accept the following resolutions, as an earnest expression of our sentiments;
>
> Whereas, we have long been sensible of the need of protecting our rights and privileges as free-born women, and are determined to defend them and our interests as workingwomen, to the fullest extent of our ability; therefore, be it
>
> Resolved, That we, the workingwomen of Lynn, known as Upper Fitters and Finishers of Boots and Shoes, do enter a most solemn protest against any reduction of wages, on any pretext whatever; and that we will not submit to any rules that do not equally affect our employers.
>
> Resolved, that we feel grateful to the shoemakers of Lynn for their interest and determination to stand by us in our time of need.
>
> Resolved, that we, the free women of Lynn, will submit to no rule or set of rules that tend to degrade and enslave us.
>
> Resolved, That we will accept no terms whatever, either with regard to a reduction of prices, notices to quit, or forfeiture of wages. That while we utterly ignore the spirit of selfishness and illiberality which prompted the late action of our would-be oppressors, we will not hesitate to resist, in a proper manner, the unjust encroachments upon our rights.
>
> Resolved, that a copy of these resolutions be given to every one of the committee, to be by them presented to each girl in every shop, and her signature thereon obtained; and should anyone of the employees of the shop be reduced in her wages, or ill-treated, we will desist from our work until she has obtained her rights.
>
> Resolved, that a copy of the above be inserted in the Lynn papers, and a large surplus number be provided for distribution among the girls.

Obviously, these women knew how to handle themselves: what to expect in the way of reprisals, how to protect themselves through united action, the mechanics of using the press, and of distributing their resolution in order to gain support in the community. They were determined as well as experienced, and as a result the employers backed down — neither the wage cut nor the dismissal notice went through at that time.

Although there is no mention of the Daughters of St. Crispin as the organization through which the women functioned on this occasion, at least some of them must have been members, for although the order declined rapidly after its brief heyday, traces of it remained longest in Lynn, up to 1876. But like many other unions, it could not weather the prolonged panic and depression, touched off by the bankruptcy of the banking firm of Jay Cooke & Company in September of 1873, which lasted until 1878.

The next surge of organization among women workers did not come until the emergence of the Knights of Labor in the 1880's. Many of the women who entered its ranks had taken part in the short-lived organizations of the '60's and '70's, but organization of women workers lacks the continuity to be found among the men. Individual women appear briefly, then vanish; a promising start in one industry or one town sputters out. Unskilled and poorly paid, the women leave one trade for another that seems more promising — or they leave work to marry and bear children. There is no money even for dues, let alone strike-funds, or the mechanics of maintaining an organization (such as Local No. 6 offered the young local of women typesetters). Women of means, with contacts and influence, such as those who kept the nascent suffrage movement alive for decades, had not yet become interested in the problems of working women, or seen the relationship between their goals; they did not do so, on any appreciable scale, until the turn of the century.

But the grievances remained — low, unequal wages, the long hours, the indignities inflicted by foremen and employers — and the unremitting, sporadic, unsuccessful attempts to organize against them also continued. However fugitive they might appear, they showed the way to those who came after, and who succeeded in building more enduringly.

## Women in the Knights of Labor and the Early A.F. of L. *

The 1880's and '90's were a period of huge and rapid industrial growth. The founding of the Standard Oil Company was followed by more "trusts," at first in the distilling, sugar-refining, and lead industries, later in steel, tobacco, and elsewhere. Railroads spread north and south, in a network all the way to the Pacific Coast, spurred by such financiers as Henry Villard, James J. Hill, and others.

Cheap tractable labor was needed for these giant enterprises: in the decade after 1880, immigration from impoverished European countries topped five million. Women workers were in rising demand, always for the lowest-paying jobs; the 2,647,000 gainfully employed in 1880 grew to 4,005,500 ten years later, from 15.2 per cent to 17.2 per cent of the total working labor force.

Outside of the large number classified as housekeepers, stewards, hostesses, and family servants of all kinds, totaling almost a million, the greatest number

*Chapter XIV.

were to be found in the same occupations they had carried on at home before the era of industrialization: making cloth and clothing, keeping these clean, and other so-called service occupations. The largest groups of women factory workers were distributed as follows:

| | | | |
|---|---|---|---|
| Clothing manufacture | 389,231 | Tobacco | 10,868 |
| Laundries and cleaning | 109,280 | Printing | 9,322 |
| Cotton textiles | 92,394 | Silk and rayon | 9,211 |
| Other textiles | 42,420 | Carpets and rugs | 7,674 |
| Shoes | 21,007 | Hats | 6,357 |
| Containers and boxes | 14,126 | | |

Although the demand for labor appeared insatiable, soaring immigration enabled employers to keep wages down. The 1880's consequently saw the first really serious attempt to build a national labor organization. The Knights of Labor, founded in 1869 as a secret fraternal order, discarded the bulk of its ritualistic features in 1881 and began organizing working men and women on an equal basis. Sometimes they were in the same "assemblies," sometimes in separate ones; these were set up on either craft or geographic lines — the Knights never achieved any standardized and stable form of organization. The first "woman's assembly" was chartered in 1881, and others were added with increasing rapidity until 1886, the year which marked the organization's high-water mark, and which also saw one hundred and thirteen women's assemblies chartered. . . .

Although the women were admitted, and their dues payments welcomed, what little effort was made to help and organize them was sparked largely by the small group of leaders from their own ranks. Miss Mary Stirling, a Philadelphia shoe worker who was the lone female delegate at the 1883 "General Assembly," as the annual conventions of the Knights were called, took an active part in the proceedings, apparently undaunted at being outnumbered by several hundred men. The next year two women were seated as delegates, one of whom, Miss Mary Hanafin, was a charter member of the first woman's assembly to be established. She proved to be sufficiently intrepid and forceful to win the convention's support against attempts by some officials to set up another assembly to rival the one she represented as a delegate. In 1885, when she was once again present at a General Assembly as a delegate, she and the two other women delegates were appointed, on her motion, to serve as a committee "to collect statistics on women's work." . . .

None of the three women appointed to the fact-finding committee had any previous experience to fit them for the task: Miss Hanafin was a sales clerk, and the other two were shoe workers. Nevertheless they went to work; they sent out a questionnaire to the women's assemblies in the Knights — the only source of information open to them — and duly reported at the convention of

1886 that the replies showed that average hours for women workers were ten a day, with wages at $5.00 a week, except in the shoe industry where they were slightly higher.

This General Assembly of 1886 in Richmond, Virginia, not only marked the high point of the Knights of Labor as an organization; it made history for working women. Of the 660 delegates, sixteen were women: the tireless Miss Hanafin, six shoe workers, five textile operatives, one machine hand, one dressmaker, one ironer, and one housewife. The housewife was Mrs. George Rodgers, who had won the position of Master Workman (or head) of the entire Knights' organization in the Chicago area, except the stockyards. The mother of twelve children, she brought the youngest, a three-weeks-old baby, to the convention, and was "interviewed" by Frances Willard (herself a member of the Order):

> Mrs. Rodgers is about forty years of age; height medium; figure neither stout nor fragile; complexion fair, clear and healthful; eye an honest gray; mouth sweet and smiling; nose, masterful Roman; head square and full; profile strong and benignant. . . . "My husband always believed that women should do anything they liked that was good and which they could do well," said Mrs. Rodgers proudly; "but for him I would never have got on so well as a Master Workman. I was the first woman in Chicago to join the Knights. They offered us the chance, and I said to myself, "There must be a first one, and so I'll go forward." "How do you speak to them?" I asked. "Oh, just as I do here to my children at home," she answered simply. "I have no time to get anything ready to say, for I do, and always have done, all my own work, but I just talk as well as I can at the time."

One of the textile operatives was Miss Mary O'Reilly from Providence, Rhode Island. Miss O'Reilly subsequently served three active years with the Order. Following passage of the first factory inspection bill in the state of Pennsylvania, she was deputy factory inspector for six years, one of the first women to hold such a position.

The outstanding member of the group was the "machine hand" from a hosiery mill in Amsterdam, New York, named Leonora M. Barry. When the group of women, serving as a committee to consider Miss Hanafin's report to the General Assembly and make suggestions for further action, recommended that a Department of Woman's Work be established with a General Investigator to inquire into "the abuses to which our sex is subjected by unscrupulous employers, [and] to agitate the principles which our Order teaches, of equal pay for equal work and the abolition of child labor," they recommended Mrs. Barry for the post.

The convention thereupon elected Mrs. Barry; for the next three and a half years she traveled around the country, investigating, speaking, and organizing, on a scale that only two other women had equaled until then: Susan Anthony and Frances Willard. The wonder grows when one realizes that both the latter were well educated by the standards of their day and had served long appren-

ticehoods in such activity; Mrs. Barry was catapulted from a stocking machine
to national leadership, and the only schooling she had to draw on was that of
experience.

She had been born in Cork, Ireland, and brought to this country when still
a young child. Her parents settled in Pierrepont, in upstate St. Lawrence
county, New York, and necessity converted her from a homemaker into a
factory hand:

> I was left, without knowledge of business, without knowledge of work, without
> knowledge of what the world was, with three fatherless children looking to me
> for bread. To support these children it became my duty to go out in the army
> of the unemployed, and in one of the largest factories of central New York, I
> went, and for four years and seven months remained a factory woman for the
> support of my little ones.

Her earnings the first day she went to work were eleven cents; for the first week
they amounted to sixty-five cents.

Little wonder that Mrs. Barry joined the Knights when the opportunity
arose. She quickly made her mark, becoming the Master Workman of an
assembly of nearly a thousand women, and delegate to the 1886 General
Assembly. By 1888, speaking as head of the Woman's Department, she could
report to the delegates once more assembled:

> There have come to the Woman's Department, from November 1, 1887 to
> October 1, 1888, 537 applications for my presence, 213 of which have been filled
> by actual service, and all others answered from the office. Communications
> requesting advice and information, 789, all of which have been answered by the
> faithful and efficient secretary, Mary A. O'Reilly.

Wherever she could find a platform — addressing members of the Knights
or its conventions, or women wishing to organize, or such bodies as the
International Council of Women — Leonora Barry raised her uncompromising and eloquent voice against the abysmal conditions under which too many
women had to earn their livelihood. . . .

Were wages low? It was not enough to state the fact: it must be documented:
"A seal-plush cloak, selling for from $40 to $75, is made by the cloak-makers
for eighty cents and $1 apiece, one being a day's work for an expert operative."
Her reports are peppered with such figures. Worst of all in her opinion was
the menace of the sweatshop, where piece-work — on garments, artificial flowers, etc. — was farmed out and completed at appallingly low pay and under
the worst possible health conditions:

> I speak of the contract sweating middleman or slop-shop plan, which works ruin,
> misery, sin and shame to toilers, and death or failure to the legitimate or regularly
> established industry with which it competes. Instance the following: Men's pants
> that retail at prices from $1 to $7 per pair, are taken by the contractor at 15 cents

per pair. Operatives are then employed and huddled together in a close stifling backroom, where the machine operatives furnish their own machines, and, in most cases, thread, and do all the machine work on pants, without basting, for 5 cents a pair. They are then passed over to the finisher, who puts on the buttons, makes buttonholes and puts on buckles for 5 cents per pair; 6 pairs is an average day's work.

Supposing 5 operatives to be employed, and there are often more than less, the contractor makes 30 cents a head, which nets him or her $1.50 per day while his or her victim gets 30 cents per day. Men's vests are contracted out at 10 cents each, the machine operative receiving 2 1/2 cents and finisher 2 1/2 cents each, making 5 cents a vest for completion. Twenty vests is a day's work. Here again, with the 5 operatives, he or she nets $1 per day for doing nothing, while his unfortunate victim has 50 cents for 11 and 12 hours of her life's energies.

Mrs. Barry was here reporting to a General Assembly of the Knights. . . . Unfortunately she was addressing an organization which was increasingly demonstrating its inability to unite on any course at all, and rapidly disintegrating in consequence. Moreover, Mrs. Barry herself admitted that in the face of such conditions as she described, the response of women to attempts at organization was disappointing, due to ignorance, apathy, hopelessness, and

the habit of submission and acceptance without question of any terms offered them, with the pessimistic view of life in which they see no ray of hope. Such people cannot be said to live, as living means the enjoyment of nature's gifts, but they simply vegetate like partially petrified creatures. Every effort has been made to perfect and extend the organization of women, but our efforts have not met with the response that the cause deserves — partly because those who have steady employment, fairly good wages, and comfortable homes seem to see nothing in organization outside of self-interest, and, because they are what they are pleased to term "all right," do not feel it incumbent upon themselves to do anything to assist their less fortunate co-workers. Again, many women are deterred from joining labor organizations by foolish pride, prudish modesty and religious scruples; and a prevailing cause, which applies to all who are in the flush of womanhood, is the hope and expectancy that in the near future marriage will lift them out of the industrial life to the quiet and comfort of a home, foolishly imagining that with marriage their connection with and interest in labor matters end; often finding, however, that their struggle has only begun when they have to go back to the shop for two instead of one. All this is the results or effects of the environments and conditions surrounding women in the past and present, and can be removed only by constant agitation and education. . . .

## Into the Mainstream of Organized Labor*

The years between 1903 and the entry of the United States into the first World War in 1917 saw the growth of the first unions composed largely of women.

*Chapter XVIII.

These unions remain a stable part of the American labor movement down to the present time.

The natural place for such unions to originate was in the garment trades, where a large proportion of the labor force was female, working under conditions which were a strong incentive to organization. Despite some progress toward factory inspection, legislation, and faint stirrings of public opinion, the establishments where clothing was made in such centers as New York, Philadelphia, and Chicago boasted of nearly every evil known to modern factory production at its worst.

For the most part the shops were small, housed in filthy old buildings which were never cleaned and where sanitary conditions and fire hazards were unbelievably bad. Windows were nailed shut and little light came in the grimy panes. The hissing of power belts and grinding of machinery were deafening. The workers were largely foreign-born, newly arrived in this country. Their limited knowledge of English, their youth, inexperience, and desperate need for work put them at the mercy of boss and foreman. There were endless fines: for talking, laughing, or singing, for stains from machine oil on the goods, for stitches either too crooked or too large which had to be ripped out at the risk of tearing the fabric, resulting in more fines. Hours not infrequently ran until ten at night, with no overtime pay and only a sandwich for supper. Not only were wages (for highly skilled work) as low as $6.00 a week; they were often withheld, and poor immigrant girls had no means of collecting the money owed them.

The earliest locals of what is now the International Ladies Garment Workers Union date back to 1900. There were some bitterly fought strikes in New York: the reefer makers in 1907, the pants makers the following year. But the first significant strike not only in the history of the union but in the organization of working women, took place in 1909 – 1910 among the shirtwaist makers in New York and Philadelphia. Organization among these workers was proceeding very slowly when resentment against the intolerable conditions erupted in two of the larger shops: Leiserson & Company and the Triangle Waist Company, which was to achieve a more gruesome notoriety two years later. Both shops went on strike in September 1909, and matters dragged on until a mass meeting of the shirtwaist workers was called on November 22 at Cooper Union to decide on further action.

The hall was jammed, and thousands who could not gain admission filled overflow halls. There were endless speeches by notables: Samuel Gompers himself, leading members of the Socialist Party (to which many garment workers belonged), Mary Dreier of the New York Women's Trade Union League, and leaders of the union. The meeting seemed in danger of petering out in speech-making, when a girl in her teens named Clara Lemlich, who worked in the Leiserson shop, stood up and asked for the floor. Despite her youth, she was known as a veteran of earlier strikes who had had several ribs broken in a police attack on a picket line. She made her way to the platform and called on the audience with electrifying effect to have done with talk and to act: "I am a working girl, and one of those who are on strike against intolerable conditions. I am tired of listening to speakers who talk in general terms. What we are here for is to decide whether or not we shall strike. I offer a resolution that a general strike be declared — now!"

She carried the crowd with her in a tremendous outburst of enthusiasm, which even caught up the chairman. He cried out, asking whether they would take the old Jewish oath: "If I turn traitor to the cause I now pledge, may this hand wither from the arm I now raise!" — and the entire hall stood up to take the pledge.

The strike which followed is variously described as the Revolt or Uprising of the Ten, Twenty or Thirty Thousand. Whatever the total figures, there is no disagreement as to its importance: not only was it the first "general strike" of its kind, but it was the first large strike of women workers, and it became a potent answer to the threadbare arguments that women could not be organized, and that they could not be counted on to hold out in a long, hard fight.

For the first time, also, the shirtwaist strike brought into existence something approximating the complex machinery of the modern strike. It was built painfully, day after day, by a small weak union and its still inexperienced allies. (The New York Women's Trade Union League went into the struggle with little preparation or experience, and came out of it a grown-up organization.) It had been thought that some 3,000 workers would go out on strike; instead, there were many thousands, 75 per cent of them women, of different nationalities. When 1,000 to 1,500 new members join an organization day after day, the clerical work alone is staggering, let alone such tasks as organizing this mass of human beings into picket lines, with responsible leadership to meet police violence and provide bail, strike relief, and welfare aid. In New York twenty-four halls were required for strikers' meetings alone, with speakers at each in Yiddish, Italian, and English. . . .

The main burden of the strike, its sufferings and sacrifices, fell on the workers themselves. In the depths of winter the shirtwaist makers, many of them between sixteen and twenty-five years of age, held out for thirteen bitter cold and hungry weeks. Not even their new-found friends, or a labor movement finally aroused to their support, could provide the needed rent, food, medical care, and other necessities for so many thousands, although it was estimated that $60,000 was expended for strike benefits, a huge sum at the time. Despite repeated police onslaughts, with dozens dragged off in "Black Maria" police vans after indiscriminate clubbings, the women picketed day after day, carrying placards with such slogans as "We Are Striking for Human Treatments" and "We Strike For Justice."

The courts thought otherwise, and did not disguise their bias. Their treatment of the strikers was so patently prejudiced that Lillian Wald, Ida M. Tarbell, Mary Simkovitch, and other citizens protested publicly in a letter published in the press. One magistrate charged a striker: "You are on strike against God and Nature, whose prime law it is that man shall earn his bread in the sweat of his brow. You are on strike against God."

This episode provided another excellent source of publicity for the strikers. Apprised of the charge, George Bernard Shaw cabled back: "Delightful. Medieval America always in intimate personal confidence of the Almighty."

In one sense the struggle, despite its heroic proportions, was unsuccessful. Settlements were made individually, shop by shop, and in some cases with few gains; on February 15 the strike was called off. But its impact on the labor movement was incalculable. Never again would it be quite so easy to argue that it was no use trying to organize women. And it led directly into the next great struggle in the industry, which took place in the men's garment trade in Chicago.

The pattern was much the same as in the shirtwaist strike. Starting with a walkout of a small group of unorganized workers in a Hart, Schaffner, and Marx shop against intolerable conditions, the strike spread throughout the trade until forty-five thousand men and women of nine nationalities and all age groups were out for fourteen weeks. In the end it too was inconclusive, except in the Hart, Schaffner, and Marx shops, where an historic agreement signed with the United Garment Workers recognized the principle of arbitration, collective bargaining, and an employees' grievance committee. . . .

The women from the shops showed their stamina again. Mrs. Robins* pointed out that not only were thousands of them mothers, but that twelve hundred and fifty babies were born to strikers or to their wives during that grim winter; she told of the young woman who lay beside a new-born infant, surrounded by three other small children, in an unheated room, and told the visitor from the League: "It is not only bread we give our children. . . . We live by freedom, and I will fight till I die to give it to my children."

When the Women's Trade Union League was organized in 1903, with the stated purpose of helping women workers in trade-union organization, membership was open to anyone "who will declare himself or herself willing to assist those trade unions already existing, which have some women workers, and to aid in the formation of new unions of women wage earners." To insure this aim, membership on the Executive Board was to be divided as follows: "The majority . . . shall be women who are, or have been, trade unionists in good standing, the minority of those well known to be earnest sympathizers and workers for the cause of trade unionism."

This balance was not achieved in fact until after 1907, the year when new leaders began to emerge in greater numbers from the ranks of the women working in the trades: Mary Anderson and Emma Steghagen of the shoe workers, Rose Schneiderman of the cap makers, Agnes Nestor and Elisabeth Christman of the glove workers (both among the handful of women who have

*Margaret Dreier Robins, a leader of the Women's Trade Union League.

ever held posts as national union officers in this country), Melinda Scott of the hat trimmers, Josephine Casey of the railway ticket takers, Stella Franklin of the department store clerks, Elizabeth Maloney of the waitresses, Maud Swartz of the typographers. The opportunity afforded by the League to such women for growth, through action and the exercise of responsibility, both largely denied them within the American Federation of Labor, can hardly be overestimated. . . .

The relations of the League to the American Federation of Labor were, on the surface, cordial and cooperative. As often as possible the League's conventions were held at the same time and place as the Federation's. But the relationship was inevitably a difficult one. The Federation gladly benefited from the new members which work by the League brought into its ranks; but to the extent that the League acted as a goad to the further organization of women by Federation affiliates, it was also an irritant. Federation leaders might praise the League for its services, particularly in such hard-fought battles as the garment strikes, but they stopped a long way short of the kind of action which would have made the League's continued existence unnecessary.

Estimates of just how many women joined unions in the first decade of the twentieth century must leave a wide margin of error. (Many unions kept no records of their membership by sex.) The estimate by Professor Wolman* gives a total of 76,748 for the year 1910, of which the largest numbers were in unions in the garment trades, textile and cloth weaving, book binding, shoe making, tobacco, retail, and in the musical and theater arts.

That this figure represented a mere 1.5 per cent of all women wage earners at that time, and only 5.2 per cent of the women in manufacturing establishments, underlines the dimensions of the task to be achieved, if women workers were to win reduction of working hours, higher wages, and an improvement in working conditions and job security. Only such gains could assure them some measure of equality in a country where living standards were rising and where democracy was growing.

It cannot be repeated too often that for women working a ten- or twelve-hour day, whose earnings were almost half those of men, whose lives were often bounded by the sweatshop, and whose relation to their employer lacked any safeguards to personal dignity or job tenure, "equal rights" was a question of more than education or getting the vote. For them equality also meant better pay for their labor, security from fire and machine hazards or the unwanted attentions of a foreman, and a chance to get home to their domestic tasks before complete exhaustion had overtaken them. Until more of them could work for these goals through a trade union, other issues were remote and unreal, a fact partially attested to by the relatively small degree of participation by such women in the suffrage movement.

*Leo Wolman, *The Growth of Trade Unions, 1880–1923* (New York, 1924), pp. 98–99.

## Women and Work

)━•━0━•━0━•━0━•━0━•━0━•━0━•━0━•━0━•━0━•━0━•━0━•━0━•━0━•━0━•━0━•━(

### President's Commission on the Status of Women

American women work both in their homes, unpaid, and outside their homes, on a wage or salary basis. Among the great majority of women, as among the great majority of men, the motive for paid employment is to earn money. For some, work has additional — or even primary — value as self-fulfillment.

When America was an agricultural country, most of both man's and woman's work was an unpaid contribution to family subsistence. As production developed in factory and city centers, many women began to do outside, for pay, what they had formerly done, unpaid, in their homes — making textiles or garments, processing food, nursing the sick, teaching children. Women's participation in paid employment importantly increases the Nation's labor force: 1 worker in 3 is a woman.

In any average month in 1962, there were some 23 million women at work; the forecast is for 30 million in 1970. Approximately 3 out of 5 women workers are married. Among married women, 1 in 3 is working; among nonwhites, almost 1 in 2. Many of these women, nearly a third, work part time; three-fifths of all part-time work is done by married women. Some 17 million women, in an average month, are full-time workers.

Their occupations range widely: the 1960 census recorded 431 geologists and geophysicists and 18,632 bus drivers. The largest concentration — 7 million — is in the clerical field. Three other main groupings — service workers (waitresses, beauticians, hospital attendants), factory operatives, and professional and technical employees (teachers, nurses, accountants, librarians) — number between 3 and 3-3/4 million each.

Though women are represented in the highly paid professions, in industry, in business, and in government, most jobs that women hold are in low-paid categories. Some occupations — nursing and household work, for instance — are almost entirely staffed by women. . . .

The existence of differentials in pay between men and women for the same kind of work has been substantiated by studies from numerous sources: an analysis of 1,900 companies, for example, showed that 1 out of 3 had dual pay scales in effect for similar office jobs.

The Commission attempted to gather informed views as to the extent to which access to jobs, rates of pay, and opportunities for training and advancement are based on the qualifications of the women who apply for or hold them, and the extent to which discriminations are made against them in these regards solely because they are women.

The reasons given by employers for differential treatment cover a consider-

From *American Women,* Report of the President's Commission on the Status of Women, 1963 (Washington, D.C.: U.S. Government Printing Office, 1963), 0-693-825, pp. 27-30, 35-39.

able range. Frequently, they say they prefer male employees because the nonwage costs of employing women are higher. They say that the employment pattern of younger women is in and out of the labor force, working for a time before marriage and thereafter putting family obligations first until their children are grown. They say that women's rates of sickness, absenteeism, and turnover are higher than men's; that the hiring of married women introduces one more element into the turnover rate because the residence of a married couple is normally determined by the occupation of the man. They say that though attendance rates of older women are often better than those of men, insurance and pensions for older workers are expensive, and that compliance with protective labor legislation applying to women is sometimes disruptive of schedules. They say that men object to working under women supervisors.

Because many personnel officers believe that women are less likely than men to want to make a career in industry, equally well-prepared young women are passed over in favor of men for posts that lead into management training programs and subsequent exercise of major executive responsibility.

Actually, situations vary far too much to make generalizations applicable, and more information is needed on rates of quits, layoffs, absenteeism, and illness among women workers and on the qualifications of women for responsible supervisory or executive positions. However, already available statistics on absenteeism and turnover indicate that the level of skill of the job, the worker's age, length of service with the employer, and record of job stability all are much more relevant than the fact that the worker is a man or a woman.

Reluctance to consider women applicants on their merits results in under-utilization of capacities that the economy needs and stunts the development of higher skills. . . .

## Labor Standards

Many of the lowest paid jobs in industry and the service occupations have historically been filled by women; driven by economic necessity, they have taken whatever jobs they could find even though conditions were damaging to health and family life. They have labored — and been exploited — as textile and needle trades workers, as laundresses and waitresses, as doers of industrial homework. Among the lowest paid workers, many have been women from minority groups.

When the formation of trade unions helped raise wages and improve working conditions through collective bargaining, some of these occupations proved — and have remained — hard to organize. Even now, nearly 30 years after the right to organize and bargain collectively was given Federal recognition in the Wagner Act. only a little over 3-1/3 million out of 24 million women in the labor force are union members.

Little by little, first in some of the States and then at the Federal level, legislation has put floors under wages and ceilings on hours. But such laws are far from uniform from State to State and are still far from adequate. At both Federal and State levels, research and regular reporting on the operation of protective labor laws would point the way to desirable future changes.

MINIMUM WAGES

In 1938, the Federal Fair Labor Standards Act (FLSA) put a floor under wages for both men and women engaged in a large number of occupations related to interstate commerce. It set minimum wages, and its requirement of premium pay for hours worked above 40 a week helped control excessive hours. But the FLSA exempts most workers, many of them women, in hotels, motels, restaurants, laundries, nonprofit organizations, and certain retail establishments.

At the same time, an estimated 6 million women are employed in intrastate work not covered by minimum wage legislation. Twenty-one States are either without minimum wage statutes or without such statutes in operation. There and elsewhere, several million women earn less than $1 an hour. Most of them are in the service trades, retailing, or domestic service.

The Federal Fair Labor Standards Act, including premium pay for overtime, should be extended to employment subject to Federal jurisdiction but now uncovered, such as work in hotels, motels, restaurants, and laundries, in additional retail establishments, in agriculture, and in nonprofit organizations.

State legislation, applicable to both men and women, should be enacted, or strengthened and extended to all types of employment, to provide minimum wage levels approximating the minimum under Federal law and to require premium pay at the rate of at least time and a half for overtime.

MAXIMUM HOURS

In the past, minimum wage and maximum hour legislation for women has been a lever for eliminating substandard conditions for both men and women, yet the benefits to be derived from such labor standards remain to be achieved for many workers. The existing range of legal working hours for women, applicable to one or more types of employment, becomes clear when the maximum hour laws of the States are compared. Seven States and Puerto Rico set no legal maximum; 4, a maximum of 60 hours a week for women workers; 14, within a range under 60 but over 48; 24 States and the District of Columbia place a ceiling at 48; the remaining State specifies a top limit of a 44-hour week and an 8-hour day.

In private employment excluding agriculture and household service, the hours actually worked in early 1963 averaged around 40 a week. Nearly 3 workers in 4 — 71 percent — work 40 hours or less; but 13.5 percent work 49 hours or more. The effectiveness over the past 25 years of the Fair Labor Standards Act in providing a deterrent in the form of premium pay designed to reduce the scheduling of excessive hours recommends this as the most practicable method of achieving future protection under normal circumstances. But while events press toward this goal, the welfare of all workers requires that where special hour protection for women represents the best so far attained it should be maintained and strengthened.

The normal workday and workweek at this moment of history should be not more than 8 hours a day and 40 hours a week. The best way to discourage excessive hours for all workers is by broad and effective minimum wage coverage, both Federal and State, providing overtime of at least time and a half the regular rate for all hours in excess of 8 a day or 40 a week.

Until such time as this goal is attained, State legislation limiting maximum hours of work for women should be maintained, strengthened, and expanded. Provisions for flexibility under proper safeguards should allow additional hours of work when there is a demonstrated need. During this interim period, efforts should continuously and simultaneously be made to require premium rates of pay for all hours in excess of 8 a day or 40 a week.

There is one group of workers, however, for whom exemption from existing maximum hour laws is desirable. Executive, administrative, and professional women frequently find that limitations on hours adversely affect their opportunities for employment and advancement. Exemptions for such occupations should be carefully drawn so as to insure against evasion of normally applicable hour laws in the case of workers who genuinely need their protection.

EQUAL PAY

In 1919, the first equal pay laws in the States were enacted; 24 States now require that women who do the same or comparable work as men in the same establishment be paid at the same rates. Lower pay rates for women doing the same work as men are not uncommon. For instance, studies made in 1960 showed area averages of women bank note-tellers with less than 5 years of experience running typically $5 — $15 a week less than the averages of men with the same years of experience, and differences of 9 to 49 cents an hour between the averages of men and women in the same power laundry occupations in a number of metropolitan areas.

In February 1962, the Commission endorsed the policy of equal pay for comparable work. A bill embodying this principle cleared both houses of Congress in 1962 but failed to reach conference before adjournment. Reintroduced in 1963, it passed and was signed by President Kennedy on June 10. The act amends the Fair Labor Standards Act of 1938 to require equal pay for equal work; it covers some 27.5 million men and women.

State laws should establish the principle of equal pay for comparable work.

GREATER FLEXIBILITY

In the case of a few State statutes, none of which currently affects large numbers of workers, the Commission believes that revision in the interest of greater flexibility is desirable. These measures, originally intended to protect women workers, have sometimes proved impracticable in their actual operation.

Restrictions that set fixed maximum limits upon weights women are allowed to lift do not take account of individual differences, are sometimes unrealistic and always rigid. They should be replaced by flexible regulations, applicable to both men and women and set by appropriate regulatory bodies.

Nightwork, especially on the graveyard shift, is undesirable for most people, and should be discouraged for both men and women. Overly rigid prohibitions, however, may work to the disadvantage of women in some circumstances. Strict regulations to prevent abuse are therefore normally preferable to prohibitions.

Prohibitions of exploitative industrial homework should remain in force. Gaps in protection should be closed, and resourcefulness exercised to arrest the development of new types of undesirable homework. However, many women who withdraw from the labor force to raise families have clerical skills; these — and editorial and research skills also — lend themselves to part-time work during years of intensive homemaking; their use is subject to exploitation and should be monitored, but it should not be made impossible by legal inflexibility.

Handicapped women, homebound for physical or psychological reasons or because of their location, should likewise not be blocked from undertaking suitable gainful employment. Offers of employment to the homebound, however, need to be carefully policed by public agencies to protect against swindles and rackets.

The women who are now without the protection of adequate Federal or State laws or collective bargaining contracts are highly vulnerable elements in the labor force. Many are women of minority groups. As labor standards have been raised, those who remain unprotected are increasingly those who suffer multiple handicaps and disabilities. This gives special urgency to completion of the task of assuring decent standards for all people who work.

THE RIGHT TO ORGANIZE

The effectiveness of unions in achieving improved working conditions, increased dignity, and essential protections has long been amply demonstrated, and the right of workers to organize and bargain collectively has been established under Federal law. In places of work solely under State jurisdiction, the difficulty of organizing women, especially those in low-paid work who are least able to risk possible loss of earnings, is augmented when employers are under no legal obligation to bargain collectively or to refrain from antiunion practices, including discharge of union members.

State laws should protect the right of all workers to join unions of their own choosing and to bargain collectively.

# Title VII of the 1964 Civil Rights Act

*Leo Kanowitz*

Some people have suggested to me that labor opposes "no discrimination on account of sex" because they feel that through the years protective legislation has been built up to safeguard the health of women. Some legislation was to safeguard the health of women, but it should have safeguarded the health of men, also.

CONGRESSWOMAN MARTHA GRIFFITHS,
Cong. Rec. 2580 (1964)

## The Background

At the beginning of the 20th century, there were in the United States 5,000,000 women workers constituting only 18 percent of the American labor force. By 1966, this figure had risen to over 27,000,000 women representing 36 percent of the U.S. total. At the present time, one-tenth of all family heads are women, and it has been observed that "most women are no longer in the labor market to supplement their husbands' income but primarily in order to provide the necessities of life for their families."

In one sense, this steady rise in the proportion of women to the total American labor force has been an encouraging development for those who seek an end to arbitrary laws that discriminate on the basis of sex. As suggested in an earlier chapter,* many legal rules that distinguish between the sexes are fashioned to a considerable extent with the employability of women in mind.

In another sense, however, the growth of the female labor contingent has not always been a positive force for eradicating male-female alienation and the female sense of "otherness" in American life. True, "society's prejudice against the worker-wife-mother combination appeared to soften in the expanding job market of the mid-sixties," and undoubtedly before then. Nevertheless, while the facts surrounding women's role in the labor market have sometimes accorded them a measure of economic and social independence, they have also often tended to exaggerate the sense of arbitrary and culturally determined difference between the sexes.

These negative effects of rising female employment upon the relations be-

From *Women and the Law: The Unfinished Revolution* (Albuquerque: University of New Mexico Press, 1969), pp. 100–102, 103–106, 108–110. Copyright by the author.

*See Leo Kanowitz, "Married Women and the Law of Support, in Chapter 5 of "Readings in Parallel."

tween the sexes have been brought about by two important economic facts. One is that women workers have received, more often than not, considerably lower wages than men performing the same work.[1] Whether such pay differentials merely reflected employers' honest beliefs that they are warranted by the difference in the sex of the employees alone, or, as some have suggested, that women, like Negroes, had become the victims of super-exploitation by profits-at-any-price employers, the positive effects upon male-female relations achieved by men and women working together in industry and commerce have been largely weakened by constant reminders of the lower economic reward for women's work than for men's.[2]

A second factor detracting from the positive effects of increased female employment in American life has been the general relegation of women, and consequently of men also, to particular types of jobs. Reflecting at times broad social prejudices, the desire of men to monopolize a particular calling, or the simple inertia of past events, the practice of dividing jobs into those for men only, those for women only, and those for both needs little documentation. A simple glance at the workaday world will reveal which sex serves as the clerk-typists, which as the automobile mechanics, which as the telephone operators, which as the pilots, and which as the overwhelming majority of physicians, lawyers[3] and architects in the United States. Though sex-based stratification of economic roles may to some extent reflect the socially condi-

1. In June, 1966, Congresswoman Martha Griffiths of Michigan stated, based on *Bureau of the Census, Current Population Reports, Series* P-60, No. 47 (1964), and *Bureau of Labor Statistics, Special Labor-Forces Report,* that "the median earnings of white men are $6,497, of Negro men $4,285, of white women $3,859, and of Negro women $2,674. This adverse differential exists in spite of the fact that white females in the labor force have 12.3 years of education on the average as compared to 12.2 years for white men; and nonwhite females have 11.1 years of education to 10 for the nonwhite males. The unemployment rate is highest for the nonwhite female. The same disparities exist when we examine the data for all workers, including temporary as well as full time." 112 CONG. REC. 13055 (1966).

2. This economic condition evoked a limited legislative response in some states. Although, until 1919, none went as far as requiring women employees to be paid the same wages as men performing equal work, many states now cover women but not men in their minimum wage legislation. Representative Martha Griffiths has noted that "the drive for these state protective laws was distorted for several reasons into laws applying solely to women." *Statement of Congresswoman Martha W. Griffiths at Hearing of the Equal Employment Opportunity Comm'n (EEOC) Concerning Proposals to Amend the Commission's Regulations on Sex Discrimination 3 (May 3, 1967).* The principal reasons were the United States Supreme Court decisions in which a New York statute limiting working hours of male and female bakery employees to 10 hours a day was invalidated, Lochner v. New York, 198 U.S. 45 (1905), and Oregon's 10-hour a day limitation on working hours for females only was upheld, Muller v. Oregon, 208 U.S. 412 (1908). Statement of Congresswoman Griffiths, *supra* at 3. Although the United States Supreme Court upheld governmental regulation of all employees' wages, hours and working conditions in the 1940's, Darby v. United States, 312 U.S. 100 (1941), the result of the earlier decisions was to convince the state legislatures that half a loaf was better than none, leading to widespread passage of protective legislation for women only. Statement of Congresswoman Griffiths, *supra* at 3-4. . . .

3. That the generally higher earnings and employability of male attorneys over female attorneys is the result of sex discrimination rather than other potential factors is persuasively demonstrated in White, *Women in the Law,* 65 MICH. L. REV. 1051, 1070-87 (1967).

tioned desires of men and women themselves, there can be little doubt of past employer resistance to the job applicant seeking employment in a position that tradition, collective bargaining agreement, or law had marked out as the exclusive preserve of the opposite sex.

Except for situations in which wage or employment opportunity discrimination was practiced by state governments or their agencies, or required by law, most discriminatory practices by employers, labor organizations, or employment agencies appeared immune to attack on substantive due process or equal protection grounds, since those constitutional safeguards are directed against governmental rather than private interferences. Moreover, even where state action was present, the United States Supreme Court, among others, had on many occasions held that sex discrimination in employment was constitutionally allowable. As a result, legislative treatment seemed the only way of curing this problem.

The pace of legislative enactments in this area has been uneven. In the equal pay field, despite scattered successes in the states, victory at the federal level was achieved in 1963 only "after 18 years of persistent, unsuccessful efforts to get an equal pay bill to the floor of Congress. . . ."

In the field of equal employment opportunities, two states — Wisconsin and Hawaii — had prohibited sex discrimination in employment by statute in 1961 and 1963, respectively. And, in 1961, the United States President's Commission on the Status of Women, established by President Kennedy's Executive Order 10980, had also been charged with reviewing progress and making recommendations in two areas: 1) private employment policies and practices, including those on wages, under federal contracts; and 2) federal government employment practices. In the same Executive Order, the Commission was asked to explore, "additional affirmative steps which should be taken through legislation, executive or administrative action to assure non-discrimination on the basis of sex and to enhance constructive employment opportunities for women." Significantly, except for its involvement with federal contracts, no reference to the private employment sector was contained in the Order.

In 1963, the Committee on Private Employment, one of the seven created by the President's Commission on the Status of Women, recommended the issuance of an Executive Order "setting forth the federal policy of equal employment opportunity and hiring, training and promotion, and establishing a President's Committee on Merit Employment of Women [which] would place main reliance on persuasion and voluntary compliance. . . ."

Despite the Committee's expansion upon its original charge by urging coverage of all employers with or without federal contracts, its recommendation was restricted severely in urging no more than an Executive Order that would be backed by persuasion to comply voluntarily rather than by more stringent enforcement measures. Nor did the Committee contemplate any recourse to the courts for more tangible relief from sex-based employment discrimination.

It is all the more gratifying, therefore, that Title VII of the Civil Rights Act of 1964 designated as an "unlawful employment practice" sex discrimination in employment practices of employers, employment agencies, and labor organizations, and provided for ultimate legal redress in the courts in the form of money damages and injunctive relief for persons aggrieved by such practices — a development that will be explored later in this chapter.

Regardless of their legislative origins, the federal Equal Pay Act of 1963, the prohibition against sex discrimination in employment in Title VII of the 1964 Civil Rights Act, and counterpart state laws enacted in their wake, have provided opportunities for developing a new era in male-female relationships in American society. Those opportunities must be seized, however, and possible restrictive interpretations of the two major federal statutes threaten the realization of their promise and potential. . . .

## The Sex Provisions of Title VII of the 1964 Civil Rights Act

### THE PECULIAR LEGISLATIVE HISTORY

Any consideration of the sex provisions of Title VII of the 1964 Civil Rights Act requires a preliminary glance at what can only be described as their peculiar legislative history. In the light of its tremendous potential for profoundly affecting the daily lives of so many Americans — both men and women — Title VII's prohibition against sex discrimination in employment had a rather inauspicious birth.

This is not to say that some species of federal legislation outlawing sex-based discrimination in employment might not have emerged eventually from a Congress in which male representatives outnumbered female representatives overwhelmingly. Agitation for such a law, after all, had been going on for many years. Moreover, Congress had acted deliberately and responsively in enacting the Equal Pay Act of 1963. But the prospects for the passage of legislation prohibiting sex discrimination in hiring and promotional practices in employment were exceedingly dim in 1964. Had the sex provisions of Title VII been presented then as a separate bill, rather than being coupled as they were in an effusion of Congressional gimmickry with legislation aimed at curbing racial and ethnic discrimination, their defeat in 1964 would have been virtually assured. We have no less an authority for this conclusion than Oregon's Representative Edith Green, whose strong advocacy of equal legal treatment for American women lends great force to her appraisal. In her view, stated in Congress, the legislation against sex discrimination in employment, "considered by itself, and . . . brought to the floor with no hearings and no testimony . . . would not [have] receive[d] one hundred votes."

In fact, it was not until the last day of the bill's consideration in Chairman Howard Smith's House Rules Committee, where it had gone after a favorable report from the judiciary committee, that there first appeared a motion to add "sex" discrimination to the other types of employment discrimination that the original bill sought to curb. That motion was defeated in committee by a vote of 8-7. But after almost two weeks of passionate floor debate in the House and just one day before the act was passed, Representative Smith, a principal opponent of the original bill, offered an amendment to include sex as a prohibited basis for employment discrimination. Under that amendment, the previously proposed sanctions against employers, unions, hiring agencies, or their agents, for discrimination in hiring or promotional practices against actual or prospective employees on the basis of race, creed, or national origin, were, with some exceptions, also to apply to discrimination based upon the "sex" of the job applicant or employee. Offering his amendment, Representative Smith remarked, "Now I am very serious . . . I do not think it can do any harm to this legislation; maybe it will do some good."

Despite Congressman Smith's protestations of seriousness, there was substantial cause to doubt his motives. For four months Congress had been locked in debate over the passage of the Civil Rights Act of 1964. Most southern representatives and a few of their northern allies had been making every effort to block its passage. In the context of that debate and of the prevailing congressional sentiment when the amendment was offered, it is abundantly clear that a principal motive in introducing it was to prevent passage of the basic legislation being considered by Congress, rather than solicitude for women's employment rights.[4]

It is not surprising, therefore, that Representative Green, expressing her hope that "the day will come when discrimination will be ended against women," also registered her opposition to the proposed amendment, stating that it "will clutter up the bill and it may later — very well — be used to help destroy this section of the bill by some of the very people who today support it."

Despite these misgivings, and despite the apparent objectives of its sponsors to block passage of the entire Act, the legislation that finally emerged contained Representative Smith's amendment intact. As a result of this stroke of misfired political tactics, our federal positive law now includes a provision that had been desired for many years by those who were concerned with the economic, social and political status of American women, but which had been delayed because of the feeling that the time had not ripened for such legislation and had been specifically opposed in this instance partly because of a belief that "discrimination based on sex involves problems sufficiently different from discrimination based on. . .other factors. . .to make separate treatment preferable."

4. *Cf.* Cooper v. Delta Airlines, Inc., 274 F. Supp. 781, 782-83 (E.D. La. 1967), where Judge Comisky remarked that "the addition of 'sex' to the prohibition against discrimination based on race, religion, or national origin just *sort of found its way* into the equal employment opportunities section of the Civil Rights Bill." (Emphasis added.)

What significance should be drawn from this peculiar legislative history of Title VII's prohibition against sex discrimination? It would be a most serious error to attribute to Congress as a corporate unit the apparently cynical motives of the amendment's sponsor. Though most members of Congress were intent on prohibiting employment discrimination based on race, religion and national origin, they did vote to do the same with respect to sex discrimination once the matter, regardless of its sponsor's apparent intentions, was brought to them for a vote. And when Congress adopts any legislation, especially a law with such important ramifications, one must infer a congressional intention that such legislation be effective to carry out its underlying social policy — which in this case is to eradicate every instance of sex-based employment discrimination that is not founded upon a bona fide occupational qualification.

Though the absence of Committee hearings on the sex provisions leaves the courts and the Equal Employment Opportunity Commission, the federal agency created by the Act to process complaints of employment discrimination, without specific guides for resolving difficult problems of interpretation — such as the relationship between those provisions and various state "protective" laws — Congress' general intentions are clear. Given those general intentions, the common law processes of the courts and of the EEOC in exercising its quasi-judicial function may constitute, in the end, the best vehicle for filling out, on a case by case basis, the broad command of the Act's prohibition against sex discrimination in employment. The important point is that for the first time in United States history, an authoritative national agency and the courts have been charged with the responsibility of developing viable equitable principles to govern the employment role of men and women in American society, and opposition to sex discrimination in employment has become official national policy.

THE IMPACT OF THE "SEX" PROVISIONS

Though born under such questionable circumstances, the prohibition against sex discrimination in employment has proved since 1964 to be much more than the toothless tiger one would have expected. As a matter of fact, the Equal Employment Opportunity Commission reported at the end of its first year of operations that over one-third of its processed complaints had involved charges of sex discrimination. Attorneys have also been encouraged, as a result of the Act, to take cases involving sex discrimination in employment. Several large cases have been settled, including one involving a back pay factor of more than $35,000, and a growing number are being decided by the courts. The volume of litigation under the sex discrimination provisions of Title VII will no doubt also be increased as a result of the recent Supreme Court decision in *Newman v. Piggie Park Enterprises,* holding that a person "who succeeds in obtaining an injunction under [Title II of the 1964 Civil Rights Act] should *ordinarily* recover an attorney's fee unless special circumstances would render such an award unjust."

In issuing its guidelines on sex discrimination, the EEOC, whose first chairman was Franklin D. Roosevelt, Jr., and which is now chaired by Clifford L. Alexander, Jr., has begun to develop a significant body of administrative law whose potential effect upon the daily relations between the sexes will no doubt be profound. Already some past patterns of sex-based job allocations show signs of cracking. Interestingly, such departures from existing employment norms have not always been in the direction of placing women in jobs previously reserved for men. The Act, after all, prohibits "sex" discrimination — and not discrimination against women. By its terms it therefore applies when men are denied a job because the one they seek has traditionally been reserved "for women only." Thus, the telephone company has already hired some males as telephone operators — to the consternation of customers who, upon hearing a male voice respond to their dialing "O," have demanded to speak to "the operator." Similar developments are occurring with regard to the employability of males as airline hosts[5] — although the right of women to be hired as pilots for the commercial airlines will undoubtedly also come up.

Aside from Title VII's specific effects upon disputes arising under it, there are a number of areas in which new legislation and other developments with respect to women's employment opportunities are directly traceable to the mood generated by the passage of Representative Smith's amendment. In 1967, for example, Presidential Executive Order 11246, which since 1965 had established a policy of non-discrimination in government employment, was amended by the addition of "sex" as a prohibited type of discrimination. And still later in the same year, President Johnson signed a law permitting women to now become admirals and generals in the United States Armed Services.[6] State fair employment legislation has also been dramatically affected by the pasage of Title VII. Prior to the 1964 Civil Rights Act, only two states, Hawaii and Wisconsin, had prohibited sex discrimination in employment. By the beginning of 1968, however, 11 other jurisdictions had joined the ranks. Though pressure for such laws undoubtedly antedated the Federal Act in some of the states it is more than a *post hoc, ergo propter hoc* fallacy to suggest that

5. On February 21, 1968, the EEOC decided by a vote of 3-1 that an airline that refuses to hire and employ members of a particular sex for the position of flight cabin attendant — whether he or she be called a purser, hostess, steward or stewardess — violates the Act. 33 Fed. Reg. 3361 (1968); *cf.* Kaiser Foundation Hosp. v. Local 399, Bldg. Service Employees, (1965-1968 Transfer Binder) CCH EMPL. PRACT. GUIDE. ¶8166 (1967), where it is held that a hospital did not violate Title VII by refusing to permit two male licensed nurses to work in the Licensed Vocational Nurse (LVN) classification where a routine requisite of such employment was "intimate care of female patients." Although this result may have been correct, the award ignored the common practices of permitting male doctors to examine intimately female patients and of allowing female nurses to perform "sensitive personal care" for male patients. . . .

6. Pub. L. No. 90-130 (Nov. 8, 1967). This law has been described as amending Titles "10, 32, and 37 of the United States Code to remove the provisions that limit the career opportunities available to women officers so that on the basis of merit they may have the same promotion and career tenure opportunities as male officers in similar circumstances." S. REP. No. 676, 90th Cong., 1st Sess. 1 (1967).

their enactment was probably hastened by the presence of the sex discrimination prohibition in the federal law.

The sex provisions of Title VII have created a momentum in American society for a re-examination of some fundamental assumptions concerning women's role in the traditional family and that larger form of family called society. The ultimate effects of Title VII are still out of sight. For the moment, however, some immediate legal and social problems raised by the passage of the Act may be considered. To do so properly requires a preliminary examination of the scope and administration of the provisions prohibiting sex discrimination in employment.

## SCOPE AND OPERATION OF TITLE VII'S "SEX" PROVISIONS

Title VII of the Civil Rights Act covers employers in industries affecting commerce, employment agencies serving such employers, and labor organizations engaged in such industries. It declares that it "shall be an unlawful employment practice" for a covered employer, because of race, color, religion, sex or national origin

> (1) to fail or refuse to hire or to discharge any individual or otherwise to discriminate against any individual with respect to his compensation, terms, conditions or privileges of employment. . .or (2) to limit, segregate, or classify his employees in any way which would deprive or tend to deprive any individual of employment opportunities or otherwise adversely affect his status as an employee. . . .

The Act thus protects the right of persons to obtain and hold a job without regard to these factors, as well as the right to equal treatment once the job has been obtained. In addition, Title VII makes it unlawful for employment agencies to discriminate in their classification or referral practices, and for labor organizations to discriminate on the same grounds in a variety of ways.[7]

An important exception to these "unlawful employment practices" is found in the "bona fide occupational qualification" provisions of section 703(e) of the Act. That section in effect permits employment discrimination based on sex, religion or national origin — but significantly not on race — "in those certain instances where religion, sex, or national origin is a bona fide occupational qualification reasonably necessary to the normal operation of that particular business or enterprise."

---

7. 42 U.S.C. § 2000e-2(c)(1964): "It shall be an unlawful employment practice for a labor organization —

(1) to exclude or to expel from its membership, or otherwise to discriminate against, any individual because of his race, color, religion, sex or national origin;

(2) to limit, segregate, or classify its membership, or to classify or refuse to refer for employment any individual, in any way which would deprive or tend to deprive any individual of employment opportunities, or would limit such employment opportunities or otherwise adversely affect his status as an employee or as an applicant for employment, because of such individual's race, color, religion, sex, or national origin; or

(3) to cause or attempt to cause an employer to discriminate against an individual in violation of this section."

The Commission has already held that sex is not a bona fide occupational qualification for the position of flight cabin attendant, and that males may not be denied such employment solely on the grounds of sex. On the other hand, the Commission has recognized that where "it is necessary for the purpose of authenticity or genuineness, [it] will consider sex to be a bona fide occupational qualification, *e.g.,* an actor or an actress." One of the knottiest problems in interpreting the bona fide occupational qualification language of the Act as applied to sex discrimination in employment, however, has been raised by the numerous state "protective" laws for women in employment.

Persons injured by the commission of an "unlawful employment practice" may ultimately procure legal redress from the federal courts. Section 706(e) allows suits by the person claiming to be aggrieved and authorizes the court to permit the United States Attorney General to intervene in cases of "general public importance." Upon finding an intentional unlawful employment practice, the federal courts may enjoin the defendant from engaging in it, and order reinstatement or hiring of employees with or without back pay. The EEOC may initiate a court proceeding on its own only to compel compliance with a previously issued order under the above provisions. If there is a pattern of intentional violations, the Attorney General may also bring a civil action in a federal district court.

Except for the last-named type of suit by the United States Attorney General, which need not be preceded by any EEOC investigation or previous referral to state or local agencies, the lawsuits authorized by Title VII represent the ultimate, or at least the penultimate, stage in the process of correcting the employment discriminations prohibited by the Act. The entire scheme of Title VII is designed to permit the EEOC to attempt to conciliate employment discrimination disputes. No private lawsuits may therefore be brought under the Act until various waiting periods have expired, during which "the Commission has been unable to obtain voluntary compliance" with Title VII. Even the Commission is prevented for prescribed periods from investigating charges on its own or on an aggrieved person's initiative if the alleged unfair employment practices are potentially subject to redress under state or local law.

Despite attempts since the bill was first introduced in the House of Representatives to give the EEOC remedial powers if conciliation failed (that is, to conduct hearings and issue orders), the Commission's power has remained limited to investigating complaints, determining whether reasonable cause exists to believe the allegations, and attempting to concilate the matter. As a result, court proceedings following the failure of conciliation by the Commission are entirely *de novo,* and nothing "said or done during and as part of. . .[the Commission's conciliation] endeavors may be. . .used as evidence in a subsequent proceeding."

Nevertheless, the Commission's investigations, findings and opinions are important, and under some circumstances attain the force of law. They may, for example, influence the Commission's decision to intervene in an aggrieved person's private suit or to refer a matter for suit by the Attorney General. In addition, good faith reliance upon and conformity with the Commission's written interpretations and opinions constitutes an absolute defense in any action or proceeding based on an alleged unlawful employment practice. Such interpretive rulings have therefore been held to have legal effect, and are important in developing the law of sex discrimination in employment.

## Job Discrimination and the Black Woman

### *Sonia Pressman Fuentes*

Civil rights is one of the principal issues facing the country today — if not *the* principal issue. But when most people talk about civil rights, they mean the rights of black people. And when they talk about the rights of black people, they generally mean the rights of black males.

They know all about the black matriarchy. They say that the black woman historically has been able to find employment, albeit in domestic service, while the black male has been chronically unemployed and underemployed. It is the black female, they say, who has been the breadwinner and who is responsible, along with Mr. Charlie, for the emasculation of the black male. So, they say, let's concentrate on improving the status of the black male — why add to an already bad scene by worrying about employment discrimination against the black female?

The trouble with the above analysis is that, in the first place, it just ain't so, and in the second place, it's irrelevant. The prevailing assumptions about the black female, like so many assumptions based on race or sex, don't match the reality. And furthermore, whatever the statistical facts about black women as a class, the individual black woman, like all individuals, should be treated in accordance with her own particular intelligence, education, experience and ability.

But first, let's set the record straight. What are the facts about the black woman?

The facts are that black women are at the very bottom of the economic totem pole. In 1967, the median wage or salary income of year-round full-time workers (14 years of age and older) by sex and race was:

From "Job Discrimination and the Black Woman," *The Crisis* (March 1970), pp. 103–108 (abridged). Copyright by Sonia Pressman Fuentes. The views here expressed are solely those of the author and do not necessarily represent official EEOC policy or opinion. [S. P. F.]

| | |
|---|---|
| White men | $7,518 |
| Black men | 4,837 |
| White women | 4,380 |
| Black women | 3,268 |

A large proportion of black working women are service workers. In June 1969, 44 per cent of working non-white women (93 per cent of whom are black) were private-household workers or service workers outside the home. In 1967, the median wage of female year-round full-time private-household workers, about 47 per cent of whom were non-white, was $1,298.

Unemployment is more severe among black women than among black men, or white women. Among teenagers, where unemployment is more widespread than among adults, non-white girls have the highest rate of unemployment.

The black woman is not generally the head of the household. The over-whelming majority of black homes, about 72 per cent of them in fact, are headed by the male.

But the burden on the black woman — and of the children dependent upon her — becomes evident when we compare their lot with that of the white woman and her children. About 28 per cent of black families are headed by a woman, and about half of those families live in poverty. Only 11 per cent of the families in the country as a whole are headed by a woman, and only 34 per cent of those families live in poverty.

Other comparisons between black and white women reveal that a higher percentage of non-white women are in the labor force, are working wives, and working mothers, and their earnings account for a larger percentage of the family income.

So there you have the real picture of the black woman: she has a significant amount of family responsibility and economic need, and a lower income than the black male or the white female.

As stated by Elizabeth Wickenden, consultant on social policy to the National Board of the YWCA, in an article on "the Moynihan Report," entitled *The Negro Family: Society's Victim or Scapegoat?:*

> Nor do the facts bear out any contention that Negro women have prospered at the expense of their male counterparts. . . . For if the plight of the under-educated, under-employed, underpaid, and undervalued Negro male is deserving of every social remedy we can bring to bear, the plight of the loyal but despised Negro mother is equally if not more so. . . . With her miserable earnings and niggardly assistance payments she fends off as best she can both starvation and the harshest impact of community rejection for her children.

Many of the myths and stereotypes about women as a class are similar to those about black people as a class and are equally invalid. Thus, it is now said about women — as it has traditionally been said about black persons — that they are frivolous, passive, content with their lot, lack ambition, and can't compete with the white male. As Kanowitz noted in his 1969 book, *Women and the Law, the Unfinished Revolution:*

> The similarities [between the legal and social situation of American women and American blacks] are indeed striking: Both groups are easily identifiable; both are objects of a discrimination largely influenced by sexual factors; both have been victims of an extraordinary economic exploitation; both have at times been denied fundamental political rights (e.g., jury service and the vote); and both have responded to social and legal injustice with widespread protest movements and civil disobedience leading, with varying degrees of success, to modifications of legal norms and a consequent restructuring of social attitudes.

In the employment sector, the forms of discrimination against women are similar to the forms of discrimination against blacks: confinement to low-skilled, low-pay jobs; wage differentials for similar work; separate lines of seniority and progression; exclusion from managerial and supervisory jobs; etc. Other methods of maintaining each group in its proper place may differ. Thus, it has been noted by Dr. Pauli Murray, a black woman attorney, writer, and teacher, that while violence has been "the ultimate weapon of resistance to racial desegregation, its psychic counterpart, ridicule, has been used to resist sex equality."

Many blacks and whites refuse to see the analogy between discrimination based on race and that based on sex. Perhaps they fear that if they did, they would have to be as morally committed to the elimination of the latter as they are to the former. The aura of moral opprobrium which today surrounds racial discrimination has not yet attached itself to discrimination based on sex. This is tragic because the economic and human waste is identical whether the cause is discrimination based on race, sex, or any other irrelevant factor. Further-more, in the treatment of the black woman, the two forms of discrimination are frequently combined. It will not be possible to eliminate discrimination against the black woman without eliminating discrimination based on both race and sex.

There is now a Federal statute which prohibits both forms of discrimination in the employment sector. It is incumbent upon the black woman to utilize this statute to achieve her rightful place in our society [there follows a description of Title VII of the Civil Rights Act of 1964 already covered in the preceding selection]. . . . [Title VII is administered by the EOCC — the Equal Employment Opportunity Commission.] Some of the highlights of EEOC rulings are as follows. As a general rule, employers may not maintain separate jobs, wage and pay scales, and seniority lines for men and women. . . .The EEOC has, for example, stated that individuals may not be refused employment because of assumptions or stereotypes about members of their sex as a class, or because of the preferences of the employer, co-workers, clients, or customers. Thus an employer may not refuse to employ qualified women for a job on the ground that the job has traditionally been held by men; requires personal characteristics not exclusive to either sex, such as attractiveness, graciousness, aggressiveness, etc.; involves work with or supervision over men; involves late night hours or work in isolated locations; or involves the lifting or carrying of heavy weights, or other strenuous activity. . . .

The EEOC has long ruled that an advertiser may not indicate a preference or limitation based on sex in the content of his classified advertising unless sex is a bona fide qualification for the job involved. On January 24, 1969, an additional EEOC guideline, dealing with the headings of classified advertising columns, became effective. By virtue of that guideline, an advertiser who places classified advertising in sex-segregated columns, such as those headed "Help Wanted — Male" and "Help Wanted — Female" thereby violates Title VII unless sex is a genuine qualification for the job involved.

The EEOC has said that, as a general rule, equal terms, conditions, and privileges of employment must be made available for men and women. Thus, an employer may not refuse to hire, nor may he discharge, women because they marry or have children, legitimate or illegitimate, unless he has a similar rule for men. The EEOC has also held that a company policy which requires the termination of unmarried pregnant employees violates Title VII where the company does not have a similar policy with regard to male employees who father illegitimate children. Moreover, the EEOC has held, in particular cases, that an employer's refusal to hire women with illegitimate children constituted unlawful race discrimination because the restriction was unrelated to satisfactory performance of the job involved and, as administered, tended to exclude more black than white employees.

An employer may not discriminate on the basis of sex with regard to medical, hospital, accident, and life insurance coverage. As a general rule, pregnant employees are entitled to a maternity leave of absence with the right of reinstatement to the job vacated, at no loss of seniority or any of the other benefits and privileges of employment. The EEOC has also stated that men and women are entitled to equality with regard to optional and compulsory retirement age privileges and that it will decide questions of difference based on sex in pension benefits, such as benefits for survivors, on a case-by-case basis.

One of the difficult questions which faced the EEOC at its inception involved the relationship between Title VII and state legislation dealing specifically with the employment of women. This legislation falls into two principal categories: (1) laws which prohibit the employment of women in certain occupations (e.g., mining, bartending), or which restrict their employment with respect to hours, nightwork, or weightlifting; and (2) laws which require benefits for women workers, such as minimum wages, premium pay for overtime, and rest periods.

The EEOC has issued a number of guidelines with respect to its handling of cases raising the conflict between Title VII and state legislation in the first category. In its guideline published on August 19, 1969, the EEOC concluded that such laws conflict with Title VII and, accordingly, do not justify discrimination against women. Similarly, recent court decisions have held that state laws restricting the hours women may work and the weight they may lift are invalid because such laws conflict with Title VII.

The EEOC's guideline contains no discussion of the Commission's position with regard to state legislation which requires benefits for women workers. The Commission has indicated that it will process cases involving such laws on a case-by-case basis.

Beginning in 1966 for employers, and 1967 for labor unions, the EEOC has required annual reports on the composition of employer units, labor unions, and on apprenticeship programs on the basis of race, national origin, and sex. The employer reports, for example, require information as to the composition of the employer's work force in categories such as officials and managers, professional employees, technicians, sales workers, office and clerical personnel, craftsmen, laborers, service workers, etc.

On March 2, 1969, the EEOC announced the release of the first nationwide employment statistics on minority group members and women. These statistics are contained in a 3-volume survey covering employment patterns for 123 cities, 50 states, and 60 major industries. The study revealed that while women account for more than 40 per cent of all white collar workers, only 1 out of every 10 management positions and 1 out of every 7 professional jobs are filled by women.

Among the significant findings of the study with particular relevance to black women are the following: black women are heavily concentrated in the low-paying laborer and service-worker categories; black women are clustered in the low-paying industries, and they are under-represented in the highest-paying industries. For black women, discrimination is especially apparent in office work: while 57 per cent of women workers for the population as a whole hold white collar jobs, only 28 per cent of black women hold such jobs.

In furtherance of its responsibilities under Title VII, the EEOC has sponsored research and held hearings on specific areas of employment discrimination. In this connection, there were several instances of particular interest to black women.

An Ohio rubber industry study, sponsored by the Ohio Civil Rights Commission and financed by the EEOC, was based on 1965 employment data filed by 70 rubber manufacturing plants in Ohio. The study focused on Akron, where reporting companies employing two-thirds of Ohio's rubber workers were located. In 1965, black women made up more than 15 per cent of the Akron city labor force. However, the study revealed that they constituted only 2.2 per cent of all females employed by Akron's four largest rubber companies (which accounted for 93 per cent of the city's rubber workers). Restrictions against black women appeared to be much tighter than those against black men. As a general rule, whatever the percent of black males among the male employees of a rubber manufacturer, the percent of black females among the same plant's female employees was smaller.

The study noted that the public transportation system in Akron and in other Ohio cities did not facilitate travel between black residential areas and outlying employers. Not every black family has two cars to get both husband and wife to separate jobs; some families do not have one car. The study pointed out that as long as black residential concentration persisted, public transportation was the key to the wide dispersion of black employment (most especially of female black employment) throughout a labor market area.

The Commission held a public forum, on January 12-13, 1967, on employment patterns in the textile industry in North and South Carolina, where 43 per cent of all U.S. textile mill production was centered in 1963. It published a summary of the transcript of that forum which revealed that black women were substantially under-represented in the work force of the 406 establishments studied in the sample; that the utilization of black workers of both sexes in the skilled craftsmen and white collar categories was minimal; and that the heavy concentration of blacks in the laborer and service occupations continued. While women made up about two-fifths of the sample studied, there were 27 white female workers employed in the establishments studied for each black female worker, and 5 black males employed for each black female. The study also revealed that recently there has been a trend toward hiring more black persons of both sexes in the Carolina mills.

In January, 1968, the Commission conducted a hearing on discrimination in white collar employment for minorities and women in New York City. In March, 1969, it conducted a hearing on such discrimination in Los Angeles, focusing on white collar employment in two industries: aerospace and communications, particularly motion picture production and radio and television. Discriminatory exclusion of women and blacks from managerial and professional positions was revealed in both hearings. . . .

In addition to the remedies available under the Civil Rights Act of 1964, there are other relevant Federal and state statutes and municipal ordinances which may be utilized by the black woman who is the victim of discrimination in employment.

On the Federal level, there are:

1. The Equal Pay Act, passed in 1963, which became generally effective in 1964. It requires equal wages and salaries for men and women in equal work, and is administered by the Department of Labor.

2. Executive Order 11375, issued by President Johnson in October, 1967, which became effective a year later. The Order, administered by the Office of Federal Contract Compliance (OFCC) in the Department of Labor, applies to government contractors. It added a prohibition against discrimination based on sex to Executive Order 11246, which previously had prohibited only discrimination based on race, color, religion, and national origin. The Order requires government contractors to develop and implement written affirmative action programs to eliminate sex discrimination or face the cancellation and future loss of government contracts.

3. Executive Order 11478, issued by President Nixon, which became effective in August, 1969, and is administered by the Civil Service Commission. This Order prohibits discrimination based on race, color, religion, sex, and national origin in covered positions in the Federal Government, including certain positions in the District of Columbia government.

4. The Age Discrimination in Employment Act of 1967, which became effective on June 12, 1968. This statute, administered by the Department of Labor, prohibits discrimination based on age between the ages of 40-65. While it does not prohibit sex discrimination, it can play a significant role in enlarging employment opportunities for women over 40 who wish to return to the labor market or change jobs.

5. The National Labor Relations Act, as amended, which is administered by the National Labor Relations Board. This Act is primarily concerned with union representation elections and unfair employment practices involving union representation. However, discrimination based on race, religion, sex, and national origin by employers and unions would also appear to come within the coverage of the Act.

On the state and local levels, there are:

1. State and municipal fair employment practices commissions which prohibit discrimination based on race, color, religion, sex and national origin. There are 34 state commissions, including one for the District of Columbia, to which the EEOC defers on charges of discrimination based on race, color, religion, and national origin. Only 19 of these commissions also have jurisdiction over discrimination based on sex.

2. State equal pay legislation, which requires equal pay for equal work regardless of sex. Thirty-five states currently have such legislation.

There are a great many new forces moving in the direction of securing equality of employment opportunity for the black woman. It is now up to the black woman to use the available means to secure her rights, and up to the rest of the country to cooperate and assist her in her struggle for equality. Hopefully, working and striving together, we will be able to achieve that democratic society which has so long been the American dream: where equal opportunity is available for all without regard to race, color, religion, sex, or national origin.

# 8. *The Doorways of Life* ━●━●━●━●━●━●━●━●━●━●━●━●━●━●━●━●━━●━●

> It has been said. . . that an education
> for women which sharpens intellectual
> curiosity and quickens the imagination
> is either a waste of time or a source of
> frustration, since the role of women as
> wives and mothers will prevent them
> from enjoying any of their intellectual
> or cultural interests. A college
> education in the liberal arts is said to be
> either unnecessary or potentially
> harmful. I find this attitude insulting,
> both to women and to education.
>
> HAROLD TAYLOR

"The most important reason for wanting to go to college," wrote an applicant for admission to Vassar in 1958, "is an insatiable desire to learn." Social mores, however, pressure a young woman to embrace other priorities, and intellectual purusits become provisional. The philosophy underlying woman's education is consequently "in case": that is, in case she doesn't marry, she should have an escape hatch. A feminine curriculum follows logically from such reasoning, for it is designed to prepare the woman graduate for gracious living in her primary orbit as family satellite. Unfortunately, the fallacy in such an approach is that utility rather than the search for truth becomes the object of learning; moreover, to engross women in irrelevancies tethers the race. Much of this is beginning to be recognized, and education for women in advanced circles is conceived not in terms of "in case" but rather as prologue and epilogue to the domestic pageant. Inherited forms of the family, however, continue virtually unquestioned. Instead, women are invited to be split personalities: to engage in a discontinuous life style, or to carry the double burden in a new fashion of part-time work or part-time education.

Speculating on the reasons for the apparent inferiority of women to men in the production of first-rank intellectual work, John Stuart Mill, in the first selection that follows, points to the mental consequences of social codification.

*Parallel readings for Chapter 8, "The Pearl in the Apron Pocket."

He even considers the recurring question of why women have not been distinguished in the fine arts, where discriminatory practices have historically been less severe than in other fields. And his answer parallels that of those opposed to the pearl-in-the-apron-pocket philosophy, namely the superiority of professionals over amateurs. Reporting on patterns of his period, time and place, he notes that at least one whole woman is required to make a family function, so that very few women have the time to concentrate and to specialize — the essential prerequisites to significant and unique accomplishment.

Charlotte Perkins Gilman tackles the same riddle, as well as the tradition of seeing in women only sex, so that their education would confine them exclusively to what have been defined as feminine interests. The opportunity to be fully human, she declares, has been denied to women, despite the fact that the most important traits are the human ones. Without the development of such human traits in mothers, the young child entrusted to essentially primitive individuals who are not qualified to teach them what is rare and precious in life. An entirely different status of women is required if we are to outgrow our tradition of androcentric (male focused) culture, if we are to achieve the power to recognize the crisis of public conditions, to judge the relative importance of social measures, and to best serve the human community.

Mirra Komarovsky, reviewing the literature of sex difference, notes that most studies reveal greater differences between members of the same sex than between the sexes. When critics cite psychological tests in support of their plea for special education for women, they ignore this overlapping. Thus, if woman's nature is violated when she is forced to imitate men in education (as has been alleged), it would also be violated if she is pressed into a feminine curriculum. The need is rather for a rich and flexible curriculum to enhance human talents. This goal is even more compelling if we consider that aptitudes are not wholly inborn and that we may, by attachment to received models, be accentuating differences that have outlived their usefulness.

In the next selection, Elizabeth L. Cless documents the rigidity of custom on campus, with its train of inherited and unexamined attitudes. These are based on the ideas of the male as prototype scholar and the female as an entity destined for shelter from economic necessity and from ambition. The author's proposals for change are nonetheless designed around the received model for the family — with assurance offered the woman that when her primary responsibility in that arena ceases, she will be welcomed and rewarded in a less personal setting. Mrs. Cless then analyzes academic procedures that might be modified to this end, suggesting that though the content and quality of education continue to be the same for the sexes, the patterns of educational involvement be adapted to their distinctive life styles. The traditional division of labor remains her underlying concept. Part-time, multi-phase patterns are offered as a Solomonic solution; the home remains intact, while the person segments herself to be all this and woman too. So, although the resultant proposals for change are enlightened and valuable, they do not challenge those culturally imposed forms that impede most women's passage through the doorways of life.

## On the Differences Between Men and Women

### John Stuart Mill

I have said that it cannot now be known how much of the existing mental differences between men and women is natural, and how much artificial; whether there are any natural differences at all; or, supposing all artificial causes of difference to be withdrawn, what natural character would be revealed. I am not about to attempt what I have pronounced impossible: but doubt does not forbid conjecture, and where certainty is unattainable, there may yet be the means of arriving at some degree of probability. The first point, the origin of the differences actually observed, is the one most accessible to speculation; and I shall attempt to approach it, by the only path by which it can be reached; by tracing the mental consequences of external influences. We cannot isolate a human being from the circumstances of his condition, so as to ascertain experimentally what he would have been by nature; but we can consider what he is, and what his circumstances have been, and whether the one would have been capable of producing the other.

Let us take, then, the only marked case which observation affords, of apparent inferiority of women to men, if we except the merely physical one of bodily strength. No production in philosophy, science, or art, entitled to the first rank, has been the work of a woman. Is there any mode of accounting for this, without supposing that women are naturally incapable of producing them?

In the first place, we may fairly question whether experience has afforded sufficient grounds for an induction. It is scarcely three generations since women, saving very rare exceptions, have begun to try their capacity in philosophy, science, or art. It is only in the present generation that their attempts have been at all numerous; and they are even now extremely few, everywhere but in England and France. It is a relevant question, whether a

From *The Subjection of Women,* 2nd ed. (London: Longmans, Green, Reader, and Dyer, 1869), pp. 125 – 137, 140 – 141.

art could have been expected, on the mere calculation of chances, to turn up during that lapse of time, among the women whose tastes and personal position admitted of their devoting themselves to these pursuits. In all things which there has yet been time for — in all but the very highest grades in the scale of excellence, especially in the department in which they have been longest engaged, literature (both prose and poetry) — women have done quite as much, have obtained fully as high prizes and as many of them, as could be expected from the length of time and the number of competitors. If we go back to the earlier period when very few women made the attempt, yet some of those few made it with distinguished success. The Greeks always accounted Sappho among their great poets; and we may well suppose that Myrtis, said to have been the teacher of Pindar, and Corinna, who five times bore away from him the prize of poetry, must at least have had sufficient merit to admit of being compared with that great name. Aspasia did not leave any philosophical writings; but it is an admitted fact that Socrates resorted to her for instruction, and avowed himself to have obtained it. . . .

But they have not yet produced any of those great and luminous new ideas which form an era in thought, nor those fundamentally new conceptions in art, which open a vista of possible effects not before thought of, and found a new school. Their compositions are mostly grounded on the existing fund of thought, and their creations do not deviate widely from existing types. This is the sort of inferiority which their works manifest. . . . When women have had the preparation which all men now require to be eminently original, it will be time enough to begin judging by experience of their capacity for originality. . . .

Who can tell how many of the most original thoughts put forth by male writers, belong to a woman by suggestion, to themselves only by verifying and working out? If I may judge by my own case, a very large proportion indeed. . . .

If women's literature is destined to have a different collective character from that of men, depending on any difference of natural tendencies, much longer time is necessary than has yet elapsed, before it can emancipate itself from the influence of accepted models, and guide itself by its own impulses. But if, as I believe, there will not prove to be any natural tendencies common to women, and distinguishing their genius from that of men, yet every individual writer among them has her individual tendencies, which at present are still subdued by the influence of precedent and example: and it will require generations more, before their individuality is sufficiently developed to make head against that influence.

It is in the fine arts, properly so called, that the *primâ facie* evidence of inferior original powers in women at first sight appears the strongest: since opinion (it may be said) does not exclude them from these, but rather encour-

mind possessing the requisites of first-rate eminence in speculation or creative

ages them, and their education, instead of passing over this department, is in the affluent classes mainly composed of it. Yet in this line of exertion they have fallen still more short than in many others, of the highest eminence attained by men. This shortcoming, however, needs no other explanation than the familiar fact, more universally true in the fine arts than in anything else; the vast superiority of professional persons over amateurs. Women in the educated classes are almost universally taught more or less of some branch or other of the fine arts, but not that they may gain their living or their social consequence by it. Women artists are all amateurs. The exceptions are only of the kind which confirm the general truth. Women are taught music, but not for the purpose of composing, only of executing it: and accordingly it is only as composers that men, in music, are superior to women. . . .

There are other reasons, besides those which we have now given, that help to explain why women remain behind men, even in the pursuits which are open to both. For one thing, very few women have time for them. This may seem a paradox; it is an undoubted social fact. The time and thoughts of every woman have to satisfy great previous demands on them for things practical. There is, first, the superintendence of the family and the domestic expenditure, which occupies at least one woman in every family, generally the one of mature years and acquired experience; unless the family is so rich as to admit of delegating that task to hired agency, and submitting to all the waste and malversation inseparable from that mode of conducting it. . . .

Now, whether the cause be natural or artificial, women seldom have this eagerness for fame. Their ambition is generally confined within narrower bounds. The influence they seek is over those who immediately surround them. Their desire is to be liked, loved, or admired, by those whom they see with their eyes: and the proficiency in knowledge, arts, and accomplishments, which is sufficient for that, almost always contents them. This is a trait of character which cannot be left out of the account in judging of women as they are. I do not at all believe that it is inherent in women. It is only the natural result of their circumstances. . . .

Besides, how could it be that a woman's interests should not be all concentrated upon the impressions made on those who come into her daily life, when society has ordained that all her duties should be to them, and has contrived that all her comforts should depend on them? The natural desire of consideration from our fellow creatures is as strong in a woman as in a man; but society has so ordered things that public consideration is, in all ordinary cases, only attainable by her through the consideration of her husband or of her male relations, while her private consideration is forfeited by making herself individually prominent, or appearing in any other character than that of an appendage to men. Whoever is in the least capable of estimating the influence on the mind of the entire domestic and social position and the whole habit of a life, must easily recognise in that influence a complete explanation of nearly all the apparent differences between women and men, including the whole of those which imply any inferiority.

## Women and Education
>━●━०━●━०━●━०━●━०━●━०━●━०━●━०━●━०━●━०━●━०━●━०━●━०━●━०━●━०━●━०━●━०━●━०━●━०━●━<

*Charlotte Perkins Gilman*

### Education

The origin of education is maternal. The mother animal is seen to teach her young what she knows of life, its gains and losses; and, whether consciously done or not, this is education. In our human life, education, even in its present state, is the most important process. Without it we could not maintain ourselves, much less dominate and improve conditions as we do; and when education is what it should be, our power will increase far beyond present hopes.

In lower animals, speaking generally, the powers of the race must be lodged in each individual. No gain of personal experience is of avail to the others. No advantages remain, save those physically transmitted. The narrow limits of personal gain and personal inheritance rigidly hem in sub-human progress. With us, what one learns may be taught to the others. Our life is social, collective. Our gain is for all, and profits us in proportion as we extend it to all. As the human soul develops in us, we become able to grasp more fully our common needs and advantages; and with this growth has come the extension of education to the people as a whole. Social functions are developed under natural laws, like physical ones, and may be studied similarly. . . .

Educational forces are many. The child is born into certain conditions, physical and psychic, and "educated" thereby. He grows up into social, political and economic conditions, and is further modified by them. All these conditions, so far, have been of androcentric character; but what we call education as a special social process is what the child is deliberately taught and subjected to; and it is here we may see the same dominant influence so clearly.

This conscious education was, for long, given to boys alone, the girls being left to maternal influence, each to learn what her mother knew, and no more. This very clear instance of the masculine theory is glaring enough by itself to rest a case on. It shows how absolute was the assumption that the world was composed of men, and men alone were to be fitted for it. Women were no part of the world, and needed no training for its uses. As females they were born

From *The Man-Made World* (New York: The Charlton Co., 1911), pp. 143-151, 156-162 (abridged).

and not made; as human beings they were only servants, trained as such by their servant mothers.

This system of education we are outgrowing more swiftly with each year. The growing humanness of women, and its recognition, is forcing an equal education for boy and girl. When this demand was first made, by women of unusual calibre, and by men sufficiently human to overlook sex-prejudice, how was it met? What was the attitude of woman's "natural protector" when she began to ask some share in human life?

Under the universal assumption that men alone were humanity, that the world was masculine and for men only, the efforts of the women were met as a deliberate attempt to "unsex" themselves and become men. To be a woman was to be ignorant, uneducated; to be wise, educated, was to be a man. Women were not men, visibly; therefore they could not be educated, and ought not to want to be.

Under this androcentric prejudice, the equal extension of education to women was opposed at every step, and is still opposed by many. Seeing in women only sex, and not humanness, they would confine her exclusively to feminine interests. This is the masculine view, *par excellence*. In spite of it, the human development of women, which so splendidly characterizes our age, has gone on; and now both women's colleges and those for both sexes offer "the higher education" to our girls, as well as the lower grades in school and kindergarten.

In the special professional training, the same opposition was experienced, even more rancorous and cruel. One would think that on the entrance of a few straggling and necessarily inferior feminine beginners into a trade or profession, those in possession would extend to them the right hand of fellowship, as comrades, extra assistance as beginners, and special courtesy as women.

The contrary occurred. Women were barred out, discriminated against, taken advantage of, as competitors; and as women they have had to meet special danger and offence instead of special courtesy. An unforgetable instance of this lies in the attitude of medical colleges toward women students.

The men, strong enough, one would think, in numbers, in knowledge, in established precedent, to be generous, opposed the newcomers first with absolute refusal; then when the patient, persistent applicants did get inside, both students and teachers met them not only with unkindness and unfairness, but with a weapon ingeniously well chosen, and most discreditable — namely, obscenity. Grave professors, in lecture and clinic, as well as grinning students, used offensive language, and played offensive tricks, to drive the women out — a most androcentric performance. . . .

Then to-day rises a new cry against "women in education." Here is Mr. Barrett Wendell, of Harvard, solemnly claiming that teaching women weakens the intellect of the teacher, and every now and then bursts out a frantic sputter of alarm over the "feminization" of our schools. It is true that the majority

of teachers are now women. It is true that they do have an influence on growing
children. It would even seem to be true that that is largely what women are
for.

But the male assumes his influence to be normal, human, and the female
influence as wholly a matter of sex; therefore, where women teach boys, the
boys become "effeminate" — a grievious fall. When men teach girls, do the
girls become —— ? Here again we lack the analogue. Never has it occurred
to the androcentric mind to conceive of such a thing as being *too* masculine.
There is no such word! It is odd to notice that which ever way the woman is
placed, she is supposed to exert this degrading influence; if the teacher, she
effeminizes her pupils; if the pupil, she effeminizes her teachers. . . .

But as a matter of humanity the male of our species is at present far ahead
of the female. By this superior humanness, his knowledge, his skill, his experience, his organization and specialization, he makes and manages the world. All
this is human, not male. All this is open to the woman as the man by nature,
but has been denied her during our androcentric culture. . . .

Their position is a simple one. "We are men. Men are human beings. Women
are only women. This is a man's world. . . .

What this world most needs to-day in both men and women, is the power
to recognize our public conditions; to see the relative importance of measures;
to learn the processes of constructive citizenship. We need an education which
shall give us facts in the order of their importance; morals and manners based
on these facts; and train our personal powers with careful selection, so that
each may best serve the community.

At present, in the larger processes of extra-scholastic education, the advantage is still with the boy. From infancy we make the gross mistake of accentuating sex in our children, by dress and all its limitations, by special teaching of
what is "ladylike" and "manly." The boy is allowed a freedom of experience
far beyond the girl. He learns more of his town and city, more of machinery,
more of life, passing on from father to son the truths as well as traditions of
sex superiority.

All this is changing before our eyes, with the advancing humanness of
women. Not yet, however, has their advance affected, to any large extent, the
base of all education; the experience of a child's first years. Here is where the
limitations of women have checked race progress most thoroughly. Here
hereditary influence was constantly offset by the advance of the male. Social
selection did develop higher types of men, though sex-selection reversed still
insisted on primitive types of women. But the educative influence of these
primitive women, acting most exclusively on the most susceptible years of life,
has been a serious deterrent to race progress. . . .

So accustomed are we to our world-old method of entrusting the first years
of the child to the action of untaught, unbridled mother-instinct, that suggestions as to a better education for babies are received with the frank derision

of massed ignorance. . . .It seems delightfully absurd to these reactionaries that ages of human progress should be of any benefit to babies, save, indeed, as their more human fathers, specialized and organized, are able to provide them with better homes and a better world to grow up in. The idea that mothers, more human, should specialize and organize as well, and extend to their babies these supreme advantages, is made a laughingstock. . . .

An ultra-male selection has chosen women for their femininity first, and next for qualities of submissiveness and patient service bred by long ages of servility.

This servile womanhood, or the idler and more excessively feminine type, has never appreciated the real power and place of the mother, and has never been able to grasp or to carry out any worthy system of education for little children. Any experienced teacher, man or woman, will own how rare it is to find a mother capable of a dispassionate appreciation of educative values. . . .The time is coming when the human mother will recognize the educative possibilities of early childhood, learn that the ability to rightly teach little children is rare and precious, and be proud and glad to avail themselves of it.

We shall then see a development of the most valuable human qualities in our children's minds such as would now seem wildly Utopian. We shall learn from wide and long experience to anticipate and provide for the steps of the unfolding mind, and train it through carefully prearranged experiences, to a power of judgment, of self-control, of social perception, now utterly unthought of.

Such an education would begin at birth; yes, far before it, in the standards of conscious human motherhood. It would require a quite different status of wifehood, womanhood, girlhood. It would be wholly impossible if we were never to outgrow our androcentric culture.

## Where Angels Fear to Tread

>=●=o=●=o=●=o=●=o=●=o=●=o=●=o=●=o=●=o=●=o=●=o=●=o=●=o=●=o=●=o=●=o=●=o=●=<

### *Mirra Komarovsky*

To be born a woman means to inhabit, from early infancy to the last day of life, a psychological world which differs from the world of the man. Much of the zest and the exasperation of life stem from this fact. The great literary

From *Women in the Modern World* (Boston: Little, Brown, 1953), pp. 18 – 30. Copyright 1953 by Mirra Heyman.

classics, no less than the "advice to the lovelorn" columns, bear witness to the preoccupation of mankind with the difference between the feminine and the masculine psyche. It is not our task, however, to present a comprehensive review of all sex differences in intellectual aptitudes and in emotional traits. We are concerned here with such differences only in so far as they may have relevance to educational policy. . . .

The first witnesses to be called to testify concerning sex differences are the psychologists.

Scores of studies conducted by psychologists in the past three decades have uncovered sex differences in intellectual and emotional traits. Among nursery school children, little boys show more restlessness, aggressiveness, insubordination. At a later age girls exhibit more introversion, dependence upon people, and neuroticism. Boys excel in mathematical and mechanical tests, girls in verbal ability. Boys are superior in speed and co-ordination of gross bodily movements, while girls excel in manual dexterity. Boys do better in tests of general information; girls are especially good at tasks involving perception of details and frequent shifts of attention.

The answer to the simple question: "But which sex is the more intelligent?" is elusive because sexes differ in the various aptitudes which enter into the measurement of intelligence. "Whether boys or girls obtain higher IQ's," write the psychologists, "depends upon the items which are included in the test. When no deliberate effort has been made to exclude sex differences from the test, there has generally been a tendency to favor girls. This follows from the fact that intelligence tests consist so largely of verbal items, on which girls are superior. Insofar as the tests depend upon memory, girls have an additional advantage." With increasing age, gifted boys are more likely to retain their high IQ's or even to show a rise, while girls with the same initial IQ's are more likely to show a drop.

As to school achievement, boys excel in arithmetical reasoning, nature study, science, and history while girls do better in reading, language usage, spelling and computation. When it comes to school *grades* as contrasted with other tests of school achievement, girls excel consistently even in the subjects which favor boys, perhaps because of their more conscientious application to studies.

In the light of these findings isn't it obvious, ask the critics, that having forced women into the curriculum originally designed for men, we have led them into ruinous competition with men in areas in which the latter had a natural advantage?

Even if we assume, for the time being, that all the observed sex differences are inborn there remains one crucial fact, neglected by the critics, which goes a long way to vitiate their argument. Psychological tests have generally revealed much greater differences between members of the same sex than between the sexes. The findings which have been cited are differences in the *average* ratings of large groups of boys and girls.

It is all too easy, upon learning, for example, that girls excel in verbal ability, to imagine that most girls surpass most boys in verbal ability, with a handful of exceptions in each sex. The truth is more nearly the reverse: Most girls are similar to most boys, with a minority in each sex creating the differences in averages. When the studies are examined in detail it becomes obvious that sexes "overlap" with regard to mental tests. A somewhat technical scrutiny of several studies will repay us in providing a truer picture of what psychological tests have actually revealed concerning sex differences.

A frequently cited study tested 189 boys and 206 girls in the third and fourth grades of a public school with respect to arithmetical reasoning and sentence completion. The boys excelled in the former while the girls did better in the latter. Shall we, then, shift the emphasis in the education of girls from arithmetic to verbal subjects? We may argue that some training in both fields is indispensable to a citizen, irrespective of his special aptitudes. But even if our aim were to develop to the fullest the unique gifts of the individual, his sex would be a poor guide to the selection of students for particular study. Though on the average the girls were inferior in arithmetic, 83 out of 206 received a score of 40+ while 68 out of 189 boys failed to attain as high a score. If training in arithmetic were to be limited only to those who demonstrate high ability, 83 girls in this group would take precedence over 68 boys. Similarly 94 boys reached a score of 35+ in sentence completion, thereby exceeding the score attained by as many as 97 girls. Again, were proficiency in sentence completion a condition for some further training, 94 boys (out of 189) would have a better claim to this training than the 97 girls (out of 206) who failed to equal the boys' score.

Turning now to tests of adolescents, we shall deliberately select those which show the sharpest sex differences. The College Entrance Examination Board in its annual report for 1949-1950 cites the scores made by candidates for admission to college.

*Percentage of Candidates Receiving a Score of 550 and Over*

Scholastic Aptitude Test

| Score | *Verbal* | | *Mathematical* | |
|---|---|---|---|---|
| | BOYS | GIRLS | BOYS | GIRLS |
| 550 | 38 | 37 | 38 | 17 |

| Score | *English Composition* | | *Social Studies* | | *Physics* | |
|---|---|---|---|---|---|---|
| | BOYS | GIRLS | BOYS | GIRLS | BOYS | GIRLS |
| 550 | 37 | 53 | 52 | 37 | 46 | 33 |

Boys are, thus, superior in the mathematical part of the scholastic aptitude test and in physics and social studies. Girls do better in English composition and are about the same in the verbal tests. But even where divergences between the sexes are great, some overlapping exists. Everybody knows that physics is a "masculine" subject. In at least one coeducational school known to the writer, girl pupils were apprehensive about enrolling in physics courses because of the widely quoted views of the physics teachers that the subject was not for girls. And, yet, on the College Entrance tests, 54 per cent of the boys fell below the scores made by the top third of the girls. If we decided that only the gifted in physics should be encouraged to develop fully their potentialities, a greater proportion of boys would, of course, be eligible. If a score of 550 were a passing grade, 46 per cent of the boys and only 33 per cent of the girls would qualify. And yet, out of every 100 girls the top 33 would surpass 54 per cent of the boys, who would, then, have to turn to social studies, English composition, or what not.

When it comes to personality, the evidence is less adequate because personality tests have lagged behind the measurement of intellectual aptitudes. One test, cited in a well-known textbook, gives women higher scores in neuroticism, introversion, submissiveness, and lack of self-sufficiency. The test itself may be imperfect, but since it is sometimes used as evidence of sex differences it bears further scrutiny. In comparing 656 college men and 544 college women with regard to neuroticism, we find that women tend to be more neurotic. If we select some arbitrary score, say 55 (the higher the score the greater the neuroticism), we find that 57 per cent of the women but only 44 per cent of the men scored higher. Nevertheless, if 55 were a passing score in mental health, many women would rate healthier than men. If some educational task demanded emotional stability, selecting students in terms of the stereotypes ("emotionally stable male" and "unstable female") would be highly misleading. The healthy group (those who rated under 55) would consist of 43 women and 56 men out of 100 of each sex. Conversely, among the failures we would find 57 women and 44 men. A similar picture of overlapping of traits among college men and women appears with respect to the other personality measures devised by the psychologist Bernreuter, such as introversion, submissiveness, and relative self-confidence. It is not claimed, of course, that college students are necessarily representative of the male and female population at large. But since our primary concern is with the college group, it is not inappropriate to deal with this selected body.

It is now clear that when the critics cite psychological tests in support of their plea for a special education for women, they ignore the facts of overlapping in mental traits. If "woman's nature" is violated by being forced to imitate men, it would also be violated by being pressed into the "feminine curriculum." It has been suggested that while taking one sex difference at a time may show considerable overlapping, were we to use a combination of mental traits, the overlapping would diminish and, conversely, the divergences between the sexes would be more pronounced. Whether or not such would be the case cannot be decided in advance. It would depend upon the degree of intercorrelations which existed between the particular traits used. Such an operation, to the best of my knowledge, has never been performed.

The moral which emerges from psychological tests is obvious: the need for a rich and flexible curriculum within which both the common and the unique talents of individuals, irrespective of sex, will be recognized and fostered.

This conclusion is all the more compelling when we remember that the differences in aptitudes as revealed in tests are not (to put it conservatively) wholly inborn but are due, certainly in part, to the different upbringing of the sexes. If some advantage of either sex is man-made we cannot, without deliberation, use this advantage to justify a further educational privilege. For all we know, we may thereby merely perpetuate and accentuate some difference in the upbringing of the sexes which has long since outlived its usefulness.

To attempt to unscramble the influences played by nature and nurture in producing psychological sex differences is to fall into the hornet's nest of an old controversy. Nevertheless, by way of illustration, let us examine the aptitude which has been termed the most masculine of all — mechanical ability. Are men born more mechanically minded?

Any man who has tried to explain to his wife the workings of a car would feel that we need go no further in search of an answer. That tests of mechanical aptitude repeatedly favor men is to him but proof of the obvious.

How early in childhood does male superiority in mechanical ability begin to register? Scheinfeld cites Gesell's findings that at the age of eighteen months boy babies do better in block building and in tests where pellets are put into a bottle. Two-year-old boys, also, do better than girls when asked to push blocks set together in imitation of a "choo-choo" train. Scheinfeld rightfully considers these findings of importance because the younger the children, the greater the likelihood that we are dealing with congenital traits.

Offsetting such evidence of superior mechanical aptitude in boys, however, are some other results of the same investigator, Gesell. He found no sex differences among the two-, three-, or four-year-olds with regard to other block tests, such as building a "bridge." When it comes to the more complex block structure of the "gate," at the age of four, the boys are more skillful than the girls in building the gate when its construction is demonstrated, but at five years 93 per cent of the girls but only 60 per cent of the boys built the "gate" directly from the model.

"It is difficult for the adult to appreciate," writes Gesell, "how much harder it is for the child to reconstruct the steps (another block construction) than to copy the gate." And yet, we note that the girls did as well as the boys in building the "steps." Tests of form discrimination calling for fitting blocks of different shapes into appropriate holes again proved equally easy for the girls. But with regard to the last-named test, another investigator using pegboards found boys at the age of a year and a half and three on the average superior but again, among the four-year-olds, girls surpassed the boys in the speed of performance.

With results so inconsistent and variable, it is not easy to assign to either sex a clear superiority in mechanical aptitudes during the early childhood period.

Several physical factors might conceivably affect performance on the tests just cited. Biological growth is accelerated in girls (though the precise acceleration varies with respect to the different parts of the organism and at different ages). And yet, the bones in boy babies are relatively bigger and thicker, and, by the age of two, boys have already greater muscular strength than girls. Boys surpass girls in the speed and co-ordination of gross bodily movements, while girls do better in the control of fine movements, perhaps because girls are ahead in bodily development and "delicate movement follows gross bodily movement within the development of the individual."

What advantage these physical factors gave to the boys in pushing the block train and to the girls in building the "gate" and so on we can only surmise. Perhaps boys are initially attracted to mechanical objects because of their greater strength and better motor co-ordination and this advantage further encourages their mechanical interests. But if this is all there is to it — it is a far cry from what is usually understood by inheritance of mechanical aptitudes. As Anastasi and Foley pointed out, if in our society we gave baby girls erector sets, toy clocks, and mechanical puzzles, their lesser strength would not handicap them in such play. With their superior manual dexterity, they, too, might have developed mechanical interests. The same writers call attention to the fact that male superiority in adulthood is more pronounced in tests depending on mechanical information than in the more abstract tests of spatial relations, which may be equally unfamiliar to both sexes.

There may exist some hereditary basis for the masculine mechanical aptitudes, but their unequivocally superior achievement in adult life does not constitute a conclusive proof of such inheritance. "Do you want a toy?" inquires a clerk. "Is it for a boy or a girl?" One mechanical toy leads to another and a more complex one. "Buddy," calls the father, "help me with the brace and bit." Knowing the use of one tool enables one to ask a sensible question about the next one. The more one knows of a subject, the more one has to learn with and to observe with. Even if the sexes were equally endowed at birth with mechanical ability, the divergence of their paths would soon tell. We all go through life perceiving but a fragment of the world before us. Early in life the different focus of interest blankets out for the girl the headline heralding a new invention and she will not "see" the diagram of some new industrial process on the pages of the magazine. Now and then a wife will knit her brows, determined to understand the technical talk of some male visitor, but while her husband learns something from the encounter, her attention soon wanders because she does not understand their references to taken-for-granted fundamentals. Against this background, it is amazing that women should have done as well as they have in defense industry during World War II.

Should educators decide that in an age dominated by machines, in a period in which defense needs may again require the replacement of men by women in industry, it would be desirable to give women a better technical education — we can safely say that there is nothing in scientific tests to discourage such a move.

To sum up, conclusive proof as to innate differences in mental aptitudes of the sexes may not be forthcoming for years to come. One prediction may be safely made. If ever confirmed, these inborn differences will be small. This is a simple inference from the fact that today, despite great divergences in the social influences impinging upon them, men and women show, with one or two exceptions, such great similarities in tests of mental aptitudes.

Women's interests and social functions may or may not dictate a different education, but nothing that psychologists have revealed about their *capacities* argues for special training.

The findings of psychological tests leave unanswered the question which is always raised in any discussion of psychological sex differences: Where are the women geniuses?

When it comes to truly great cultural innovations, the record of women is unimpressive. While for some this slender yield constitutes prima facie evidence of women's limited capacity for creative achievement, the inference is by no means conclusive. We are reminded that many male geniuses were not deterred by poverty, discouragement, and even persecution and that, consequently, women who had it in them would have also surmounted environmental handicaps. But the environment that counts is not merely the external one of favorable laws and opportunities. It is the inner environment, the self-image and the level of aspirations, which is at the root of motivation. This self-image, subtly molded by society, has been, and still is, inimical to the full development of whatever creativity women may possess.

Creation of a high order requires a fierce concentration. A man need not have always paid for it by the sacrifice of other goals normally desired, such as love or marriage. But even when supreme sacrifices were entailed, the man in making them need not have suffered the added penalty of corroding self-doubt. Any woman who was prepared to make such sacrifices was condemned as a "freak" and, being a child of her society, inevitably suspected that the verdict was just. Self-doubt at this sensitive core of one's being, apart from external handicaps, tended to block creativity in women. In the light of the conflicts. . .the surprising thing is not the absence of women geniuses but the great number of highly competent women in the arts and in professions. We must remember that men geniuses are rare, too, and that thousands of men are stimulated and trained in various spheres before one genius emerges.

Interesting as it is to speculate upon women's chances to join the ranks of the great creators, it is hard to see that the design of college education needs to take this speculation into account. It is the main body of students, not the occasional genius, which is the basic concern in devising a curriculum.

# A Modest Proposal for the Educating of Women

*Elizabeth L. Cless*

"Why can't a woman be more like a man!" This musical complaint in *My Fair Lady* comes from the lips of Professor Higgins. Eight centuries of shaping higher education to meet the needs of men have produced a system that finds women at best a nuisance, at worst an irrelevance. Universities emerged under the wing of a medieval church that considered women an aberration and, barring a brief period during the Italian Renaissance, this attitude has continued to prevail.

Higher education in the United States was designed exclusively for the white, upper- or middle-class male. Its procedures, its rigid uninterrupted timetable, and its cost all but prohibit its use by women despite well-meaning, sometimes desperate, twentieth-century attempts to provide appropriate schooling for every qualified American citizen.

The masculine attitudes that govern the procedures and structures of American higher education are not consciously vicious, merely unexamined, discriminatory by inheritance. Even thoughtful men, educational liberals, assume that the pattern that worked for them is, therefore, the best pattern for all humans; that if women are not able to realize their full intellectual potential within existing academic procedures the fault lies with women, not with the structure. It is demonstrable that women, who make up half of American society, are not assuming their share of leadership. Many men, including

From "A Modest Proposal for the Educating of Women," *The American Scholar*, vol. 38, no. 4 (Autumn 1969), pp. 618–627. Copyright 1969 by the United Chapters of Phi Beta Kappa. By permission of the publishers.

Presidents Kennedy and Johnson, have raised an alarm about the declining proportion of women in management, technology and the professions. Many women retort with charges of discrimination. Both groups have verifiable evidence; both sincerely encourage women to accept responsibility for solving problems, creating beauty, healing the sick, building cities. Incredibly, neither group looks behind the scarcity of women in responsible positions to the educational fallacy that produces the scarcity.

Gestures toward coeducation in the nineteenth century consisted of little more than the addition of schools of home economics. The first excellent American women's colleges patterned themselves as closely as possible on the examples of Harvard and Yale. Unfortunately, as Eli Ginzberg has written in *Life Styles of Educated Women,* "Education for women was fashioned during the few generations when only a handful of female students had career objectives, and when even fewer women graduates pursued occupational goals after they were married." This mid-Victorian fashioning has left only two academic options, neither of them designed to bring out the best in today's woman who would be educated. On the one hand, if she wishes to become economically and socially productive, she must follow paths that Ginzberg suggests "are geared to the prototype of a man moving along steadily from one stage of educational and career development to the next, except for a possible interruption for military service; a prototype which is no longer valid, even for men." Or she yields to the siren song of a Victorian education meant for women perpetually sheltered against economic necessity or ambition.

The intelligent American woman cannot be, and does not want to be, like a man. And, whether we like it or not, she cannot, in our world, live a sheltered life of indulgence. She humanly demands the opportunity to be both a woman and a person. She wants to marry; to help her husband become successful; to bear and raise children. But she needs to do it in the context of the great, wide world, not in the semi-isolation of the P.T.A. and the car pool. More important, she must have the assurance that when her primary responsibility ceases to be the family she will be welcomed, and rewarded, in a less personal setting. Her valuable, equal and authoritative contribution to society must cease to be seen as a threat to, or diminution of, men's particular capabilities.

If a woman's marriage continues to be viewed by men as a sign of intellectual weakness, the number of women who choose not to marry may increase, now that spinsterhood no longer implies frustration. The equation of marriage and lack of intellectual motivation is implicit in the genteel "feminized" curricula of some colleges and, more destructively, in overt refusal of graduate schools to admit more than a token number of women "because they'll just get married, anyway." As if to prove their lack of bias most masculine heads of graduate departments or professional schools are loud in praise of the ability and dedication of their few women students, yet continue to sanction a frankly discriminatory admission quota. The result is a shortage of serious women students, which the country can ill afford.

Today, more then 75 percent (some estimates are as high as 95 percent) of all intellectually qualified youngsters who do not enter college are girls. Approximately 50 percent of all women who enter college drop out before receiving their first degrees. All the sources recently examined by Jencks and Riesman for *The Academic Revolution* suggest that women with B.A.'s are less than half as likely as men to earn a graduate degree, despite the fact that, on the average, they have better undergraduate records. Jessie Bernard's unimpeachable research on women who survive to become part of the prevailing educational system justifies her statement (in *Academic Women*): "Students of symbolism could undoubtedly explain why it is that colleges and universities are pictured as females. It is not immediately obvious."

The coeducational colleges, of course, have assumed that women are glad to accept masculine goals and procedures. It is a rare one that appoints its Dean of Women as a counsel on matters curricular, a rarer one that deliberately seeks a woman member for its top administration. Harold Taylor's glibness does not disguise the logic of his view of the situation: "[Women] . . . should be given the same inadequate education that men are given on the grounds that no matter how bad men's education is, women are entitled to it too."

Most segregated American women's colleges were founded to protect their students from masculine competition and distraction. The "tender flower" stereotype of women is a romantic male invention, as medical statistics prove. Submission and shelter are positive human necessities, common to both sexes; to base any educational system on them alone seems unrealistic.

Colleges cast in the Victorian mold offer glimpses of the life of the mind that tantalize the intelligent girl, but all too often frustrate her when she tries to translate that life of the mind into the life of the community. Many excellent protective women's colleges treasure the finishing aspect of their education to such a degree that their students intent on graduate or professional training must petition the faculty to be allowed to take the specialized courses necessary for graduate school admission. The antifeminist view that intensity of purpose in a woman is unnatural and therefore unladylike has been largely unexamined since the crinoline disappeared. It is treasured by many women (usually alumnae) and their teachers. Lazy women and wishful professors will undoubtedly perpetuate this view as long as society will pay for it.

In spite of current worship of the higher degree, the graduate and professional school picture is particularly bleak for aspiring women. According to a 1968 *Special Report on Women and Graduate Study*,[1] 72 percent of all women receiving the bachelor's degree in 1961 planned to attend graduate

1. *Resources for Medical Research, Report No. 13*, June 1968. U. S. Dept. of Health, Education and Welfare, National Institutes of Health.

school and 76 percent of them had high academic records. By 1964, 42 percent had enrolled for graduate study, but only two-fifths of those were full-time students. Kenneth M. Wilson's similar study for the College Research Center at Vassar shows that 77 percent of all seniors in the class of 1966 in three quite different women's colleges had plans for postgraduate study, either immediately or later. An interesting fact, which we emphasize for later discussion, is that although 32.3 percent of this group intended to go directly from college to graduate study, 44.7 percent expected to engage in graduate study at a later date.[2] Since 1940, there has been a decline of 16 percent in the number of women in professional and technical occupations, most of which require study beyond the B.A.

Statistics tell us that masculine-oriented education fails to capitalize on indentifiable feminine ability. A search for the "why" of this failure is more subjective. To turn back to Jessie Bernard: ". . . A major grievance of men with respect to women. . .is that they refuse to compete for the values men set up. . . Willingness to compete is a sign that one accepts the values competed for." While men, in this rather negative way, encourage women to adopt their system, the woman who tries it is branded "aggressive." Intellectual aggressiveness, as a given basis for academic or economic success, is seen as a male virtue but a female vice. Later rewards for a woman's acceptance of the values men set up include neither the status nor the salary of men with comparable backgrounds. Many intelligent women opt out of higher education, rather than risk the emotional punishment incurred by a woman who dares to enter a system built by men for men.

The primary problem for women is the timing of higher education. The expectation that the years between eighteen and twenty-five will be devoted to uninterrupted study and career choice works well for men. The average age of marriage for an American woman is twenty. Her last child is born when she is twenty-six. (We all know of women who manage to take that final exam on the way to the delivery room. This may encourage wisdom, but leaves much to be desired as a deliberate educational technique.) Professional literature recognizes that girls, having intellectually outperformed boys in prepuberty, often fall behind the boys at the very time that the need of both boys and girls for higher education is assumed. Karem Monsour, a psychiatrist, suggests, in *Education and a Woman's Life,* that a woman cannot be educated effectively when she is in love or having a baby. If we want to capture a woman's abstract imagination, perhaps she should not be forced, during the peak years of her

2. The N.I.H. Report adds a significant dimension to approximately the same statistical finding; women of low socio-economic status are most likely to plan graduate study (78 percent as against 67 percent with high socio-economic status). However, 59 percent of those women expected to have to delay their entrance to graduate school. The lesson for financial aid offices is clear.

reproductive life, into an intellectual structure that ignores her psychosomatic difference from men. Striking evidence has appeared in programs of women's continuing education that no matter how well a girl of eighteen to twenty-one performs in college, she does better when she returns to formal study after the age of thirty.

Procedural custom seldom allows the free flow of students in and out of colleges and universities at times of individual, rather then institutional, choice. Educational record-keeping, methods of student evaluation, entrance procedures, all are predicated on the masculine habit of uninterrupted progress from kindergarten to the highest professional degree — with a year or two out to earn money, serve in the armed forces or with VISTA, perhaps, but never with fifteen years out to raise a family.

The prevailing request, on college admissions forms, for letters of evaluation from recent teachers serves to illuminate the system that locks in the most imaginative college officers and locks out older students. College presidents themselves have been heard to admit that they would not now be considered for entrance to their own institutions if they had to present their high school transcripts and take the scholastic aptitude tests required of incoming freshmen. SAT's are not all that difficult, but they rest on the supposition that the examinee has recently studied a defined set of facts. The Educational Testing Service has been experimenting, for the College Entrance Examination Board, with college-level examinations to test "untraditionally" acquired knowledge, in an effort to certify adults for further study after a period of years away from the classroom. The lack of attention and the misinterpretation with which these experiments have been met in admissions offices are sad proof of the sanctity of our locked-in, inherited single-form system.

The residence requirement for a degree is an anachronism that militates against the able woman in a mobile society. A young woman may have fulfilled her requirement at college A before she married. Following her new husband to another part of the country, she transfers to college B and begins to rack up the necessary credits in residence again, since B has its own requirement and will not accept time served at A. Her husband is moved again. When college C insists that residence at colleges A and B is useless for its degree, and her original admitting college refuses its degree if completed *in absentia*, a sensible — and sensitive — young woman becomes a weary dropout.

The simple transfer of credits from one college to another poses a related problem. The unacceptability of tested knowledge obtained at another institution is justified parochially as protection of the "ethos" of a specific college's degree. "Ethos" is expendable. Education cannot depend upon sentiment. Accreditation is the official seal of approval issued to educational institutions by one of the six Regional Accreditation Commissions of Higher Education, composed of educators from that specific region. These six watchdogs of academic quality are linked in a national federation where, one gathers, fairly uniform standards of academic quality are agreed upon. Given these circumstances of voluntary submission to the periodic scrutiny of one's peers, it might be expected that credit for similar courses at different institutions would be automatically interchangeable among the accredited colleges or universities; that prerequisites for advanced courses would be mutually acceptable; that requirements for the field of concentration would be similar. The fallacy of this assumption would seem to lie in its simplicity. The educational penalty for mobility is not simple.

Colleges and universities pay much lip service to the "learning of living" but most of them still jealously refuse to consider credit for nonclassroom learning. This means that a woman leaving the lecture hall to be married at twenty and returning at thirty-two, when her last child enters the first grade, presumably has learned nothing in the intervening twelve years that could be measured and recorded as progress toward a diploma. With increased life expectancy and sustained vigor there is no valid reason why one cannot profitably begin either undergraduate or graduate study at the age of thirty-five. Colleges and universities must begin to look for ways to utilize nonclassroom learning within the degree system if older women are to ease existing and predicted shortages of professional manpower. It is possible to give academic credit for experience gained outside the classroom — as colleges honoring VISTA, the Peace Corps, and ghetto tutoring are finding; as Antioch, Bennington and Berea have demonstrated for years. Able women may deserve advanced educational placement when they return to formal education after work in the League of Women Voters, a cooperative nursery school or a secretarial job. Colleges and universities concerned with the education of women will have to admit that raising a family and serving a community are learning experiences as valid in fact, if not in kind, as sitting in a history classroom or standing in a biology laboratory.

The compulsive uninterrupted full-time study sequence of high school, bachelor's degree, then the master's degree followed by the Ph.D., M.D. or LL.D., can be broken, or pursued more slowly, with no diminution of quality. Part-time study must be recognized as natural, desirable and just as effective as full-time study. Higher education, at all levels, must cease its current punishment of failure to follow an academic pattern consecutive in time and specialized in content, if able women are to contribute fully to the future. Far from damaging the excellence of education, an acceptance that the intellectually productive periods of a woman's life may be different in time from those of a man will produce a response from the feminine student to her preceptors that is impossible when that student is forced into an ill-fitting masculine mold. We can accept the different life patterns of men and women while rewarding them equally for planned, purposeful progression.

It is impossible for a young woman in her late teens or early twenties to know where, or exactly how, she will be living for the rest of her life. She may not be able to plan the details of her future, but she can be helped to see the general pattern into which most women's lives now fall. She — and we — must be reminded constantly that there is no longer an option between marriage or a career. The girl of sixteen to twenty-five is so physiologically determined to perpetuate the human race that she consistently underrates the importance and the potential of her intellect. Marriage in these years now often eclipses educational plans entirely. Final career choice at this stage seems usually to be made at a much lower level than the woman's basic ability would dictate. Current research is beginning to suggest that the growth of normal intelligent women includes a marked change of intellectual interest sometime between the ages of thirty and forty. This suggests that professional choice should be tentative for many until their middle years. The girl who has purpose enough to be singleminded about her professional direction early in life must, of course, be given every opportunity to move through the educational system swiftly and effectively.

The last hundred years have been spent verifying the fact that women can indeed meet the intellectual demands of men's education. The testing has been done. There is no doubt left about the equal educability of men and women. Gordon Blackwell has said, ". . .we are, therefore, now able to move from the proving ground to the experimental field of education for women." The optional content, and the quality, of education for men and women must be the same. But men and women are not the same, any more than all men are the same, or all women are the same.

Procedural flexibility to meet individual differences is possible. Undergraduate colleges must assume lifelong academic counseling responsibility for their entering students. By the simple fact of admission, a college indicates its confidence in the potential of the young woman student; it therefore cannot abandon responsibility for that student as she leaves the campus for marriage, for motherhood or for a job. Whenever, and wherever, a woman wishes to resume formal education, her original admitting college must stand ready to encourage and facilitate that return. This means an immediate joint attack by all responsible institutions concerned with women's education at every level on the problems of admissions procedures, credit transfer, residence requirements, and informal accumulation of learning. It means a new approach to record-keeping, perhaps a national academic credit bank under the auspices of the Federation of Accreditation Commissions.

The United States Department of Labor predicts that the now young American woman who never marries can expect to have a paying job for forty years; the woman who does marry will work outside her home for thirty years, some of them undoubtedly on a part-time basis. The undigested challenge for education is that most women who now join the labor force do so after the age of thirty-five, in jobs well below their capability. Higher education, particularly at its upper levels, lacks techniques that would encourage able, sophisticated women to qualify for professional and managerial positions where severe shortages exist and will continue. Colleges, graduate and professional schools should be the obvious places to learn the flexibility and adaptability that women must find over and over again. But to teach such traits, institutions must first embrace them.

American educators, under pressure, are creating new opportunities for the economically and culturally underprivileged. Women, the intellectually and occupationally underprivileged, suffer in comparative safety; indeed, many of them are taught to prefer educational deprivation, which allows them to avoid the social responsibility required by a changing world. Perhaps as a result, women seldom are mentioned in plans for new educational opportunity, except as they share minority ethnic characteristics with men. The existing scarcity of serious women students, both under and over twenty-five, with its attendant damage to the social mechanism of our future, is another result of that lack of empathy and foresight that denied education to children of the poor, the black, the inhabitant of the reservation.

Some women have made it through men's educational system, often, it is stated, at the price of the femininity men claim to value. Women, single and married, value their real femininity, too, and cannot lose it through exercise of the mind. Men — and women — correctly infer that willingness to accept man's educational patterns shows lack of pride in that femininity. Therefore this modest proposal. The alternative — the educated woman receiving recognition only as a pseudo man — appeals to women no more than it does to men. Professor Higgins must not be given tenure!

## 9.  *Women in the Establishment* ━●━○━●━●━●━●━○━●━●━●━●━●━○━●━

> Truth is the name we give to errors
> grown hoary with the centuries.
>
> SPINOZA

Women are off camera in most of the pictures of the past handed down to us, for it has long been assumed that they were extraneous to public endeavor. Nevertheless, scattered data impugn these preconceptions. There are hints in the lore and legend of ancient peoples that women were once members of the establishment: hunters and warriors, priestesses and queens; that even in the kinship order their social significance was very different when the capacity to be fruitful and multiply was a crucial variable, when domestic economy was all the economy there was. In response, therefore, to Freud's question, "What does woman want?" the answer is she wants to re-enter the world; there is no other. She wants once again to be an insider.

Reporting on the patterns of African tribal societies, Annie M. D. Lebeuf takes note of traditional assumptions. "By a habit of thought deeply rooted in the Western mind, women are relegated to the sphere of domestic tasks and private life, and men alone are considered equal to the task of shouldering the burden of public affairs." Attitudes of this kind, she remarks, may be at the bottom of erroneous ideas about the real authority exercised by women in other cultures, and may impel "intruding colonial powers" systematically to exclude women from the social forms they initiate. Yet tribal tradition and the accounts of early travelers testify to the exploits of African women who

---

*Parallel readings for Chapter 9, "Remembrance of Things Past."

founded cities, led migrations, and conquered kingdoms. The selection that follows includes a survey of how women have been associated, directly and indirectly, with the structure of power. Evidence is also adduced about women's importance in commerce and in agriculture and the powerful organizations formed to advance these purposes. Although their strength is not as great as it was, the significance of such groups can be measured by the 1929 Ibo movement known as "the war of the women." Following a rumor that the government planned to introduce a tax on women's property, more than two million people — very few of whom seem to have been men — were mobilized. This is scarcely a picture of the sequestered and immutable woman.

Phyllis McGinley, exploring a very different milieu, also reveals that the work of the world was not always the special prerogative of the masculine gender. If we wish to glimpse the New Woman of a different age, we need look no further, she remarks in her wry style, than the female saints: articulate, vigorous, and unsubduable. Some were queens and some were peasants. They were celebrated as educators and diplomats, as abbesses and judges, as scholars and rulers. Accusations hurled against them have a familiar ring: "She is ambitious and teaches theology as though she were a Doctor of the Church." The selection included here contains vignettes of five saints taken from different ages and varying nations. They constitute further evidence that "there have been towering women since the world was invented."

# The Role of Women in the Political Organization of African Societies

>—•—•—•—•—•—•—•—•—•—•—•—•—•—•—•—•—•—•—•—•—•—•—•—•—•—<

*Annie M. D. Lebeuf*

By a habit of thought deeply rooted in the Western mind, women are relegated to the sphere of domestic tasks and private life, and men alone are considered equal to the task of shouldering the burden of public affairs. This anti-feminist attitude, which has prevented political equality between the sexes from being established in our country until quite recently (and even so, the equality is more *de jure* than *de facto*), should not allow us to prejudge the manner in which activities are shared between men and women in other cultures, more particularly, so far as we are concerned, in those of Africa. And we are entitled

From "The Role of Women in the Political Organization of African Societies," in Denise Paulme (ed.), *Women of Tropical Africa,* trans. by H. M. Wright (Berkeley and Los Angeles: University of California Press, 1963), pp. 93–107, 113–114. Originally published by the University of California Press; reprinted by permission of The Regents of the University of California.

to ask ourselves if it is not an attitude of this kind that is at the bottom of many erroneous ideas about the very real authority exercised by women in African political systems; and whether it has not contributed, to a certain extent, to the initiation of policies which deprive women of responsibilities that used to be theirs.

The role of women in political organization may be defined in terms of their participation, direct or indirect, in the activities of government, or, in societies without a State, in the activities of groups or sub-groups which exercise authority.

To facilitate analysis, the very large number of African political systems has been assigned to two main categories of societies: on the one hand, societies in which there is an organized State with centralized authority and administrative machinery, and in which an economy based on the profit motive has created social classes between which there is an unequal distribution of wealth and differences in status; on the other, societies in which the political structure is more or less fused with kinship organization, kinship ties being the basis of social relations. In the case of the latter, authority rests with the heads of lineages and of families, who act in concert with the various social segments based principally upon age-sets and ritual functions.

Thus African societies offer a large variety of types of political organization, from monarchy — very rarely of the absolute variety — to democracy, from the administration of a vast State to that of a single village. In some places, hierarchical systems have been reconstructed, on a very much reduced scale, following upon the collapse of great kingdoms, whereas in others large populations are divided up into smaller political units coterminous with lineages or with clans, each one independent of the other.

Everywhere the political picture is a complex one. It seldom appears in a political guise as such, being more often manifested in terms of social institutions in which the political element is merged with functions of another kind, social, economic, or ritual — this providing multiple opportunities to individuals and to groups for participation in the general life of the community.

Everywhere, too, the functioning of these institutions has been abruptly disturbed by the imposition of the colonial system. Even if earlier forms of social organization still, in most places, underlie the new system imposed upon them, they have nevertheless been profoundly altered for the worse, and have rapidly been reduced to a level upon which they no longer answer the needs they were designed to fulfil and the demands which are made on them.

Women have suffered from this even more than men, for, having had their role in earlier forms of organization, they now find themselves systematically excluded from any participation in the new set-up which has been hastily formulated by the intruding colonial powers. Completely swept aside by this new development, they found that both the material and the psychological basis upon which their authority had rested had crumbled, and that gradually their privileges were disappearing. This state of affairs leads to the necessity of entering into a certain amount of historical reconstruction if we are to attempt to form a picture of what their former position was.

On turning towards the past, it is noticeable that exploits performed by women are a preponderant feature in African legends and historical traditions, and justification for this is provided by local chronicles and the accounts of early travellers.

In the Niger and Chad regions and in Hausa territory, women founded cities, led migrations, conquered kingdoms. Songhai groups still remember the names of celebrated ancestresses who governed them: in Katsina, Queen Amina became famous during the first half of the fifteenth century through her widespread conquests. She extended her influence as far as the Nupe, built many cities, received tribute from powerful chiefs, and is still held to have been responsible for introducing the kola nut to the region. In a neighbouring state, south of Zaria, another woman called Bazao-Turunku appears in the tradition at the head of a group of warriors who established themselves in a town, the ruins of which are still extant. In the myths concerning the establishment of the So in North Cameroon it was also often a woman who chose the site of a city, held the insignia of power, or governed a district.

The Lango, a Nilotic tribe, recount tales about the feats of arms performed by women; and long before we heard of the exploits of the "Amazons" of the kings of Dahomey, Gezo, Glegle and Behanzin, there were written accounts celebrating the courage of the female legions who fought in the armies of Monomotapa and reporting the privileges they enjoyed.

In West Africa, among the Ashanti and other Akan-speaking peoples, oral tradition frequently tells of women founding small states such as Mampong, Wenchi, Juaben. And if, in this area, the rule of matrilineal descent provides a possible explanation for this, no such interpretation comes into play in explaining the fact that, on the west coast and in the Cameroons and the Congo, many groups, although patrilinear, yet trace their genealogies back to eponymous ancestresses.

In many of the traditions concerning the founding of kingdoms there is a constantly recurring theme with variations of a woman, the queen or the daughter of a chief, who marries a stranger to whom she hands over the insignia of the power invested in her. There is the Queen of Daura who, according to the Kano chronicle, married Abayejidu, the progenitor of the Hausa kings, after he had killed the sacred serpent. Or the hunter Kongolo marrying the woman who governed the country where he founded the first Luba kingdom, while the second kingdom had similar origins in the marriage of a stranger to the Ndalamba Bulanda, the king's own sister. In the high Kasai the Lunda trace back their dynasty to Lueji, the daughter of a local chief, who, before marrying a man from the north, the hunter Ilunga Kibinda, promised him that he would be ruler of the region.

The early travellers have also left us accounts of the role played by women in such matters. Ibn Batuta tells of the intrigues carried on by the women of the Melle court and describes Queen Kassa, wife of Mansa Suleyman, as taking part with him in the government. Then in the sixteenth, seventeenth and eighteenth centuries various authors mention with astonishment the prerogatives and privileges of Wolof, Serer, Vili or Bakongo princesses such as may still sometimes be found in our own times.

This hasty survey should provide sufficient examples to show that when Africans turn to their past they do not forget the part played by women in it, but on the contrary assign to them a place that in many respects is theirs no longer. Moreover, it should also show that there are no valid historical grounds for explaining the present lack of interest in political matters so often found among African women as being a heritage of the past.

Most of the traditional social systems, viewed from the political angle, provide scope for women to play their part, although their participation may assume different forms. The opportunities open to them differ enormously according to whether the form of government in question is one based on relations between social classes, or one based on kinship relations. Further, various other aspects of the society, such as the system of descent, the mode of life, the economic structure, the ritual pattern, may provide limiting or favourable factors with regard to their rights and obligations, which again may vary, within the same community, according to the position held in the family system, or to seniority, or to general activities.

None of these criteria taken in isolation permits making any valid classification by means of which it would be possible to define the corresponding feminine roles. With such knowledge as is at present available, it seems preferable to start off by examining the various forms which feminine authority assumes as observed in specific examples, whether these be cases where women have effective exercise of power, or where they fulfil functions, either individually or collectively, which are associated either directly or indirectly with the structure of power.

It seldom occurs that a woman is invested with supreme sovereignty, occupying an isolated position at the summit of the social hierarchy; but on the other hand, in most of the monarchical systems there are either one or two women of the highest rank who participate in the exercise of power and who occupy a position on a par with that of the king or complementary to it.

The example provided by the tribes inhabiting the North-Eastern Transvaal, the Lovedu and their neighbours, who grant to women sole exercise of supreme power, is unique. This cultural trait distinguishes them from the Sotho tribes with whom they are linked in other ways. It seems to have been intruduced about 150 years ago by the last Lovedu king, Mugodo, whose predecessors, since the foundation of the kingdom in the sixteenth century by a small group of Karanga immigrants inheriting the traditions of Monomotapa, had always been men. During the past century three women have reigned. The first, Mujaji I, was Mugodo's daughter, and after a time of great trouble and misfortune, she came to the throne at her father's wish, after having consented to commit incest with him. At her death, her place was taken by her daughter, Mujaji II, who died in 1894 and was succeeded by Mujaji III, the daughter of her "sister" and "principal spouse."

The kingdom has about 40,000 inhabitants, who practice agriculture, whose rule of descent is patrilineal, with patrilocal residence, and among whom the legal status of women is, in general, comparatively high, although it is a function of their position in the kinship system, their rights as elder sister or father's sister being greater than the rights enjoyed by wives as such.

From the administrative point of view, the kingdom consists of a confederation of districts governed by district heads — either men or women — who have great local autonomy but who recognize the superior authority of the government at the capital, where the queen, to whom they are linked by a complex system of reciprocal ties, has her seat.

The prestige of the queen rests primarily upon the supernatural power with which she is invested — the power to "make rain," and to make it for her own people and prevent it from falling upon their enemies. Any failure on her part to carry out this essential task entails the risk of deposition, and since men depend on her performance of it for their wealth and security as plants and animals do for their growth and fertility, it is to her very person that all are linked, and it is her personal behaviour that guarantees the cyclic regularity of the seasons. The belief in the queen's power and the sacred duties demanded of her mean that she is bound in a network of obligations and ritual prohibitions of so rigorous a nature that they even include putting a term to the length of her reign, which must end by ritual suicide at the end of the fourth *vudiga,* an initiation ceremony held every ten years or so.

In return for the security and prosperity which she ensures, nobles, local chiefs and sometimes foreign chiefs send their daughters and their sisters to be her "wives." She does not have the right to be officially married to a man, although she may have children whose father will be chosen from among her close kin, but she is obliged to keep a "harem."

Through her "wives" she stands in the relationship of *tsetse,* "fiancé" or "son-in-law," to a great many of her subjects, and this affinal link creates mutual obligations between them that reinforce other relationships.

Sometimes some of the wives have children, who are regarded as belonging to the queen and may eventually become claimants to the throne. Further, the queen may marry some of her wives to men chosen by her, thus extending the network of affinal relationships, which carries on into the subsequent generation through her right to demand in return one of the daughters of these marriages, in accordance with the prevailing rules of kinship. She thus directs this system to political ends, seeking always to exert her influence in the direction of peace, conciliation and harmony.

In her capacity as head of the judicial system, she is assisted by the "mothers of the kingdom" who represent the various districts and are appointed by the queen to act as her intermediaries with the people of the district. Her authority is not supported by any military organization, but relies essentially on her divine nature.

As a result of the fame of Mujaji I, which spread as far as the Swazi and the Zulu, the first queens appeared in the neighbouring Khaha and Mamaila tribes, an example later to be followed by the Letswalo (or Narene) and the Mahlo.

A much more frequent occurrence is that in which a woman exercises joint sovereignty, and in many states the monarchy consists either of a couple — the king and a woman of rank; or a triad — the king and two women. I prefer, for the moment, not to give these women any precise title in case this should impute to them a role which is not borne out by the facts. In order to give an exact translation of an African title, it is first of all necessary to know precisely how it is interpreted by the people concerned. Now as often as not these women were called Queen-Mothers or Queens, even when the king was neither son nor husband, and what confronts us here is a complex system of correspondences in which symbol and reality interpenetrate yet do not coincide.

In the Ruanda of former times "it may be said," writes J. Maquet, "that the royal power was invested in two persons equally, without any differentiation in duties or privileges." The *Umu-Gabe-Kazi,* who was the mother of the *Mwami,* shared with him all the responsibilities of power. If she died before the king, she was replaced by another woman; if the contrary happened, she retired.

Among the Swazi the *Indlovukati,* mother of the king, is, along with her son, at the head of the political hierarchy. They each have their own residence in separate villages, their own court, their own officials. Their relations are regulated by a series of obligations. Together they control the age classes, allocate land, dispense justice, preside over religious ceremonies. They assist each other in all these activities, but not so much, it would appear, by sharing the same prerogatives, as by wielding power separately, but in such a way as to complement or balance each other in all the various spheres in which they operate.

In legal matters, for instance, the king alone could pronounce the death sentence, but in the highest court where such cases were discussed with him, the counsellors of the *Indlovukati* could appear, and men sentenced to death could take refuge in her hut. In the same way, the king controls the entire army, but the commander-in-chief resides with his own regiments in the capital of the queen-mother, while she has regiments under the leadership of princes at the capital of the king. In ritual matters, she takes part with the king in rain-making rites and in the ancestral cult; she is the custodian of the regalia, but they are not effective without the co-operation of the king.

She is the Elephant, the Earth, the Beautiful, the Mother of the Country; the king is the Lion, the Sun, the Great Wild Animal.

Among the Lunda, a matrilineal tribe ruled over by a patrilineal aristocracy, the *Mwata Yamvo* has by his side the *Lukonkeketha,* a woman chosen by his four chief dignitaries, who must be a kinswoman of his, and who was originally his classificatory sister. She takes part in all matters concerning the administration. She has her own court, her own officials, and collects her own taxes. She may marry, but her husband does not apparently fill any definite role. She is regarded as the mother of the kingdom.[1]

Among the Bamileke in South Cameroon, the *Mafo,* mother of the *Fong,* is regarded by the whole tribe as being equivalent to the chief himself. She partakes of his divine nature, and at her death she is accorded the same rites. She does not, however, share all responsibilities with her son, although she exercises authority in some spheres in which the *Fong* does not intervene. She has her own residence, and her own estates, which do not come under the control of her son, and over which he has no rights of jurisdiction and thus they are a place of refuge. She directs all feminine activities, thereby controlling the agricultural work of the whole community. Dressed in masculine attire, she takes part in the deliberations of the *kamvə ,* the administrative council, where she takes precedence over the chief himself. She presides over all the women's secret societies and belongs to those of the men unless they are of a military nature. Her status is completely different from that of any other woman, and she has her own property, may undertake commercial transactions as she thinks fit, may choose a husband, has the right to commit adultery, and in general enjoys complete freedom and immunity. All her children belong to her and not to their father, which is contrary to the accepted rule of descent.

In the Benue region, one of the most important officials among the Chamba of Donga is the *Mala,* the paternal aunt, or elder sister, or daughter of the paternal aunt, of the king or *Gara.* She rules over all the women, and her duties correspond to those of the *Angwu Tsi* of the Jukun. She has judicial functions and intercedes with the *Gara* for all those who have incurred his displeasure. She also exercises important religious functions, being in charge of the strictly female cult, the *Vonkima,* while in addition she takes part along with the king in the ancestral cult. When the king is away, she presides at all the rites performed for his safety and for the success of his mission. She can be married,

1. J. Slaski; Irstam considers that she is both queen and queenmother; L. de Heusch, *Essai sur le symbolisme de l'inceste royal en Afrique* (Brussels: Institut de Sociologie Solvay, 1958, 266 pp.), p. 121, regards her as representing the ideal, but forbidden, incestuous spouse.

but her husband remains a comparatively unimportant person. At her death, she is buried with the same rites as those accorded to chiefs.

In the kingdoms of the west which are characterized by matrilineal descent, one of the Akan peoples, the Ashanti, have an *Ohemaa,* the name given to "the chief's female counterpart". She is the senior female of the royal lineage, either the mother or the classificatory sister of the *Ohene,* and as joint ruler she holds prerogatives far greater than those of any man.

She inhabits a different palace from that of the king, and like the mother of the Swazi king, maintains a court and numerous functionaries. She directs and supervises all feminine matters, concerning herself with marriages, births, and children's education, settling disputes in cases of adultery or divorce, and, most important of all, presiding at the initiation ceremonies held for girls when they have reached puberty, and at the rites performed by women for ending periods of drought. Being the custodian of the consecrated stools of her predecessors, she shares in the royal ancestral cult and participates with the king in certain rites.

She enjoys great prestige as a genealogist, responsible for maintaining traditions and preserving customs. When a new king is to be elected she is consulted and has to decide the legitimacy of the rights of the various claimants. At the nomination of the new king, she has to present him to the people, and takes part in the enthronement ceremonies. Throughout her life she remains the only person in the kingdom who may give him advice, guide him, and criticize him to his face, even in public.

In time of war, when the king is absent, it is she who takes his place. In spiritual matters, she incarnates the feminine, and in particular the mother, aspect of Nyame, the Supreme Being, while the king represents the masculine aspect. She is the moon, while the king is the sun.

In the royal family of the Bemba (in North-Eastern Rhodesia) the *Candamukulu,* who is either the mother or the oldest uterine relative of the king, also plays an important role. She takes part in tribal councils and herself governs several villages. Like the *Mafo* of the Bamileke she enjoys great sexual freedom. The same pattern is found among the Bushongo of the Kasai. Among the Loango, the *Makunda* formerly held a similar position as joint ruler with the Vili king.

In these various matrilineal systems, although the female element as such acquires greater significance than in the systems mentioned earlier, yet the functions of those women who are, so to speak, the symbolic representatives of the matrilineal principle, do not exceed the functions fulfilled by women in the general division of labour between the sexes that is found in the societies in question, where the role of women does not impinge upon purely masculine activities any more than it does in societies where patrilineal descent is the rule.

In the examples that follow, a third figure appears — again that of a woman — at the head of the government. This tripartite rule does not essentially differ from the systems described in the foregoing examples, for it would be impossible to maintain that the specific functions allotted to the third figure are not already latent within these other systems.

In the region of the Great Lakes the title of Kabaka is borne by three people: the king, his mother *(Namasole),* and one of his classificatory sisters, the *Lubuga,* who is at the same time his official spouse. She is enthroned along with him and must remain childless. Their offices are superior to those of the twelve principal chiefs of the kingdom. They have spearate residences from that of the king, and own estates in each district from which they receive taxes in addition to receiving their portion of the taxes collected by the king. Their ritual functions are important, and the *Lubuga,* after the king's death, becomes the guardian of his tomb, where she keeps up his cult and pronounces oracles.

In Kitara the mother of the claimant to the throne is involved in his activies even before he mounts the throne, and takes part in the struggle against his brothers from which he has to emerge the victor in order to become king. As soon as he is nominated, his mother takes the official title of *Nyina Mukuma* and receives special insignia. She is supposed to lead a chaste life, and must never see her son again, although they keep in contact through certain functionaries who act as intermediaries. She has her own court and her own estates, with power of life and death over the people on them. But her primary importance lies in her custodianship of the royal crown which by implication gives her a protective role over the whole kingdom. When she dies she is replaced by a woman of her own clan. A similar position is held by the *Mugole wa Muchwa,* a half-sister of the king chosen by him to be his only official wife, who, as in Ganda, must not have any children. She enjoys prerogatives similar to those of the queen-mother, having her own court, her own estates, and the power of life and death over her own people. When the king dies she retires to an estate that is given to her.

In the same way, the monarchy in Ankole consists of three persons: the king or *Mugabe,* his mother, and one of his classificatory sisters who, however, is not, as elsewhere, his wife, and who is free to marry and have children. At one time they all three enjoyed equal status.

Neither of the women has a special title, and they are simply called *nyinya omugabe,* king's mother, and *omunyana omugabe,* king's sister. The mother of the *Mugabe* has her own residence and estates. The king visits her as often as he wishes. If she falls seriously ill, he administers the ritual poison and chooses another maternal kinswoman to be her successor.

Both he and the king's sister have their herds, their armies, and their officials, and formerly they levied the *ekyitoro* tribute on Bahima cattle, as well as receiving a share of cattle taken in raids. The king's mother also has judicial and administrative functions, sits beside the *Mugabe* at all judicial cases, and decides on questions of war and peace. No man may be executed without her consent. It is she who receives foreign ambassadors before they are presented to the king. With the king's sister, she has direct say in the choice of the prime minister, the *Enganzi.* Her function is eminently that of protector, as with the queen-mother of Kitara. By performing the appropriate rites, she protects the king against maleficent spirits and fends off the vengeance of slain victims. She takes part with him in the ritual connected with the worship of the ancestors, and at the new moon makes offerings on the altar in her own dwelling that is consecrated to them.

The *omunyana omugabe* performs a special function of a purificatory nature at the enthronement ceremony, and she is in charge of her brother's health. If she falls seriously ill, she is not given the royal poison. In general, both women are closely linked with all rites performed to ensure the prosperity of the kingdom.

Among the Bateke it is also a triad that rules: the king, *Ma Onko,* and two women, the *Wanfitɛre* and the *Ngasa.* Their functions, although essential, are predominantly spiritual and ritual rather than political, or at least this is so nowadays, when the political aspect suffers from the confusion resulting from the process of emancipation from European rule at present taking place in this district.

The title of *Wanfitɛre* implies that this is a hereditary office transmitted to women within one particular family according to the rules of patrilineal descent observed by the whole Bateke tribe. The primary function of the woman who holds it is to initiate the king and his wife, the *Ngasa,* and the importance of her role is most marked during the period which extends from the death of the king to the enthronement of his successor, a period which may last for years. She is, during this time, the sole custodian of the regalia, and owing to this her power is greater than that of the heir, whom she has officially chosen with the help of the chief officials of the dead king. She maintains this position of authority until the day when she allows the heir and his wife to take over from her, after they have gone through a series of tests to which she submits them and which they must pass successfully. These tests take place during the coronation ceremonies for which she herself has fixed the date and which she directs. As soon as the coronation rites are over, she chooses from within her own family a senior woman who, on behalf of the new king, will manipulate the sacred objects, look after his fire, and do the cooking for him and for the queen — to which end she has been cultivating a field specially reserved for this purpose — and who will agree to renouncing all sexual relations.[2]

2. The last woman to be given this title, who was known as Queen Ngalifuru, reigned over the Bateke plateaux between 1892 (the date of the death of the *Onko* by the side of whom she held this position) and 1956, when she passed away, having been the chief authority recognized by the French administration; it was she to whom her unfortunate subjects owe the schools and dispensaries that have been established. Her role was reinforced by the fact that she never allowed the regalia to be taken from her, so that none of the numerous kings who succeeded were able

The *Ngasa* also belongs to one particular family. She may have been the king's wife before his nomination and have had children by him, but as soon as she has been enthroned and has received her official title, she must have no more children. She rules over the entire female population and directs the agricultural work that is their principal occupation. Her life is intimately bound up with that of the *Onko* with whom she shares the same dwelling and whom she assists at religious ceremonies. Formerly, if she was the first to die, the king was put to death, but now he is merely dismissed from office. If she survives him, she loses her position and goes into retirement, although still surrounded with special marks of esteem.

The Bateke interpret the functions of these women as a projection in the physical world of mythological events, thus conjoining the monarchical system with the cosmic order. In their view, the world was created by a hermaphrodite spirit, the *Nkwembali,*[3] and arranged by it into a fixed number of species in a fixed hierarchy, at the summit of which is placed a pair of individuals who are unique of their kind, and to whom it is permitted to recover the knowledge and power originally possessed by the primordial twins but subsequently lost by them. The *Wanfitere*, commonly called "mother of the kingdom," is an embodiment of this spirit, and the rites during the crucial period of the enthronement of the king and queen are a re-enactment of the drama of the loss and recovery of knowledge, after which she enables them to acquire the power of the primordial twins whose substitutes they have become.

In the countries that have adopted Mohammedanism in Nigeria and the Chad, these feminine roles have lost much of their earlier importance and are more in the nature of survivals.

At the Nupe court (Nigeria) the Fulani have retained the two former titles of *Nimwoye* and *Sagi,* which are bestowed on the king's mother, paternal aunt, sister or daughter. They must be women of about 40-50 years, and they take part in the king's council. Although they have lost most of their political prerogatives, they still have great moral authority. They live in the *Etsu's* house and used to have their own estates, officials and regiments. They still settle quarrels between women, especially women of noble families, and officially represent the court at certain ceremonies.

Among the Bolewa (Kanuri), the Kotoko and the Bagirmians, the king is assisted by two women: the *Magira* or *Magara* and the *Glimsu* or *Gumsu.* The first of these is the mother or the classificatory sister of the king.[4] She lives

---

to survive after their enthronement. The *Onko* at present on the throne refused to allow her to enthrone him, fearing to suffer the fate of his predecessors, and he contents himself with exercising very much reduced powers.

3. This name is also given to the chief emblem of royalty, which is always considered to belong to the *Wanfitere,* even when held by the *Onko.*

4. Among the Kotoko, until fairly recent times, the title of *Magira* was never borne by the king's mother, since she was ritually put to death by her son on the day of his enthronement; cf. M. Griaule and J. P. Lebeuf, "Fouilles dans la région du Tchad," *Journal de la Société de*

in a part of the royal capital specially assigned to her, has her court, her officials, and her estates over which she has jurisdiction. She levies taxes, and her domain is regarded as a place of refuge. Her principal functions, as with the *Gumsu,* are concerned with women's activities. At her death she is replaced by another woman of her family. It should be noted that in Bagirmi a man may be appointed *Magira* in the same way as a woman, fulfilling the same functions and wearing female clothes for the ceremonies.

Upon the election of the king, the title of *Gumsu* is conferred on one of his wives chosen from among those who have not borne him a son. Among the Kotoko of the Chari delta, it is the daughter of the chief official of the kingdom, the *Iba,* chief of the land, on whom the title is bestowed. In distinction to the other royal wives, she must never have any children, and she does not live in the same part of the palace as they do. She lives in the southern part of the building, according to a strict system of correspondence between functions and spatial directions. Along with the *Magira* she rules over the women of the kingdom, and she helps to choose some of the officials, in particular the army leaders whom she appoints personally, having chosen them from among the officials attached to her own house. She plays an important part in the septennial ceremonies for ensuring the perpetuation of the kingdom. She is associated with the morning star, the mother of all the stars, and is regarded by the people as the mythical mother of all the nobles.

In general, her power is such that it provides a constant counterbalance to that of the king, the entire political system being conceived as a delicate balance between masculine and feminine, right and left, north and south, that must be maintained in the power-relations of individuals, in all their activities, and even in their spatial location.

In all the political systems which have either one or two women at the top of the hierarchy, these women belong to a very restricted group drawn from a social class which already confers on them, even before they occupy their special roles, rights and privileges which are in marked contrast to those of the rest of the female population. The woman who fills the chief role always belongs to the generation senior to that of the king, and her position in the royal lineage, whatever it may be, is just as important as the kinship relation between her and the king. In general, she is regarded as his "mother," and acts as guide, protector, or initiator. Almost everywhere, it is she who has to choose the woman who will play the second role in sharing power with the king. This second woman, either a classificatory sister of the king or the daughter of some powerful family in the kingdom, is, with the exception of the sister of the *Mugabe* of Ankole, his official "wife." But as wife she has a completely

*Africanistes,* XXI (Paris, 1951), 1-95, p. 22. This practice is also found among the Yoruba; cf. S. Johnson, *The history of the Yoruba from the earliest times to the beginning of the British Protectorate,* Routledge, 1921, pp. 46–48, according to L. de Heusch, *Essai sur le symbolisme de l'inceste royal en Afrique,* p. 125.

different status from that of the other wives, which places her on an entirely different level. Emphasis is everywhere laid on the importance of both these roles, closely linked with the king as they are, either through his life, or in the period from the opening of his reign until the enthronement of his successor. When the women who fill them die, they are replaced by another member of their family, except in the case of the *Ngasa*, whose death entails that of the king.

In general, the relations between the two queens and the king, whether he be their son, their brother or their spouse, are of an exceptional nature, quite without parallel in the ordinary course of life. Thus to understand the association of all three, it is necessary not only to determine the position they occupy in relation to each other, but also to see this within the whole pattern of the royal lineage system.

We have seen that queens may take their full share in the responsibilities of power, either by performing the same functions as the king, or by carrying out tasks which are complementary to his; or they may have a restricted field in which they operate, although this in no way impairs their authority.

There is no doubt, however, that it is in the moral and ritual spheres that their importance lies. Or at any rate it is here that we can most easily observe the importance of their role, for these are the spheres that have suffered least from the recent political upheavals, since the spiritual values on which institutions are based long outlast the institutions themselves. But it would be wrong to view the queens' participation in state affairs from this angle alone and make them out to be nothing more than performers of sacred rites. If this function now eclipses all their other functions, this is because of the collapse of the system as a whole; and it may well be the case that this aspect of the queens' role has acquired increased significance because of the restrictions placed upon their judicial and administrative activities. . . .

While it is a general tendency for women to form groups for the purpose of carrying out their various activities in wealthy and populous areas like Southern Nigeria, such groups, owing to the importance of women in commerce and agriculture, have become powerful organizations which have been in existence for a long time.

An example of a complex system of groups of this kind is provided by the Yoruba. Its development was partly due to the existence of large towns, and its objectives are mutual aid, defence of common interests, and the organization of markets, for the attainment of which women in every town have formed producers', sellers', and buyers' associations. The Oyo associations are called *Egbe Iyalode* (literally: association of the *Iyalode*), the *Iyalode* being the title of the leader of these associations; and they are consulted by the political authorities. An *Iyalode* is often an important figure. The *Iyalode* of Ibadan, for instance, was a member of the Council of State down to 1914.

Ibo villages all have their women's councils, and in large towns each district

nominates its own spokeswoman, these together forming the council. There is
no hierarchy between the various councils, but their members maintain permanent relations with each other as between one urban or village area and
another. Each council is presided over by a woman elected, not on account of
her seniority or wealth, but because of her personality and experience. These
councils are responsible for everything concerning agriculture and the interests
of women in general. They fix the timetable for all the important agricultural
tasks, look after the protection of crops, and regulate all the ceremonies
involved. If anyone, man or woman, contravenes any of their decisions, they
can take sanctions against them, and they have great authority in judicial
matters. When the interests of a woman have to be defended, the council meet
to discuss the matter with her family, or, if she is married, with her husband's
family.

Although their powers are not so great as they used to be, their strength
and cohesion can be measured by the widespread nature of the movement for
the assertion of their rights which they organized in 1929, which was known
as "the Aba Riots" or "the war of the women." Following upon a rumour that
the government was on the point of introducing a tax on women's property,
they started making demonstrations which broke out first in Aba and then
spread through the two provinces of Owerri and Calabar, mobilizing more
than two million people, very few of whom seem to have been men. The
rapidity with which the trouble spread and the gravity of the situation which
resulted illustrate the tremendous strength of the women's organizations.

African women have a tradition of practical participation in public affairs.
Among many peoples the very conceptions on which power is based associate
them closely with the exercise of power, and although it is usually men who
are called upon to rule, the norms which regulate the position of individuals
within a community often permit a woman, under special circumstances, to
take the place of a man. In general, the profound philosophical ideas which
underlie the assignment of separate tasks to men and women stress the complementary rather than the separate nature of these tasks. Neither the division
of labour nor the nature of the tasks accomplished implies any superiority of
the one over the other, and there is almost always compensation in some other
direction, for the actual inequalities which result from such a division.

## Saint-Watching

>−●−●−●−●−●−●−●−●−●−●−●−●−●−●−●−●−●−●−●−●−●−●−●−●−●−●−●−●−●−●−●−●−●−●−●−●−●−●−●−●−●−●−●−●−●−

*Phyllis McGinley*

History must always be taken with a grain of salt. It is, after all, not a science but an art, as the Greeks knew; so that when they were parceling out the deities, they gave history a Muse of her own just as they assigned one each to poetry and playwriting and music and other explosions of the imagination.

I was reminded of this truth only yesterday morning. I had picked up for an hour's refreshment that exquisite but perverse essay of Virginia Woolf 's, "A Room of One's Own." One bleak sentence caught my skeptical eye. "Nothing," it said flatly, "is known about women before the eighteenth century."

Now Mrs. Woolf the novelist is a delight. Mrs. Woolf the historian is something else again. If I put my trust in her I must believe that until recently women had been a voiceless, hopeless multitude, without power or influence in the world. I must take for granted the odd idea that we moderns who write and paint and manage corporations and elect Presidents sprang full-panoplied from the forehead of the Nineteenth Amendment. I am perfectly willing to grant my sex an astonishing adaptability, but I cannot give such a theory as Mrs. Woolf 's a full assent.

Naturally I'm grateful for the ballot and my Rights just as I'm grateful for automatic dish-washers, air-conditioning, penicillin, and other latter-day luxuries. But I doubt that, even unenfranchised, our ancestresses were so under-privileged a group as feminist history makes them out. They did not lash themselves to railings in their drive toward equality with men, or go on hunger strikes. But in that they admitted no impediment to their abilities, they were, in a way, the first feminists. And anyone who contends that there were no great women before the eighteenth century has not read history with any care.

What about Bridget of Sweden, born in 1303, who made peace treaties as other women now run up slip covers? Or Lioba, who brought learning, gentleness, and the arts to heathen Germans in the seventh century? Or Joan of Arc, burned not for her sex but for her politics? What, in short, about the saints?

For from the beginning of the Christian era women, no matter what their position in society, knew another outlet for their talents beside the purely domestic. They had only to step from the hearth to the cloister and find there a bracing freedom. If we wish to catch a glimpse of the New Woman as typified in a different age, we need look no farther than the female saints. From old abbesses of desert monasteries to the nineteenth century's Mother Javouhey — whom Louis-Philippe of France called "that great man" — there they stand, articulate, vigorous, and unsubduable. Some of them were queens; some of them were peasants. They lived in times of storm or of calm. They were as well educated as Hilda or as illiterate as Catherine of Siena. But not one of them seems to have found her sex a barrier to greatness. I could count them by hundreds if I had need, valiant women all and powers in their generations. But five does as well as fifty. The five I mean to mention come from different ages and from varying nations. They have in common only their genius and the fact that they star the saintly Calendar.

I suppose, of the list, Teresa of Avila seems nearest to us. Although she lived in fanatic Spain more than four hundred years ago, her unconquerable charm works on us today just as it did on the kings, townspeople, and recalcitrant nuns of her own time. She was that near contradiction, a reformer with a sense of humor.

"God deliver us from sullen saints!" she used to cry, and there was never one less long-faced than she. Only a genius could have spoken with such familiarity to God — "No wonder You have so few friends when You treat the ones You have so badly" — and sounded not like a scold but a lover.

Teresa's story runs counter to that of many men and women who worked great changes on society. Her vocation seems unapparent in her youth. As a girl in the province of old Castile, she was pretty, clever, romantic, and lively, but no more than that. It is true that at seven she and her brother, Rodrigo, decided to run away to find martyrdom among the Moors in Africa. Carrying a stock of dried raisins (Teresa was always practical), they got as far as the open country outside Avila's walls before they were met by their Uncle Francisco and brought back home. But such an escapade was rather like a modern child's running away to join a circus, a common romantic dream. Otherwise Teresa lived the ordinary life of a Spanish young lady of good family. She read novels, attended balls, and took pains with her dress. We know that she was attractive and aware of the fact. At a party a few days before she entered the Carmelite Convent, a young man was admiring her pretty feet in their dancing slippers. "Take a good look, sir," Teresa told him. "You won't be getting another chance."

It was only at past twenty when she decided after much heart-searching to become a nun that she caught fire — became, indeed, a conflagration which burned up the corruption of her day. For that religion was corrupt then does not stand in doubt. The Inquisition had terrorized but not cleansed Spain. The convent where Teresa went as a novice and eventually presided as its prioress had once been strict, poor, and holy. Now it was like half the other establishments of its kind, a twittering bird cage of femininity with its rules relaxed and its practices tarnished. Girls came there not for love of God but to "find a home," and they continued to be as worldly as if they still lived in society. They gave concerts and parties, wore jewelry, dined on delicacies sent by their families, and entertained friends in the parlors. It was Teresa's lifelong task to recover the ancient Rule of the Carmelites and to bring not only her foundation but the whole of Spain back to pure practices of religion.

That she did not do it without outcry, controversy, and discouragement goes without saying. She was as beleaguered and reviled as any suffragette of the nineteenth century agitating for the vote. Nuns and priests who did not wish to change their soft ways of living demonstrated violently against her. Avila for a while ostracized her. She was examined by the Inquisition. An irate Papal Nuncio called her a "restless gadabout" and cried, "She is ambitious and teaches theology as though she were a Doctor of the Church." (The joke after some centuries is on him, for Teresa *is* now regarded, if unofficially, as a Doctor of the Church.) She seems, however, to have been as little afraid of nuncios as she was of princes, prioresses, or the surly muleteers who carried her on her interminable journeys.

Merry and undaunted, she "traipsed" as she says, about Spain, re-establishing the Unmitigated Rule in convent after convent, reforming, exhorting, and captivating the countryside.

With her eloquence and charm she won over the Archbishop of Seville, who instead of permitting her to kneel to him fell on his own knees in front of her. She successfully lectured the Pope. Even the formidable King Philip found his letters from her studded with good advice. She traveled continually, enduring floods, cold, heat, lack of provisions, and unspeakable country inns with the hardihood of an old soldier. "God gives us much to suffer for Him," she wrote, "if only from fleas, ghosts, and bad roads."

Yet, for all her traveling, she found time to write the great books, *The Way of Perfection* and *The Interior Castle,* on which rest her literary fame, as well as to take a lively interest in her horde of friends, to look out for the welfare of her beloved family, and to bring up various little nieces sent her from time to time in the casual Spanish fashion. For Teresa, besides being an inspired executive and a holy woman, was also an enchanting companion. She believed that joy was quite as essential to sanctity as faith or good works. She used to leave her prayers in order to visit with her community when they begged for her company. She set the nuns dancing to castanets on feast days and encouraged laughter and music as heartily as she discouraged sullen faces and sin. That what she did was done for love of God rather than for human satisfaction does not blur her charm even for the agnostic. In fact, anyone who writes about Teresa finds himself falling in love with his subject. Here is Woman as Reformer at her merry best — talented, original, unself-conscious, and powerful, filled like other geniuses with the "large drafts of intellectual day" which Crashaw ascribes to her.

Because Teresa was herself a writer we come close to her. We can look at another famous woman, Hilda of Whitby, only through the eyes of her biographer, the Venerable Bede. That busy little English monk wrote history with a pen dipped in incense. All his stories are nosegays, sweet-smelling as pinks or freesias. But Hilda, even engarlanded, comes through with her capabilities intact. She was no journeyer like Teresa, but then her country, in the early seventh century, was no place for journeys; it was barely scratched by civilization. The Romans had gone, leaving their walls and their roads and their villas to crumble away in the forests. The Saxons had only recently conquered the Druid Celts, who worshiped oak trees and burned human sacrifices alive. It seems almost unthinkable that such a great woman could have risen to acclaim in so savage a land. Yet when we meet Hilda in her thirties, she is already abbess of the great double monastery at Streaneschalah (afterward re-named Whitby by the Danes) and in charge of both the monks and the nuns there. To be sure, this coeducational kind of establishment was not rare in those days. Evidently women were more highly considered in rough-and-tumble times than we believe. Although the two communities lived apart, coming together only to sing their Office in choir, many a group of monks obeyed an abbess rather than an abbot.

Perhaps men then were like their counterparts today, inclined to leave teaching and the small arts to women while they went about their business of making a living or waging war or bringing home the venison for the pot, so that abbesses were more likely to know Latin and Greek than their brothers. Or it might simply have been that women proved the better dormitory mistresses, less jealous of authority and better equipped to see to creature comforts. At any rate, Hilda was one of those abbesses, and a famous one. She was famous for her learning; she was renowned for her charity. She was celebrated as an educator and statesman. And this in the darkest period of what we call the Dark Ages, when, we are told, a woman knew little more than how to keep a fire burning under the kettle or the best way of mending her husband's tunic. It shows how histories disagree.

Hilda insisted on study. All her community read the Scriptures, and copied and pored over what books they could acquire in that long-ago time nearly eight hundred years before the invention of the printing press. They illuminated manuscripts. They worked at involved mathematical riddles. She herself, in addition to scholarship, labored at looking after the welfare of all who lived in the territory governed by her monastery. Bede writes that "not only ordinary people but even kings and princes asked and accepted her advice."

So highly was she regarded that when the Great Synod of 664 was called to decide on certain Church doctrine, Whitby was chosen on account of its reputation for learning. One wonders if Hilda's equal reputation for hospitality might not have also influenced the committees. Although she ate sparingly herself, she "kept a dainty table," and bishops are seldom averse to a tasty dinner.

But if Hilda had done nothing else worth reporting we could still love her for one famous deed. She came close to inventing English literature.

There lived in her abbey, as a servant, a man named Caedmon, who according to Bede had never been able to sing or to play the harp until in a dream someone called him by name, saying "Caedmon, sing to me."

"What shall I sing?" he asked.

"Sing me of Creation," came the answer, and Caedmon at once began "to sing in praise of God."

The dreamer mentioned his new gift to the alderman of the town; the alderman told Hilda. And Hilda at once took him under her motherly wing.

"Then the Abbess began to accept and to love the gift of God to this man and she advised him that he leave the world and receive monkhood; and he consented to that gladly. And," continues Bede, "his song and his poetry were so winsome that his teachers wrought and learned at his mouth."

It may be that Hilda personifies all women everywhere who have been accused of inheriting no genius comparable to man's. Perhaps like her they have been kept so occupied persuading men to sing or to paint or to explore the stars, that they have had little time to conquer the arts themselves. Certainly literature would have been poorer without Hilda's patronage of the first native English poet.

Hilda is only the most eminent of dozens of great abbesses who ruled and dispensed justice and kept learning alight during those dark old times. Elburga, Radegund, Agnes, Hildegard, Mildred — one could count them off like a litany. There was Lioba, already mentioned, who thought nothing of following her cousin, Saint Boniface, into the astonishing wilderness of Germany to convert the pagans there, and to whom all of Hesse and Saxony came "in peril of fire and tempest and sickness." There was Caesaria, who fourteen hundred years ago drew up a course of study for her community and saw to it that they "studied two hours of every day." There was Walburga, who practiced skillfully such medicine as existed in the eighth century and suffered after death an unusual fate. She was one of the band of brave women who accompanied Lioba on her travels, and she became as renowned on the Continent as in her native England. But her name took on a sea change in the northern countries, where the most common version of it is Walpurgis. It was on her feast day, evidently, that wild revels of Walpurgis Night took place, a queer tribute to this kindly saint.

Saint Audrey, the abbess of Ely, suffered an even quainter metamorphosis. She reigned over a populous community in the seventh century and must have been one of the most beloved of Anglo-Saxon holy people, since so many old churches in England are named for her. Whatever else she did, she added an adjective to the language. Her feast, like Walburga's, was kept with such enthusiasm for many years that, like other holy days which turn into a time for secular romping, June 23 became famous for its annual fairs. The fairs drew customers and the customers wanted things to buy; so cheap necklaces and other trumperies were always on sale, and eventually the name "Saint Audrey" was corrupted into "tawdry." It seems a poor memento for a useful life.

But not all feminine saints were prioresses. Margaret of Scotland entered no convent and took no vows. She was a mother, a wife, and a queen who ran her realm, Scotland, like the talented headmistress of a turbulent boarding school. "Margaret," says one biographer, "had queenship thrust upon her." When she was a girl of not much more than twelve, in 1057, she was sent to the English court of Edward the Confessor to be reared and educated. After Edward died and the Normans reigned in England, Margaret took refuge in Scotland with Malcolm Canmore, called "the Great Leader." Margaret was "as good as she was beautiful," and Malcolm fell in love with her. He was an exemplary soldier but not much of a courtier or a scholar, and it took his pretty Queen some years to tame him. As a matter of fact, although she taught him to leave off his rougher ways, to go to church, to "be attentive to the works of justice, mercy, almsgiving, and other virtues," he seems never to have learned to read. But "he would turn over and examine books which the Queen used either for her devotions or her study; and whenever he heard her express especial liking for a particular book, he also would look at it with special interest, kissing it and often taking it into his hands." What an appreciative husband he appears to have been!

Indeed, there in the eleventh century, he seems a prototype of all those husbands whom psychologists rather scold today. He fought the wars but Margaret did the ruling. She had a strange, disturbed country for her domain. The clergy kept to their Celtic calendars and observed their Celtic feasts instead of following the Latin pattern. The people were wild, superstitious, and ignorant. Highwaymen flourished, common as heather on the moors, and a traveler went in fear of his life. Margaret stirred herself to root out as many evils as one woman could manage in a lifetime. She insisted on education for both clergy and lay people. She built hostels for strangers, ransomed captives, founded almshouses and hospitals for the sick and the poor. She was politician, statesman, mother-confessor to the land. Like Hilda, she also presided over a great synod which separated the Celtic Church from its old practices and wrestled it into line with the rest of Christendom. "It was Margaret's tremendous achievement," says one authority, "to open her doors to the full wealth of the Western European tradition, not by way of conquest and bloodshed but by the joyous generosity that is the gift of the saint."

She was also a pioneer in another sphere. Bands of women met together at her invitation to study, discuss the Scriptures, and embroider vestments and altar cloths for the churches. So we can call Margaret the inventor of the Women's Club.

She had a further capability, one perhaps rarer even than her other gifts. She was a wise mother. "Her children surpassed in good behavior many who were their elders; they were always affectionate and peaceable among themselves." Across ten centuries I, for one, salute her. No wonder she was able to bequeath to her adopted country "the happiest two hundred years of its history."

But, one might argue, thrones make greatness possible. Besides, Margaret lived during the Middle Ages, before the strictures and anxieties of urbanized civilization had hardened nations and religion into rigid formalism. Contrary to superstition, the society of her time was an open one. Ideas flowed freely from country to country. Christian spoke to infidel with less than anger. Women held both pride and place. By the fourteenth century things had changed enough to corrupt an innocent and universal Christianity and to push many women back into a sort of purdah.

The most shining name of that troubled century, however, is that of Catherine, Siena's saint and still most famous citizen. And she was neither noble nor a scholar. She at whose bidding princes put down their arms and popes changed their ways of life was born in 1347, the youngest of the twenty-five children of Giacomo Benincasa, a dyer, and his wife Lapa. Poor Lapa. She has not come off very well at the hands of biographers. They make her out a temper-ridden woman, cross and sharp-tongued. But having to cope with twenty-five lively children as well as a disobedient mystic seems to me excuse enough for a hard word now and then.

Actually, her only faults appear to have been that same quick tongue and the perfectly natural ambition that her yellow-haired Catherine should make a good marriage. She was no visionary but a mother, and she could not for the life of her understand why her daughter should be plagued with extravagant holiness. One fancies her saying to herself, "Adolescents! Forever dramatizing themselves! We'll see what a bit of discipline will do for those day dreams."

So she nagged the girl to marry until Catherine in a gesture of defiance cut off all her beautiful hair. Any mother might well be annoyed at that, and Lapa did her best to exorcise what she thought of as the devil out of her stubborn child. She set her doing the hardest work of the household, deprived her of her bedroom, and forced her to wait on the rest of the family like a servant. Catherine, however, was a match for her peppery parent. She simply did as she was told so charmingly that in frustration her father and finally her mother gave way in everything. Catherine was allowed to lead her own extraordinary life — to shut herself up to prayer and meditation in a little cell of her own. Almost all saints begin so. They spend an early time of physical inactivity and mystical exercise, like athletes preparing for a contest. Indeed, that is what they are: athletes of the spirit. Catherine was a prodigy, and long before she was twenty her preparations were done and she left her cell to begin a mission to the world.

At first she went into the hospitals and the houses of the poor. A plague swept Italy, and she nursed the sick with the same single-mindedness she had expended on her prayers. The sweetness of her nature and the success of her work so endeared her to Siena that in a year or two she became the center of a group of notable disciples. This fellowship, called the Caterinati, consisted of "old and young, priests and laymen, poets and politicians," most of whom she had rescued from lives of illness, idleness, or vice. One of them was the artist Andrew Vanni, who painted the portrait we still have of her. Another was Neri de Landoccio, the poet. The rest followed a dozen different professions. They were united only as followers of this indomitable girl whom they affectionately called "Mama" although she was younger than any of them.

From Siena her fame spread to all of Italy and eventually to the rest of Europe. She advised kings. She intervened between political war parties. She helped draw up treaties of peace. At this time the Pope was living in exile in Avignon, and Rome had nearly fallen apart for lack of central government. Catherine performed the tremendous feat of coaxing a timorous pontiff back to his proper see in the face of hostility and the arguments of France, which preferred that the Pope live in its sphere of influence. Although Catherine never learned to write, she did learn to dictate, and her letters, addressed to half the great of Europe, are famous for their persuasive skill and boldness of insight. She also composed two books, *The Dialogues of Catherine* and *A Treatise of Divine Providence,* which theologians for years discussed and pondered.

She died at thirty-three, so renowned that she has been called "the greatest woman in Christendom." The whole world wept for her. Her character was so original and inflexible that she does not come through to us so delightfully as does, say, Teresa. But her political and moral triumphs were as enormous as her personal prestige. The historian who belittles feminine talent before the eighteenth century is unwise to overlook her.

Catherine, although all the civilized earth was affected by her life, scarcely ever left home. Mother Javouhey, fifth in this gallery of the great, scarcely ever stopped traveling.

Like the Apostle Paul, she found herself "in journeys often," sailing back and forth across oceans, making her way through jungles and forests and fever-teeming swamps, riding when she could, walking when she must, tramping the roads of earth like a saint and a soldier. Indeed, "General Javouhey" was her nickname in France. Her principal work lay among Africans and Indians, among the slaves, colonists, and savage tribes whom France had recently taken under treaty in Martinique, Guadeloupe, Madagascar, Miquelon, Oceania, the Comoro Archipelago, French Guiana, and a dozen lesser islands. Land swarming with tropical snakes and insects, countries full of gold and of adventurers in search of gold, provinces of torrential rains or murderous heat — those were the parishes of this amazing woman, born Anne Marie Javouhey in 1779, in prosperous, wine-growing Burgundy.

Her father, Balthazar, was a well-to-do peasant with his own vines and acres. On the face of it one might think a Burgundian farm no place to foster a career of adventure, but Anne Marie, whom everybody affectionately called

"Nanette," grew up in an adventurous time, the time of Revolution and the Reign of Terror. In many ways France then was like France under the German Occupation twenty-five years ago. To be out of sympathy with the regime was to go in terror of one's life. There were a Resistance Force and an Underground movement, of which Burgundy was the center. Instead of sheltering British or American fliers as in the last war, the Javouheys and their neighbors rescued priests with a price upon their heads or members of titled families destined for the guillotine. As a child of twelve or thirteen, Nanette made quite a name for herself in the countryside, carrying messages, hiding the hunted under the very noses of the Secret Police, protecting fugitives fleeing to England. No wonder she was too restless to settle down later to a staid life as the wife of some substantial farmer or as her father's helper on the land. Balthazar had hoped for the latter. He called Nanette his "clever son" and said she was the best farmer in the family.

But saints' parents seem to have little say in the matter of their children's career. Nanette, once the Revolution was over, determined to follow a religious life where she could continue to help those in need of help. The habit of kindness thrives on practice. Charity is an infection hard to shake off. Since schools had been disrupted during the long troubles of France, the girl came to the conclusion that she could most usefully work among neglected children. And Balthazar was no Lapa. If his daughter insisted on feeding the hungry and teaching the illiterate, she should have her way. With a saintlike patience of his own he not only let her take vows and carry off her three sisters and a brother to do the same, but for a while constituted himself the prop and stay of Nanette's new little order of Saint Joseph of Cluny. He gave them a house. He would turn up with a wagonload of food, frequently in the nick of time, when the sisters had nothing left in the cupboard to eat.

After early trials, the order flourished. Mother Anne Marie grew famed as teacher, nurse, worker of wonders among the poor, the ill, and the insane. In the Napoleonic Wars she nursed French and Austrians impartially, an early Florence Nightingale. But oddly enough she had always dreamed of taking care of "black men." Opportunity came along, as it often does for genius. The governor of Bourbon Island had recently arrived in Paris with tales of ignorance, immorality, and squalor among settlers and natives there. Who in France was brave enough to undertake that mission? "I know just the person for you," said the Minister of the Interior. "Mother Javouhey. She hasn't an ounce of fear in her."

So began her years of work and wandering. Her mission started in Bourbon, went on to Senegal, embraced finally the entire African and South American empire of the French state. It would seem a miraculous accomplishment at any time. But remember that this was the early eighteen hundreds, the Jane Austen period of curls, fainting fits, and helpless femininity. The Sisters of Saint Joseph either were a hundred years ahead of their time or had never been told that they should faint and sigh. We have an amusing picture of what they did expect from themselves. When the Prince de Joinville visited their leper settlement in Guiana, he asked one of the sisters what he could give her as a gift. "Something really useful for you, Sister," he insisted. She asked — and got — a fine gun. After that her invalids had fresh game once or twice a week.

Mother Javouhey had many times to wish that "men were as resolute as women" when she was battling alone with her nuns in the jungle against climate, accident, and the incompetence of administrations. Still, it was a good time for Anne Marie's abilities. The Revolution, horror that it was, had still left behind one legacy of good — the idea of freedom for all peoples. Emancipation was in the air. . . . Man after man, governor after governor had already failed. Mother Javouhey set out to succeed where they had not.

She was successful in Bourbon and Senegal, even being asked by the British to take over their hospitals along with her own. She was successful in Guadeloupe, Martinique, Saint-Pierre, Pondicherry. She knew how to farm. She knew how to manage people. She was adept at country trades. First she set up hospitals and leper colonies; then she established schools. After that she began to train natives and settlers for the skills they needed to survive in an agricultural community. Not for nothing had Anne Marie learned to work in the fields with her father. Now she applied that knowledge to a new world.

"Grow rice for food," she told the colonists. "When you plant banana trees, place them twelve feet apart in all directions so that coffee can grow between them." She stocked the farms with fat cows, sheep, goats, pigs, donkeys. She built a brickyard so there would be material for houses and churches and town offices. Nothing was too large and nothing too small for Mother Javouhey to take an interest in, so long as it helped her flock.

Eventually she was asked to take on the most difficult task of all, the colonization of the Mana district in Guiana. It was a tremendous request. What she was expected to do was nothing less than to bring civilization to the most primitive forests of South America. No one had plans to offer her, only a chart of repeated failures. Anne Marie invented her own plan and it was masterful. With thirty-six nuns, a number of French artisans, and fifty Negro laborers, she set out for Guiana and in four years had there a prosperous settlement. As she civilized, she also extended her deeds of mercy, buying up runaway slaves to save them from the lash, healing the sick, founding villages for lepers — all as part of the day's work. Once the colony was self-sustaining, she sailed home, only to be asked at once to return to Guiana.

The government proposed to free a group of slaves in Mana and to permit them to be citizens. But they must be taught to read and write and work. Would Mother Javouhey undertake this task — invent, as it were, a master chart for liberation everywhere?

She would and she did. Back she sailed to beard the wrath of French planters, who did not at all like being deprived of cheap slave labor. Considering the temper of the times, it is rather as if a woman were to set out to teach hostile Afrikaners how to do away with apartheid. Angry planters even bribed someone to upset a boat with Mother Javouhey in it. She proved unsinkable. What she did do was found a state within a state. She selected six hundred natives, to whom she taught reading, writing, religion, and mechanical and africultural arts. When in 1838 they were solemnly freed, a sum of money, a piece of land, and a cottage were waiting for each family — arranged for by Anne Marie. Eventually all of Mana became a free colony under her supervision and the Negroes gained the right to elect their delegate to the French Parliament. To a man they cast their votes for Mother the French Parliament. To a man they cast their votes for Mother Javouhey. When it was explained that a woman could not sit for them, they refused to cast a ballot at all. . . .

She was only one of a long tradition. The peculiar genius which is sanctity has for two thousand years been finding an outlet for its energies. She and hundreds of abbesses and prioresses and queens and peasant-saints had spent their lives proving that compassion and kindness, as well as greatness, are the special prerogatives of neither sex.

No influential women before the eighteenth century? Again, nonsense! There have been towering women since the world was invented.

# 10. *A Case of Identity* ●━○━●━○━●━○━●━○━●━○━●━○━●━○━●━○━●━○━●━○━(

> We must separate the instinctive
> equipment from the stereotypes.
>
> WALTER LIPPMANN

The assumption of unambiguous norms in history, that things "have always been that way," is rooted in an even deeper conviction that woman has always been "that way," that is, in durance to her organism. To test this assumption, one must ask to what extent it is biologically imperative and to what extent it is socially relevant. This implies a consideration of the concept of the weaker sex as it relates to differentials of physical strength and of generative function, for together they are viewed as universal constants debarring women, by definition, from independent social range and from integrated social role.

With respect to strength and stature, it has been demonstrated (1) that secondary sex characteristics are greatly affected by cultural factors, and (2) that despite such differentials, women have never been exempt from heavy labor. With respect to reproduction and rearing, revolutions of fertility choice and population pressure imply entirely new patterns of human increase. Yet custom regarding woman's place, and laws regarding woman's mating — and its consequences — continue to be rooted in the philosophy of woman as a body who belongs to somebody. Perhaps in this era of equalization, however, we are on the verge of discovering that women and men are alike in their humanness, that all children are our children, that together we are wrapped in the same bundle of destiny.

*Parallel readings for Chapter 10, "The Living Fossil."

Ethel Albert, using the data of anthropology, points to the varied patterns of institutional role that contravene assumptions of biological determinism, and concludes that with femaleness, as with other external signs, one cannot learn about persons from physical appearances. That is not to say there is no difference between the sexes, only that it is not *the* difference, the *decisive* difference that distinguishes human beings. "What remains problematic is this: for any physical-biological difference, what difference does the difference make?" Biology makes us male and female; society makes us men and women. And society is a variable organism.

Laurel Limpus, reflecting the reasoning of Reich and of Marcuse (and speaking for one segment of the new Women's Liberation Movement), also dissents from biological determinism, which she sees as a social myth aimed at human repression. She regards the idea that child bearing and rearing are women's destiny — and can constitute complete fulfillment in life — as the most destructive myth of all, for it not only imprisons women but also mutilates children. In searching for the causes of such myths and distortions, and for their effects in arrested development and sexual neurosis, the author points to the institutional framework. Society, according to Reich, systematically produces people — through the agency of the family — who are incapable of love and sexual surrender because it needs such people to perpetuate itself in its present patterns of mechanized existence. Society, according to Marcuse, requires suppression for continued survival and effective control. Psychological imperatives are thus related to social needs, and even sexual repression is dictated by the Reality Principle. In this view differentials presented as aspects of nature are not in fact absolutes. On the whole, we have here an analysis of hope, for it suggests that such differentials and their heritage of distortions are subject to change in a reconstituted society.

## The Roles of Women

*Ethel M. Albert*

Objectivity is one of the first requirements of scientific study. But who is qualified to make an objective investigation of women? Merely being a woman is not in itself a promising qualification. First, nobody seems quite sure what a woman really is. Second, any favorable statement about women by a woman

From "The Roles of Women: Question of Values," in Seymour M. Farber and Roger H. L. Wilson (eds.), *Man and Civilization: The Potential of Woman* (New York, 1963), pp. 105–115. Copyright 1963 by McGraw-Hill, Inc. Used by permission of McGraw-Hill Book Company.

is suspect as either wishful thinking or blind loyalty to her sex. But any negative statement about women by a woman is suspect as cattiness or sick self-hatred. On the other hand, merely being a man, that is, not being a woman, is hardly a more likely qualification. If a man speaks well of women, he is suspect as uxorious. But if he speaks out against them, he is neurotic or worse. Not being female, moreover, men are necessarily excluded from direct access to some of the primary data. Yet, every investigator is either a man or a woman, whatever these terms designate.

Objectivity in the study of women will then be, at best, difficult to achieve. In this, however, the study of women is not essentially different from any study of human beings by human beings. The dilemma is the same: How can we be objective about our own kind? How can we really understand those from whom we are very different? The resolution is in the selection of a suitable frame of reference and suitable objectives and methods of inquiry. The necessary degree of objectivity can be achieved by attending to the object studied. Making explicit the assumptions of inquiry is prerequisite to clarity, and cross verification by different investigators neutralizes the distorting effects of the personal equation. Sufficient progress in the study of humanity has now been made to justify optimism as to the possibility of objective studies of women. Despite the expression of misgivings and doubts by some, women are human, and the study of women is part of the study of human behavior and human nature. The same techniques can be and are being used. Qualified observers *may* be either male or female; they *must* be well trained in the methods and theory of their specialization.

Approaching the study of women through the social-behavioral sciences is, of course, only one of many ways of dealing with the topic. In no small part, objectivity requires keeping a safe distance from such other approaches as those of the poet lamenting the perfidy of a lost love; of politicians seeking the women's vote; of legislators debating the issue of equal pay for equal work; of a particular woman coming to terms with the problems generated by the particular society she lives in; to say nothing of the husband and wife discussing — if that is the correct word — the relative merits of a trip to Europe or a quiet spell at a hunting lodge for this year's vacation. There is no necessary incompatibility among the different ways of dealing with the character, nature, and roles of women. Each is surely legitimate, but all are different in goal and method. We are far from clarity about the possible interrelations of the esthetic, practical, legal, political, personal, and scientific approaches to this or to any other human subject. Here, the concern is entirely with the social-behavioral-science study of women and with the data and theory of anthropology in particular, as they affect the scientific quest for reliable information and theory about human behavior, including woman's behavior.

Instead of attempting to relate the different ways of approaching the question of woman's nature, let us attempt to relate the investigation of woman as such to other inquiries that have started from some biological characteristic as the basis for the description and prediction of behavior. Perhaps "pseudobiological" is the better term in the present context. For, biology as science is very different from traditional notions associated with simplistic theories of biological determinism. Specifically, we are confronted by an ancient and honorable but naive and unscientific way of classifying human beings according to easily visible differences and with a causal theory that such visible differences as those of gender, or skin color, or height of forehead, or other physical traits are a reliable index to intelligence, artistic ability, mechanical aptitude, emotional stability, leadership skills and other critical characteristics of persons.

Some categories are less useful than others for scientific purposes, when we mean by scientific purposes adequate description and prediction, and when the utility of a category is defined as follows: the characteristic chosen to define the category is a good predictive index of other shared characteristics. We can be quite sure that red hair is not a reliable index to ill temper; that fatness does not predict jollity; that skin color, while it is a useful index to probable color of eyes and hair, proportion of limbs to body, and the like, has no predictive value for intelligence, skills, or any other personal or behavioral characteristics. A study of woman, conducted on the assumption that gender predicts significantly no non-sex-linked phenomena is almost certain to be a scientific failure. What do we know about a human being, when we know the gender? We can assert with confidence that if any person is a mother, that person is surely a woman, or, at least, is surely female. The same certainty attaches to statements about individuals designated as wife, sister, daughter, aunt, mother-in-law, daughter-in-law. They are bound to be female — though a few seem to have arrived at this enviable status via Copenhagen and the surgeon's knife. But we cannot judge whether any of them are intelligent or stupid, mentally well or ill, tenderhearted or tough as nails, industrious or lazy, attractive or ugly, happy or wretched. And if we do not know these things, we do not know much of value. With femaleness, as with skin color or height of forehead or other external signs, we cannot learn about persons from appearances.

Let me hasten to offer this reassurance. I am not at all asserting, as did overzealous egalitarians of a generation ago, that there is no difference between male and female. This is rather to overstate the case. I am unconditionally on the side of those who say, "*Vive la difference.*" That males and females are different from each other at least physiologically is one of the few relatively clear and simple facts of life. But the male-female difference is *a* difference, not *the* difference. What remains problematic is this: for any physical-biological difference, what difference does the difference make? This is the crucial question for interpreting the behavioral significance of any physiological characteristic singled out for special study. And it is here that the simplistic pseudobiological categories fail.

The rejection of broad, obvious categories like race or sex or body type is perfectly compatible with the view that physiological factors are indispensable elements in the description and prediction of human nature and behavior. Long-standing arguments about biological determinism as opposed to some sort of antibiological or nonphysical determinism only get in the way of clarity. All human behavior is biological; but it is never only that. Mankind is a sociocultural being. Biological variations and sociocultural variations, not simplified stereotypes, are the object of serious, scientific inquiry. What any individual becomes depends in part on nature and in part on sociocultural values and ideal role-models, as these are worked out in the specific circum-stances of each individual life history. For the study of sex differences, we may say that nature — biology, if you will — makes us male or female; the values and norms of the society in which we develop make us men or women; and the interrelations of these factors with the other biological, sociological, and situational components of experience make us the kinds of persons we become. No single factor explains the complex totality of any individual personality or of the human species.

A sampling of anthropological data will help us to judge what behavioral difference the biological male-female difference makes. The relevant data are scattered throughout the voluminous monographic literature of anthropology, for the description of any society must include a description of its women as well as its men. A systematic assembling of data and some illuminating inter-pretations may be found in Margaret Mead's study, *Male and Female*. Even a very small selection of the ideas and ideals of the feminine found in other societies than our own is illuminating, and so too is an examination, however cursory, of the curious interrelations of cultural ideals with situational and behavioral realities. Such data are useful for developing theory, but they may also suggest the kinds of information to look for when we face the hard task of studying the place of woman in our own culture.

No human society overlooks so patent a biological contrast as that between male and female. But we find cross-cultural differences of great magnitude in what various societies think is female nature, as distinct from male nature; in what different societies construct as the ideal woman and the ideal man; and, if that were not diversity enough, we find that everywhere actual behavior is permitted to diverge to a greater or lesser degree from society's ideals and role-models.

First things first. Let us start with this question: is the male or the female by nature the more sexually agressive? As every nice girl in Western culture knows, it is the male who is the aggressor, while the passive female submits with good or bad grace. But if we ask this question of Africans or of American Indians, we do not get the same reply. Obviously, they tell us, women are more driven by sex than men. Among the Zuni Indians as among ourselves, there are stories of fearful newlyweds facing up to the terrors of the first night of marriage. But the Zuni stories feature the groom, not the bride, in a state of fear. I suspect that not a few males from other societies, possibly even our own, understand the Zuni groom's sentiments very well, but unlike the Zuni, they have been brought up to believe that the male is the fearless aggressor and that any display or feeling of fear is unmasculine. Now, I do not know which version is "biologically" true. Perhaps social expectations work on nature's endowment, which is probably variable to begin with, so that some grow up hot, some grow up cold, and those fare best whose biology is in harmony with the prevailing sociocultural notion about what is natural.

Next question: which of the sexes is by nature better fitted for heavy manual labor? In the madonna-and-child value system of middle- and upper-class European and American culture, it is plain that women are the more delicate, the weaker sex. Heavy work is for men, in fact, for he-men, who are more muscular, stronger, and generally coarser. But if we change the social stratum or continent or historical era, the pale, delicate, weaker sex disappears from view. In the not so remote American past, pioneer women were and had to be strong, quick on the trigger when the Indians raided, able and willing to help with farming and other heavy chores. In any peasant or subsistence economy, past and present, women are considered as fit as men for hard manual labor. The chief agricultural labor force of Africa is its women, and it is generally believed that women are better suited than men for hard work. This among other lessons about the presumed biological nature of men and women was brought home to me during a research stint in Central Africa some years ago. My African neighbors had become accustomed to the idea that my country engaged in all manner of nonsensical practices. They were usually tactfully tolerant, but when I said that in my country, it was the men who did the heavy work, that women were not considered fit for it, they did not conceal disapproval. This was a mistake, they maintained. Everybody knows that men are not suited by nature for heavy work, that women are stronger and better workers. Men drink too much and do not eat enough to keep up their strength; they are more tense and travel about too much to develop the habits or the muscles needed for sustained work on the farms. And this was all confirmed by observation of actual behavior. It should be noted that the society in question was an old-fashioned patriarchal feudal kingdom, in which nobody had ever heard of equality of the sexes.

Emotional stability is another axis of variation. It is obvious, to some, that women are by nature less stable emotionally than men, that it is natural for women to cry easily and otherwise show their feelings, whereas men are more easily able to control and conceal them. But again, the belief about what is natural and whether observed behavior corresponds to belief depend on where we happen to be. Edward T. Hall, in his book, *The Silent Language*, offers as his illustration of this point the views of male-female difference in Iran. There — in a thoroughly patriarchal society, where men are deemed the superiors of women — it is expected that women will be practical, cool, and calculating, whereas men are expected to show emotions, to be sensitive and intuitive, to prefer poetry to logic. And so it is.

The last item we shall look at for a general idea of diversity in views of male and female nature is intelligence. In a comparison of an American Indian community—the Zuni mentioned above—with a nearby group of Anglo-Americans, an investigating anthropologist made this assumption: if Anglo-Americans, living in a society in which the male is the dominant, superior sex, generally believe that men are intellectually superior to women, then the Zuni, living in a matrilineal society where decisions are made by women, would believe that women are intellectually superior to men. But projecting our culture-bound views or merely reversing them is not sound procedure. The Zuni replies to the question "Which are more intelligent, men or women?" took this general form: "Well, some men are more intelligent than some women, and some women are more intelligent than some men. That's because some men are intelligent and some are not, and some women are intelligent and some are not." Any comment on such a judicious verdict could be only an anticlimax.

To present further cases would only be to labor the point: there is universal recognition of differences between males and females—let us be thankful for small favors—but whatever the differences, they are not so strikingly uniform that human beings everywhere must come to the same conclusions about them. We have, moreover, a hint of part of the answer to the question "What difference does a difference make?" What is believed to be true of the nature of males and females influences significantly the content of ideal models constructed for the formation of character. Within a given society, there is a statistical tendency to develop according to socially defined ideals of appropriate behavior. But viewing humanity on a world-wide scale, we find no consensus. Again, nature makes us male or female, but the beliefs and values of our society make us the kinds of men or women we become. It would nonetheless be again erring in the direction of oversimplification to assert, as some social scientists have done, that observed behavior is fully explicable by social definitions of roles. Each individual perforce has a multiplicity of biological characteristics, sexual and otherwise, which may or may not be compatible with role expectations. Actual behavior is the product of complex and usually unconscious negotiations among the demands of diverse roles and diverse individual characteristics. In the dynamics of everyday life, there is much more room for individuality than is suggested by descriptions of societal norms and ideals. Permissiveness with respect to departures from established norms varies from one place to another. However, in no society is there a demand for complete conformity. Secondary norms are regularly set up to permit scope to the multiplex character of any concrete individual.

For at least a preliminary view of the complicated relationship between a cultural ideal of woman and the behavorial realities, I am much indebted to my friends, male and female, in the African Kingdom I mentioned briefly above. What follows is drawn from my paper, "The Status of Women in Burundi," in a volume on *Women of Tropical Africia*. As I said, this is an old-fashioned, feudal, patriarchal society in the grand manner. Women may not call their husbands by their given names, for this would be lacking in respect. They serve their husbands from a kneeling position. Political power, judicial rights, ownership and inheritance of cattle and lands, and the right of independent action are traditionally for men only. A wife is paid for, so that the husband owns all the children borne by the woman during the marriage and has a right to her labor on his farms and in the home. Obedience, fertility, graciousness as a hostess, industriousness, respect for her husband are among the chief feminine virtues. All this and more is taken as serious, literal truth by men and women alike, irrespective of caste, age, or other variables. Yet, in point of fact, there are women — and not a few — who enjoy considerable authority, who own or control cattle, lands, and other forms of wealth, command large numbers of feudal inferiors, and in general realize the central values presumably intended only for their fathers and brothers. There are many charming but formidable matriarchs who rule with an iron will all those who come within their reach. Unstinted admiration is accorded to women who succeed. It seems not to have occurred to anyone that such women are unwomanly or unfeminine. What a woman cannot do as a woman she manages very well indeed to do as a person, as a member of her society.

The scope of feminine activity in Burundi is limited rather by caste than by sex, for wealth and power are distributed that way. Still, even the poorest woman can be a politician on the scale permitted by her circumstances. What is needed are the personal qualities of cleverness, ambition, energy, courage, and application — and, incidentally, men willing to do one's bidding for a share of the profits. There are always a good many of them available for projects, large and small.

A woman of Burundi who has just served her husband his dinner from the accepted kneeling position will, on leaving the house, order about her workmen or servants with the greatest authority and efficiency. This is part of her job, and there is no conflict. Each role requires different behavior, and any reasonably socialized individual goes from one to the other as naturally as breathing. While all agree that men are supposed to be more intelligent and emotionally stable than women, exceptions are readily recognized, and a stupid husband values a clever wife. Intelligence is not to be wasted. When it is applied to the advantage of husband or father or local ruler, it is duly rewarded. By the exercise of good judgment, by giving good advice, a woman earns gifts of cattle and lands. Her voice will be heard in private conclave and respected — but in public, women do not depart from the ideal of modest silence in the presence of men. There are no love songs in the otherwise rich poetic tradition of Burundi; but when a wife has proven intelligent, capable, and loyal, her husband composes a praise-poem for her, of the same form used to praise princes and generous patrons.

To be sure, there is a seamy side. Many women are not especially bright, and nobody seeks their advice and gives them gifts to reward them for judicious decisions. Some intelligent women, instead of helping their husbands, plot against them and destroy them. Many who find father, brother, or husband less than tractable take control of the affections of a son, in such fashion that Momism, Burundi style, makes the American version look very tame indeed. We need not go into the high cost of patriarchal systems. The point to be made is clear. Even — perhaps especially — where sex-linked role-models are rigid, individual differences are in fact permitted scope for activities which are not in accord with the ideal models but which are nevertheless socially acceptable, even praiseworthy.

What conclusions can we draw, from our brief excursion into other cultures, about women, real and ideal, in our own society and about the potential of woman? An adequate descriptive account of women would have to include the variety of beliefs about the nature of women, the variety of ideal role-models assigned to women as women but also to women as persons, and the crooked course of the flow of actual behavior relative to ideal models. Even within one society, there is so high a degree of heterogeneity in the actualities that one is led to suspect that although there are millions of females in this world, there is no such thing as "woman." To study "woman," or even "women," is to study a figment of our traditional classification of humanity. For, if anything is true of "woman," it must be true of women in all times and places. To study women as female persons is another matter. Specifically feminine roles and characteristics can then be viewed in their relationship with other types of roles and characteristics, and these all add up to meaningful totals.

Studies of women in Western culture encounter a peculiar problem. In most societies, ideals are kept within hailing distance of realities. They are understood as prescribing and proscribing behavior, thus as limiting development by channeling it. In the Western tradition, however, ideals tend to be so far above and beyond common reality that their realization is not likely, except perhaps in the rare instance. They are thought to elevate their object, to give it wings to raise it above the common. Denis de Rougemont, in his study of love in the western world, gives us a sensitive historical account of the development of the romantic ideal and a somber sociological analysis of the damage done to both sexes by the etherealization of the female. Mere flesh and blood — or, if you will, "a rag, a bone and a hank of hair" — what can any woman do to bring to reality the fictions and fancies that have gone into the construction of "the ideal woman"? It is perhaps momentarily flattering to be raised high on a pedestal, but the higher the pedestal, the harder the bump when it crumbles beneath the weight of realities. It is probably a sign of great esteem to idealize any object. But those of us who have read some history profoundly mistrust idealizers. What has been done to human beings in the name of ideals of religion, of civilization, of progress, is painful to contemplate. Ideals of "true femininity," of "woman," of "motherhood," are emotionally pleasing, but they, too, are suspect as selfish, unconsidered wish-fulfillment for the idealizer, as delusive flattery for the idealized that can all too easily become merciless mutual exploitation.

Extravagant glorification is not the remedy for traditional degradation. Exploration of the potential of women is part of the world-wide exploration of the potential of humanity generally. Ideals too easily realized do not sufficiently spur us on to optimum growth. But we must distinguish between ideals which stimulate constructive action and the fictional products of dreams and unfulfilled needs. Impossible ideals do not bring out the best in us. They are as restrictive and deforming as the worst kind of tyranny. The construction of viable ideals for the future requires reliable factual information about humankind, male and female, not to cut down ideals to what has been achieved or can be done without much effort but rather to fit them to what can be achieved in fact, rather than in fancy, and to provide some assurance that we will be protected against the disappointments that flights from reality almost surely bring in their train. Being fully human is a high enough ideal for all; it contains the potential for woman and the potential for man, inextricably linked together. By all means, let imagination and hope soar, but untrammeled by false notions and untroubled by false problems.

# Sexual Repression and the Family

*Laurel Limpus*

This is an attempt to deal with some of the theoretical problems of the liberation of women, particularly as they relate to sexuality and sexual repression Obviously the problem of sexuality is a dual one: when I speak of female liberation, I mean liberation from the myths that have enslaved and confined women in their own minds as well as in the minds of others; I don't mean liberation from men. Men and women are mutually oppressed by a culture and a heritage that mutilates the relationships possible between them.

One of the reasons we find it difficult to deal with the problem of female

From "Sexual Repression and the Family," *Liberation of Women* (Spring 1969). Boston: New England Free Press.

liberation is because the problem is so pervasive, so all encompassing; it involves the total realm of bourgeois consciousness. We are facing oppression that is both psychological and ideological; it concerns people's definitions of themselves and of each other and of the roles that are possible between them. It is, therefore, difficult for us to grasp it with any theoretical rigor and clarity. The problem is compounded by the fact that women make up a very peculiar social group: they are not a class; their position of oppression is unique; and the mental repression that stifles them stifles at the same time the men who on the surface appear to be their oppressors.

Juliet Mitchell, in her article, "Women: The Longest Revolution," has summed up the peculiarly unique situation of women as a group very well:

> They are not one of a number of isolable units, but half a totality: the human species. Women are essential and irreplaceable; they cannot therefore be exploited in the same way as other social groups can. They are fundamental to the human condition, yet in their economic, social and political roles, they are marginal. It is precisely this combination — fundamental and marginal at one and the same time — that has been fatal to them.

## 1

The central problem is that this society had produced an image and a mythology of women that has deprived them of their humanity and creative role in society. For a variety of reasons, one of the central agents of this oppression has been the institution of the family. Many factors come together when we look at the family. For one thing, as we shall see later, the family seems, at the present time, to be the primary agent of sexual repression in this society. For another, it is by defining women primarily within the family that this society has deprived her of her humanity and her creativity. If women are to liberate themselves, they must come squarely to grips with the reality of the family and the social forces that have produced it at this particular period in history.

Both Simone de Beauvoir in *The Second Sex* and Juliet Mitchell have stressed what I have found to be [a] very useful distinction between the mythologized roles of men and women: using de Beauvoir's terminology for a moment, men are encouraged to play out their lives in the realm of transcendence, whereas women are confined to immanence. This simply means that men work, create, do things, are in positions of authority, create their own histories; whereas women are confined to the home, where their function is not to create, but to maintain: Women keep house and raise children. Of course the reality is not quite like this, since work in capitalist society is usually alienating, stifling, and stunting, and most men engaging in it could hardly be described as creating their own histories by transcending themselves. Within the present social context, however, it is still true that men are trained to go out, work, shape their own lives; and that women are not, and that thus, even within the context of the alienating nature of their work, they often have more opportunities to satisfy their needs for creativity than do women. The point that must be made here is that ideologically men are urged towards creativity and that women are not. As Juliet Mitchell says:

> But women are offered a universe of their own: the family. Like woman herself, the family appears as a natural object, but it is actually a cultural creation. There is nothing inevitable about the form or role of the family any more than there is about the character or role of women. *It is the function of ideology to present these given social types as aspects of nature herself.* (Emphasis mine.)

Mitchell's use of the word ideology here is very important, because now she is talking about the dimension of consciousness; she is saying that women are ideologically oppressed; that they are defining themselves in a culturally created way which they believe is natural. The myth that women's natural place is in the home and that naturally she will find the fulfillment of her creativity in bearing and raising children and in submitting to a man is just that: a myth. More than that, it is a terribly destructive myth, like most of the mythology of bourgeois society. As long as it is believed and adhered to by women as well as by men, it systematically destroys their real potential to develop as individuals rather than as marionettes. And I firmly believe that it is to women, and not to men, that this point has to be made, because the most disturbing aspect of this whole question is the extent to which *women* cling tenaciously to these very conceptions of themselves which stunt their humanity.

I want to consider first how a woman's role as a wife and the socializer of children acts as a stunting influence upon her creativity. Then I will look at the very complex question of the repression of female sexuality, and the resulting mutilation of male sexuality and the resulting disintegration of love relations in this society.

One of the most pervading conceptions in the present ideology is that the family is a natural, inevitable phenomenon. Once this is accepted, because of the apparent universality of the family, women are relegated automatically to a separate but (perhaps) equal status. As Mitchell says:

> The causal chain then goes: Maternity, Family, Absence from Production and Public Life, Sexual Inequality. The lynch-pin in this line of argument is the idea of the family.

It is the family, and the ideology that confines a woman to it, that prevents her from fully entering into the arena of production, not her relation to a man. A woman may still work while living with a man, although much of the mythology of the "wife" who maintains a home for her husband and lives for him and through him rather than for and through herself remains to be dealt with; but it is her relationship to her children which prevents her from seriously committing herself to a job. That doesn't mean, of course, that the job is going to be creative.

Most of the jobs open to most women are unpleasant — (waitresses, salesclerks, nurses, secretaries, clerks, typists, etc.). The mere opening up of job opportunities to women thus does not solve the problem of women in production. Further, the nature of these jobs often makes marriage seem more attractive, thus backing up the mythology. As Simone de Beauvoir says:

> Modern woman is everywhere permitted to regard her body as capital for exploitation. It is natural enough for many women workers and employees to see in the right to work only an obligation from which marriage will deliver them. As long as the temptations of convenience exist — in the economic inequality that favors certain individuals and the recognized right of woman to sell herself to one of these privileged men — she will need to make a greater moral effort than would a man in choosing the role of independence. It has not been sufficiently recognized that the temptation is also an obstacle, and even one of the most dangerous. Here it is accompanied by a hoax, because in fact there will only be one winner out of thousands in the lottery of marriage.

Marriage, finally, which is made to seem attractive and inevitable, is a trap. For girl children as well as mothers. Most women do not grow up to see themselves as producers, as creators — instead they see their mothers, their sisters, their women teachers, and they pattern themselves after them. They do not see women making history. As de Beauvoir says again:

> She has always been convinced of male superiority; this male prestige is not a childish mirage; it has economic and social foundations; men are surely masters of the world. Everything tells the young girl that it is for her best interests to become their vassal.

But to become a vassal, to live through another human being, is a deeply frustrating experience, and the subjected wife takes the revenge of the frustrated. Ultimately, it is a terrible revenge.

I should note here that much of this pattern of wifely subservience is changing, and I would like to make it quite clear that I am referring to those women (who still comprise a large part of the total population) who would define themselves as *wives* and who do not work or have another project. Their husbands have projects; they do not. They revenge themselves upon the agent of their own emptiness, and thus the man is mutilated by his supposedly subservient wife. I also want to make it clear that I am not talking about men *oppressing* women here. This is a situation which arises out of expectations and role definitions that are ideological and that imprison both men and women:

> "Men," writes de Beauvoir, "are enchained by reason of their very sovereignty; it is because they alone earn money that their wives demand checks; it is because

they alone engage in a business or profession that their wives require them to be successful; it is because they alone embody transcendence that their wives wish to rob them of it by taking charge of their projects and successes. If the wife seeks desperately to bend him to her will, it is because she is alienated in him. *He will free himself in freeing her.*" (Emphasis mine.)

Martha in "Who's Afraid of Virginia Woolf?" is exactly the kind of wife who is out to get her husband for both his transcendence and his lack of it. George's worldly failure is a constant source of humiliation to her for which she continually torments him. Her own energies have found no other outlet, except in fantasies of motherhood, which brings us to the next aspect of women's exploitation in the family.

The myth that childbearing and rearing is the fulfillment of a woman's destiny is by far, in my opinion, the most damaging and destructive myth that imprisons her. Having children is no substitute for creating one's own life, for producing. And since so many women in this culture devote themselves to nothing else, they end up by becoming intolerable burdens upon their children because in fact these children *are* their whole lives. Juliet Mitchell has caught the situation exactly:

> At present, reproduction in our society is often a kind of sad mimicry of production. Work in a capitalist society is an alienation of labour in the making of a social product which is confiscated by capital. But it can still sometimes be a real act of creation, purposive and responsible, even in conditions of the worst exploitation. Maternity is often a caricature of this. The biological product — the child — is treated as if it were a solid product. Parenthood becomes a kind of substitute for work, an activity in which the child is seen as an object created by the mother, in the same way as a commodity is created by a worker. Naturally, the child does not literally escape, but the mother's alienation can be much worse than that of the worker whose product is appropriated by the boss. No human being can create another human being. A person's biological origin is an abstraction. The child as an autonomous person inevitably threatens the activity which claims to create it continually merely as a *possession* of the parent. Possessions are felt as extensions of the self. The child as a possession is supremely this. Anything the child does is therefore a threat to the mother herself who has renounced her autonomy through this misconception of her reproductive role. There are few more precarious ventures on which to base a life.

So we have the forty-or fifty-year-old woman complaining to her grown child: "But I gave you everything," This is quite true; this is the tragedy. It is a gift the child hardly wanted, and indeed many children are daily mutilated by it. And it leaves women at the waning of their years with the feeling that they have been deceived, that their children are ungrateful, that no one appreciates them because they have come to the realization that they have *done* nothing.

This is not to say that there are not women who genuinely love their children or anything of the kind. It merely points out that the prevailing ideology leads many women into the mistake of thinking that having children will be the ultimate *project* (to use de Beauvoir's terminology again) of their lives. Just because women bear children does not *necessarily* mean that they must rear them. It certainly does not mean that this is *all* they should do. But this society has seen to it that there are no other institutions for the rearing of children except the nuclear family.

2

The second problem — that of repressed female sexuality — is so vast, unexplored and variegated that what I have to say only represents a few scattered thoughts largely taken from my own experience and those of my friends. I'll try later to relate them to the work of Marcuse and Wilhelm Reich.

The problem of sexuality again clearly illustrates that men and women are oppressed together in an institutional framework which makes inhuman demands of them and inculcates destructive beliefs about themselves. I want to stress, though, that we women shouldn't become obsessed with freeing ourselves from sick male sexuality. It is more important to free ourselves from the structures which make both male and female sexuality sick. The male definition of virility which makes woman an object of prey is just as much a mutilation of the human potential of the male for a true love relationship as it is of the female's. Although we as women experience this predatory attitude and are often outraged by it, we must realize that our own hangups often contribute to it, and that in any case we will get nowhere by venting our hostility upon men. We must both be liberated together, and we must understand the extent to which our fear and frigidity, which has been inculcated in most of us from infancy onwards and against which most of us have had to struggle for our sexual liberation, has hurt and mutilated them.

Since the myths emphasize male virility and female chastity, within the family men have been inculcated with predatory attitudes while women have been filled with profound sexual fear. From early infancy women have had deep sexual inhibitions instilled within them, and these fears and inhibitions are so tenacious that even when you consciously reject the morality of your parents, you often find that your body will not obey the dictates of your mind. You can believe in sexual freedom and still be frigid. For many years that was certainly true for me.

I have talked to very many women about this subject and have found that almost all of them have had the same experience or similar ones; they found that their ideas had changed, but that they still could not respond sexually. Many of these women, including myself, have finally succeeded in responding sexually, but only after a long and anguished period of doubt and fear and struggle. Many young girls, who feel only revulsion when they think they should feel ecstasy, react with immense relief when they are told that this is a quite common experience. Since of course this is not the kind of problem one ordinarily talks about, they did not know that anyone else had been through this, and they had thought that they were monsters.

The repression of these young women is matched only by their sexual ignorance, which is of course integrally related to it. When I went into the dorms at the University of Toronto to talk about birth control, about half of the girls there didn't understand the mechanics of menstruation. One of them asked me if when a man comes the sperm can actually be seen, like little tadpoles. This may sound funny, but it is really tragic. How will women like this react in a sexual situation, and what will be the effect upon the men who initiate them. Although there is a great deal of talk about sexual liberation and promiscuity floating around, my guess would be that the reality of the situation of many couples engaging in sexual relations is frigidity, fear, impotence, inhibition, and ignorance.

One of the most subtly destructive effects the myth of female chastity has had is to make women lie about the nature of their own sexuality. While the prevailing myths about virility make men feel they must be predatory, the prevailing myths about female sexuality often make even semi-liberated women demand to be treated as prey. This is a very complicated point; but I think it is important enough to be treated at length because it illustrates the interrelationship between male and female sexual sickness. Even though it is generally admitted even now that women have desires and are supposed to respond sexually, I have noticed that even in supposedly radical circles girls can still be labelled "promiscuous." There are tremendous residual moral condemnations of female sexuality in all of us, in spite of our radical rhetoric. A woman, even a relatively sexually liberated one, often finds it hard to approach a man sexually the way a man can approach her. Needless to say, less liberated women will be even more dishonest about their desires. A man I know once remarked that he knew few women who could look at him sexually (for example, stare at his genitals without embarrassment) the way he could look at a woman. I have found these residual fears in myself, and I know other women who experience the same thing. This means that since women will often be dishonest about their desires and encourage the man to pursue them, they force him to become the very predatory person that radical women object to.

Sexual repression is clearly structural, and the central agent of repression is the family, which has inculcated both the subservience of women and sexual taboos. From infancy onwards we are all subjected to this process, and this process is obviously related to the institutions of society.

Much of the resentment of liberated women against men is sexual, because they feel they are being treated as objects (as in fact they are). Fashion, advertising, movies, Playboy Magazine, all betray the fact that women are culturally conceived of as objects and, worse still, often accept this definition and try to make themselves into a more desirable commodity on the sexual market. We must remember, however, that every month some woman is more than willing to be the playmate of the month and that the problem exists in her consciousness as much as in that of the men who stare at her. This is ideology, self-definition, conscious acceptance of myths, and these things are related to institutions, to economic and social structures.

Wilhelm Reich and Herbert Marcuse both tried to deal with the institutional background of this mutilation of erotic life. While the *agent* of sexual repression and mutilation is the family, it reflects, in microcosm, the demands of society. Reich argues that our society is systematically producing people through the family who are incapable of love and sexual surrender because it needs such people in order to perpetuate itself. Parental repression in childhood, especially of sexuality, cuts down the vital vegetative side of life — the antithesis to the present mechanization of existence — and has led to the building in the individual of an intricate character armour. A neurosis has been created; and most of us share it. This armour is essentially fearful and protective, and prevents one from loving, because it keeps repressed and dammed up those life energies which would ordinarily flow outwards as love, which would let us surrender. So we fear love and sexuality, and are anxious and guilty about love-making.

Reich postulates that sexual orgastic impotence is directly related to the existence of this character armour, and that when this armour is broken down, the individual's loving, creative, and sexual energies are released. He also postulates that the neurotic character armoured individual is a necessity for the present authoritarian mechanized capitalistic society, and that people freed of this armour find that they can no longer function in this society as successfully as before:

> Quite spontaneously, patients began to feel the moralistic attitudes of the environment as something alien and queer. They began to feel a strong need for some vital work in which they could have a personal interest. If the work in which they were engaged lent itself to the absorption of real interest, they blossomed out. If, however, their work was mechanical, as that of an employee, a merchant or a clerk, it became an almost unbearable burden, and they felt a sharp protest of the organism against empty, mechanical work.

These same people also found themselves, because of their new sexual responsiveness, much more serious about the importance of interpersonal relationships than before:

> Their previous behavior had been the result of the fact that they experienced no sensations in the sexual act whatsoever; whereas now, they experienced full sensation in the act and therefore regarded it as an important part of their lives, not to be dealt with as lightly as their former behavior would indicate. That, in

other words, they became more "moral" in the sense of wanting only one partner
—one who loved and satisfied them.

Thus, a released sexuality appeared to lead not to the so-called promiscuity
of the frigid woman, but to the desire to establish a serious love relationship.

It is obvious that the changes that Reich observed in his patients who
became capable of full sexual response have deep social and political implications. As he says: "The picture presented at the end by all of them was that
of a different kind of society," namely one in which work was human and
creative, sexuality was unrepressed and spontaneous, and love relationships
replaced the present moralistic compulsive and often repressed marriage system. This leads Reich to hypothesize that the present system of sexual repression has a social function:

> The purpose of the demand for sexual abstinence is that of making the adolescent
> submissive and capable of marriage. The children destined for this kind of
> marriage are brought up in sexual abstinence; they show neuroses and those
> character traits with which we are familiar. Their sexual abstinence has the
> function of making them submissive. *Sexual suppression is an essential instru-*
> *ment in the production of economic enslavement.* (Emphasis mine.)

It is important to realize exactly what Reich is saying here. He is saying that
a society of sick individuals has been created, largely through the suppression
of sexuality, the life function, in order to create men fit to work in a social order
where the priorities are not human, but profit. He also makes it clear that in
order to change society we must also attempt to change the individuals created
by it: "The cultural revolution requires the alteration of the psychic structure
of the mass individual."

While this analysis may seem oversimplified to some, it clearly points in the
direction of the kind of exploration that has to be done about the social
function of sexual suppression.

Marcuse moves in the same direction, although in dealing with the question
of sexual suppression in its social context, he expands it throughout history.

Marcuse begins with what has been considered to be the Freudian idea that
the suppression of the libido at an early age is absolutely necessary for the
continuation of society; otherwise civilization would not continue to exist,
since men must work to survive, and the libido militates against work. Eros
uncontrolled is a fatal danger; therefore the history of mankind has been a
history of repression. This Freud formulates in the opposition of the Pleasure
and Reality principles: the first geared to erotic gratification and constantly
suppressed, finding relief in fantasy, art, or psychological distortions; the
second, the Reality principle, geared [to] the maintenance of civilization
through work. Marcuse, however, points out that all societies have been maintained according to certain systems of domination; certain classes have been
in control and have not worked. Therefore simply to postulate scarcity of

resources as the reason for sexual repression in order to make men work is not enough. He also points out that the advances of technology now make the argument of scarcity untenable, at least in the developed countries, and yet there is still repression.

In other words, technology would now make it possible for necessary work to be reduced to a minimum, and, if sexual repression persists, there must be some other reason for it than scarcity. This reason according to Marcuse is the interest of domination, and he calls the repression necessary for this surplus repression. Even though it would now be theoretically possible for men to be comparatively freed from work, they are still being suppressed to make them work. The Reality principle does not operate independently of history; it is not just the fact, but also the *organization* of scarcity, that creates repression. In other words, as Reich also said, psychological realities are related to political needs, and men are being sexually repressed in order to exploit them.

As Reich does, Marcuse identifies the sex instincts with the life instincts, and he further postulates that the suppression of these instincts was necessary to the development of Western civilization, which defined itself in terms of reason, productivity, and the domination of nature.

With the development of a different kind of civilization with different values, made possible for the first time by advanced technology, Marcuse sees the possibility of a change in the Reality principle, which is not something inevitable and mystical, but historically determined. With the passing away of both resource scarcity and, he hopes, the present systems of political and social domination and economic exploitation, he sees the Reality principle merging more and more with the repressed Pleasure principle, and a whole new form [of] erotically liberated life [made] possible. As he says:

> We have suggested that the prevalent instinctual repression resulted, not so much from the necessity of labour, but from the specific social organization of labour imposed by the interest in domination — that repression was largely surplus repression. Consequently, the elimination of surplus repression would per se tend to eliminate, not labour, but the organization of human existence into an instrument of labour.

Very much like Reich, Marcuse envisions man freed from surplus repression as capable of a much more receptive relationship both with the environment and with other people. He is therefore postulating a new form of social organization related to a new kind of character organization. He calls this "a total revolution in the mode of perception and feeling" and makes it clear that it is only possible in a society in which production is the means, and not the end, of human activity: "Possession and procurement of the necessities of life are the prerequisite, rather than the content, of a free society." He describes at length during the second half of *Eros and Civilization* what the content of such a free society and a free consciousness might be.

Both Marcuse and Reich have begun arguments that I think are crucial for any discussion of female liberation. All the oppressive phenomena which we experience as women clearly are related to social institutions and structures, and this includes the sexual inhibition which we experience and the problem of the woman's role as defined in the family. Since the problems that face women are related to the structure of the whole society, ultimately our study of our particular situation *as women* will lead us to the realization that we must attempt to change this whole society.

## 11. *The Nature of Nurture* ━●━●━●━●━●━●━●━●━●━●━●━●━●━●

The self is made up of the reflected appraisals of others.

HARRY STACK SULLIVAN

The third assumption, also based on the imperative of the organism, stems from the idea that the feminine psyche is a pattern fundamentally woven into the human fabric, that woman's personality, like woman's place, is biologically imprinted. Somatic design is presumed to determine personality configuration. But what configuration? Authorities differ in their catalogue of traits but agree in their conviction that there must be one. "So far," however, "those who believe in such organic correlations of constitution with psyche traits have not isolated its mechanisms." Instead, the most important finding of recent investigations into sex-typing seems to be the intricacy of the process of growing and being; the most important result seems to be the inadequacy of single factors and causal weights to account for the dynamism and complexity of human life. Human nature and human nurture are regarded as interdependent. The personality, it has been determined, has an evolution.

Viola Klein, in the initial reading in this section, gives an overview of the effect of events and of intellectual climate on concepts of women. For centuries, doctrine touching the capacities of women found authority in religion; later with the development of the natural sciences, rationalizations were sought in biological tendencies and evolutionary trends. More recently, the emphasis has shifted to the modifiability of human nature. It has found its reflection in the "basic thought that the world is not to be comprehended as a complex of ready-made things, but as a complex of processes." One such process was the French Revolution, with its ideology of liberty and equality.

*Parallel readings for Chapter 11, "Portrait of a Lady."

Another was the industrial revolution, with its extrusion of women from the public sphere — to which they have had ever since to demand readmission. Similarly, concepts of inherent sex nature can only arise in a culture where women are excluded from all social functions except those connected with sex.

Such a scientific approach to ideas led to a critical examination of assumptions. This took the form of cross-cultural studies, like those of Margaret Mead, and of psychological investigations, like those of Helen B. Thompson. Viola Klein summarizes the work of the latter at the University of Chicago between 1898 and 1900, in the first scientific attempt to apply the experimental method to the subject of mental sex differences. It is interesting to learn that, so far back, such differences as were revealed were strikingly small; they reflected, in Miss Thompson's view, two different social ideals: manliness with its spectrum of active, and femininity, with its spectrum of passive, traits.

The range in standardization of sex temperaments among the peoples she studied caused Margaret Mead to conclude that many, if not all, of the personality traits that have been called masculine or feminine are as lightly linked to sex "as are the clothing, the manners, and the form of head-dress that a society . . . assigns to either sex." The evidence rather attests, she believes, to the strength of social conditioning; the same infant can be developed into a full participant in a wide spectrum of human societies. Granting this, there still remains the question, how do diversities arise? Dr. Mead's hypothesis is that within the arc of possible human personalities, each culture tends to standardize certain temperaments. The history of the social definition of men and women is an example of this tendency to select a few traits from the compass of human endowment and specialize them by sex.

The final selection by Paul H. Mussen is, I believe, the most fascinating of the Readings in Parallel. It reveals to what extent sophisticated researchers, studying the internalization of norms, have themselves internalized those norms. As a consequence, they fail to ask the penetrating questions that relate to concepts beyond the given. It is as though they are constrained by an invisible chalk mark from trespassing beyond the range of established possibilities. The result is, to quote Paul Goodman once again, "a bland affirmation of clashing contradictions" as Freudian typology is employed — and revised — in response to the current intellectual climate. Change affects traditionalists, but only to the point of preserving an old corpus in new amber.

For the specialists, whose hypotheses and data are here reviewed, seek to determine the process by which an individual develops sex appropriate attitudes as defined by a specific society. In such investigations, one would expect that they would ask: 1) what are the norms? 2) what are the tokens of such norms? 3) how are these norms integrated? The studies under discussion, however, tend to accept 1) and 2) as received, focusing not on the models inculcated nor on the symbols by which they have been institutionalized, but solely on the riddle of their internalization. The concern is with the "how" rather than with the "why" and the "wherefore."

Assuming that one can derive truth from such a research design, appropriate criteria for determining "the link between the ascriptive act by the society . . . and the role performance of the child" pose a problem. More often than not, these tend to reflect the very social definitions which are being examined, and to shift from study to study. Again, as Mussen observes, the correlations between the tests are generally low. And, although it is acknowledged that sex-typing results from a complex process, designated criteria tend toward wanton simplification. Thus, the careful student reading this selection will come upon the very pre-formed patterns of certainty, the very stereotypes and assumptions that this volume has sought to analyze — carried as stowaway cargo in the reasoning of the experts.

Moreover, none of the theories of sex-role development here summarized accounts for the range of phenomena that bear on the process. This may be due to the avoidance by the psychological disciplines of what C. Wright Mills has called the principle of historical specificity. He writes: "The relevance of earlier experience, 'the weight' of childhood in the psychology of the adult character, is itself relative to the type of childhood and the type of social biography that prevail in various societies. It is, for example, apparent that the role of 'the father' in the building of a personality must be stated within the limits of specific types of families, and in terms of the place such families occupy within the social structure of which these families are a part."

On the other hand, the evidence that sex-typing is now studied, not assumed, testifies to profound modifications in the universe of discourse. There seems to be agreement among these scholars that the process is, by and large, a cultural one, that it develops rapidly in the early years, and that it is firmly established by the age of three or four. This marks a substantial shift away from biological determinism. Clearly, even traditionalists no longer assert that psychological traits have automatic sex linkages.

## Sex and Psychology

*Viola Klein*

It is interesting to note how, in the theoretical discussions of the problem of woman, the terms of reference have changed. Both parties, those advocating

From "First Investigations in Experimental Psychology: Helen B. Thompson," *The Feminine Character* (London: Kegan Paul, 1946), pp. 91–103. (slightly abridged).

male superiority as well as those championing equality of the sexes or even feminine superiority, had for centuries looked to theology to supply them with arguments. The supporters of masculine rule naturally made use of the Bible and of St. Paul's pronouncements, such as: "For a man indeed ought not to cover his head, forasmuch as he is the image and glory of God; but the woman is the glory of the man. For the man is not of the woman; but the woman of the man. Neither was the man created for the woman, but the woman for the man." (I Cor., xi.7-9.) Or, in Milton's words:

> My author and Disposer, what thou bidst
> Unargued I obey; so God ordains;
> God is thy law, thou mine; to know no more
> Is Woman's happiest knowledge, and her praise.

But the opposition as well, in arguing their point, had recourse to the authority of the Scriptures. In one of the first "feminist" books ever written, *Of the Nobility and Superiority of the Female Sex* (first published in 1505), the author, Heinrich Cornelius Agrippa von Nettesheim, justifies his plea for feminine superiority by an exegesis of his own: "Adam means Earth; Eve stands for life; ergo, Adam is the product of nature, and Eve the creation of God. Adam was admitted to the Paradise for the sole purpose that Eve might be created . . ."[1]

It was natural, then, to argue in theological terms, and it was equally "natural" later to discuss the problem in terms of Natural Science. Mainly during the nineteenth century justifications of all points of view on the question of woman were sought in biological tendencies and evolutionary trends. The solutions were sought, so to speak, in the germ plasm.

More recently, the emphasis has again been shifted, and the main attention been directed towards the modifiability of human nature under the impact of personal experience and cultural milieu.

This new attitude towards human nature arose at a certain stage in historical development when the quiet flow of tradition was disturbed and changes became drastic and obvious enough to make themselves felt in all walks of life.

The growing restlessness of the middle and lower classes preceding the French Revolution had already produced various plans to cure the ills of society. Babeuf, Saint-Simon, Fourier, Robert Owen, had put forward their schemes of social reconstruction. They, in their turn, followed a number of philosophers whose attention had been attracted to problems of historical evolution by the social development they were witnessing: Montesquieu, Diderot, Condorcet, Turgot, Voltaire, are French examples. David Hume and

---

1. Quoted from Joseph Tenenbaum: *The Riddle of Woman* (London: John Lane, 1939).

Adam Smith in this country [England], Lessing, Herder, Kant and Hegel in Germany, manifest the same trend.

The French Revolution and the growing imprint of industrialization on the most various aspects of the social order further increased the general interest in the social forces at work. Auguste Comte's endeavours, for instance, to establish the principles of an "ordered progress" which would involve "neither restoration nor revolution," and which resulted in the foundation of Sociology as a science, were the outcome of his profound alarm at the effects of the Revolution. He, as well as others of his contemporaries, felt that in the social sphere evolution was not necessarily identical with progress, and the need for and interest in social reform grew increasingly.

Attention was, moreover, directed towards the mechanisms of change and the pliability of human nature by the closer contact with different social and cultural systems, made possible by expanding capitalism. The study of foreign peoples, their customs and mores, offered a wide field of comparison and numerous objects of meditation.

Finally, migratory movements on a large scale, due to the colonization of other continents, created a kind of social laboratory for new experiments. The immigration to North America, in particular, which gave rise to an integrated national and cultural unit out of racially and culturally most diverse elements, afforded a strong incentive to social study. (To the present day the interest in social sciences is, for this reason, more acute in the United States than it is, for instance, in this country [England]. The number of sociological books published every year, the number of social research institutes and professorial chairs in the U.S.A. are far above the corresponding figures in this country [England].)

Each of these factors contributed to an attitude which no longer took for granted things as they were, but began to doubt traditional values and institutions. Together they led to an emphasis on change, movement and development, to an atmosphere of relativity and a readiness to overhaul traditional thoughts, beliefs and ideals.

This change of attitude found expression not only in the social sciences, but affected the scientific outlook in general. The "basic thought that the world is not to be comprehended as a complex of ready-made things, but as a complex of processes" (as Fr. Engels said) — the fact that it was no longer static objects but activities which became the centre of interest and scientific investigation — is one of the major events in the development of scientific thought in recent time. The relativist outlook, the emphasis on dynamic processes, and the willingness to re-examine all, even our most elementary concepts and all phenomena of ordinary everyday life itself, are characteristic features of present-day culture. They have found expression in contemporary art no less than in all branches of science. Doubt as a heuristic principle has, from the days of Descartes on, been the foundation and the most distinctive characteristic of Modern Man. Now once more it became active and invaded all departments of thought: Physics found it necessary to reconsider the fundamental notions of time and space; analytical psychology re-examined under its magnifying glass such elementary emotions as parental and sexual love. Music disposed of the old conceptions of harmony; modern painting cleared away ancient ideas of form. Sociology, a new science altogether, came into being in order to make an inventory of assets and liabilities, to study the mechanisms of the dynamic social processes and to investigate the underlying principles.

The motives responsible for the new scientific outlook in general, and for the foundations of Sociology as a new science in particular, are the same motives which account in great part, if not exclusively, for the ever increasing interest in our special problem: the psychological traits of woman. . . .

The most important ideological influence was undoubtedly the ideal of Human Rights, based on a philosophy of "equality" and "liberty" disseminated by the French Revolution. This philosophy implied — even if it did not state expressly — equal rights for women no less than for men. The first publications in support of the emancipation of women were, in fact, the *Declaration des Droits des Femmes,* submitted to the French National Assembly in 1798, and the *Vindication of the Rights of Woman,* by Mary Wollstonecraft, in 1792, in this country [England]. The very wording of these titles testifies sufficiently to their spiritual origin in French Revolutionary ideology. In different ways and various expressions this appeal has made itself heard ever since and has enormously increased both in weight and in volume all over the world.

The decisive economic factor in the rise of the problem of woman was, as we have seen before, industrialization, with the consequent transfer of productive activities from the family to the factory and the creation of an enormous leisure-class of bourgeois women who henceforth strove for improved educational facilities and for re-admission into the economic process.

A further incentive to the study of both the social and psychological aspects of this problem of woman was the growing knowledge of foreign cultures and mainly of primitive peoples. The examination of different institutions afforded the "duality" necessary for adequate judgment. It is impossible to understand and to criticize a situation as long as one is oneself entirely part of it. Only if one has an adequate observation point which ensures a view of things in their proper perspective can one pass a proper judgment. As long as the patriarchal family tradition was undisturbed and no other contrasting patterns were known, whatever was established in social tradition was regarded as part of human nature. As there was only one way of life to be considered, this was thought to be the only possible, the "natural" course. The first perceptible break in that tradition, as well as the background provided by the study of primitive cultures, sharpened critical awareness of established institutions. Such publications as J. J. Bachofen's *Mutterrecht* (1861), L. H. Morgan's *Ancient Society, Researches in the Lines of Human Progress from Savagery through Barbarism to Civilization* (1877), F. Engels' *Origin of the Family* (1884), E. A. Westermarck's *History of Human Marriage* (1891) and others, increased not only the knowledge of different family systems but the criticism of the existing pattern. The fact that comparisons between contrasting cultural patterns arouse a critical attitude has been known and used by critics of their social system ever since Montesquieu first published his *Lettres Persanes.* But progressing anthropological research has brought this literary technique out of the sphere of imagination and speculation and put it on the firmer basis of established facts. Characteristically, for instance, J. Kirk Folsom uses this device in his sociological study of the family. His book is preceded by a number of pages on which he confronts attitudes and beliefs, held in our Western civilization with regard to various problems of marriage and family life, with respective attitudes towards the same problems in Melanesian society. He thereby succeeds in stressing the peculiarities of our own institutions and in creating an atmosphere of greater objectivity.

More recently, changes in our society have become so marked that comparisons between present and past standards within our own civilization afford bases for comparison similar to those between different cultures. The adoption of a relativistic outlook has consequently been greatly increased.

That woman should have become a problem is therefore due to a set of general changes in the new era: to a new trend in economic development, to a new philosophy of life, and to a new scientific outlook.

But in addition to these general changes, the special interest which the problem of woman has evoked is due to two factors of a specific kind: The first is the development of medicine in general, and the improvement of birth control methods in particular. It had two significant effects on the actual emancipation of woman: relieved from the burden of constant child-bearing she could envisage taking up a career and could compete with men in the economic field on more equal terms. And, secondly, the separation of sex from procreation — in the sense of an inevitable consequence — created a new attitude towards love. It is not our task here to evaluate the revolutionary changes involved in this separation of two hitherto closely linked notions. Our aim is to show that birth-control has, if not fully, at least to a considerable extent, reduced woman's dependence on what Nature seemed to have destined for her, and it enabled her to choose and to accept the responsibility for her love-life (as men have always done). Both in work and in love, therefore, woman became a more equal partner to man.

The other important specific factor contributing to the scientific interest in Woman was the changing attitude towards the problem of Sex.

Introduced by Havelock Ellis and furthered mainly by Sigmund Freud and his school, sex has increasingly become a subject of scientific interest. Unpleasant as the reminder of this connection may be to the emancipated woman, who thinks of herself first of all as an individual and not as an object of merely or mainly sexual interest, the fact must not be overlooked that the scientific interest in the personality of woman developed alongside the scientific interest in sex. Only when sex ceased to be considered a sin could woman be regarded as a human being and not as either a "temptress" or as the incorporation of a necessary evil. In this light Weininger's statement that women are first of all interested in matters of sex is correct, though not in the sense Weininger meant it. Only after society had been freed from an ideology which regarded sex as sinful in itself could women be seen as individuals in their own right instead of as instruments of the devil. This has nothing to do with an "inherent sexual nature" of women but is the natural outcome of a man-made culture in which women of the upper and middle classes were excluded from all but those social functions directly or indirectly connected with sex. With the development of science and the growing influence it exerted on the public mind a number of religious taboos lost their original strength, the taboo on the discussion of sex among others.

An interesting light on the way in which primitive taboos linger on persistently in the form of prejudices and social habits until, in the end, they are dispelled by the more enlightened attitude created by modern science, is thrown by the example of menstruation. The primitive taboo attaching to woman's "uncleanness" lived on in feelings of shame and physical inferiority on the part of women, and in numerous myths, such as the belief that a menstruating woman cannot make butter "set" in the churn, or preserve fruit or jam, that she should not touch meat in a pickle tub nor flowers in a pot for fear they would decay. Many of these and similar superstitions still survive in the popular mind. Even medical science used to treat the problem of menstruation with awe as a kind of mysterious disease and regarded women as "naturally invalid." "Women," said Galiani in his *Dialogue sur les Femmes,* "only have intervals of health in the course of a continual disease." More recently, however, doctors are inclined to regard it as a normal process in healthy women and not as an illness and to attribute a great part of the pains and nervousness connected with it to psychological causes, such as, for instance, the "expectation of troubles."

> The mischief [says a report by the Hygiene Committee of the Women's Group on Public Welfare in 1943][2] is, however, far more serious owing to the survival, in an atmosphere of mystery which surrounds the subject, of the tribal outlook upon it. Women themselves are generally unaware of the extent to which this function is present in the minds of responsible persons in judging of their capacity to enter fresh fields, but startling light was thrown upon it when the alleged incompetence of women in menstruation to be trusted with the lives of passengers was made the ground for refusing to grant them the Pilot's B Certificate for flying. A committee of women doctors had to be set up to contest this decision, which they did successfully.

2. *Our Towns. A Close-up* (Oxford University Press, 1943).

The all-round progress of the sciences has produced a critical attitude towards institutionalized habits and traditional prejudices. It opened the way for a study of the feminine character which was released from the emotional bonds of religious taboos and was, in its intention at least, objective.

The research was carried out along two main lines. One was the attempt first to establish in a scientific way and to ensure what characteristic mental differences of sex are to be found, here and now, without enquiry into their origin.

The other approach was mainly concerned with the problem of causation, biological, psychological, social, etc., and has produced a great number of varying theories. Sociology is, first of all, interested in the possibilities and limits of social conditioning, that is, in the problem of the extent to which the character structure of modern civilized woman is the result of a certain mode of existence, of social institutions, traditions, and ideologies. It is based on the assumption that, notwithstanding the conditions of his physical and intellectual equipment, man is to a large extent a product of his surroundings, and that — even after allowance has been made for the limits imposed on a man's variability by his constitution and innate tendencies — the margin within which his nature is alterable is still wide enough to be of essential interest and to call for special investigation. . . .

The first scientific attempt to apply experimental methods to the investigation of mental sex differences was carried out in the psychological laboratory of the University of Chicago by Dr. Helen Bradford Thompson during the years 1898 to 1900. Its results were published under the title of *The Mental Traits of Sex* in Chicago in 1903. It is a report of a series of experiments and tests applied to a selected group of twenty-five college men and twenty-five college women, all students of the (co-educational) University of Chicago. They were all of one age-group and came from more or less the same social background. In this way the number of variables was reduced to a minimum, but Miss Thompson herself makes the following comment:

> In order to make a trustworthy investigation of the variations due to sex alone, it is a pre-requisite to obtain individuals for comparison who are near the same age, who have the same social status, and who have been subjected to like training and social surroundings. The complete fulfilment of these conditions, even in the most democratic community, is impossible. The social atmosphere of the sexes is different from the earliest childhood to maturity.

Miss Thompson tries to take this obvious source of error into account as much as possible. The main objection which may be raised against the method of her enquiry is the limited number of individuals subjected to examination and the resulting danger of too rash generalizations and too little allowance being made for individual differences. Confronted with the choice between a thorough investigation of a small number of cases and a necessarily more or less superficial study of a great number of individuals, she preferred to sacrifice the volume of her research to its intensity and exactitude. Being a pioneer she had not yet at her disposal a perfected method of mental testing which would have enabled her to deal with great numbers equally or more thoroughly.

Comparisons were made between the measured aptitudes in men and women of motor ability, skin and muscle senses, taste and smell, hearing, vision, affective processes, of such intellectual faculties as memory, association and ingenuity, and of their general knowledge in English, history, physics, mathematics, biology and science.

The careful measurement of all those faculties shows some slight difference between men and women which, however, are strikingly small and resolve themselves, in the light of Miss Thompson's investigation, mainly into differences in attitudes towards the problems in question and not into innate differences of abilities.

There is, for instance, a certain feminine superiority in association and in memory, both with regard to the rapidity of memorizing and to duration, and a masculine superiority in ingenuity.

The question is [as Miss Thompson puts it] largely one of the distribution of attention. A large part of a boy's attention goes towards his activities — the learning of new movements, the manipulation of tools, the making of contrivances of various sorts. A girl's less active existence must be filled with some other sort of conscious process. The only possibility is that sensory and perceptual processes should be more prominent. [And she goes on]: On the more purely intellectual level it is only natural that in the absence of a sufficient social spur toward originality and inventiveness they should depend more upon memory for their supply of ideas.

The measurable differences in ingenuity on the one hand, memory on the other, are in Miss Thompson's view expressions of two different social ideals: The ideal of manliness which encourages individuality, independence in thought and action, and readiness to experiment; and the ideal of femininity which breeds a spirit of obedience, dependence and deference. According to these contrasting ideals different characteristics are developed which are, however, only different manifestations of one psychic energy.

This assumption is corroborated by more recent sociological theories which regard the individual's social role and his conception of his role as among the most important factors in the shaping of personality.

Miss Thompson can find no difference according to sex in the total amount of general information possessed by men and women who have had the same course of education, and no marked difference in the character of affective processes, in the strength of emotions, in the form of their expression, or the degree of impulsiveness in action. There seems to be, however, a greater tendency in women to inhibit the expression of their emotions.

The tendency to introspection, as well as the clearness of thinking, are found to be the same in both sexes. In intellectual interests, and what are considered the easiest and hardest branches of study, and in methods of work, there are only trifling divergences.

Miss Thompson discards the view, which occupies such a prominent place in Havelock Ellis's theory, of a universally greater variability in men than in women. She thinks it necessary to discriminate between normal and abnormal variations. "A class," she says, "which presents the greatest number of abnormalities in character might not be the class which displays the widest normal variations of that character." Her view is based on the extensive studies on variations by the statistician K. Pearson,[3] who draws attention to the need for measurement of variability around the average and who calls the principle that men are more variable than women a "pseudo-scientific superstition."

More recently L. S. Hollingworth has also contested Havelock Ellis's assumption of a greater variability in males.[4] She points out that the smaller number of feeble-minded women found in institutions is due to the fact that many feminine occupations are of an uncompetitive character and therefore render the detection of mental defectiveness in women more difficult. On a mental level which would make men liable to detention, women are able to live outside institutions with their families or to earn their livelihood with domestic work or prostitution. Thus, although there may be more mentally defective men inside institutions, more feeble-minded women are living outside. In order to rule out environmental influences Hollingworth, moreover, collected a great number of physical measurements of infants at birth[5] and could not find any consistent sex difference in variability. Mental differences, however, which are the main point in the controversy about the differential variability of the sexes, cannot be measured at that age, and this contention of Hollingworth's therefore does not seem relevant.

Summing up the general result of her investigation Miss Thompson says:

> The point to be emphasized as the outcome of this study is that, according to our present light, the psychological differences of sex seem to be largely due, not to difference of average capacity, nor to difference in type of mental activity, but to differences in the social influences brought to bear on the developing individual from early infancy to adult years. The question of the future development of the intellectual life of women is one of social necessities and ideals, rather than of the inborn psychological characteristics of sex.

Miss Thompson's findings are, of course, open to the objection that the principle guiding the selection of individuals for her experiment led her to study a very particular, unrepresentative group of persons. Women who in the

3. K. Pearson: "Variations in Man and Woman" in *The Chances of Death,* Chap. VIII (E. Arnold, London, 1897).

4. L. S. Hollingworth: "Differential Action upon the Sexes of Forces Which Tend to Segregate the Feeble-minded" *(Jour. Abn. Psych.,* No. 17, 1922).

5. L. S. Hollingworth and H. M. Montague: "The Comparative Variability of the Sexes at Birth" *(Amer. Jour. Sociol.,* No. 20, 1914–15).

eighteen-nineties, in spite of conventional prejudices and the generally inimical attitude towards "blue-stockings," took up university studies must be considered the exception rather than the rule. They represented an *élite* with regard to their intellect as well as with regard to their character. The results obtained in a study of twenty-five university women prove nothing more nor less than the fact that there are women — whether many or only a few cannot be judged from the data — who equal masculine standards. Miss Thompson's research, therefore, interesting as it is as a beginning, is only of limited value.

Her work was, however, only the first of its kind and was followed by an increasing number of similar studies. The development of psychometric methods on the one hand, and social changes which brought women into the sphere of masculine occupations on the other, led to an intensified study of psychological sex differences.

During the First World War, women were called upon to play an important part in many fields of action and they acquitted themselves beyond all expectations. This fact greatly strengthened their social position and earned them political rights in many countries. The impoverishment of the middle-classes which followed that war, and which increased during the years of economic crisis, brought to middle-class women a share in the economic life of society. The coincidence of economic crisis with woman's entry into the economic field was, in many respects, unfortunate. Although the critical economic situation was, as we have seen, a pre-condition of woman's liberation in the sense that it prepared the ground for her development and allowed her to disentangle herself from the tight grip of tradition, it was, at the same time, a danger to woman's emancipation. The atmosphere of uncertainty, restlessness, and general dissatisfaction, caused by the economic crisis, was in many minds associated with the fact that women now had jobs, and in women themselves it aroused doubts as to the value of a liberation purchased, as they saw it, at the price of security and happiness. The fact that millions of men were out of work and family life was upset, while, at the same time, women provided cheap labour, created in many people a longing for the "good old times," when women had no rights but certain privileges, and it made them wonder whether woman's place was not the hearth, after all. A movement "back to the home" spread and it was particularly marked in Germany, where it became one of the strong-points of Nazi ideology.

As a consequence of these circumstances the centre of gravity of the problem was shifted. The question was no longer one of capability but became one of social expediency. It was increasingly evident that in a highly mechanized economy, such as ours, which necessitates a huge administrative apparatus, there were very many jobs which could be done as well by women as by men and which women were willing to perform. The problem, as it presents itself to us to-day, is no longer the question: What are women able to do?, but: What are the limits to which society can go in granting women equality, without endangering its continued existence and the happiness of individuals? From an enquiry into causes the problem became an enquiry into the effects. This is another instance to show how the way a question is put in the Social Sciences depends on the social configuration in which it originates. At a time when women crash-dive in combat-planes or present themselves to a not even surprised public as record-breaking snipers, the question has ceased to be one of qualitative differences. Instead, it has become one of ends and means. The ends being a successful and well-functioning human society, the change undergone with regard to our specific problem reflects the change in progress in the social structure at large. The problem of women presents only one particular instance exemplifying the transition from the individualism of a liberal society to the organization of a planned society.

Before the development of Individualism the problem of woman's emancipation and, concurrently, the enquiry into her aptitudes, could not arise; after its decline and the move towards a society which thinks primarily in terms of social welfare, it could, in its original form, not survive. Only a liberalistic ideology, with its emphasis on individual achievement, created an atmosphere in which the question was primarily focussed on psychological abilities. Such ideals as the utmost development of the individual's faculties or "equal chances for everybody" bred an attitude of curiosity as to the peculiarities and possibilities of human character. This attitude was very typical for the era of expanding capitalism and it is largely responsible for the enormous progress of scientific psychology within the last decades.

## Sex and Temperament
>=—o=—o=—o=—o=—o=—o=—o=—o=—o=—o=—o=—o=—o=—o=—o=—o=—o=—o=—o=—o=—o=—o=—o=—o=—o=—o=—<

*Margaret Mead*

### The Standardization of Sex-Temperament

We have now considered in detail the approved personalities of each sex among three primitive peoples. We found the Arapesh — both men and women — displaying a personality that, out of our historically limited preoccupations, we would call maternal in its parental aspects, and feminine in its sexual aspects. We found men, as well as women, trained to be co-operative, unaggressive, responsive to the needs and demands of others. We found no idea that sex was a powerful driving force either for men or for women. In marked contrast to these attitudes, we found among the Mundugumor that both men and women

Reprinted with omissions by permission of William Morrow & Company, Inc. from *Sex and Temperament in Three Primitive Societies* (pp. 279-289, 290-309, Chapters XVII and XVIII). Copyright 1935, 1950, © 1963 Margaret Mead.

developed as ruthless, aggressive, positively sexed individuals, with the maternal cherishing aspects of personality at a minimum. Both men and women approximated to a personality type that we in our culture would find only in an undisciplined and very violent male. Neither the Arapesh nor the Mundugumor profit by a contrast between the sexes; the Arapesh ideal is the mild, responsive man married to the mild, responsive woman; the Mundugumor ideal is the violent aggressive man married to the violent aggressive woman. In the third tribe, the Tchambuli, we found a genuine reversal of the sex-attitudes of our own culture, with the woman the dominant, impersonal, managing partner, the man the less responsible and the emotionally dependent person. These three situations suggest, then, a very definite conclusion. If those temperamental attitudes which we have traditionally regarded as feminine — such as passivity, responsiveness, and a willingness to cherish children — can so easily be set up as the masculine pattern in one tribe, and in another be outlawed for the majority of women as well as for the majority of men, we no longer have any basis for regarding such aspects of behaviour as sex-linked. And this conclusion becomes even stronger when we consider the actual reversal in Tchambuli of the position of dominance of the two sexes, in spite of the existence of formal patrilineal institutions.

The material suggests that we may say that many, if not all, of the personality traits which we have called masculine or feminine are as lightly linked to sex as are the clothing, the manners, and the form of head-dress that a society at a given period assigns to either sex. When we consider the behaviour of the typical Arapesh man or woman as contrasted with the behaviour of the typical Mundugumor man or woman, the evidence is overwhelmingly in favour of the strength of social conditioning. In no other way can we account for the almost complete uniformity with which Arapesh children develop into contented, passive, secure persons, while Mundugumor children develop as characteristically into violent, aggressive, insecure persons. Only to the impact of the whole of the integrated culture upon the growing child can we lay the formation of the contrasting types. There is no other explanation of race, or diet, or selection that can be adduced to explain them. We are forced to conclude that human nature is almost unbelievably malleable, responding accurately and contrastingly to contrasting cultural conditions. The differences between individuals who are members of different cultures, like the differences between individuals within a culture, are almost entirely to be laid to differences in conditioning, especially during early childhood, and the form of this conditioning is culturally determined. Standardized personality differences between the sexes are of this order, cultural creations to which each generation, male and female are trained to conform. There remains, however, the problem of the origin of these socially standardized differences.

While the basic importance of social conditioning is still imperfectly recognized — not only in lay thought, but even by the scientist specifically concerned with such matters — to go beyond it and consider the possible influence of variations in hereditary equipment is a hazardous matter. The following pages will read very differently to one who has made a part of his thinking a recognition of the whole amazing mechanism of cultural conditioning — who has really accepted the fact that the same infant could be developed into a full participant in any one of these three cultures — than they will read to one who still believes that the minutiae of cultural behaviour are carried in the individual germ-plasm. If it is said, therefore, that when we have grasped the full significance of the malleability of the human organism and the preponderant importance of cultural conditioning, there are still further problems to solve, it must be remembered that these problems come *after* such a comprehension of the force of conditioning; they cannot precede it. The forces that make children born among the Arapesh grow up into typical Arapesh personalities are entirely social, and any discussion of the variations which do occur must be looked at against this social background.

With this warning firmly in mind, we can ask a further question. Granting the malleability of human nature, whence arise the differences between the standardized personalities that different cultures decree for all of their members, or which one culture decrees for the members of one sex as contrasted with the members of the opposite sex? If such differences are culturally created, as this material would most strongly suggest that they are, if the new-born child can be shaped with equal ease into an unaggressive Arapesh or an aggressive Mundugumor, why do these striking contrasts occur at all? If the clues to the different personalities decreed for men and women in Tchambuli do not lie in the physical constitution of the two sexes — an assumption that we must reject both for the Tchambuli and for our own society — where can we find the clues upon which the Tchambuli, the Arapesh, the Mundugumor, have built? Cultures are man-made, they are built of human materials; they are diverse but comparable structures within which human beings can attain full human stature. Upon what have they built their diversities?

We recognize that a homogeneous culture committed in all of its gravest institutions and slightest usages to a co-operative, unaggressive course can bend every child to that emphasis, some to a perfect accord with it, the majority to an easy acceptance, while only a few deviants fail to receive the cultural imprint. To consider such traits as aggressiveness or passivity to be sex-linked is not possible in the light of the facts. Have such traits, then, as aggressiveness or passivity, pride or humility, objectivity or a preoccupation with personal relationships, an easy response to the needs of the young and the weak or a hostility to the young and the weak, a tendency to initiate sex-relations or merely to respond to the dictates of a situation or another person's advances — have these traits any basis in temperament at all? Are they potentialities of all human temperaments that can be developed by different kinds of social conditioning and which will not appear if the necessary conditioning is absent?

When we ask this question we shift our emphasis. If we ask why an Arapesh man or an Arapesh woman shows the kind of personality that we have considered in the first section of this book, the answer is: Because of the Arapesh culture, because of the intricate, elaborate, and unfailing fashion to which a culture is able to shape each new-born child to the cultural image. And if we ask the same question about a Mundugumor man or woman, or about a Tchambuli man as compared with a Tchambuli woman, the answer is of the same kind. They display the personalities that are peculiar to the cultures in which they were born and educated. Our attention has been on the differences between Arapesh men and women as a group and Mundugumor men and women as a group. It is as if we had represented the Arapesh personality by a soft yellow, the Mundugumor by a deep red, while the Tchambuli female personality was deep orange, and that of the Tchambuli male, pale green. But if we now ask whence came the original direction in each culture, so that one now shows yellow, another red, the third orange and green by sex, then we must peer more closely. And leaning closer to the picture, it is as if behind the bright consistent yellow of the Arapesh, and the deep equally consistent red of the Mundugumor, behind the orange and green that are Tchambuli, we found in each case the delicate, just discernible outlines of the whole spectrum, differently overlaid in each case by the monotone which covers it. This spectrum is the range of individual differences which lie back of the so much more conspicuous cultural emphases, and it is to this that we must turn to find the explanation of cultural inspiration, of the source from which each culture has drawn.

There appears to be about the same range of basic temperamental variation among the Arapesh and among the Mundugumor, although the violent man is a misfit in the first society and a leader in the second. If human nature were completely homogeneous raw material, lacking specific drives and characterized by no important constitutional differences between individuals, then individuals who display personality traits so antithetical to the social pressure should not reappear in societies of such differing emphases. If the variations between individuals were to be set down to accidents in the genetic process, the same accidents should not be repeated with similar frequency in strikingly different cultures, with strongly contrasting methods of education.

But because this same relative distribution of individual differences does appear in culture after culture, in spite of the divergence between the cultures, it seems pertinent to offer a hypothesis to explain upon what basis the personalities of men and women have been differently standardized so often in the history of the human race. This hypothesis is an extension of that advanced by Ruth Benedict in her *Patterns of Culture*. Let us assume that there are definite temperamental differences between human beings which if not entirely hereditary at least are established on a hereditary base very soon after birth. (Further than this we cannot at present narrow the matter.) These differences finally embodied in the character structure of adults, then, are the clues from which culture works, selecting one temperment, or a combination of related and congruent types, as desirable, and embodying this choice in every thread of the social fabric — in the care of the young child, the games the children play, the songs the people sing, the structure of political organization, the religious observance, the art and the philosophy.

Some primitive societies have had the time and the robustness to revamp all of their institutions to fit one extreme type, and to develop educational techniques which will ensure that the majority of each generation will show a personality congruent with this extreme emphasis. Other societies have pursued a less definitive course, selecting their models not from the most extreme, most highly differentiated individuals, but from the less marked types. In such societies the approved personality is less pronounced, and the culture often contains the types of inconsistencies that many human being[s] display also; one institution may be adjusted to the uses of pride another to a casual humility that is congruent neither with pride nor with inverted pride. Such societies, which have taken the more usual and less sharply defined types as models, often show also a less definitely patterned social structure. The culture of such societies may be likened to a house the decoration of which has been informed by no definite and precise taste, no exclusive emphasis upon dignity or comfort or pretentiousness or beauty, but in which a little of each effect has been included.

Alternatively, a culture may take its clues not from one temperament, but from several temperaments. But instead of mixing together into an inconsistent hotchpotch the choices and emphases of different temperaments, or blending them together into a smooth but not particularly distinguished whole, it may isolate each type by making it the basis for the approved social personality for an age-group, a sex-group, a caste-group, or an occupational group. In this way society becomes not a monotone with a few discrepant patches of an intrusive colour, but a mosaic, with different groups displaying different personality traits. Such specializations as these may be based upon any facet of human endowment — different intellectual abilities, different artistic abilities, different emotional traits. So the Samoans decree that all young people must show the personality trait of unaggressiveness and punish with opprobrium the aggressive child who displays traits regarded as appropriate only in titled middle-aged men. In societies based upon elaborate ideas of rank, members of the aristocracy will be permitted, even compelled, to display a pride, a sensitivity to insult, that would be deprecated as inappropriate in members of the plebian class. So also in professional groups or in religious sects some temperamental traits are selected and institutionalized, and taught to each new member who enters the profession or sect. Thus the physician learns the bed-side manner, which is the natural behaviour of some temperaments and the standard behaviour of the general practitioner in the medical profession; the Quaker learns at least the outward behaviour and the rudiments of meditation, the capacity for which is not necessarily an innate characteristic of many of the members of the Society of Friends.

So it is with the social personalities of the two sexes. The traits that occur in some members of each sex are specially assigned to one sex, and disallowed in the other. The history of the social definition of sex-differences is filled with such arbitrary arrangements in the intellectual and artistic field, but because of the assumed congruence between physiological sex and emotional endowment we have been less able to recognize that a similar arbitrary selection is being made among emotional traits also. We have assumed that because it is convenient for a mother to wish to care for her child, this is a trait with which women have been more generously endowed by a carefully teleological process of evolution. We have assumed that because men have hunted, an activity requiring enterprise, bravery, and initiative, they have been endowed with these useful attitudes as part of their sex-temperament.

Societies have made these assumptions both overtly and implicitly. If a society insists that warfare is the major occupation for the male sex, it is therefore insisting that all male children display bravery and pugnacity. Even if the insistence upon the differential bravery of men and women is not made articulate, the difference in occupation makes this point implicitly. When, however, a society goes further and defines men as brave and women as timorous, when men are forbidden to show fear and women are indulged in the most flagrant display of fear, a more explicit element enters in. Bravery, hatred of any weakness, of flinching before pain or danger — this attitude which is so strong a component of *some human* temperaments has been selected as the key to masculine behaviour. The easy unashamed display of fear or suffering that is congenial to a different temperament has been made the key to feminine behavior.

Originally two variations of human temperament, a hatred of fear or willingness to display fear, they have been socially translated into inalienable aspects of the personalities of the two sexes. And to that defined sex-personality every child will be educated, if a boy, to suppress fear, if a girl, to show it. If there has been no social selection in regard to this trait, the proud temperament that is repelled by any betrayal of feeling will display itself, regardless of sex, by keeping a stiff upper lip. Without an express prohibition of such behaviour the expressive unashamed man or woman will weep, or comment upon fear or suffering. Such attitudes, strongly marked in certain temperaments, may by social selection be standardized for everyone, or outlawed for everyone, or ignored by society, or made the exclusive and approved behaviour of one sex only.

Neither the Arapesh nor the Mundugumor have made any attitude specific for one sex. All of the energies of the culture have gone towards the creation of a single human type, regardless of.class, age, or sex. There is no division into age-classes for which different motives or different moral attitudes are regarded as suitable. There is no class of seers or mediums who stand apart drawing inspiration from psychological sources not available to the majority of the people. The Mundugumor have, it is true, made one arbitrary selection, in that they recognize artistic ability only among individuals born with the cord about their necks, and firmly deny the happy exercise of artistic ability to those less unusually born. The Arapesh boy with a tinea infection has been socially selected to be a disgruntled, antisocial individual, and the society forces upon sunny co-operative children cursed with this affliction a final approximation to the behaviour appropriate to a pariah. With these two exceptions no emotional role is forced upon an individual because of birth or accident. As there is no idea of rank which declares that some are of high estate and some of low, so there is no idea of sex-difference which declares that one sex must feel differently from the other. One possible imaginative social construct, the attribution of different personalities to different members of the community classified into sex-, age-, or caste-groups, is lacking.

When we turn however to the Tchambuli, we find a situation that while bizarre in one respect, seems nevertheless more intelligible in another. The Tchambuli have at least made the point of sex-difference; they have used the obvious fact of sex as an organizing point for the formation of social personality, even though they seem to us to have reversed the normal picture. While there is reason to believe that not every Tchambuli woman is born with a dominating, organizing, administrative temperament, actively sexed and willing to initiate sex-relations, possessive, definite, robust, practical and impersonal in outlook, still most Tchambuli girls grow up to display these traits. And while there is definite evidence to show that all Tchambuli men are not, by native endowment, the delicate responsive actors of a play staged for the women's benefit, still most Tchambuli boys manifest this coquettish play-acting personality most of the time. Because the Tchambuli formulation of sex-attitudes contradicts our usual premises, we can see clearly that Tchambuli culture has arbitrarily permitted certain human traits to women, and allotted others, equally arbitrarily, to men.

If we then accept this evidence drawn from these simple societies which through centuries of isolation from the main stream of human history have been able to develop more extreme, more striking cultures than is possible under historical conditions of great intercommunication between peoples and the resulting heterogeneity, what are the implications of these results? What conclusions can we draw from a study of the way in which a culture can select a few traits from the wide gamut of human endowment and specialize these traits, either for one sex or for the entire community? What relevance have these results to social thinking? Before we consider this question it will be necessary to discuss in more detail the position of the deviant, the individual whose innate disposition is too alien to the social personality required by his culture for his age, or sex, or caste ever to wear perfectly the garment of personality that his society has fashioned for him.

## The Deviant

What are the implications for an understanding of the social deviant of the point of view outlined in the last chapter? Under the term "deviant" I include any individual who because of innate disposition or accident of early training, or through the contradictory influences of a heterogeneous cultural situation, has been culturally disenfranchised, the individual to whom the major emphases of his society seem nonsensical, unreal, untenable, or downright wrong. The average man in any society looks into his heart and finds there a reflection of the world about him. The delicate educational process that has made him into an adult has assured him this spiritual membership in his own society. But this is not true of the individual for whose temperamental gifts his society has no use, nor even tolerance. The most cursory survey of our history is enough to demonstrate that gifts honoured in one century are disallowed in the next. Men who would have been saints in the Middle Ages are without vocation in modern England and America. When we take into account primitive societies that have selected far more extreme and contrasting attitudes than did our own ancestral cultures, the matter becomes even clearer. To the extent that a culture is integrated and definite in its goals, uncompromising in its moral and spiritual preferences, to that very extent it condemns some of its members — members by birth only — to live alien to it, in perplexity at the best, at the worst in a rebellion that may turn to madness.

It has become the fashion to group together all of those by whom the cultural norm is not accepted as neurotics, individuals who have turned from "reality" (that is, the present-day solutions of their own society) to the comfort or inspiration of fantasy situations, taking refuge in some transcendental philosophy, in art, in political radicalism, or merely in sexual inversion or some other elaborated idiosyncrasy of behaviour — vegetarianism or the wearing of a hair shirt. The neurotic is furthermore regarded as immature; he has not grown up sufficiently to understand the obviously realistic and commendable motivations of his own society.

In this blanket definition two quite different concepts have become blurred and confused, each one rendering the other nugatory. Among the deviants in any society, it is possible to distinguish those who are physiologically inadequate. They may have weak intellects or defective glands; any one of a number of possible organic weaknesses may predetermine them to failure in any but the simplest tasks. They may — very, very rarely such an individual is found — have practically all of the physiological equipment of the opposite sex. None of these individuals are suffering from any discrepancy between a purely temperamental bent and social emphasis; they are merely the weak and the defective, or they are abnormal in the sense that they are in a group which deviates too far from human cultural standards — not particular cultural standards — for effective functioning. For such individuals any society must provide a softer, a more limited, or a more special environment than that which it provides for the majority of its members.

But there is another type of neurotic that is continually being confused with these physiologically handicapped individuals, and this is the cultural deviant, the individual who is at variance with the values of his society. Modern psychiatric thought tends to attribute all of his maladjustment to early conditioning and so places him in the invidious category of the psychically maimed. A study of primitive conditions does not bear out such a simple explanation. It does not account for the fact that it is always those individuals who show marked temperamental proclivities in opposition to the cultural emphases who are in each society the maladjusted persons; or for the fact that it is a different type of individual which is maladjusted among the Mundugumor from the type which is maladjusted among the Arapesh. It does not explain why materialistic, bustling America and a materialistic, bustling tribe in the Admiralty Islands both produce hoboes, or why it is the individual endowed with a capacity to feel strongly who is maladjusted in Zuñi and Samoa. Such material suggests that there is another type of unadjusted person, whose failure to adjust should be referred not to his own weakness and defect, not to accident or to disease, but to a fundamental discrepancy between his innate disposition and his society's standards.

When society is unstratified and the social personalities of both sexes are fundamentally alike, these deviants are drawn indiscriminately from both sexes. Among the Arapesh the violent man and the violent woman, among the Mundugumor the trustful, co-operative man and the trustful, co-operative woman, are the deviants. Too much positive self-feeling predetermines one to maladjustment among the Arapesh, too much negative self-feeling is an equal liability among the Mundugumor. In earlier chapters we have discussed the personalities of some of these deviating individuals, and shown how the very gifts that Mundugumor society would have honoured were disallowed among the Arapesh, how Wabe and Temos and Amitoa would have found Mundugumor life intelligible, and Omblean and Kwenda would have been well placed among the Arapesh. But the alienness of both these groups in their own cultures, although it impaired their social functioning, reducing the uses to which their gifts might have been put, nevertheless left their psycho-sexual functioning unimpaired. Amitoa's positive drive made her behave not like a man, but like a woman of the Plains. Ombléan's love for children and willingness to work strenuously in order to care for a number of dependents did not make him suspect that he was like a woman, nor did it provoke in his associates an accusation of effeminacy. In loving children and peace and order, he might be behaving like some white men or some tribe they had never seen, but certainly no more like a Mundugumor woman than like a Mundugumor man. There was no homosexuality among either the Arapesh or the Mundugumor.

But any society that specializes its personality types by sex, which insists that any trait — love for children, interest in art, bravery in the face of danger, garrulity, lack of interest in personal relations, passiveness in sex-relations; there are hundreds of traits of very different kinds that have been so specialized — is inalienably bound up with sex, paves the way for a kind of maladjustment of a worse order. Where there is no such dichotomy, a man may stare sadly at his world and find it essentially meaningless but still marry and rear children, finding perhaps a definite mitigation of his misery in this one whole-hearted participation in a recognized social form. A woman may day-dream all her life of a world where there is dignity and pride instead of the mean shop-keeping morality that she finds all about her, and yet greet her husband with an easy smile and nurse her children through the croup. The deviant may translate his sense of remoteness into painting or music or revolutionary activity and yet remain in his personal life, in his relations to members of his own and the opposite sex, essentially unconfused. Not so, however, in a society which, like that of the Tchambuli or that of historical Europe and America, defines some temperamental traits as masculine, some as feminine. In addition to, or aside from, the pain of being born into a culture whose acknowledged ends he can never make his own, many a man has now the added misery of being disturbed in his psycho-sexual life. He not only has the wrong feelings but, far worse and more confusing, he has the feelings of a woman. The significant point is not whether this mal-orientation, which makes the defined goals of women in his society intelligible to him and the goals of the man alien and distasteful, results in inversion or not. In extreme cases in which a man's temperament conforms very closely to the approved feminine personality, and if there is in existence a social form behind which he can shelter himself, a man may turn to avowed inversion and transvesticism. Among the Plains Indians, the individual who preferred the placid activities of the women to the danger-ous, nerve-racking activities of the men could phrase his preference in sex terms; he could assume women's dress and occupations, and proclaim that he really was more a woman than a man. In Mundugumor, where there is no such pattern, a man may engage in feminine activities, such as fishing, without its occurring to him to symbolize his behaviour in female attire. Without any contrast between the sexes and without any tradition of transvesticism, a variation in temperamental preference does not result in either homosexuality or transvesticism. As it is unevenly distributed over the world, it seems clear that transvesticism is not only a variation that occurs when there are different personalities decreed for men and women, but that it need not occur even there. It is in fact a social invention that has become stabilized among the American Indians and in Siberia, but not in Oceania. . . .

This discussion is concerned neither with the congenital invert nor with overt behaviour of the practising homosexual. There are, it is true, ways in which the different types of maladjustment intersect and reinforce each other, and the congenital invert may be found among those who have found shelter in transvesticism. But the deviants with whom we are concerned here are those individuals whose adjustment to life is conditioned by their temperamental affinity for a type of behaviour that is regarded as unnatural for their own sex and natural for the opposite sex. To produce this type of maladjustment, not only is it necessary to have a definite approved social personality, but also this personality must be rigidly limited to one of the two sexes. The coercion to behave like a member of one's own sex becomes one of the strongest implements with which the society attempts to mould the growing child into accepted forms. A society without a rigid sex-dichotomy merely says to the child who shows aberrant behaviour traits: "Don't behave like that." "People don't do that." "If you behave like that, people won't like you." "If you behave like that you will never get married." "If you behave like that, people will sorcerize you" — and so on. It invokes — as against the child's natural inclination to laugh or cry or sulk in the wrong places, to see insult where there is none, or fail to see insult that is intended — considerations of human conduct as socially defined, not of sex-determined conduct. The burden of the disciplinary song is: "You will not be a real human being unless you suppress these tendencies which are incompatible with our definition of humanity." But it does not occur to either the Arapesh or the Mundugumor to add: "You aren't behaving like a boy at all. You are behaving like a girl" — even when actually this may be the case. It will be remembered that among the Arapesh, boys, owing to their slightly different parental care, do cry more than girls and have temper tantrums until a later age. Yet because the idea of sex-difference in emotional behaviour is lacking, this real difference was never invoked. In societies without a sex-dichotomy of temperament, one aspect, one very basic aspect, of the child's sense of its position in the universe is left unchallenged — the genuineness of its membership in its own sex. It can continue to watch the mating behaviour of its elders and pattern its hopes and expectations upon it. It is not forced to identify with a parent of opposite sex by being told that its own sex is very much in question. Some slight imitation of a father by a daughter, or of a mother by a son, is not seized upon and converted into a reproach, or a prophecy that the girl will grow up to be a tomboy or the boy a sissy. The Arapesh and Mundugumor children are spared this form of confusion.

Consider in contrast the way in which children in our culture are pressed into conformity: "Don't act like a girl." "Little girls don't do that." The threat of failing to behave like a member of one's own sex is used to enforce a thousand details of nursery routine and cleanliness, ways of sitting or relaxing, ideas of sportsmanship and fair play, patterns of expressing emotions, and a multitude of other points in which we recognize socially defined sex-differences, such as limits of personal vanity, interest in clothes, or interest in current events. Back and forth weaves the shuttle of comment: "Girls don't do that." "Don't you want to grow up to be a real man like Daddy?" — tangling the child's emotions in a confusion that, if the child is unfortunate enough to possess even in some slight degree the temperament approved for the opposite sex, may well prevent the establishment of any adequate adjustment to its world. Every time the point of sex-conformity is made, every time the child's sex is invoked as the reason why it should prefer trousers to petticoats, base-ball-bats to dolls, fisticuffs to tears, there is planted in the child's mind a fear that indeed, in spite of anatomical evidence to the contrary, it may not really belong to its own sex at all. . . .

Such social pressure exerts itself in a number of ways. There is first the threat of sex-disenfranchisement against the child who shows aberrant tendencies, the boy who dislikes rough-and-tumble play or weeps when he is rebuked, the girl who is only interested in adventures, or prefers battering her playmates to dissolving in tears. Second, there is the attribution of the emotions defined as feminine to the boy who shows the mildest preference for one of the superficial sex-limited occupations or avocations. A small boy's interest in knitting may arise from a delight in his own ability to manipulate a needle; his interest in cooking may derive from a type of interest that might later make him a first-class chemist; his interest in dolls may spring from no tender cherishing feelings but from a desire to dramatize some incident. Similarly, a girl's overwhelming interest in horseback riding may come from a delight in her own physical co-ordination on horseback, her interest in her brother's wireless set may come from pride in her proficiency in handling the Morse code. Some physical or intellectual or artistic potentiality may accidentally express itself in an activity deemed appropriate to the opposite sex. This has two results: The child is reproached for his choice and accused of having the emotions of the opposite sex, and also, because the occupational choice or hobby throws him more with the opposite sex, he may come in time to take on much of the socially sex-limited behaviour of that opposite sex.

A third way in which our dichotomy of social personality by sex affects the growing child is the basis it provides for a cross-sex identification with the parents. The invocation of a boy's identification with his mother to explain his subsequent assumption of a passive role towards members of his own sex is familiar enough in modern psychiatric theory. It is assumed that through a distortion of the normal course of personality development the boy fails to identify with his father and so loses the clue to normal "masculine" behaviour. Now there is no doubt that the developing child searching for clues to his social role in life usually finds his most important models in those who stand in a parental relationship to him during his early years. But I would suggest that we have still to explain why these identifications occur, and that the cause lies not in any basic femininity in the small boy's temperament, but in the existence of a dichotomy between the standardized behaviour of the sexes. We have to discover why a given child identifies with a parent of opposite sex rather than with the parent of its own sex. The most conspicuous social categories in our society — in most societies — are the two sexes. Clothes, occupation, vocabu-lary, all serve to concentrate the child's attention upon its similarity with the parent of the same sex. Nevertheless some children, in defiance of all this pressure, choose the parents of opposite sex, not to love best, but as the persons with whose motives and purposes they feel most at one, whose choices they feel they can make their own when they are grown. . . .

Before considering this question further, let me restate my hypothesis. I have suggested that certain human traits have been socially specialized as the appropriate attitudes and behaviour of only one sex, while other human traits have been specialized for the opposite sex. This social specialization is then rationalized into a theory that the socially decreed behaviour is natural for one sex and unnatural for the other, and that the deviant is a deviant because of glandular defect, or developmental accident. Let us take a hypothetical case. Attitudes towards physical intimacy vary enormously among individuals and have been very differently standardized in different societies. We find primitive societies, such as those of the Dobu and the Manus, where casual physical contact is so interdicted for both sexes, so hedged about with rules and categories, that only the insane will touch another person lightly and casually. Other societies, such as that of the Arapesh, permit a great deal of easy physical intimacy between individuals of different ages and both sexes. Now let us consider a society that has specialized to one sex this particular temperamental trait. To men has been assigned the behaviour characteristic of the individual who finds casual physical contact intolerable, to women, as their "natural" behaviour, that of individuals who accept it easily. To men, the hand on the arm or across the shoulder, sleeping in the same room with another man, having to hold another man on the lap in a crowded automobile — every contact of this kind would be, by definition, repellent, possibly even, if the social conditioning were strong enough, disgusting or frightening. To women in this given society, however, physical contact that was easy and unstylized would be, by definition, welcome. They would embrace each other, caress each other's hair, arrange each other's clothes, sleep in the same bed, comfortably and without embarrassment. Now let us take a marriage between a well-brought-up man in this society, who would be intolerant of any physical casualness, and a well-brought-up woman, who would consider it as natural when displayed by women and never expect it among boys or men. To this couple is born a girl who displays from birth a *noli me tangere* attitude that nothing her mother can do will dispel. The little girl slips off her mother's lap, wriggles away when her mother tries to kiss her. She turns with relief to her father, who will not embarrass her with demonstrations of affection, who does not even insist upon holding her hand when he takes her for a walk. From such a simple clue as this, a preference that in the child is temperamental, in the father is socially stabilized male behaviour, the little girl may build up an identification with her father, and a theory that she is more like a boy than like a girl. She may come in time to be actually better adjusted in many other ways to the behaviour of the opposite sex. The psychiatrist who finds her later in life wearing mannish attire, following a male occupation, and unable to find happiness in marriage may say that identification with the opposite sex was the cause of her failure to adjust as a woman. But this explanation does not reveal the fact that the identification would not have occurred in these terms if there had been no dichotomy of sex-attitudes in the society. The Arapesh child who is more like a reserved father than like a demonstrative mother may feel that it resembles its father more than its mother, but this has no further effects on its personality in a society in which it is not possible to "feel like a man" or "feel like a woman." The accident of a differentiation of sex-attitudes makes these chance identifications dynamic in the adjustment of the child.

This example is admittedly hypothetical and simple. The actual conditions in a modern society are infinitely more complicated. To list merely some of the kinds of confusions that occur should be sufficient to focus attention upon the problem. One of the child's parents may be aberrant, and therefore be a false guide to the child in its attempt to find its role. Both the children's parents may deviate from the norm in opposite ways, the mother showing more pronounced temperamental traits usually specialized as male, the father showing the opposite traits. This condition is very likely to occur in modern society, in which, because it is believed marriage must be based upon contrasting personalities, deviant men often choose deviant women. So the child, groping for clues, may make a false identification because its own temperament is like that decreed for the opposite sex, or a false identification because, while it is itself fitted for easy adjustment, the parent of its own sex is maladjusted.

I have discussed first identification along temperamental lines, but the identification may also be made in other terms. The original identification may be through intelligence or specific artistic gifts, the gifted child identifying with the more gifted parent, regardless of sex. Then, if the double standard of personality exists, this simple identification on the basis of ability or interest will be translated into sex terms, and the mother will lament: "Mary is always working with Will's drafting instruments. She hasn't any more normal girl's interests at all. Will says it's a pity she wasn't born a boy.". . .

Worth mentioning here is the way in which the boy's plight differs from the girl's in almost every known society. Whatever the arrangements in regard to descent or ownership of property, and even if these formal outward arrangements are reflected in the temperamental relationships between the two sexes, the prestige values always attach to the occupations of men, if not entirely at the expense of the women's occupations, at least to a great extent. It almost always follows, therefore, that the girl "who should have been a boy" has at least the possibility of a partial participation in activities that are surrounded by the aura of masculine prestige. For the boy "who should have been a girl" there is no such possibility open. His participation in women's activities is almost always a matter for double reproach: he has shown himself unworthy to be categorized as a man, and has thereby condemned himself to activities with a low prestige value.

Furthermore, it is seldom that the particular attitudes and interests which have been classified as feminine in any society have been given any very rich expression in art or in literature. The girl who finds the defined masculine interests closer to her own can find for herself forms of vicarious expression; the boy who might have found similar outlets if there were a comparable feminine art and literature is denied such satisfactory escape. . . .

This perplexity is likely to remain throughout life. The woman who either by temperament or accident of training has become more identified with the interests of men, if she cannot adjust to the current sex-standards, loses out since a great part of the artistic symbolism of his society is rendered unavailable and there is no substitute to which he can turn. He remains a confused and bewildered person, unable to feel as men "naturally" feel in his society, and equally unable to find any satisfaction in roles that have been defined by women, although their social personality is more akin to his temperament.

And so, in a thousand ways, the fact that it is necessary to feel not only like a member of a given society in a given period, but like a member of one sex and not like a member of the other, conditions the development of the child, and produces individuals who are unplaced in their society. Many students of personality lay these multiple, imponderable maladjustments to "latent homosexuality." But such a judgment is fathered by our two-sex standard; it is *post hoc* diagnosis of a result, not diagnosis of a cause. It is a judgment that is applied not only to the invert but to the infinitely more numerous individuals who deviate from the social definition of appropriate behaviour for their sex.

If these contradictory traits of temperament which different societies have regarded as sex-linked are not sex-linked, but are merely human potentialities specialized as the behaviour of one sex, the presence of the deviant, who need no longer be branded as a latent homosexual, is inevitable in every society that insists upon artificial connexions between sex and bravery, or between sex and positive self-feeling, or between sex and a preference for personal relations. Furthermore, the lack of correspondence between the actual temperamental constitution of members of each sex and the role that a culture has assigned to them has its reverberations in the lives of those individuals who were born with the expected and correct temperament. It is often assumed that in a society which designates men as aggressive and dominating, women as responsive and submissive, the maladjusted individuals will be the dominant, aggressive woman and the responsive, submissive man. Theirs is, indubitably, the most difficult position. Human contacts of all sorts, and especially courtship and marriage, may present insoluble problems to them. But consider also the position of the boy naturally endowed with an aggressive, dominating temperament and reared to believe that it is his masculine role to dominate submissive females. He is trained to respond to responsive and submissive behaviour in others by a display of his self-conscious aggressiveness. And then he encounters not only submissive females, but also submissive males. The stimulus to dominating behaviour, to an insistence upon unquestioning loyalty and reiterated statements of his importance, is presented to him in one-sex groups, and a "latent homosexual" situation is created. Similarly, such a man has been taught that his ability to dominate is the measure of his manhood, so that submissiveness in his associates continually reassures him. When he encounters a woman who is as naturally dominating as he is himself, or even a woman who, although not dominating temperamentally, is able to outdistance him in some special skill or type of work, a doubt of his own manhood is set up in his mind. This is one of the reasons why men who conform most closely to the accepted temperament for males in their society are most suspicious and hostile towards deviating women who, in spite of a contrary training, show the same temperamental traits. Their hold upon their conviction of their own sex-membership rests upon the non-occurrence of similar personalities in the opposite sex.

And the submissive, responsive woman may find herself in an equally anomalous position, even though her culture has defined her temperament as the proper one for women. Trained from childhood to yield to the authority of a dominant voice, to bend all of her energies to please the more vulnerable egotism of dominant persons, she may often encounter the same authoritative note in a feminine voice and thus she, who is by temperament the ideal woman in her society, may find women so engrossing that marriage adjustments never enter the picture. Her involvement in devotion to members of her own sex may in turn set up in her doubts and questions as to her essential femininity.

Thus the existence in a given society of a dichotomy of social personality, of a sex-determined, sex-limited personality, penalizes in greater or less degree every individual born within it. Those whose temperaments are indubitably aberrant fail to adjust to the accepted standards, and by their very presence, by the anomalousness of their responses, confuse those whose temperaments are the expected ones for their sex. So in practically every mind a seed of doubt, of anxiety, is planted, which interferes with the normal course of life.

But the tale of confusions is not ended here. The Tchambuli, and in a milder degree parts of modern America, represent a further difficulty that a culture which defines personality in terms of sex can invent for its members. It will be remembered that while Tchambuli theory is patrilineal, Tchambuli practice gives the dominant position to women, so that the position of the man with aberrant — that is, dominating — temperament is rendered doubly difficult by the cultural forms. The cultural formulation that a man has paid for his wife and can therefore control her continually misleads these aberrant individuals into fresh attempts at such control, and brings them into conflict with all their childhood training to obey and respect women, and their wives' training to expect such respect. Tchambuli institutions and the emphases of their society are, to a certain extent, at odds with one another. Native history attributes a high development of dominating temperaments to various neighbouring tribes, whose women have for many generations run away and married the Tchambuli. In explanation of its own inconsistencies, it invokes the situation that was just frequent enough among the Arapesh to confuse the adjustments of men and women there. These inconsistencies in Tchambuli culture were probably increased by a diminshed interest in war and head-hunting and a greater interest in the delicate arts of peace. The importance of the women's economic activities may also have increased without any corresponding enhancement of the men's economic role. Whatever the historical causes, and they are undoubtedly multiple and complex, Tchambuli today presents a striking confusion between institutions and cultural emphases. And it also contains a larger number of neurotic males than I have seen in any other primitive culture. To have one's aberrancy, one's temperamental inability to conform to the prescribed role of responsive dancing attendance upon women, apparently confirmed by institutions — this is too much, even for members of a primitive society living under conditions far simpler than our own.

Modern cultures that are in the throes of adjusting to women's changing economic position present comparable difficulties. Men find that one of the props of their dominance, a prop which they have often come to think of as synonymous with that dominance itself — the ability to be the sole support of their families — has been pulled from beneath them. Women trained to believe that the possession of earned income gave the right to dictate, a doctrine which worked well enough as long as women had no incomes, find themselves more and more often in a confused state between their real position in the household and the one to which they have been trained. Men who have been trained to believe that their sex is always a little in question and who believe that their earning power is a proof of their manhood are plunged into a double uncertainty by unemployment; and this is further complicated by the fact that their wives have been able to secure employment.

All such conditions are aggravated in America also by the large number of different patterns of decreed behaviour for each sex that obtain in different national and regional groups, and by the supreme importance of the pattern of intersex behaviour that children encounter within the closed four walls of their homes. Each small part of our complex and stratified culture has its own set of rules by which the power and complementary balance between the sexes is maintained. But these rules differ, and are sometimes even contradictory, as between different national groups or economic classes. So, because there is no tradition which insists that individuals should marry in the group within which they were reared, men and women are continually marrying whose pictures of the interrelationships between the sexes are entirely different. Their confusions are in turn transmitted to their children. The result is a society in which hardly anyone doubts the existence of a different "natural" behaviour for the sexes, but no one is very sure what that "natural" behaviour is. Within the conflicting definitions of appropriate behaviour for each sex, almost every type of individual is left room to doubt the completeness of his or her possession of a really masculine or a really feminine nature. We have kept the emphasis,

the sense of the importance of the adjustment, and at the same time we have
lost the ability to enforce the adjustment.

# Early Sex-Role Development

)━●━●━●━●━●━●━●━●━●━●━●━●━●━●━●━●━●━●━●━●━●━●━●━●━●━●━●━●━●━●━●━●━●━(

*Paul H. Mussen*

It is a banal truth that the individual's sex role is the most salient of his many
social roles. No other social role directs more of his overt behavior, emotional
reactions, cognitive functioning, covert attitudes and general psychological
and social adjustment. Linton observed that "the division of the society's
members into age-sex categories is perhaps the feature of greatest importance
for establishing participation of the individual in culture" (Linton, 1945, p. 63).

Nor is the ascription of any role more fundamental for the maintenance and
continuity of society. Activities, tasks, characteristics and attitudes are assigned differentially to men and women in all cultures. But, as Margaret Mead
(1935) demonstrated so effectively in her now-classic study of three New
Guinea tribes, there are marked differences among cultures in the specific
activities and personality characteristics ascribed to males and females, and in
the degrees of differentiation between the two sex roles. Among the Arapesh,
both men and women are cooperative, unaggressive, responsive to the needs
of others — characteristics typically associated with the feminine role in Western culture. In marked contrast, the Mundugumor would be regarded as
"masculine" by our cultural standards, for both men and women tend to be
ruthless, aggressive, severe, and unresponsive. Neither of these tribes put any
emphasis on the contrast between the sexes. In the third tribe, the Tchambuli,
the personality characteristics of the two sexes are the reverse of what is usual
in our own culture. Tchambuli women are dominant, impersonal and managing; the men are less responsible and emotionally dependent (Mead, 1935).

Although each culture has its own definitions of male and female roles and
characteristics, there are some impressive cross-cultural regularities, some core
concepts of masculinity and femininity (d'Andrade, 1966). For example, the
majority of societies around the world organize their social institutions around
males, and in most cultures men are more aggressive and dominating, have
greater authority and are more deferred to than women. They are generally

From "Early Sex-Role Development," *Handbook of Socialization Theory and Research*,
edited by David A. Goslin (Chicago: Rand McNally, 1969), pp. 707-729.

assigned the physically-strenuous, dangerous tasks and those requiring long periods of travel. Women, on the other hand, generally carry out established routines, ministering to the needs of others, cooking, and carrying water. The husband-father role is *instrumental,* i.e., task-oriented and emotion-inhibited in nearly all cultures, and the wife-mother role is customarily more *expressive,* i.e., emotional, nurturant, and responsible (Parsons, 1955).

These almost universal sex differences are apparent among children. Systematic ethnographic observations indicate that boys in most cultures are much more likely to engage in conflict and overt aggression, and girls are more likely to be affectionate, cooperative, responsive, sociable, and succorant (d'Andrade, 1966).

These cross-cultural regularities in sex differences might be interpreted to mean that male and female roles and personality characteristics are biological "givens." Indeed they are, to some extent, based upon biological factors such as the male's superior strength and endurance. But there are a few cultures, such as the Tchambuli, in which the usual sex-role assignments do not apply or may even be reversed. Moreover, in most cultures, there are some biologically normal individuals whose behavior and characteristics are like those of the opposite, rather than their own, sex. From these facts, it must be concluded that, by and large, sex-role differences do not stem directly from biological factors. Being born a boy does not mean that the individual will *automatically* become masculine in the sense of acquiring masculine behavior, affective responses, characteristics, and cognitive responses.

The term sex-typing refers to the process by which the individual develops the attributes (behavior, personality characteristics, emotional responses, attitudes, and beliefs) defined as appropriate for his sex in his own culture. "This process is the link between the ascriptive act by the society (namely the parents, at first) and the role performance by the child. . . . There is nothing automatic about the connection between ascription and role adoption; sex-typing is a . . . complex process" (R. R. Sears, 1965, p. 133). Sex-typed or sex-appropriate behavior, reactions, characteristics, beliefs and attitudes — overt as well as covert — are the *products* (or outcomes, derivatives, or consequents) of this complex process.

Although there is a substantial body of research and theory on sex-typing, our understanding of the process is far from complete. The primary purpose of this chapter is to review the major explanatory hypotheses related to this process — those dealing with the fundamental antecedents and underlying mechanisms — and relevant empirical data. The discussion is largely confined to the early phases of sex-typing; first, because the first few years are of critical importance in this process and, secondly, because most of the theories link the process to the child's earliest *social,* particularly familial, experiences. Undoubtedly the sex-typing process is influenced in critical ways by extra-familial relationships (with peers, teachers and others in the community), and by experiences of later childhood and adolescence. These have not as frequently

teristics of masculinity or femininity, the derived scores or ratings should be been the foci of theory or research and hence we will make no attempt to deal with them systematically in this chapter.

Theories of sex-typing can best be understood in the context of current knowledge of developmental trends in sex-role acquisition and the stability of sex-typed characteristics. A brief, very much summarized account of the pertinent findings follows.

## Developmental Trends in Sex-Role Development

METHODOLOGICAL PROBLEMS

The major problems in research on sex-typing are related to the selection of criteria, i.e., the assessment of sex-role development. Many investigations make use of tests of masculinity and femininity. For example, in one test for young children the subject is presented with a line of fourteen toys, seven that appeal to girls (e.g., dolls, cribs, dishes) and seven that appeal to boys (e.g., knives, boats, racing cars). He is instructed to rank in order of preference the toys he would like to play with (Rabban, 1950). In another test, the child is first shown a sexless stick figure, IT, and then given groups of pictures of masculine and feminine toys, activities, objects, and clothes. He is asked to designate, in order, the objects and activities IT prefers, the assumption being that the choices attributed to IT reflect the child's own preferences. Older children, adolescents, or adults are asked to indicate their agreement or disagreement with statements indicative of masculine and feminine attitudes or interests (e.g., I enjoy participating in active sports).

All these tests may be scored from complete masuclinity to complete femininity. The rationale underlying the scoring is empirical: objects or items presented (or agreement with statements) are chosen significantly more frequently by members of one sex than by the other. Does the subject choose toys and activities typically chosen by boys? Does he respond to questions (or agree with statements) in characteristically masculine ways?

In other studies, behavioral manifestations of sex-typed characteristics in natural settings or in structured situations have been used as indices of sex-role development. These have included frequency of aggressive (masculine) behavior or dependent (feminine) behavior on the playground or in specially devised doll-play situations (P. Sears, 1951). In one recent intensive study of nursery school children, conducted by Sears, Rau and Alpert (1965), measures of "gender role" included behavioral observations, observer's ratings of each subject's masculinity or femininity and an area usage score — the amount of time the child was observed in a nursery school area predominantly used by members of his own sex. In addition, doll-play sessions yielded several measures relevant to sex role (e.g., the extent to which male and female dolls were used as agents of sex-typed activities).

Since all these tests or observations presumably reflect generalized charac-

correlated positively with each other. Unfortunately, however, the correlations are generally low. Masculine interests are correlated with masculine personality characteristics (as rated by observers) among adolescents (Mussen, 1961), but most studies have failed to demonstrate strong relationships. Thus, the intercorrelations among the five nursery school and assessment measures used in the Sears, Rau and Alpert study, ranged from 0 to .71 for girls, with a median of .36, while the median for boys was only .15. On the basis of these intercorrelations the authors concluded that the products of sex-typing are not well integrated at nursery school age but there is a "higher integration of femininity than of masculinity" (Sears et al., 1965, p. 180).

The generally low intercorrelations among the measures may make it difficult to interpret the results of studies of sex-typing. The findings of one study may not support (or may even contradict) those of another, not because the conclusions based on one set of data are faulty, but rather, because the studies used vastly different, uncorrelated operational measures of sex-typing.

TRENDS IN SEX-TYPING

What is known about developmental trends in sex-typing? Apparently the process begins very early — though not by means of instinctive, innate, constitutional, or automatic mechanisms. Dramatic evidence for this statement is found in research on hermaphrodites or pseudohermaphrodites, individuals born with genital anomalies that make their physical sex ambiguous. Parents or physicians generally assign a sex role to such individuals in early infancy, and the child ordinarily begins to assume the behavior and characteristics appropriate to this role. This assignment may subsequently be shown to be contradictory to the individual's biological (chromosomal, gonadal or hormonal) sex. Even under these circumstances, however, sex-typed characteristics and reactions congruent with the initial label or sex-role assignment, including affectional orientation toward the "opposite" sex, are maintained. Moreover, attempts to reassign sex in accordance with the predominant physical attributes are usually unsuccessful and may result in severe psychological stress, unless the change is made *before the child is two years old* (Hampson, 1965).

Clearly, then, the very first years are of crucial importance for sex-role development. Once established, the individual's sex role appears to be fixed and irreversible. In this sense, the first two years seem to constitute a critical period in sex-typing.

A number of relevant empirical studies of normal children's sex-typing of interests, activities and attitudes also show that the process develops rapidly in the early years. According to these studies, generally employing the kinds of techniques of sex-role assessment described earlier, by the age of three or four, boys express clear-cut preferences for masculine activities, toys and objects (Brown, 1957; Hartup & Zook, 1960; Kagan & Moss, 1962; Rabban,

1950). Sex-typed behavior becomes progressively more firmly established with age thereafter (Rabban, 1950).

In general, boys show earlier and sharper awareness of sex-appropriate behavior and interests. Age trends for sex-typed preferences for girls are somewhat more variable and less clear-cut. While most girls adopt patterns of behavior, interests and activities that are congruent with the feminine stereotypes, many girls between the ages of three and ten show rather strong preferences for masculine games, activities and objects (Brown, 1957; Hartup & Zook, 1960). Very few boys of this age prefer feminine activities and young boys have stronger preferences for masculine toys than girls for feminine toys. For both sexes, age trends in preference for peers of the same sex roughly parallel those for sex-typed preferences for objects and activities. Almost all boys prefer other boys as friends during the early school years, and many girls of this age prefer their male peers. Furthermore, a substantial number of girls wish they were boys or "daddies" but very few boys want to be girls or "mommies" (Brown, 1957). This may be a reflection of the girl's incipient awareness of the relative devaluation of the female role in the culture.

Subgroups within our own culture differ in degree and timing of sex-typing. Boys and girls of the lower class become aware of their appropriate sex-role patterns earlier than their middle-class peers and their preferences conform more closely to the male and female stereotypes. Thus, lower-class boys reached a stable, high level of sex-appropriate choices by the time they were five, while middle-class boys did not do so until they were six. Analogously, lower-class girls made definite sex-appropriate choices by the age of six, but middle-class girls had not reached this level even by the age of eight (Rabban, 1950). Perhaps this is due to the clearer differentiation between adult masculine and feminine roles in the lower class, and the lower-class mothers' more energetic and consistent encouragement of appropriate sex-typing.

STABILITY OF SEX-TYPING

Are these early developed sex-typed characteristics stable and continuous over time? Is the highly masculine young boy likely to become a highly masculine adolescent or adult, and the highly feminine nursery school girl a highly feminine woman? The answers to these questions require longitudinal study. Unfortunately, there are very few such studies and data are consequently relatively sparse. What little evidence we have, however, suggests that the answers are affirmative. For example, Kagan and Moss (1962) studied the relationship between the childhood and adult characteristics of the subjects in the Fels Research Institute's longitudinal population. Their subjects, intensively observed at four developmental periods during childhood, were rated on such characteristics as aggression, passivity, dependency, achievement motivation, anxiety, heterosexual behavior and sex-typed activities. Adult status on each characteristic was assessed from intensive interviews when the subjects were between twenty and thirty years of age.

Traits congruent with appropriate sex-typing were found to be relatively stable from childhood to maturity. For example, girls high in passivity and dependence during childhood manifested these characteristics as adults, although passive dependent boys were not likely to retain these characteristics. Analogously, for males, high levels of aggression and heterosexual behavior in childhood predicted anger arousal and strong sexual orientation in adulthood. This prediction did not hold for females. It was concluded that "behavioral stability depended on congruence with sex-role standards" (Kagan, 1964, p. 155).

In this same population, the tendency to act in sex-appropriate ways was highly stable from early childhood to adulthood for both sexes (Kagan & Moss, 1962). These findings are consistent with some others based on other longitudinal data that showed that aggressive adolescent boys become aggressive, easily angered, men. Among these boys, the ones with appropriate sex-typed patterns of interest and behavior were likely to become masculine, "instrumental" adults — self-sufficient but lacking in sociability and introspection. Those who were more feminine in interest patterns during adolescence became more emotionally expressive men, less self-sufficient, more dependent, more sociable and interested in others (Mussen, 1961).

To summarize, there is substantial evidence that sex-typing begins very early and becomes crystallized during the first few years of the child's life. Once sex-typed characteristics are strongly established, they tend to be maintained over a considerable span of time.

What are the factors underlying this remarkably rapid course of growth and development and the stability of sex-typing? The corpus of theory relating to the process outweighs the available solid, systematic data. Attention in the following section will therefore be centered on theories, but, wherever possible, pertinent research findings will be cited.

## Theories of Sex-Role Development

Three general types of explanatory hypotheses about sex-role development may be differentiated. The first, a social-learning theory of sex-typing, emphasizes factors such as tuition (teaching), reward and punishment, generalization and imitation, in the development and strengthening of sex-typed behavior. The second type of hypothesis, which is related to the first — particularly to the concept of imitation learning — views sex-typing as a product of *identification*. According to the third explanatory hypothesis, recently proposed and elaborated by Kohlberg (1966), sex-typing is a natural concomitant of cognitive development and maturation, emerging quite independently of specific training and learning experiences.

### SOCIAL-LEARNING THEORY
Social-learning theory explanations of sex-typing are the most traditional, best-known and probably the most widely accepted. Moreover, some of the

basic principles of learning, such as those concerned with the effects of reward and punishment, are universally included in the folk wisdom about child-training.

Most experts in the field of socialization speak of the child's "learning a sex role" which is taught to him by the agents of socialization, most particularly by his family. "Many agencies share in teaching a child the expected behavior of his sex, but the family is pre-eminent" (Elkin, 1960, p. 53). Sex-role training is seen as beginning at birth, with the use of blue blankets for boy infants and pink ones for girls; the roles are "drilled in" intensively and continuously throughout childhood.

In their explanation of sex-typing, social-learning theorists invoke well-known, experimentally verified principles of learning. The factors that are central are differential and selective rewards and punishments, generalization, mediation, modeling and vicarious learning.

Stated in the simplest terms, social-learning theory holds that sex-appropriate responses are rewarded (reinforced) by parents and others, and hence are repeated (increased in frequency). Sex-inappropriate behavior, on the other hand, is likely to be punished and hence to diminish in strength and frequency, i.e., to become extinguished.

On a common-sense basis, this argument seems irrefutable. Moreover, there is abundant experimental evidence showing that, even within the first few weeks of life, infants can learn to make specific responses to specific stimuli. For example, they can learn to turn their heads, smile, and vocalize in response to the approach of others, if these responses are frequently rewarded (Rheingold, 1956).

Is there evidence that the theory is applicable to the very early learning of sex-typed responses? Certainly, parents are keenly aware of the cultural definition of sex-role behavior, and it may be inferred that they reward their children's sex-appropriate responses and punish those that are inappropriate. Moreover, children feel that their parents want them to adopt sex-appropriate behavior (Fauls & Smith, 1956).

Middle-class fathers freely admit that they would be concerned if their sons showed a lack of responsibility and initiative, inadequate school performance, insufficient aggression or too much passivity, ineptitude in athletics, over-conformity, excitability, too much crying or other childish behavior (Aberle & Naegele, 1952). Presumably these fathers would punish their sons for manifesting such characteristics and would reward them for the opposite kinds of behavior. But this could not be done during infancy, for such characteristics would not be apparent until later on. Yet, as noted earlier, sex-typing begins very early in the child's life. If social-learning theory is applicable, there must be rewards for sex-typed behavior beginning in the first year or two. The argument may be compelling, but firm supportive data are lacking. In fact, there is very little evidence that infant boys and girls receive any significant differential treatment by either, or both, parents. Thus, in their comprehensive study of child-training practices, Sears, Maccoby and Levin (1957) found no sex differences in most aspects of feeding or toilet training, or surprisingly, in training for modesty and the inhibition of sex play. Mothers were somewhat more indulgent and warmer toward their infant daughters than toward their infant sons, however.

More rigorous and detailed observation and analysis of infant-parent interactions might reveal that parents do reward and punish their sons and daughters differently, especially for responses related to sex-typing. So far, however, such data are not available.

Direct rewards appear to be effective in fostering sex-appropriate behavior later in childhood. Even here, however, the evidence, although consistent with social-learning theory, is not impressive. In an excellent summary of the social-learning point of view as applied to the sex-typing of aggression and dependency, Mischel says:

> The greater incidence of dependent behaviors for girls than boys, and the reverse situation with respect to physically aggressive behavior, seems directly applicable in social-learning terms. Dependent behaviors are less rewarded for males, physically aggressive behaviors are less rewarded for females in our culture and consequently there are mean differences between the sexes in the frequency of such behaviors after the first few years of life.
>
> Unfortunately, present evidence that the sexes are indeed treated differentially by their parents with respect to the above behaviors is far from firm and much more detailed investigations are needed of the differential reward patterns and modeling procedures used by mothers, fathers and other models with boys and girls in the natural setting. The current empirical evidence is equivocal, although consistent with a social-learning view (adapted from Mischel, 1966, p. 75).

For example, among the middle-class preschool and kindergarten boys and girls studied by Sears et al.,

> aggression was the area of child behavior in which the greatest sex distinctions were made by parents. Boys were allowed more aggression in their dealings with other children in the neighborhood, and were more frequently encouraged to fight back if another child started a fight (Sears et al., 1957, p. 403).

A number of mothers apparently felt that being "boylike" implied being aggressive, especially in self-defense, with playmates. As social-learning theory would predict, since they are rewarded for aggressive behavior, boys manifest greater physical aggression and more negativistic behavior.

Girls, on the other hand, receive more praise for "good" behavior (obedience, conformity, sweetness and non-aggressiveness). They are more often subjected to punishment and withdrawal of love for aggression and disobedience. And, as learning theory would predict, girls are, in fact, more obedient and conforming in their relationships with others.

Unfortunately, the data of this study came exclusively from maternal interviews and hence may be biased. There are no definitive studies relating reliable and objective observations of parental rewards and punishments to children's sex-typed behavior.

Other evidence consistent with the social-learning point of view comes from a cross-cultural study involving 110 cultures. In the vast majority of cultures surveyed, sex differences in child-training practices seemed clearly designed to produce sex-typed characteristics. Girls in most cultures are subjected to greater pressures (rewards and punishments) that lead to the development of nurturance, obedience and responsibility and boys all over the world are more trained to achieve and to be self-reliant. In other words, patterns of child-rearing practices seem to be oriented toward molding the prescribed adult sex-appropriate characteristics, thus minimizing what Benedict termed "discontinuities in cultural conditioning" (Barry, Bacon & Child, 1957).

*Generalization.* Of course, social-learning theorists do not argue in favor of the simplistic notion that direct rewards and punishment are the only sources of the development of sex-typed responses. Other important principles of learning are also central in their explanations of the development and maintenance of sex-typed behavior. There is, for example, the principle of generalization, which states that when a response has been learned to one stimulus, it is likely to occur in response to other, similar stimuli. The greater the degree of similarity between the original stimuli and those in a new situation, the greater the likelihood that the response will occur. Applied to the learning of sex-typed behavior, this principle would assert that if the boy is rewarded for expression of aggression toward other children in his own backyard, he is likely to behave aggressively in his interactions with children in other situations such as nursery school. Similarly, the little girl's compliance or obedience, rewarded by her mother, is likely to generalize to her relationships with other adults, such as teachers.

Certain broad patterns of behavior, attitudes, and characteristics that are related to later sex-typing may be established early in childhood as a consequence of parental rewards and punishments. This was demonstrated in the recent study of Sears et al. (1965) in which many child-rearing variables were correlated with measures of sex-typing. They discovered two clusters of child-rearing variables that were associated with sex role. One was related to permissiveness with respect to sex play, and the other to disciplinary methods and aggression. Sex permissiveness was correlated with masculinity and non-permissiveness with femininity *for both sexes.*

> ... the more freedom these children had for sexual play (i.e., the more permissive the parents were), the more masculine (or non-feminine) they became. This would occasion no surprise if we had been measuring the child's active sex play itself, but the measures showing this effect are quite detached from such overt sexuality. The choice of toys and occupations, in particular, seemed distant from sex behavior. Whatever the mechanism by which encouragement or discouragement of active sexual behavior was translated into the liking or disliking of other

gender role activities, there is little doubt that discouragement produced a passive, non-masculine quality in a boy's behavior and a passive femininity in the girls' (Sears et àl., 1965, p. 190).

Severity of socialization during nursery school — i.e., strong demands for good table manners, severe toilet training, maternal punishment for aggression and high use of physical punishment — also tends to femininize children of both sexes.

These masculine and feminine responses manifested by these children in nursery school may be interpreted as generalizations of behavior learned at home. In relatively relaxed, permissive homes, a child of either sex is rewarded for exploring, experimenting, seeking outgoing activity, and aggression, i.e., for displaying essentially stereotyped masculine behavior and qualities. These responses become stronger and are likely to generalize. In nursery school and test situations, these generalized responses will be manifested in his preference for energetic, adventurous, masculine games and activities. In a restrictive milieu, on the other hand, the child is rewarded for — and learns — obedience, passivity, and the inhibition of strong overt reactions, responses that are generally considered feminine. These reactions and characteristics, established in the home, generalize to other situations, and are reflected in an orientation toward feminine interests and activities.

As the child's cognitive development progresses, he forms concepts, and attaches labels to objects and events. These labels may then serve as the bases for further generalization, i.e., all stimuli with the same label may elicit the same reactions. This is called *verbal mediation,* or *mediated generalization.*

It is easy to see how mediated generalization facilitates development and crystallization of sex-typing. The boy's social learning experiences are likely to result in associations between terms such as "good boy," "boys' games" and "that shows you're strong" and parental approval and reward. Consequently, responses and activities having these labels become attractive to the boy and he is likely to learn them. Analogously, for boys, labels such as "sissy," "girlish," "nice" are likely to be linked with parental disapproval (punishment) and interests, activities and behaviors labeled in these ways will be avoided.

*Imitation.* Recently Bandura and other social-learning theorists have dealt systematically with the enormously potent influence of imitation — also called observational learning, vicarious learning, and modeling — on behavior development. The major conclusion of a vast amount of research is that simply by observing a model's behavior, the child may acquire responses, including sex-typed ones, that were not previously included in his behavioral repertoire. This may be true even if the child does not perform imitative responses, or receive reinforcement at the time he is observing the model. For example, in several studies, Bandura and his colleagues have shown that after exposure to aggressive models children will imitate many novel aggressive responses (Bandura, 1966; Bandura, Ross & Ross, 1961; Bandura & Walters, 1963).

It is impossible to determine how much of the child's repertoire of sex-typed responses develops as a result of the imitation of models. But there is little doubt that from very early childhood onward, children learn by imitating models, either because they are instructed to do so, or because they simply "want to." If the child's imitative behavior is rewarded frequently "a secondary tendency to match [imitate] may be developed and the process of imitation becomes the derived drive of imitativeness" (Miller & Dollard, 1941, p. 10).

The questions of why and how the process of imitation develops remain unanswered. But clearly, once imitation begins, it becomes a highly significant means of acquiring new responses. Many of the child's sex-typed responses may develop simply through imitation of his like-sexed parent's behavior.

A note of caution must be sounded. On the basis of their recent research, summarized above, Sears et al. (1965) rejected the imitation hypothesis as an explanation for the acquisition of sex-typed behavior, concluding that it is "deceptively simple." Bandura's research had shown that powerful and nurturant models were more likely to be imitated than models lacking these characteristics. But the study of Sears et al. yielded no data supportive of a "modeling" hypothesis which stated that "if the father is more nurturant and more powerful than the mother, the child will use him as the more-to-be-imitated model, and will thus be more masculine" (Sears et al., 1965, p. 187).

Nor were there any significant correlations between their parental power and nurturant scales and measures of sex role for either sex. The investigators attributed this negative finding to the fact that the responses imitated in the Bandura studies were simple and easily recognized, while Sears et al. were concerned with the emulation of "that very complex quality of gender role exemplified in parental behavior" (Sears et al., 1965, p. 186).

IDENTIFICATION

The acquisition and development of many complicated sex-typed patterns of behavior, personality characteristics, motives and attitudes do not yield readily to analysis in terms of social-learning theory. Many such responses appear to develop spontaneously, without direct training or reward and without the child intending to learn. A more subtle process, identification, has been hypothesized to account for such developments.

> ... sex-typing has been interpreted by non-psychoanalytic theorists as an instance of primary identification. Gender roles are very broad and very subtle. It would be difficult to imagine that any kind of direct tuition could provide for the learning of such elaborate behavioral, attitudinal, and manneristic patterns as are subsumed under the rubrics of masculinity and femininity (Sears et al., 1965, p. 171).

The concept of identification originated within the framework of psychoanalytic theory. Freud defined it as the process which "endeavors to mold a person's own ego after the fashion of one that has been taken as a model" (Freud, 1921, p. 62).

Because of its extensive, explanatory powers, the concept also appeals to many non-psychoanalytic theorists. Learning theorists conceptualize identification as "learned drive" or "motive" to be like a model (e.g., parents). The child's identification with his parents is seen in his attempts to duplicate or emulate their ways of behaving, thinking, and feeling and to adopt their ideals, attitudes and opinions.

Clearly, imitation and identification are concepts that have much in common and it is frankly difficult to make precise or rigorous differentiations between them. In fact, Bandura and Walters deny that such a differentiation is possible:

> . . . observational learning is generally labeled "imitation" in experimental psychology and "identification" in theories of personality. Both concepts, however, encompass the same behavioral phenomena, namely the tendency for a person to reproduce the actions, attitudes, or emotional responses exhibited by models (Bandura & Walters, 1963, p. 89).

These theorists prefer to use the term "imitation" to refer to "the occurrence of any matching responses" (Bandura & Walters, 1963, p. 90).

Although this argument has considerable merit, most students of socialization — and of sex-typing in particular — find the concept "identification" a very useful one. It is generally used to denote a particular kind of imitation: the spontaneous duplication of a model's complex, integrated pattern of behavior (rather than simple, discrete responses), without specific training or direct reward but based on an intimate relationship between the identifier and the model. Phenomenologically — from the child's viewpoint — identification is manifested by the belief that he possesses some of the model's attributes and feelings (Kagan, 1958).

> If a six-year-old boy is identified with his father, he necessarily regards himself as possessing some of his father's characteristics, one of which is maleness or masculinity. Moreover, if a child is identified with a model, he will behave, to some extent, as if events that occur to the model are occurring to him. If a child is identified with his father, he shares vicariously in the latter's victories and defeats; in his happiness and in his sorrow; in his strengths and in his weaknesses (Kagan, 1964, p. 146).

The outcomes or products of the process are assumed to be relatively stable and enduring and highly resistant to change. Broad, pervasive aspects of personality and character, such as inner control or conscience, and sex-typing are presumably assimilated or absorbed by means of identification. Obviously identification with the like-sexed parent enhances the child's sex-typing considerably. As Kagan points out,

> The boy with a masculine father gains two products from an identification with him — the vicarious power and strength that facilitate future attempts to master sex-typed skills, and the continued exposure to sex-typed behavior. This exposure

facilitates the acquisition of sex-typed responses (Kagan, 1964, p. 148).

Three major hypotheses about the origins and development of identification have been proposed: defensive identification, the original psychoanalytic hypothesis; the developmental identification hypothesis, based essentially on the principles of learning; and the role-playing hypothesis, derived from sociological conceptualizations.

*Defensive identification.* The original, psychoanalytic formulation of defensive identification linked the process to the resolution of the Oedipus complex. The young boy, having libidinous feelings toward the mother, begins to see his father as a competitor for the mother's love and attention and, therefore, as an object of antagonism, envy and hostility — "a rival who stands in his way and whom he would like to push aside" (Freud, 1949, p. 91).

But the boy soon begins to fear that his father will castrate him in retaliation for his envy and hostility, as well as for his sexual strivings toward the mother. This fear, together with the boy's realization that he cannot succeed in this struggle, lead to the resolution of the Oedipus complex. Instead of competing with his father and feeling hostile and jealous, the boy *identifies* with him. Identification in a sense *replaces* the Oedipal conflict. It is as though the boy said, "if I *am* him, he can't hurt me."

Identification then serves the functions of reducing the boy's fear of the father and permitting him to enjoy the mother's love vicariously. (If he *is* the father, he possesses the mother's love.) Such identification has also been labeled "aggressive identification," and "identification with the aggressor" (A. Freud, 1946; Bronfenbrenner, 1960; Mowrer, 1950, pp. 573-616).

Two recent theorists, Kagan (1958) and Whiting (1960), also suggest that envy (though not exclusively of a sexual kind) is a central factor in the development of identification. The child envies a broad range of the model's powers and capabilities as well as his efficient control and enjoyment of resources. The child covertly practices the roles of the model so that, at least in fantasy, he is like the envied model, controlling and consuming the valued resources he lacks in reality. Underlying the child's development and maintenance of identification is a desire "to experience or obtain positive goal states that he perceived that the model demands" (Kagan, 1958, p. 298).

The classical psychoanalytic hypothesis that identification is motivated by fear of castration clearly cannot explain the girl's identification with her mother. To explain this, Freud postulated the mechanism of anaclitic identification, rooted in the girl's love and attachment as well as her need to insure the continuation of her dependency relationship with the mother. Fear of the loss of the mother's love, and the frustration and deprivation this would entail, motivate the girl to identify with her mother.

*Developmental identification.* The hypothesis of developmental identification, which is related to the concept of anaclitic identification, maintains that love and affection for the model are the principal factors instigating identification. If the child has pleasant, nurturant, rewarding interactions with the parent, that parent's behavior — his activities, speech, and mannerisms — acquire positive value or, in learning theory terms, secondary reward value. The child, being dependent on the nurturant parent, feels frustrated when he is absent. But by performing some of the acts ordinarily performed by that parent, the child is able to provide himself with some of the rewarding feelings originally associated with the parent's presence. Developmental identification, manifested in the child's imitation of the parent's behavior, is motivated by the child's desire to "reproduce bits of the beloved and longed-for parent" (Mowrer, 1950, p. 615).

Developmental identification can readily explain the girl's identification with her mother, but accounting for the boy's father-identification is theoretically more troublesome. Since the mother is the primary source of nurturance and affection for all infants, both boys and girls should at first identify with her. To identify with his father, the little boy must, in some way, "abandon the mother as a personal model and shift his loyalties and ambitions to his father" (Mowrer, 1950, p. 607).

Mowrer has suggested that the infant's first identification with his mother is undifferentiated, i.e., it is with the mother as an adult human being, not specifically as a man or a woman. After the child becomes aware of sex differences,

> the father, who has played a somewhat subsidiary role up to this point, normally comes forward as the boy's special mentor, as his proctor, guide, and model in matters which will help the boy eventually to achieve full adult status in society, not only as a human being, but also in the unique status of a *man* (Mowrer, 1950, p. 608).

This shift to father-identification is based on affection and love for the father. This usually occurs at the age of three or four, when

> the good father tends to "take [his son] on," to accept responsibility for him in a way that he does not do for his little girls. The boy becomes *my boy, my son;* the father permits the child to accompany him in his work, if possible, and otherwise creates special opportunities for excursions and experiences which the mother could not well provide. The father, in other words, begins to open up for the child a glimpse into "man's world" (Mowrer, 1950, p. 610).

*Role theory and identification.* For role theorists, identification is equated with "role-playing," e.g., identification with the father is synonymous with "playing the father's role." The child's role-playing is purposive because it provides practice for significant adult behavior (Maccoby, 1959).

Two factors determine the extent of the child's role-playing or the strength of his identification: (1) frequency and intensity (or intimacy) of the child's interaction with the model; and (2) the model's power over the child, i.e., his control of resources that are valuable to the child (Maccoby, 1959). From the child's point of view, the model's power may involve both giving nurturance and reward (the major determinants of developmental identification) and the ability to threaten and punish (of paramount importance in producing defensive identification) (Mussen & Distler, 1959).

*Studies of identification and sex-typing.* Identification with the like-sexed parent is often regarded as a *sine qua non* of appropriate sex-typing. Whether or not such a sweeping generalization is valid, there is evidence that *lack* of such identification has deleterious effects on sex-typing. For example, three- and four-year-old boys reared without fathers in their homes are retarded in acquiring typically masculine aggressive patterns of behavior, presumably because they did not have masculine models available (Sears, Pintler & Sears, 1946). Such boys also have difficulties establishing relationships with their peers, perhaps because of their inadequate development of the masculine skills and orientations necessary for successful peer interactions (Lynn & Sawrey, 1958).

*Homosexuality.* More dramatic, and perhaps more relevant, evidence comes from investigations of the backgrounds of homosexuals, individuals who have not acquired the most essential attribute of adequate sex-typing, sexual orientation (object choice) toward the opposite sex. Clinical evidence suggests that the male homosexual is overly attached to his mother, identifying with her rather than with his father (Bieber et al., 1962). This may be due to rejection by the father, together with acceptance by the mother, or perceptions of the mother as the more dominant and powerful parent. If either of these conditions obtains, the boy does not shift from early identification with his mother, remains excessively dependent on her, and does not identify with his father or other adult males. If he maintains his identification with the mother, he will, as a consequence, assume her sex-object choice.

"If mother (like women in general) is sexually oriented toward men, and if the boy's strongest personal alignment remains with her, then he too, as a consequence of his persistent mother-identification, will tend to be sexually oriented toward men" (Mowrer, 1950, p. 612).

In order to test the Freudian hypothesis that male homosexuals show stronger identification with their mothers and less identification with their fathers, Chang and Block (1960) assessed the identification patterns of twenty overt homosexual male adults and a matched group of twenty men who were not homosexuals. Their data supported the hypothesis, showing clearly that overt male homosexuals were relatively more strongly identified with their mothers than with their fathers. In brief, failure to identify with the like-sexed parent seems to be an antecedent of homosexuality or inappropriateness of sex-object choice.

*Sex-typing of nursery school children.* Measures of sex-typing have been used as indices of identification in a number of systematic studies involving normal children from intact families. In one study designed to test the relative truth values of the developmental, defensive and role-playing hypotheses of identification, boys' masculinity scores were related to their perceptions of their fathers (Mussen & Distler, 1959). The questions underlying the study were: Do highly masculine boys view their fathers as nurturant and rewarding, as the developmental hypothesis would predict; as punitive and threatening, in accordance with the defensive identification hypothesis; or, as powerful controllers of resources (rewards and punishment), as role theory would hold? Thirty-eight five-year-old boys were given the IT Scale, a projective test of sex-role preference (Brown, 1956) and the ten most masculine boys and the ten least masculine were selected for further study. These twenty boys completed a series of incomplete, semi-structured doll-play stories, that revealed their perceptions of their parents. As would be predicted from the developmental identification hypothesis, the highly masculine boys significantly more frequently portrayed their fathers as nurturant and rewarding. There was also some slight support for the defensive identification hypothesis, however, with highly masculine boys perceiving their fathers as more punitive.

These boys also scored higher than the boys low in masculinity in *father power,* a score reflecting both the extent of the child's interaction with his father and the degree to which the latter has power over him, i.e., controls rewards and punishments. This last finding may be regarded as evidence in support of the role theory of identification. It may be concluded that this study, designed to evaluate the three theories, yielded some support for all of them. The evidence for the developmental hypothesis is the most clear-cut and impressive, however.

Interviews with the mothers of the boys generally corroborated the doll-play findings. The fathers of the highly masculine boys were reported to be warmer and more affectionate toward their sons and more interested in them. These results, too, may be interpreted as supportive of the developmental and role-theory hypotheses of identification, but they provide no support for the defensive identification hypothesis.

In a replication and extension of this study, the IT Test was administered to five- and six-year-old boys and girls who completed the same incomplete stories in doll-play (Mussen & Rutherford, 1963). In addition, each mother was interviewed intensively and both parents answered personality questionnaires and a "play and games list" dealing with the parent's encouragement or discouragement of the child's participation in certain typical sex-typed activities.

The study yielded further evidence for the developmental identification hypothesis as applied to both sexes. Appropriate sex-typing among boys was again found to be related to perceptions of fathers as warm, nurturant, and rewarding. The findings for girls paralleled those for the boys. Highly feminine, appropriately sex-typed girls described their mothers in doll-play as significantly warmer, more nurturant, affectionate and gratifying than the other girls did. The data from maternal interviews buttressed these findings, mothers of highly feminine girls reporting more interest in their daughters and warmer relationships with them. None of the evidence fitted the defensive identification model.

Other factors were also found to be conducive to the young girl's feminization. Mothers' self-acceptance and fathers' masculinity of interests and orientation, as well as the fathers' encouragement of their daughters' participation in feminine activities, were associated with high degrees of femininity in the girls.

It must also be noted that not all investigations of identification and sex-typing have yielded positive results. Sears et al. (1965) found no significant correlations between their scales of parental nurturance and power, on the one hand, and their measures of their nursery school subjects' sex-role behavior. Judging from their data,

> There is no evidence that the feminine girls' mothers were warm or set high standards (except for table manners) or used love-oriented discipline, or specified themselves as models. The masculine boys' parents, in the home, were not warm, nor did they use love-oriented discipline or refer to themselves as models . . . the primary identification theory as an explanation of gender role is poor (Sears et al., 1965, p. 194).

It is difficult to determine exactly why these results are so vastly different from those obtained in the studies reviewed above, but a number of possible reasons may be suggested. For one thing, the subjects of the Sears et al. study were at least a year younger than the subjects of the other studies and perhaps their patterns of identification were not yet well-enough crystallized. Moreover, they were all from highly intelligent, well-educated families where sex roles may be less clearly differentiated than they are in lower-middle class, more poorly educated families from which the subjects of the other studies came. Most importantly, different operations were used in assessing sex-typing: preferences for obvious, easily recognized masculine and feminine activities and objects in the IT Test versus actual choices of objects and activities plus more subtle, more complex qualities of sex role in the Sears et al. study (1965). In any case, the findings of the latter study make it clear that, at least during the nursery school period, developmental identification does not seem to be a complete and adequate explanation of sex-typing.

COGNITIVE-DEVELOPMENTAL THEORY OF SEX-TYPING

A theoretical interpretation of the acquisition of sex-typed behavior and attitudes that contrasts sharply with learning theory identification interpretations has recently been proposed by Kohlberg (1966). The theory is linked to two prominent recent developments in psychology: the renaissance of cognitive developmental theory, stimulated by the work of Piaget and his followers, and the new stress on motives such as curiosity, mastery, exploration, competence and effectance.

Kohlberg's intriguing theory is based on the assumption that the basic patterning of sexual attitudes is to be found neither in biological instincts nor in arbitrary cultural norms, but in universal aspects of "the child's cognitive organization of his social world along sex-role dimensions" (Kohlberg, 1966, p. 82). The development of sex-typing is conceived as an aspect of cognitive growth which involves basic, qualitative changes with age in the child's modes of thinking and concomitantly, in his perceptions of the physical and social world, including his sense of self, and of his sex role. Learning, particularly observational learning, plays some role in sex-role acquisition, but the most significant factor is the child's *cognitive activity* — his active selection and organization (structuring) of his perceptions, knowledge and understanding.

The child's initial conception of sex role stems from

> important, "natural" components of patterning; i.e., aspects of sex-role attitudes which are universal across cultures and family structures and which appear relatively early in the child's development. This patterning of sex-role attitudes is essentially "cognitive" in that it is rooted in the child's conceptions of physical things, the bodies of himself and of others, as he relates body concepts to his conceptions of a social order which makes functional use of sex categories in quite culturally universal ways. Rather than biological instinct, it is the child's cognitive organization of social role concepts around universal physical dimensions that accounts for the existence of universals in sex-role attitudes (adapted from Kohlberg, 1966, p. 82).

Sex-typing is initiated by the very early sex *labeling* of the child which begins with hearing and learning the words "boy" and "girl." By the age of two or three, children know their own self-labels, and in the next couple of years, they label others according to conventional cues. The child regards his sex-identification as an "abstract self-concept" which, when stabilized, is practically fixed and irreversible, "maintained by a motivated adaptation to physical-social reality and by the need to preserve a stable and positive self-image" (Kohlberg, 1966, p. 88). The child's basic sexual self-concept (his self-categorization as "boy" or "girl") becomes the major organizer and determinant of many of his activities, values, and attitudes. The boy in effect says, "I am a boy, therefore I want to do boy things, therefore the opportunity to do boy things (and to gain approval for doing them) is rewarding" (Kohlberg, 1966, p. 89).

The child's sex self-concept or gender identity becomes stabilized at about five or six years of age, at the same time that the child begins to understand the principle of conservation — the fact that physical properties such as mass, number and weight are stable and invariant. With further cognitive development, he acquires a number of cross-cultural stereotypes of masculine and feminine behavior — of males as active, dominant, powerful and aggressive, and females as more nurturant. These are not derived from parental behavior or direct tuition, but rather, stem from universal perceived sex differences in bodily structure and capacities.

Once established, basic sex-role concepts generate new sex-typed values and attitudes. Kohlberg postulates five mechanisms by which sex-role concepts become directly translated into masculine-feminine values:

(1) The first, an expression of Piaget's notion of *assimilation,* is the child's "tendency to respond to new activities and interests that are consistent with old ones" (Kohlberg, 1966, p. 112). By the age of two, there are clear-cut sex differences in interests, activities and personality characteristics. New objects or activities consistent with established interests and preferences are assimilated, while discrepant ones are not.

(2) Children make value judgments consistent with their self-concepts of sex role. The three-year-old has a "naive or egocentric tendency to value anything associated with or like himself" as best (Kohlberg, 1966, p. 113), and hence values and seeks objects and activities that are representative of his own sex.

(3) Young children tend to associate positive, self-enhancing values with sex-role stereotypes and these values are motivating. For example, masculinity is associated with values of strength, competence, and power, and for the boy, acquiring this stereotype produces a motivation to enact a masculine role, to conform to the stereotype. According to Kohlberg, this is true regardless of the rewards associated with the role.

(4) The child perceives his gender role as normative and hence generates judgments that conformity is morally right and deviations are morally wrong.

(5) Modeling or identification is the fifth mechanism, but Kohlberg's analysis of the process is strikingly different from the psychoanalytic or learning interpretations discussed earlier. Sex-typing is not conceived as a *product* of identification; quite the contrary, identification is a consequence of sex-typing. Boys model themselves after males because they already have masculine interests and values; "for the boy with masculine interests and values, the activities of a male model are more interesting and hence more modeled" (Kohlberg, 1966, p. 129).

Once the modeling process begins, it continues, with widespread effects. The child begins to imitate not only individually admired acts; but he wants to be like the model in general and hence needs a continuing relationship to him to attain this goal (Kohlberg, 1966, p. 134).

> In summary, then, the boy's general competence motivation leads him to prefer and imitate masculine roles and models on a twofold base, first because

they are "like self" and second because the boy awards superior prestige, power and competence to such roles. These tendencies lead him to develop preferential imitation and approval seeking from the father, but only after a delay period. This delay period occurs because cognitive growth is required before the father's role is categorized in terms of "we males," and before the father's occupational and familial role is perceived as more prestigeful than the mother's in terms of economic, occupational, and instrumental functions. During this period, the boy's identification with the father tends to be assimilated to general stereotypes of the masculine role having little to do with the father's individual role and personality (adapted from Kohlberg, 1966, p. 136).

Since the cognitive-developmental theory of sex-typing was proposed very recently, there have not yet been direct tests of specific hypotheses derived from theory and adequate evaluation is not possible. Nevertheless, Kohlberg's presentation is intriguing, thoughtful, stimulating, and plausible. It cites relevant, supportive evidence and emphasizes a number of important problems neglected by other theories of sex-typing.

The stress on early sex labeling, underplayed in other theories, seems warranted in view of facts reviewed earlier. Most importantly, Kohlberg's stress on the critical roles of cognitive growth and changes in cognitive organization seem a much needed antidote for the neglect of these phenomena in traditional learning theory and psychoanalytic hypotheses about identification and sex-typing. His arguments in these matters are compelling. There is little doubt that the child's cognitive abilities — his perceptions and understanding of his environment — strongly influence the development of sex-role behavior. Unfortunately, however, the mechanisms underlying cognitive development have not been carefully specified or adequately analyzed, changes being attributed to "natural" (i.e., unexplained) events.

The theory is a descriptive-developmental one and is not primarily concerned with antecedent-consequent relationships in sex-typing. As a result, it gives less adequate attention to individual differences in degrees of sex-typing, i.e., within-sex differences in strength of sex-typed responses. Kohlberg views these fundamentally as the outcomes of differences in level or rate of cognitive development. This hardly seems a satisfactory explanation, however, for in any group of boys of the same age and of equal intelligence, there are wide variations in degrees of masculinity of interests, attitudes and behavior. Kohlberg acknowledges that "a family climate of warmth, expressiveness, security . . . and high social participation" may facilitate sex-typing because it "allows for the exploration and integration of the new and the problematic" in development (Kohlberg, 1966, p. 156). But in general his theory underemphasizes the potency of reinforcement of sex-typed responses, modeling, and identification in the sex-typing process.

## A Synthesis and Point of View on Sex-Role Development

As this review demonstrates, there is a variety of theories of sex-typing and acquisition of sex role. Each undoubtedly contains some truth and each has some empirical support. Yet none of the theories by itself is able to account for all the observed phenomena and all the data on the acquisition of sex-typed behavior.

A comprehensive theory of sex-role development — if such is possible — will have to incorporate aspects of all three theories, and in addition, include some factors not explicitly handled in any of them. Furthermore, such a theory must explain individual differences in sex-typing as well as general age developmental trends in the process.

It may be hypothesized that normally, for most children, learning, identification and cognitive organization all contribute to the development and growth of sex-typing and sex-role acquisition. It seems likely that learning is of paramount importance in the very early phases of sex-role development and that identification and cognitive growth play vital, facilitating roles later on. That is, the first established components of sex role are probably learned by means of reinforcement and imitation. Certainly specific and discrete sex-typed responses can be trained and learned in this way, and, probably more importantly, so can broad, pervasive sex-typed personality characteristics, attitudes and approaches — products of generalizations from specific responses — which, once formed, generalize to many situations.

If children between the ages of one and four were reared in a highly controlled, laboratory setting (God forbid), their training — and consequently their learning — could probably be programmed in such a way as to produce stereotypical sex-appropriate behavior, profoundly reversed sex roles, or something in between. Undesirable as this would be from other points of view, it would be theoretically possible for the child to acquire the overt aspects (and probably some of the covert attributes) of sex-role behavior in this way, without forming an identification relationship with a like-sexed adult.

But happily, reinforcement learning is not ordinarily the only process involved in sex-role development. In the course of growing up, most children form affectionate relationships with their parents, identify with them, and take them as behavior models.

The sequence of critical events in sex-role development, as we view it, is labeling, tuition (training), and identification. Obviously, training is not entirely superseded by identification when the latter process begins. Rather, training and learning continue with broader, more striking consequences after the child has identified with his parents.

As Kohlberg suggests, labeling the child properly initiates the process of sex-typing. But the simple act of labeling is not sufficient to set the process in operation. The assigned label must be salient for the child and must be regarded as positive, valuable, and rewarding. The fifteen-month-old child who is appropriately labeled, but is at the same time restricted, given no freedom for self-expression and made to feel inadequate, will not be highly motivated to act in sex-appropriate ways. In order to be effective (i.e., to promote sex-typing), labeling must occur within a context of a "sense of autonomy" (Erikson, 1950), i.e., feelings of self-reliance, worthiness, and adequacy. If the label is applied with signs of love and affection, with clear indications of acceptance and approval, it will be associated with positive feelings (rewards). Under these circumstances, the boy will like to hear himself called a boy and he will be motivated to perform more "boy" activities. In other words, the label becomes an incentive for acquiring more sex-typed behavior. What is important, then, is not only the label itself, but its associations and the context within which it is assigned.

Parents have two major tasks in promoting their child's sex-typing. The first is *tuition,* i.e., teaching the child appropriate sex-typed responses through rewards and punishments, and guiding his behavior, directing it into the proper channels. The second is *providing a model* of the proper general attitudes and personality characteristics for the child to emulate.

Fortunately, most parents can perform these tasks without great difficulty because they themselves have absorbed and incorporated sex-appropriate responses, characteristics, and attitudes and they have clear conceptions of appropriate masculine and feminine behaviors. They expect different responses from their sons and daughters and, from early childhood on, properly reward and encourage sex-appropriate responses (or intimations that the child is trying to behave in sex-appropriate ways), including early imitation of sex-appropriate models. Sex-inappropriate behavior, and and attempts to imitate opposite-sex responses, are punished and discouraged.

But parents do not wait passively for the occurrence of sex-typed responses that they reward. They participate in their child's sex-typing more actively, guiding his activities by providing him with sex-appropriate objects and toys and then rewarding with approval his interest and his manipulations of these. Thus many little girls of two are presented with dolls and carriages and rewarded for their play with these toys. Through these experiences they acquire many sex-typed responses, become more keenly aware of, and evaluate highly, the kinds of activities that are sex-appropriate (Hartley, 1964).

As his sex-appropriate responses and characteristics become progressively strengthened as a consequence of reinforcement, the child's cognitive abilities increase. His perceptions, understanding and interpretation of the world become more mature, adult-like and realistic. His concepts of his own sex role become more comprehensive and accurate, and in turn, lead to further channelization of his behavior, ready assimilation of sex-appropriate responses, and rejection of the inappropriate.

The principle of conservation or invariance is applicable to conceptions of sex role, too. When he has acquired the principle, the child is more aware of the essentially constant, invariant components of masculine and feminine roles as well as of those which, though often associated with one of these roles, are not necessary components. Thus, the more mature cognitive organizations facilitate the selection of behaviors to be emulated, imitated, and thus acquired.

Identification with the parent of the same sex plays an analogous, and critical, facilitating role in sex-typing. Undoubtedly superficial, overt sex-typed characteristics (e.g., aggression) can be acquired and strengthened without any substantial identifications. Boys whose fathers do not live at home may learn masculine responses and may take on other male models or identificands. Social pressures soon convince the child that his rewards come from sex-appropriate responses and from emulation of models of his own sex.

Yet, some profound and subtle aspects of masculinity and femininity would not develop without identification with the like-sexed parent. Both clinical case studies and systematic investigations make it clear that such identification is an important antecedent of the formation of heterosexual orientation, probably the most important single component of sex role (Chang & Block, 1960), and of general, pervasive sex-typed interests and attitudes (Mussen, 1961; Payne & Mussen, 1956). In brief, identification with his like-sexed parent directs the child in the development of a broad range of new, subtle, and highly significant aspects of sex role — role behaviors not readily acquired through simple reinforcement learning.

In addition, the tendency to imitate the like-sexed parent may also generalize. The boy who finds emulation of his father rewarding is motivated to imitate other male models (including some more masculine than his father) and thus further to enhance the sex-typing process.

There are, of course, in both sexes, a wide range of individual differences in degrees of sex-typing achieved, i.e., in the closeness of fit between the individual's behavior and stereotyped sex-typed patterns of behavior. The boy who is closely identified with his "all-American" father is likely to possess all the characteristics and behaviors that comprise the stereotyped masculine pattern. In contrast, the son of a relatively effeminate man will lack many of these characteristics and patterns if he is strongly identified with his father.

Does the level of sex-role development affect general psychological or social adjustment? There are no data to answer this question adequately, but clinical experience suggests that the factors of paramount importance are the individual's acceptance of the behaviors and characteristics, and his confidence that these fulfill adequately, if not completely, the cultural prescriptions for members of his sex. It may be hypothesized further, that such self-acceptance and confidence are characteristic of individuals whose sex-role development is rooted in substantial identification with his like-sexed parent.

## REFERENCES

ABERLE, D. F., & NAEGELE, K. D. Middle class fathers' occupational role and attitudes toward children. *American Journal of Orthopsychiatry,* 1952, 22, 366–378.

BANDURA, A. Social learning through imitation. In M. R. Jones (Ed.), *Nebraska symposium on motivation,* 1962. Lincoln: Univer. of Nebraska Press, 1962.

BANDURA, A. Vicarious processes: A case of no-trial learning. In L. Berkowitz (Ed.), *Advances in experimental social psychology.* Vol. II. New York: Academic Press, 1966.

BANDURA, A., ROSS, DOROTHEA, & ROSS, SHEILA. Transmission of aggression through imitation of aggressive models. *Journal of Abnormal and Social Psychology,* 1961, 63, 575–582.

BANDURA, A., & WALTERS, R. H. *Social learning and personality development.* New York: Holt, Rinehart and Winston, 1963.

BARRY, H., BACON, M., & CHILD, I. L. A cross-cultural survey of some sex differences in socialization. *Journal of Abnormal and Social Psychology,* 1957, 55, 327–332.

BIEBER, I., DAIN, H. J., DINCE, P. R., DRELLICH, M. G., GRAND, H. G., GUNDLACH, R. H., KREMER, M. W., RIFKIN, A. H., WILBUR, C. B., & BIEBER, T. B. *Homosexuality.* New York: Basic Books, 1962.

BRONFENBRENNER, U. Freudian theories of identification and their derivatives. *Child Development,* 1960, 31, 15–40.

BROWN, D. G. Sex-role preference in young children. *Psychological Monographs,* 1956, 70, 1–19. No. 14.

BROWN, D. G. Masculinity-femininity development in children. *Journal of Consulting Psychology,* 1957, 21, 197–202.

CHANG, J., & BLOCK, J. A study of identification in male homosexuals. *Journal of Consulting Psychology,* 1960, 24, 307–310.

D'ANDRADE, R. Cross-cultural studies of sex differences in behavior. In Eleanor Maccoby (Ed.), *The development of sex differences.* Stanford, Calif.: Stanford Univer. Press, 1966.

ELKIN, F. *The child and society.* New York: Random House, 1960.

ERIKSON, E. H. *Childhood and society.* New York: Norton, 1950.

FAULS, L. B., & SMITH, W. D. Sex role learning of five-year-olds. *Journal of Genetic Psychology,* 1956, 89, 105–117.

FOSTER, J. C. Play activities of children in the first six grades. *Child Development,* 1930, 1, 248–254.

FREUD, ANNA. *The ego and the mechanisms of defense.* New York: International Universities Press, 1946.

FREUD, S. *Group psychology and the analysis of the ego.* London: Hogarth Press, 1921.

FREUD, S. *An outline of psychoanalysis.* New York: Norton, 1949.

HAMPSON, J. L. Determinants of psychosexual orientation. In F. A. Beach (Ed.), *Sex and behavior.* New York: Wiley, 1965. Pp. 108–132.

HARTLEY, RUTH. A developmental view of female sex-role definition and identification. *Merrill-Palmer Quarterly,* 1964, 10, 3–16.

HARTUP, W. W., & ZOOK, E. A. Sex-role preferences in three- and four-year-old children. *Journal of Consulting Psychology,* 1960, 24, 420–426.

JONES, M. C. The later careers of boys who were early or late maturing. *Child Development,* 1957, 28, 113–128.

JONES, M. C., & MUSSEN, P. H. Self conceptions, motivations, and interpersonal attitudes of early and late maturing girls. *Child Development,* 1958, 29, 491–501.

KAGAN, J. The child's perception of the parent. *Journal of Abnormal and Social Psychology,* 1956, 53, 257–258.

KAGAN, J. The concept of identification. *Psychological Review,* 1958, 65, 296–305.

KAGAN, J. Acquisition and significance of sex typing and sex role identity. In Hoffman & Hoffman (Eds.), *Review of child development research,* Vol. I. New York: Russell Sage Foundation, 1964.

KAGAN, J., & LEMKIN, J. The child's differential perception of parental attributes. *Journal of Abnormal and Social Psychology,* 1960, 61, 446–447.

KAGAN, J., & MOSS, H. A. *Birth to maturity.* New York: Wiley, 1962.

KOHLBERG, L. A cognitive-developmental analysis of children's sex-role concepts and attitudes. In Eleanor Maccoby (Ed.), *The development of sex differences.* Stanford, Calif.: Stanford Univer. Press, 1966.

LANSKY, L. M., CRANDALL, V. J., KAGAN, J., & BAKER, C. T. Sex differences in aggression and its correlates in middle class adolescents. *Child Development,* 1961, 32, 45–58.

LINTON, R. *The cultural background of personality.* New York: Appleton-Century-Crofts, 1945.

LYNN, D. B., & SAWREY, W. L. The effects of father absence on Norwegian boys and girls. *Journal of Abnormal and Social Psychology,* 1958, 59, 258–262.

MACCOBY, ELEANOR. Role-taking in childhood and its consequences for social learning. *Child Development,* 1959, 30, 239–252.

MEAD, MARGARET. *Sex and temperament in three primitive societies.* New York: Morrow, 1935.

MILLER, N. E., & DOLLARD, J. *Social learning and imitation.* New Haven: Yale Univer. Press, 1941.

MISCHEL, W. A social learning view of sex differences in behavior. In Eleanor Maccoby (Ed.), *The development of sex differences.* Stanford, Calif.: Stanford Univer. Press, 1966.

MOWRER, O. H. *Learning theory and personality dynamics.* New York: Ronald Press, 1950.

MUSSEN, P. H. Some antecedents and consequents of masculine sex-typing in adolescent boys. *Psychological Monographs,* 1961, 75, 1–24. No. 2.

MUSSEN, P. H., & DISTLER, L. Masculinity, identification, and father-son relationships. *Journal of Abnormal and Social Psychology,* 1959, 59, 350–356.

MUSSEN, P. H., & JONES, M. C. Self-conceptions, motivations and interpersonal attitudes of late and early maturing boys. *Child Development,* 1957, 28, 243–256.

MUSSEN, P. H., & JONES, M. C. The behavior inferred motivations of late and early maturing boys. *Child Development,* 1958, 29, 61–67.

MUSSEN, P. H., & RUTHERFORD, E. Parent-child relations and parental personality in relation to young children's sex-role preferences. *Child Development,* 1963, 34, 589–607.

PARSONS, T. Family structures and the socialization of the child. In T. Parsons & R. F. Bales (Eds.), *Family, socialization and interaction process.* Glencoe, Ill.: Free Press, 1955.

PAYNE, D. E., & MUSSEN, P. H. Parent-child relations and father identification among adolescent boys. *Journal of Abnormal and Social Psychology,* 1956, 52, 358–362.

RABBAN, M. Sex-role identification in young children in two diverse social groups. *Genetic Psychology Monographs,* 1950, 42, 81–158.

RHEINGOLD, HARRIET. The modification of social responsiveness in institutional babies. *Monograph of Social Research and Child Development,* 1956, 21. No. 2.

SEARS, P. S. Doll play aggression in normal young children: Influence of sex, age, sibling status, father's absence. *Psychological Monographs,* 1951, 65. No. 6.

SEARS, R. R. Identification as a form of behavioral development. In D. B. Harris (Ed.), *The concept of development.* Minneapolis: Univer. of Minnesota Press, 1957. Pp. 149–161.

SEARS, R. R. Development of gender role. In F. A. Beach (Ed.), *Sex and behavior.* New York: Wiley, 1965. Pp. 133–163.

SEARS, R. R., MACCOBY, ELEANOR, & LEVIN, H. *Patterns of child rearing.* Evanston, Ill.: Row, Peterson, 1957.

SEARS, R. R., PINTLER, M. H., & SEARS, P. S. Effect of father separation on preschool children's doll play aggression. *Child Development,* 1946, 17, 219–243.

SEARS, R. R., RAU, LUCY, & ALPERT, R. *Identification and child rearing.* Stanford, Calif.: Stanford Univer. Press, 1965.

WHITING, J. W. M. Resource mediation and learning by identification. In I. Iscoe & W. Stevenson (Eds.), *Personality development in children.* Austin, Texas: Univer. of Texas Press, 1960. Pp. 112–126.

# SUGGESTED READINGS

With the resurgence of interest in the status of women, reflections of other periods are being discovered anew and contemporary reports are being rushed into print. To encompass the literature on the second sex becomes increasingly a task equivalent to drawing up a catalogue of works on mankind. What follows is, therefore, not a comprehensive bibliography, but a personal one. I have included those studies that were for me most rewarding: as information source, as stimulus — both positive and negative — and as analytical instrument.

## Feminism: The Feminine Idea, The Feminine Experience

Baker, Elizabeth F. *Technology and Woman's Work.* New York: Columbia University Press, 1964. Traces the relationship between woman's labor force participation and technological change.

Bernard, Jessie. *Academic Women.* University Park, Pa.: Pennsylvania State University Press, 1964. An authoritative study of the role of women on campus: as students and as faculty.

Bird, Caroline, with Sara Welles Briller. *Born Female.* New York: David McKay Co., 1968. A lively report in popular style on the range of discrimination in the employment market, particularly at the executive and professional levels.

Brenton, Myron. *The American Male.* New York: Coward-McCann, 1966. Describes the penalties of rigid sex-typing as experienced by both men and women. A work of intelligent journalism.

Calverton, V. F., and S. D. Schmalhausen (eds.). *Sex in Civilization.* Garden City, New York: Garden City Publishing Co., The Macaulay Co., 1929. A collection of essays, some of them dated, but nevertheless of historical interest. See especially "Freud's Theory of Sex: A Criticism" by Abraham Myerson.

De Beauvoir, Simone. *The Second Sex.* New York: Knopf, 1953, first published in 1949. Translated from the French by H. M. Parshley. The initial salvo of the second feminist revolution. It is marred by obscure language and existentialist references, but is perceptive and original in content, especially in Part III, "Myths."

Friedan, Betty. *The Feminine Mystique.* New York: Norton, 1963. A popular treatment of the dilemmas of the middle class American woman in the split-level suburb. Somewhat ahistorical, but useful for an analysis of the media, and of other contemporary phenomena that form female images.

Gilman, Charlotte Perkins (Stetson). *Women and Economics.* Boston: Small, Maynard and Co., 1898. The author was the principal theorist of the first feminist revolution in the United States. She writes lucidly, in an astringent style, with brilliant flashes of insight. Her viewpoint is socialist, but her attendant biases are in some instances sentimental. On balance, however, this is a valuable work.

Holtby, Winifred. *Women.* London: John Lane, The Bodley Head, Ltd., 1934. Reflects the issues that concerned the Woman's Movement in England during the years between the wars.

Kanowitz, Leo. *Women and the Law: The Unfinished Revolution.* Albuquerque: University of New Mexico Press, 1969. A scholarly analysis of the legal status of women in the United States today. The section treating the Equal Rights Amendment is of particular interest.

Klein, Viola. *The Feminine Character: History of an Ideology.* New York: International Universities Press, 1949. (This edition is out of print. A new edition is in press to be published by the University of Illinois Press.) Since women are invisible, the sociology of women has been a nonfield. The subject has therefore been largely pre-empted by journalists, who often search out the data intelligently, but lack the theory, historical perspective, and profundity of the scholar. This synthesis of views on women from the vantage points of various disciplines is one of the rare exceptions, a book by a fine sociologist. It is the best I know on the subject.

Komarovsky, Mirra. *Women in the Modern World: Their Education and Their Dilemmas.* Boston: Little, Brown, 1953. Another work based in sound scholarship. Especially valuable in its analysis of proposals for a feminine curriculum and in vignettes it offers of women with varying life styles.

Kraditor, Aileen S. (ed.). *Up From the Pedestal: Landmark Writings in the American Woman's Struggle for Equality.* Chicago: Quadrangle Press, 1968. A discriminatingly chosen selection of documents and speeches, made more meaningful by the editor's focusing essay.

Marder, Herbert. *Feminism and Art: A Study of Virginia Woolf.* Chicago and London: University of Chicago Press, 1968. A sensitive study of the writings of Virginia Woolf, including her novels, from the standpoint of her ideas on the position of women in society.

Mill, John Stuart. *The Subjection of Women.* London: Longmans and Company, 1906 (first published in 1869). One of the classics in the field, written by an English philosopher and economist.

Millett, Kate. *Sexual Politics.* Garden City, New York: Doubleday, 1970. Reflects some of the thinking of the Women's Liberation Movement. The relationship between the sexes is seen as a power struggle. Of particular interest is the analysis of the work of Lawrence, Miller, Mailer, Genet, in the section titled: "The Literary Reflection."

Mitchell, Juliet. "The Longest Revolution," in *New Left Review,* vol. 40 (November-December, 1966). A study of women from the Marxist vantage, with a critique of the treatment of the subject in socialist theory and thought.

Newcomer, Mabel. *A Century of Higher Education for American Women.* New York: Harper, 1959. Offers a valuable perspective on the development of women's college education in the United States.

Schmalhausen, S. D., and V. F. Calverton (eds.). *Woman's Coming of Age.* New York: Horace Liveright, Inc., 1931. An interesting collection of essays from another period. See especially "How Christianity Has Treated Women" by Joseph McCabe.

Schreiner, Olive. *Woman and Labor.* New York: Frederick A. Stokes Company, 1911. A reflective work of style and remarkable prescience.

Schwabacher, Albert E., Jr. "Women and Money," in *Vogue,* April 1, 1963. Distinguishes between the property women own: that which they own in name only, and that which they actually manage.

Smuts, Robert W. *Women and Work in America.* New York: Columbia University Press, 1959. Reviews the history of women in the marketplace. Especially useful for a picture of the early sweatshops.

Wollstonecraft, Mary. *A Vindication of the Rights of Women.* New York: Norton, 1967 (first published 1791). Eighteenth-century classic by a woman committed to the challenging view.

Woolf, Virginia. *A Room of One's Own.* New York: Harcourt, Brace, 1929. A moving description of the dilemmas of the dependent woman, particularly of the dependent woman artist, and an eloquent plea for change.

## *Other Perspectives: History, Anthropology, and Cross-cultural Patterns*

Abbott, Edith. *Women in Industry: A Study in American Economic History.* New York: Appleton, 1913. Traces the position of women at work, noting that women have always been an important factor in American industry, early public moralists rigidly insisting that women earn their own keep.

Beard, Mary. *Woman as a Force in History.* New York: Macmillan, 1946. Contrasts the myths of woman's social role with the reality of woman's life in various historical periods.

Clark, Alice. *Working Life of Women in the Seventeenth Century.* London: George Routledge and Sons, Ltd., 1919. Contrasts the myths of woman's exclusion from the productive process with the conditions of life in England before the full impact of the industrial revolution. Based on exhaustive study of original sources, such as parish records.

Dodge, Norton T. *Women in the Soviet Economy.* Baltimore: Johns Hopkins Press, 1966. A careful analysis of the concrete conditions of women's status in the U.S.S.R. and the extent of their integration into productive life.

Donaldson, Sir James. *Woman: Her Position and Influence in Ancient Greece and Rome, and Among the Early Christians.* London: Longmans Green and Company, 1907. An interesting compendium of data on the classic periods. Particularly noteworthy on the concepts of the early Christians about woman as temptress.

Flexner, Eleanor. *Century of Struggle: The Woman's Rights Movement in the United States.* Cambridge, Mass.: Belknap Press of Harvard University Press, 1959. An authoritative account of the struggle of American women for education, employment, and suffrage. It begins with the position of women in this country up to 1800 and ends with the adoption of the Nineteenth Amendment in August 1920. This work is a splendid example of the qualitative difference between a first-rate piece of scholarship and an able piece of journalism.

Paulme, Denise (ed.). *Women of Tropical Africa.* Translated by H. M. Wright. Berkeley and Los Angeles: University of California Press, 1963. Six essays by professional ethnologists — all women — based on recent fieldwork in French-speaking Africa. Corrects the usual preconceptions about the inferior position of women in African tribal societies.

Pinchbeck, Ivy. *Women Workers and the Industrial Revolution, 1750-1850.* London: George Routledge and Sons, Ltd., 1930. Picks up the thread of woman and labor in the English economy for the period following that documented by Alice Clark. A thoroughgoing analysis.

## Woman and the Family

Aries, Phillipe. *Centuries of Childhood: A Social History of Family Life.* New York: Random House, 1962. Translated from the French by Robert Balick. Examines the concept of childhood and shows to what extent our model is a modern phenomenon.

Goode, William J. *World Revolution and Family Patterns.* New York: Free Press of Glencoe, 1968. One of the leading authorities on the family examines the relationship between economic and technological development and family forms.

Mace, David and Vera Mace. Garden City, N.Y.: Doubleday, 1963. A report on family patterns among the western republics of the Soviet Union, based on readings and on a motor trip. Written in popular style by a team of family sociologists. Their bibliography is included.

Nye, F. Ivan, and Lois W. Hoffman. *The Employed Mother in America.* Chicago: Rand McNally, 1963. Brings together a comprehensive body of research on the effect of the employment of mothers on children, on the husband-wife relationship, and on the adjustment of the woman herself.

Schur, Edwin M. (ed.). *The Family and the Sexual Revolution.* Bloomington: Indiana University Press, 1964. A collection of essays on changing sex standards, fertility choice, and the social status of women. They are, on the whole, too brief to serve as more than an introduction. See, however, "Does Communal Education Work? The Case of the Kibbutz" by Bruno Bettelheim.

Spiro, Melford E. *Kibbutz: Venture in Utopia.* Cambridge, Mass.: Harvard University Press, 1956. The standard work on collective settlements in Israel and their patterns of family life.

Stern, Bernhard J. (ed.). *The Family: Past and Present.* New York: Appleton, 1938. A classic source book on the changing form of the family in time, and on contemporary trends in family life.

Zimmerman, Carl C. *Family and Civilization.* New York: Harper, 1947. A detailed historical review of designs in family living, which includes a discussion (and refutation) of various aspects of evolutionary theory respecting such development.

## Sex Differentials

Beach, Frank A. (ed.). *Sex and Behavior.* New York: Wiley, 1965. A compilation at the technical level of the most recent findings on this subject. See particularly "Determinants of Psychosexual Orientation" by John L. Hampson and "Development of Gender Role" by Robert R. Sears.

Hulse, Frederick S. *The Human Species: An Introduction to Physical Anthropology.* New York: Random House, 1965. Includes interesting data on sexual dimorphism. Also valuable on the relationship between biology and culture.

Maccoby, Eleanor E. (ed.). *The Development of Sex Differences.* Stanford: Stanford University Press, 1966. A collection of findings by authorities in the field. See especially "Sex Hormones in the Development of Sex Differences" by David A. Hamburg and Donald T. Lunde, "Sex Differences and Cultural Institutions" by Roy G. D'Andrade, and "Sex Differences in Intellectual Functioning" by Eleanor E. Maccoby.

Montagu, Ashley. *On the Natural Superiority of Women.* New York: Macmillan, 1968. A popular treatment by a knowledgeable educator of some of the findings about physical sex differences that contradict prevalent assumptions. Marred by unsubstantiated concepts of temperamental dichotomy.

Scheinfeld, Amram. *Women and Men.* New York: Harcourt, Brace and Company, 1944. One of the earliest books on sex differentials. Many of the data still are useful.

Stoller, Robert J. *Sex and Gender.* New York: Science House, 1968. Based on studies conducted at the California Gender Identity Center, and the conflict – in a population of anomalies – between biological identity and gender assignment. Marred by assumptions respecting masculine and feminine temperamental traits.

Vaerting, Mathias, and Mathilde Vaerting. *The Dominant Sex.* Translated by Eden and Cedar Paul. New York: George H. Doran Company, 1923. Relates the social subordination of women to attitudes of the prevailing social structure, and therefore seeks to compare psychological attributes of women in settings where they were dominant with that of the dominant sex today. Although the pendulum aspect of their theory is not accepted by contemporary scholars, they developed some striking evidence of the position of women in the ancient civilizations of Egypt, Libya and Sparta.

## Sources: Of Detailed Accounts and of Data on Woman's Place

*Annals of the American Academy of Political and Social Science.* See especially: "Women in the Modern World: The Changing Educational, Political, Economic Relationships of Women in the United States" edited by Viva B. Boothe, 143 (May 1929); "Women's Opportunities and Responsibilities" edited by Louise M. Young, 251 (May 1947); "Women Around the World" edited by Althea K. Hottel, 375 (January 1968).

Briffault, Robert. *The Mothers.* 3 vols. New York: Macmillan, 1927. Written by one of the mavericks who tackled the fundamental riddle of historic change. This work, triggered by the ethnocentric vision of Westermarck who postulated monogamy as part of the eternal human condition, became a lifetime obsession of the author, who searched out a mass of illustrative material to contravert that and other preconceptions. Briffault's theories of social mutation are not accepted by contemporary anthropologists, but his dynamic approach and his absorption with the larger questions of cultural evolution are remarkably pertinent to today's concerns. His work is a unique repository of data on women in other periods and in other places.

*Encyclopedia of the Social Sciences,* 15 vols. Edwin R. A. Seligman (editor in chief). New York: Macmillan, 1937. This set is no longer current but it has very useful articles on women in history, and on the history of the family, as well as in other categories of interest to the student of women in society. (Articles on these topics in more recent compilations are not comparable, in terms of profundity of treatment.)

*Handbook on Women Workers.* Women's Bureau of the United States Department of Labor. Washington, D. C., 1969. This valuable source of data on women's income, education, employment, occupations, as well as family and legal status, is usually issued every two years. The latest issue also contains a bibliography relating to employment and education.

*History of Women's Suffrage,* 6 vols. Edited by Susan B. Anthony, Elizabeth Cady Stanton, Mathilda Joclyn Gage, and Ida Husted Harper. Rochester, New York, 1881, 1886, 1902; New York, N. Y., 1922. The basic source book on the American movement.

*Report of the President's Commission on the Status of Women — American Women.* Washington, D.C.: U.S. Government Printing Office, 1963. The Commission was appointed by President Kennedy and chaired, until her death, by Eleanor Roosevelt. Its report has sections on the position of women in education, employment, in the community, and under the law. There have been later supplements updating the findings, all obtainable from the Government Printing Office. See also *Reports* by the various State Commissions on the Status of Women.

Veblen, Thorstein. *The Theory of the Leisure Class.* New York: The Viking Press, 1931 (first published in 1899). Another of the mavericks who tackled questions of transformation in the human condition. Especially interesting to students of women because of the author's theory respecting the role of the second sex in conspicuous consumption.

# INDEX

425